AF791118

Liability Law for Failed Contract Negotiations

This book provides the European structure of liability for failed contract negotiations through a comparative lens, with wider lessons for an international context.

The book demonstrates that all the analyzed legal systems, in Belgium, France, Germany, Italy, and the Netherlands, can be best understood through a binary structure in their approach to pre-contractual liability, or *culpa in contrahendo*. This structure consists of two key elements: first, a general liability framework that allows for compensation of pure economic loss based on certain qualified conduct, such as negligence; and second, an implicit obligation to contract, which, though not explicitly recognized, is presumed in most systems. The book argues that this dual framework provides valuable insights into ongoing scholarly debates and the challenges practitioners face in cases of failed contract negotiations. Drawing on these insights, it proposes a more effective approach to the obligation to contract: one that encourages parties to collaborate in reaching an agreement voluntarily rather than imposing one upon them.

This book will be of interest to researchers in the field of comparative contract and tort law, European private law, and private law theory.

Tom Hick is Senior Research Fellow at the Max Planck Institute for comparative and international private law in Hamburg. He conducts research on comparative law of obligations, comparative succession law, and private law theory with a focus on questions relating to social justice and sustainability. Previously, he has been a research and teaching assistant at the Institute for the Law of Obligations at the KU Leuven, Belgium, where he defended his doctoral dissertation in 2024. He also is a member of various international research groups and of the Friday Group, a Belgian think-tank striving to integrate young Belgian citizens into the public debate on important societal issues.

Liability Law for Failed Contract Negotiations

A Comparative, Structural, and Historical Analysis

Tom Hick

Routledge
Taylor & Francis Group
LONDON AND NEW YORK

First published 2026
by Routledge
4 Park Square, Milton Park, Abingdon, Oxon OX14 4RN

and by Routledge
605 Third Avenue, New York, NY 10158

Routledge is an imprint of the Taylor & Francis Group, an informa business

© 2026 Tom Hick

The right of Tom Hick to be identified as author of this work has been asserted in accordance with sections 77 and 78 of the Copyright, Designs and Patents Act 1988.

All rights reserved. No part of this book may be reprinted or reproduced or utilised in any form or by any electronic, mechanical, or other means, now known or hereafter invented, including photocopying and recording, or in any information storage or retrieval system, without permission in writing from the publishers.

Trademark notice: Product or corporate names may be trademarks or registered trademarks, and are used only for identification and explanation without intent to infringe.

British Library Cataloguing-in-Publication Data
A catalogue record for this book is available from the British Library

ISBN: 978-1-032-95668-8 (hbk)
ISBN: 978-1-032-98530-5 (pbk)
ISBN: 978-1-003-59916-6 (ebk)

DOI: 10.4324/9781003599166

Typeset in Times New Roman
by Apex CoVantage, LLC

Contents

Acknowledgements

This book is the result of a part of my doctoral dissertation, defended on 4 June 2024 and researched from roughly the end of 2018 to early 2024 at the KU Leuven, Belgium.

Thanking those who have made this process possible, and a joy, matters. That is, first and foremost, Professor Dr. Sophie Stijns for having been my ever-patient, trusting, and kind supervisor throughout this process. That certainly is also true of Professor Dr. Annick De Boeck for her engagement with the subject matter and for her supportive availability whenever needed. The same goes for the remaining members of my jury, whom I thank for their time, sincere engagement with my writings, and support throughout: Prof. Dr. Ekaterina Pannebakker, Prof. Dr. Bert Keirsbilck, and Prof. Dr. Dr. h.c. mult. Reinhard Zimmermann. To the latter, I wish to address a special word of gratitude for offering me a postdoc position in his team. I'd also like to thank Prof. Dr. Evelyne Terryn for her willingness to chair my public defence and Prof. Dr. Marieke Wyckaert for being so kind and gracious when called upon last minute. I am also grateful for Prof. Dr. Jan Smits and Prof. Dr. Bert Demarsin for having acted as members of my supervisory committee.

Those are the professors, colleagues, and friends along the way, specifically at the institute for the law of obligations, the department for private law, and the faculty of law and criminology of the KU Leuven. I'd also like to thank those I met during my research stays in Copenhagen, Hamburg, and Rome, as well as those I met during many conferences and exchange programmes. I'd also like to mention my new colleagues in Hamburg for the open and warm welcome they gave me.

Lastly, I thank my dog, my close friends, and particularly my family for their support, trust, and all the beautiful moments I've spent with them.

To all: my heartfelt gratitude for the privilege it has been!

Tom Hick
Hamburg, 5 November 2024

Abbreviations

Codes and model laws

ABGB	Austrian Civil Code (Allgemeines Bürgerliches Gesetzbuch)
Be. Civ. C.	Belgian Civil Code (French: *Code civil Belge*; Dutch: *Belgisch Burgerlijk Wetboek*; German: *Belgisches Bürgerliches Gesetzbuch*)
BGB	German Civil Code (*Bürgerliches Gesetzbuch*)
DCFR	Draft Common Frame of Reference
Fr. Civ. C.	French Civil Code (*Code civil Français*)
GWB	German Act against Restraints of Competition (*Gesetz gegen Wettbewerbesbeschränkungen*)
It. Civ. C.	Italian Civil Code (*Codice civile*)
NBW	Dutch Civil Code (*Nederlands Burgerlijk Wetboek*)
Nap. Civ. C.	Napoleonic Civil Code (*Code Napoléon*)
PECL	Principles of European Contract Law
PELUE	Principles of European Law on Unjustified Enrichment
UPICC	Unidroit Principles of International Commercial Contracts

Regulations and directives

DMA	Digital Markets Act (*EU Regulation 2022/1925 of 14 September 2022 on contestable and fair markets in the digital sector and amending Directives (EU) 2019/1937 and (EU) 2020/1828*)
B2PR	Business to Platform Regulation (*Regulation (EU) 2019/1150 of the European Parliament and of the Council of 20 June 2019 on promoting fairness and transparency for business users of online intermediation services*)
UTPD	Unfair Trading Practices Directive (*Directive 2019/633 on unfair trading practices in business-to-business relationships in the agricultural and food supply chain*)

Courts

Bundesgerichtshof	Supreme Court of Germany
Hoge Raad	Supreme Court of the Netherlands
Cour de Cassation belge/Hof van Cassatie	Supreme Court of Belgium
Cour de Cassation française	Supreme Court of France
Corte di Cassazione italiano	Supreme Court of Italy

General vocabulary

GTC	General Terms and Conditions
UTP	Unfair Trading Practices
c.i.c.	*culpa in contrahendo*

Introduction

1. To get the right answers, one must ask the right questions. If I were to ask for a loaf of bread at my local bakery when wanting to receive a cake, chances are I get a loaf of bread instead of the desired cake. In law, this is no different. In *Gesetzliche Schuldverhältnisse. Eine historische Strukturanalyse*, Nils Jansen writes that in this article he would like "to ask to what extent our dogmatic concepts, metaphors and models provide a value-appropriate, comprehensible picture of the law of legal obligations."[1] That is, put perhaps more sophisticatedly, providing the right questions. Liability for failed contract negotiations, generally referred to as pre-contractual liability, or *culpa in contrahendo*, revealed itself as an area in which the wrong questions have been asked frequently and persistently, and consequentially, wrong answers have been obtained frequently and persistently.

2. Take the way in which compensable harm is framed when negotiations have culpably been broken-off. It is generally explained that the compensable harm covers the so-called negative interest – that is, to be compensated for the costs made in the negotiation process. Exceptionally, the positive interest, covering the expected benefits under the negotiated contract, could be compensated. Upon reflection, such a rule-exception reasoning is alien to the determination of the extent of damages. The extent of damages is established by assessing what harm is causally linked to the invoked fault. This can, in many cases, correspond to what is described as negative interest but not because it is the negative interest but because it is causally linked to the fault. Liability law 101. Oddly enough, this seems to be disregarded when negotiations fail. Were one to decide based on this rule-exception reasoning what compensation should be granted, the results would be highly arbitrary ("*Billigkeitsrechtsprechung*").[2] Wrong questions, after all, tend to lead to wrong answers.

1 Nils Jansen, "Gesetzliche Schuldverhältnisse Eine historische Strukturanalyse," *AcP* 216 (2016). p. 116. Free translation. Original version: "*Ich möchte fragen, wie weit unsere dogmatischen Begriffe, Metaphern und Leitbilder ein wertungsangemessenes, fassliches Bild des Rechts der gesetzlichen Schuldverhältnisse bieten.*"

2 As is strongly and, in that respect, rightly criticized in Hans Stoll, "Tatbestände und Funktionen der Haftung für culpa in contrahendo," in *Festschrift für Ernst von Caemmerer zum 70. Geburtstag*, ed.

DOI: 10.4324/9781003599166-1

3. The fact that wrong questions are asked, I argue, is explained by the failure to see that through liability for contract negotiations, two distinct questions are supposed to be answered by one answer. Inevitably, this must lead to a malaise.

The duality of questions stems from a duality of interests that can be protected via this liability: the integrity of the patrimony, on the one hand, and on the other, the freedom of contract of the person that suffers the no-contract scenario. This duality of protected interests translates into a dual or two-pronged structure of this liability. First, a general liability applicable in contract negotiations that protects negotiating parties from suffering pure economic loss in the context of contract negotiations. Second, an obligation to contract or to negotiate which protects the freedom of contract of the party to whom negotiations are broken-off or the conclusion of a contract is refused and explains that this latter act was unlawful.

4. Essentially, the point just made boils down to saying that the structure, one may say the architecture, of liability for contract negotiations is unsettled. It is the functioning of and the interaction between different criteria of application which are unclear. As with all theory, unclarity on this level tickles down to the practitioner. Complementing the earlier citation of Jansen: "I want to ask to what extent our dogmatic concepts, metaphors and models provide a value-appropriate, comprehensible picture of the law of legal obligations. *Such questions are anything but academic. . . . Practitioners in particular are therefore dependent on a suitable dogmatic language that expresses the relevant judgements in a directly understandable way*."[3]

Specific to the context of failed negotiations, Wolfgang Küpper's findings formulated in 1988 in his dissertation *Das Scheitern von Vertragsverhandlungen als Fallgruppe der culpa in contrahendo* still hold true today:

> "If there is agreement in this respect, liability arising from culpa in contrahendo in general and from the failure of contractual negotiations in particular is generally recognised but is still highly controversial in terms of its prerequisites and content, and for the most part also controversial in its foundations."[4]

Hans Claudius Ficker and Detlev König (Tübingen: Mohr Siebeck, 1978). p. 436. More recently, for instance, in Dieter Medicus and Jens Petersen, *Grundwissen zum Bürgerlichen Recht* (München: Vahlen, 2019). p. 91, nr. 2.

3 Jansen, "Gesetzliche Schuldverhältnisse Eine historische Strukturanalyse," p. 116. Free translation. Original version: "*Ich möchte fragen, wie weit unsere dogmatischen Begriffe, Metaphern und Leitbilder ein wertungsangemessenes, fassliches Bild des Rechts der gesetzlichen Schuldverhältnisse bieten. Solche Fragen sind alles andere als akademisch. . . . Gerade die Praxis ist also auf eine passende dogmatische Sprache angewiesen, die die einschlägigen Wertungen unmittelbar verständlich zum Ausdruck bringt*."

4 Wolfgang Küpper, *Das Scheitern von Vertragshandlugen als Fallgruppe der culpa in conrahendo* (Berlin: Duncker & Humblot, 1988). p. 19. Free translation. Original text: "*Besteht insoweit Übereinstimmung, so gilt für die Haftung aus culpa in contrahendo im allgemeinen wie für diejenige aus dem Scheitern von Vertragsverhandlungen im besonderen, dass sie generell zwar anerkannt, in Voraussetzung und Inhalt dagegen immer noch lebhaft, größtenteils auch grundsätzlich umstritten ist*."

5. To remedy this lack of architectural understanding of liability for contract negotiations, this book deals with the underlying structural elements, valuations, and rules of liability for failed contract negotiations.[5] This is first done by identifying the function fulfilled by liability for contract negotiations, both from a historical-evolving and contemporary perspective. According to that function, the *type* of liability law necessary to fulfil those functions can be established. Once the necessary type of liability law has been clarified and shown to be identical in all analysed legal systems, I turn to the architecture of this type of liability law system.

Overall, I believe that this architectural ambition resonates with Reinier Kraakman *et al.*'s ambition formulated in *The Anatomy of Corporate Law*.[6] In the relevant parts, they explain:

> "We join an emerging tendency in comparative law scholarship by seeking to give a highly integrated view of the role and the structure of corporate law that provides a clear framework within which to organize an understanding of individual systems, both alone and in comparison, with each other. Moreover, while comparative law scholarship often has a tendency to emphasize differences between jurisdictions, our approach is to highlight similarities as well. Doing so illuminates an underlying commonality of structure that transcends national boundaries. It also provides an important perspective on the basis for the international cross-fertilization of corporate law that has become more common in the wake of the growth of global economic activity.
>
> . . .
>
> we wish to offer a *common language* and a general *analytic framework* with which to understand the purposes that can potentially be served by corporate law, and with which to compare and evaluate the efficacy of different legal regimes in serving those purposes. Indeed, it is our hope

5 See similarly in Nils Jansen, "Konturen eines europäischen Schadensrechts," *JZ*, no. 4 (2005). p. 160. See also: "After all, it is not about the presentation of a concrete normative system, but about the connecting dogmatic structures of a multitude of positive legal systems. Of course, legal dogmatics in general is not exhausted in the presentation and interpretative specification of written norms. In the foreground is, on the one hand, the reconstructive formulation of general legal principles, and on the other hand, the analytical and synthetic presentation of normative connections that go beyond the assertion of a norm but are nevertheless at least indirectly related to legal norms and explain them in a typically generalising legal form." Nils Jansen, "Dogmatik, Erkenntnis und Theorie im europäischen Privatrecht," *ZEuP* (2005). pp. 753–754. Citations omitted. Free translation. Original text: "*Denn es geht ja gerade nicht um die Darstellung eines konkreten Normsystems, sondern um die verbindenden dogmatischen Strukturen einer Vielzahl positiver Rechtsordnungen. Dabei erschöpft die Rechtsdogmatik sich freilich ganz allgemein nicht in der Darstellung und auslegenden Präzisierung geschriebener Normen. Im Vordergrund steht zum einen die rekonstruktive Formulierung allgemeiner Rechtsgrundsätze, zum anderen die analytische und synthetische Darstellung normativer Zusammenhänge, die über die Behauptung einer Norm hinausgehen, gleichwohl aber zumindest mittelbar auf Rechtsnormen bezogen sind und diese in einer typischerweise generalisierenden Form juristisch erklären.*"

6 Reinier Kraakman et al., *The Anatomy of Corporate Law A Comparative and Functional Approach*, 3rd ed. (Oxford: Oxford University Press, 2017), xvii+281 p.

> that the analysis offered in this book will be of use not only to students of comparative law, but also to those who simply wish to have a more solid framework within which to view their own country's corporation law.
>
> . . .
>
> Rather, we are seeking to set out a conceptual framework and a factual basis with which that and other important issues facing corporate law can be fruitfully explored."[7]

Except for stating that the subject matter of the present study is not corporate law but liability for contract negotiations and by extension delictual and contractual liability law, there seems to be little I need or could add to my methodological approach. Perhaps that I have found a historical approach as developed in Reinhard Zimmermann's *The Law of Obligations*[8] very helpful and enlightening. As Susanne Hähnchen writes, "everything that is can only be understood if one knows how it has come to exist."[9] This historical approach, however, only serves to pave the way for the comparative analysis that follows and is not an aim in and of itself.

6. In that comparative exercise, I have looked into Belgian, Dutch, French, German, and Italian law as national legal systems and the Draft Common Frame of Reference (DCFR), the Principles of European Contract Law (PECL), and the Unidroit Principles on International Commercial Contracts (UPICC) as harmonization models.

The choice of analysed legal systems made should provide sufficient points of reference for other left-out systems to situate themselves within the established framework. At least, it is my hope that by providing the architecture of liability for failed contract negotiations, the reader will find in it a generalisable framework or matrix for looking at systems of pre-contractual liability rather than a snapshot of the analysed legal systems. Indeed, the structured comparative approach is meant to provide the reader with the relevant tools to look at any kind of system of pre-contractual liability and assess the coherence of the system in question.

7. Concerning language, I want to assure that I read and speak all languages compared with – except for Latin in as far as that is relevant. In the text, I have always cited in English and provided the original language version in the footnotes. The cited translations have been made by DeepL under my close supervision. All remaining inadequacies are thus of my own responsibility.

7 Kraakman et al., *The Anatomy of Corporate Law A Comparative and Functional Approach*, pp. 3–5. Citations omitted.

8 Reinhard Zimmermann, *The Law of Obligations. Roman Foundations of the Civilian Tradition* (Cape Town: Juta & Co, 1990), lxiv+1241 p.

9 Susanne Hähnchen, *Obliegenheiten und Nebenpflichten. eine Untersuchung dieser besonderen Verhaltensanforderungen im Privatversciherungsrecht und im allgemeinen Zivilrecht unter besonderer Berücksichtigung der Dogmengeschichte*, Jus Privatum, (Tübingen: Mohr Siebeck, 2010). p. 3. Free translation. Original text: "*Alles was ist, kann nur verstanden werden, wenn man weiß, wie es geworden ist.*"

Where available, I have relied on official translations of the texts I worked with, especially when it comes to statutory provisions. For the French Civil Code, I have relied on the translation provided by John Cartwright, Bénédicte Fauvarque-Cosson, and Simon Whittaker.[10] The translation of the Belgian Civil Code has been done by my colleague Christopher Borucki and is unfortunately not yet publicly available. The translation of the Dutch Civil Code is the one available at the Dutch Civil Code,[11] while the one of the BGB is the one from *Gesetze im Internet*.[12]

Freely translated statutory translations have been indicated as such; if nothing is specified, translations stem from the translation just explained. Scholarly articles that do exist in a translated version but have been read in their original language have been freely translated, relying here on DeepL as well – in order to spare me the laborious work of looking up the translations and finding the corresponding passages. May the reader excuse my lack of patience for such work.

8. To provide the right questions to ask, this book is structured in three substantial parts which are preceded by the present introductory part and succeeded by a concluding one. The first substantial part will, broadly speaking, set out the structure of no-contract law. That is to say, to explain why and how within what is generally dealt with as pre-contractual liability, or *culpa in contrahendo*, in fact, two separate questions exist yet are often dealt with interchangeably. This part will also explain some terminological decisions I have made in order to provide a smoother and more coherent terminology. The second substantial part will deal specifically and in much detail with the general liability applicable in contract negotiations to protect the patrimonial integrity of parties to negotiations, where it is deemed worthy of protection. The third substantial part will be devoted to the obligation to negotiate or to contract and the consequences of their non-performance. As per usual, the concluding part will bring together all relevant findings and leave the reader with some more general takeaways from the research that has led to the present book.

With having stated what this book will be, it is also worthwhile to close this introduction by stating what this book is *not*. It, overtly, is neither a general handbook on liability for failed contract negotiations nor a discussion of all existing scholarship on the subject matter dealt with. By consequence, this book will not discuss in minute detail questions of practical application of the doctrines it presents. This would detract from the main purpose of providing insight into the underlying functioning of the discussed doctrines. The practitioner will thus not find "*prêt-à-porter*" answers. Instead of answers, he will find questions – but the right questions to ask to get the right answers.

10 In which not all texts are still up to date with the texts applicable today. URL: https://www.trans-lex.org/601101/_/french-civil-code-2016/ (consulted on 8 December 2023).

11 URL: http://www.dutchcivillaw.com/civilcodegeneral.htm (consulted on 8 December 2023).

12 URL: https://www.gesetze-im-internet.de/englisch_bgb/ (consulted on 8 December 2023).

Part I

Structure of liability for contract negotiations and obligations to contract

1 Function of pre-contractual liability

1. *Culpa in contrahendo*

1.1. Jhering's construction

1. THE ISSUE JHERING FACES – In order to assess what the function of pre-contractual liability is, it appears plausible to start with the beginning. That is, for our purpose, with Jhering's *culpa in contrahendo* which he unveils to the world in his *Culpa in contrahendo oder Schadensersatz bei nichtigen oder nicht zur Perfection gelangten Verträgen*, published in 1861.[1] He departs his observation from the discovery of what he considered to be a lack in the state of the law of his time, namely, that a party who committed a mistake in the conclusion of the contract could not be held liable to compensate for the costs arising from the nullity ensuing from the mistake.[2] Jhering used the example of a person who wants to order 100 gramm of some product but instead writes down 100 kilogramm. Upon arrival, the buyer refuses to reception the 100 *kilo*gramm.[3] Jhering asks who would have to bear the additional transportation costs for returning the excessive quantity of the ordered product. As Jhering cannot find a satisfying answer to this question in his contemporary literature, he famously

1 See on this point MüKoBGB/Emmerich, 9. Aufl. 2022, BGB § 311 nr. 38; Ulrike Babusiaux, "Liability for Negotiations," in *Commentaries on European Contract Laws*, ed. Nils Jansen and Reinhard Zimmermann (Oxford: Oxford University Press, 2018). p. 349, nr. 1; Carsten Nickel, *Die Rechtsfolgen der culpa in contrahendo* (Berlin: Buncker & Humblot, 2004). p. 52.

2 Rudolf Jhering, "Culpa in contrahendo oder Schadensersatz bei nichtigen oder nicht zur Perfection gelangten Verträgen," *Jahrbücher für die Dogmatik des heutigen römischen und deutschen Privatrechts* 4 (1861). p. 2: "In my lectures on the doctrine of essential error, one point has been causing me great difficulty for years, and I have been unable to give a satisfactory answer to it, namely the question of whether the erring party is not liable to compensate the opponent for the damage caused by his fault?" Free translation. Original text: "*Bei dem Vortrage der Lehre vom wesentlichen Irrthum in meinen Vorlesungen machte mir schon seit Jahren ein Punkt große Schwierigkeit, auf den ich eine befriedigende Auskunft zu ertheilen nicht im Stande war, nämlich die Frage: ob nicht der irrende Theil dem Gegner auf Ersatz des durch seine Schuld ihm verursachten Schadens Hafte?*"

3 I take the case as presented by Jhering without any personal analysis.

DOI: 10.4324/9781003599166-3

acclaims that the seeming inexistence of such a claim for damages hurts his feeling or intuition for justice ("*Rechtsgefühl*"):

> "Who does not feel that a claim for damages is needed here?"[4]

To Jhering, "the inequity and practical bleakness of such an outcome is obvious,"[5] and he is not willing to accept it.[6] The issue he faces when trying to grant damages to the harmed party is that no legal action appears to be readily available. Indeed, given that the contract in question will be void in the cases he faces, a contractual claim seems excluded.[7] By consequence, Jhering sets out to explore whether a non-contractual claim could provide relief. He does so, as usual in his days, based on considerations of Roman sources.[8]

2. Non-contractual pure economic loss – Two non-contractual grounds for liability appear possibly useful for Jhering's endeavour: the *actio de dolo* and the *actio legis Aquilia*. Yet in the territories which were to become Germany in 1871, both actions are limited in their scope in such a way that they do not allow to compensate pure economic loss based on culpable conduct:[9] While the *actio legis Aquilia* was a non-contractual fault-based liability, it did not allow for the compensation of pure economic loss. Inversely, the *actio de dolo* was a non-contractual liability which allowed for the compensation of pure economic loss but required a *dolus*, an intentional wrong.[10] His extra-contractual, fault-based liability compensating pure economic loss would have to hold the middle ground between the *actio legis Aquilia* and *actio de dolo*:

> "This would result in an action that would hold the middle ground between the two, borrowing culpa from the latter [*actio legis Aquilia*] and indifference to the form of the damage from the former [*actio de dolo*],

4 Jhering, "Culpa in contrahendo oder Schadensersatz bei nichtigen oder nicht zur Perfection gelangten Verträgen." p. 5. Free translation. Original text: "*Wer fühlt nicht, dass es hier einer Schadensersatzklage bedarf?*"

5 Jhering, "Culpa in contrahendo oder Schadensersatz bei nichtigen oder nicht zur Perfection gelangten Verträgen." p. 2. Free translation. Original text: "*Die Unbilligkeit und praktische Trostlosigkeit eines solchen Resultats liegt auf der Hand.*"

6 Elke Nüsslein, *Die Integration der culpa in contrahendo in das BGB nach der Schuldrechtsreform* (Berlin: Peter Lang, 2018). p. 71.

7 Jhering, "Culpa in contrahendo oder Schadensersatz bei nichtigen oder nicht zur Perfection gelangten Verträgen." p. 4.

8 For a discussion, see f.i. Nüsslein, *Die Integration der culpa in contrahendo in das BGB nach der Schuldrechtsreform*. pp. 66–70.

9 Jörg Benedict, *Culpa in Contrahendo*, Vol. I (Tübingen: Mohr Siebeck, 2018). p. 189; Nils Jansen, "Developing legal doctrine: fault in the German law of delict," in *The Development and Making of Legal Doctrine*, ed. Nils Jansen (Cambridge: Cambridge University Press, 2010). p. 101: "there was no extracontractual liability for negligently caused purely economic loss and especially for negligent misstatements."

10 Dieter Medicus, "Zur Entdeckungsgeschichte der culpa in contrahendo," in *Iuris Professio Festgabe für Max Kaser zum 80. Geburtstag*, ed. Hans-Peter Benöhr et al. (Wien: Hermann Böhlaus, 1986). p. 170. See also Babusiaux, "Liability for Negotiations." pp. 349–350, nr. 2.

> or in other words, the legal proposition that extra-contractual culpa per se gives rise to an obligation to pay damages."[11]

As such an action did not exist under "German law," no claim is available to the harmed party of a voided contract. Jhering could have drawn inspiration from the Napoleonic Civil Code, whose articles 1382 and 1383 allow for the compensation of pure economic loss on a fault-based liability. However, such a claim appeared excessively broad and vague to "German" scholars[12] and Jhering himself:

> "In non-contractual relationships, no one can demand from the other a guarantee of the reliability and truth of his statement and communication; the law protects him only against dolus, not against culpa, and he has himself to blame if he suffers damage through blind trust in the statements of third parties, for he must have known their non-binding force."[13]

3. Contractual fault-based liability – This impasse forces Jhering to construct the *culpa in contrahendo*, a liability based on a fault in contracting. Absent any useful non-contractual ground for liability, he inevitably must turn to a contractual ground for liability.[14] Indeed, in the contractual realm, a fault-based liability compensating pure economic loss was possible:[15]

> "This is a general law of the theory of contract, according to which each party must compensate the other for the damage caused to him by his *culpa*."[16]

11 Jhering, "Culpa in contrahendo oder Schadensersatz bei nichtigen oder nicht zur Perfection gelangten Verträgen." p. 24. Free translation. Original text: "*Man würde dadurch eine Klage bekommen, welche die Mitte zwischen ihnen beiden hielte, von der letzteren [actio legis aquilia] die culpa, von der ersteren [actio de dolo] die Gleichgültigkeit der Form der Beschädigung entlehnte oder mit anderen Worten den Rechtssatz, dass die außercontractliche culpa schlechthin eine Verpflichtung zum Schadensersatz begründe.*"

12 Babusiaux, "Liability for Negotiations." p. 350, nr. 3; Christian von Bar, *The Common European Law of Torts*, Vol. I (Oxford: Clarendon Press, 1998). p. 25, nr. 17.

13 Jhering, "Culpa in contrahendo oder Schadensersatz bei nichtigen oder nicht zur Perfection gelangten Verträgen." 42. Free translation. Original text: "*In außercontractlichen Verhältnissen kann Niemand von dem anderen die Garantie für die Zuverlässigkeit und Wahrheit seiner Äußerung und Mittheilung verlangen, das Recht schützt ihn nur gegen dolus, nicht gegen culpa, und er hat es sich selbst zuzuschreiben, wenn er durch blindes Vertrauen auf Aussagen Dritter in Schaden kommt, denn er mußte die unverbindliche Kraft derselben kennen.*" See in this context Benedict, *Culpa in Contrahendo*, I. pp. 59–60; Nüsslein, *Die Integration der culpa in contrahendo in das BGB nach der Schuldrechtsreform*. p. 78.

14 Irritatingly, a considerable part of French-speaking scholarship (f.i. Jacques Ghestin, "La responsabilité délictuelle pour rupture abusive des pourparlers," *JCP (éd Gen.)* 20–21 (2007). p. 15, nr. 3.) follows the erroneous interpretation of Jhering's piece as meaning that the liability would be contractual because some sort of negotiation agreement would have been implied in Jhering's judgment. This is wrong, but it is not clear where exactly this misconception comes from.

15 Benedict, *Culpa in Contrahendo*, I. p. 60.

16 Jhering, "Culpa in contrahendo oder Schadensersatz bei nichtigen oder nicht zur Perfection gelangten Verträgen." p. 40. Free translation. Original text: "*allgemeines Gesetz der Contractstheorie*

The problem Jhering faces in the contractual realm is that in the case of a voided contract, no contract exists to base a contractual claim on. To overcome this difficulty, he needs to argue that (i) a contractual liability indemnifying pure economic loss exists independently of the validity of the contract and (ii) that such a contractual liability exists as of the moment of the conclusion of the contract.

4. (I) PURPOSE OF CONTRACT – The first argumentative step consists in distinguishing between the main purpose of the contract and what could be described as residual effects of the contract. In Jhering's understanding, the main purpose consists in the performance of contractual obligations. Yet where this main purpose cannot be fulfilled, this does not imply that no legal effects follow from the contact:

> "the expression nullity, if it is to be used appropriately, can therefore only have a limited sense, predicating not the absence of all, but only certain effects. The purpose of every contract is fulfilment; the intended effect therefore consists in the creation of an obligation to fulfilment. If this effect is excluded because of the lack of some necessary requirement, and the actual purpose of the contract is thus frustrated, we call it null and void; we therefore determine the concepts of validity and nullity of the contract according to the main practical purpose of the contract. It is quite compatible with this that the contract may give rise to other kinds of obligations, provided that they are not directed towards fulfilment."[17]

5. *CULPA* – Granted the voidance of a contract only annuls the main purpose of the contract, what are then the remaining "other kinds of obligations" which "are not directed towards fulfilment"? For Jhering, the remaining obligations are some to act in accordance with this *diligentia*. In a more contemporary terminology: duties of care or of conduct. The party to the voided contract who fails to act diligently, and Jhering will generally discuss this matter looking at the seller,[18] acts culpably – hence, *culpa*.

---

unter, dem, dass jeder Theil dem anderen für den ihm durch seine culpa zugefügten Schaden aufkommen muss."

17 Jhering, "Culpa in contrahendo oder Schadensersatz bei nichtigen oder nicht zur Perfection gelangten Verträgen." p. 29. Free translation. Original text: "*der Ausdruck der Nichtigkeit kann also, wenn er passend gebraucht sein soll, nur einen beschränkten Sinn haben, nicht die Abwesenheit sämtlicher, sondern nur bestimmter Wirkungen prädicieren Der Zweck eines jeden Vertrages ist die Erfüllung, die beabsichtigte Wirkung besteht mithin in der Hervorbringung einer Verbindlichkeit auf Erfüllung. Ist nun diese Wirkung wegen Mangels irgend eines nothwendigen Erfordernisses ausgeschlossen, der eigentliche Zweck des Vertrages also vereitelt, so nennen wir ihn nichtig, wir bestimmen demnach die Begriffe der Gültigkeit und Nichtigkeit des Contracts nach dem praktischen Hauptzweck des Vertrages. Allein damit verträgt sich sehr wohl, dass der Vertrag Verbindlichkeiten andere Art hervorbringen kann, insofern dieselben nur nicht auf Erfüllung gerichtet sind.*" See also p. 32. See also Küpper, *Das Scheitern von Vertragshandlugen als Fallgruppe der culpa in conrahendo*. p. 23.

18 Benedict, *Culpa in Contrahendo*, I. p. 63.

6. POSITIVE AND NEGATIVE INTEREST – With this understanding of the contract and its voidance being set,[19] Jhering's distinction between the positive and the negative interest, based on Friedrich Mommsen's *Zur Lehre von dem Interesse*,[20] becomes both clear and necessary.[21] Jhering will use the distinction between the positive and negative interest to distinguish respectively between the equivalent of the performance of the contractual obligations and other damages following from this residual *culpa*:

The positive interest ("*positives Interesse*") describes the position a party would have been in, had the obligation been properly performed.[22] Therefore, it is contemporarily rather designated as the expectation or performance interest.[23] As I find the term "performance interest" much clearer and more precise, I will use this terminology. Furthermore, it prevents confusion between expectation and reliance interest, both notions which are semantically speaking close but designate different realities.

The negative interest ("*negatives Interesse*") describes the position a party would have been in had no contract been concluded.[24] As it covers the loss of the party that has *relied* on the validity of the contract, it nowadays is called the reliance interest ("*Vertrauensinteresse*").[25] More specifically, the negative interest describes the suffered damage when a contract has been voided to the exclusion of the performance of the contract.

Take the voided sale of the 100 kg of a given product (*supra* Chap. 1, nr. 1). The positive interest describes the net advantage of having 100 g of a given product, *i.e.* the monetary equivalent of the advantage of being able to use the product. The negative interest covers the loss suffered due to the fault, *i.e.* the expenses of sending back the 99 kg of a product. As Jhering himself made explicit, the head of damage subject to compensation does not say anything about the *actual extent of damages* that can be obtained. It may very well be that the negative

19 See likewise Claus-Wilhelm Canaris, "Ansprüche wegen 'positiver Vertragsverletzung' und 'Schutzwirkung für Dritte' bei nichtigen Verträgen. Zugleich ein Beitrag zur Vereinheitlichung der Regeln über die Schutzpflichtverletzungen," *JZ* (1965). p. 476.

20 Referencing Mommsen in fn. 17. Friedrich Mommsen, *Beiträge zum Obligationenrecht II: Zur Lehre von dem Interesse* (Braunschweig: Schwetschke, 1855). XIII+301 p.

21 Benedict, *Culpa in Contrahendo*, I. p. 63; Nüsslein, *Die Integration der culpa in contrahendo in das BGB nach der Schuldrechtsreform*. p. 78; Nickel, *Die Rechtsfolgen der culpa in contrahendo*. p. 53.

22 Jhering, "Culpa in contrahendo oder Schadensersatz bei nichtigen oder nicht zur Perfection gelangten Verträgen." p. 16. For a contemporary view on the topic Isabel Zuloaga, *Reliance in the Breaking Off of Contractual Negotiations* (Intersentia, 2019). pp. 170–171.

23 Attributed to LL Fuller and WR Perdue, "The Reliance Interest in Contract Damages: 1," *Yale LJ* (1936). p. 54.

24 Jhering, "Culpa in contrahendo oder Schadensersatz bei nichtigen oder nicht zur Perfection gelangten Verträgen," p. 16. For a contemporary view on the topic Zuloaga, *Reliance in the Breaking Off of Contractual Negotiations*. pp. 170–171.

25 Nickel, *Die Rechtsfolgen der culpa in contrahendo*. pp. 41–42.

interest is equal to the positive interest. Only the justification and thus availability of the different heads of damages are distinct:

> "The negative interest can possibly reach the level of the positive interest, . . . but, as can be seen from the above, for a completely different reason."[26]

Indeed, the reason for the compensation of the positive interest is justified by the non- or bad-performance of a valid contractual obligation; the reason for the compensation of the negative interest is a negligent conduct which has led to the voidance of the contract.

7. (II) DILIGENCE IN THE CONTRACT CONCLUSION – The second argumentative step Jhering had to take was to delimit the claim. As he did not want to extend the claim beyond the contractual realm, he had to specify that one could be held liable "for contracting" – hence, *in contrahendo* – but not prior to the contract conclusion:[27]

> "He who contracts thereby passes from the purely negative obligation of extra-contractual intercourse into the positive one of the sphere of contract, from the sphere of mere culpa in faciendo to that of culpa in non faciendo, of positive diligentia, and the first and most general obligation he thereby assumes is that of already expending the necessary diligentia in contracting itself. Not only the existing, but also the emerging contractual relationships must be protected by the rules on culpa, if contractual intercourse is not to be severely exposed on this side, and if every contracting party is not to be exposed to the danger of becoming the victim of someone else's negligence."[28]

26 Jhering, "Culpa in contrahendo oder Schadensersatz bei nichtigen oder nicht zur Perfection gelangten Verträgen." 21. Free translation. Original text: "*Das negative Interesse kann unter Umständen die Höhe des positiven erreichen, . . . aber, wie aus dem bisherigen hervogeht, aus einem ganz anderen Grund.*"

27 Mauro Orlandi, "Responsabilità precontrattuale," *Enciclopedia del diritto* (2021). p. 999, nr. 3; Benedict, *Culpa in Contrahendo*, I. p. 60; Nüsslein, *Die Integration der culpa in contrahendo in das BGB nach der Schuldrechtsreform.* pp. 75 and 77; Tomasz Giaro, "Culpa in contrahendo: eine Geschichte der Wiederentdeckung," in *Das Bürgerliche Gesetzbuch und seine Richter*, ed. Ulrich Falk and Heinz Mohnhaupt (Frankfurt am Main: Vittorio Klostermann, 2000). p. 117.

28 Jhering, "Culpa in contrahendo oder Schadensersatz bei nichtigen oder nicht zur Perfection gelangten Verträgen." pp. 41–42. Free translation. Original text: "*Wer contrahirt, tritt damit aus dem rein negativen Pflichtverhältnis des außercontractlichen Verkehrs in den positiven der Contractsphäre, von dem Gebiete der bloßen culpa in faciendo auf das de culpa in non faciendo, der positiven diligentia, aud die erste und allgemeinste Verpflichtung, die er damit übernimmt, ist die: beim Contrahieren selbst bereits die nöthige diligentia aufzuwenden. Nicht bloß die bestehenden, sondern bereits die entstehenden Contractsverhältnisse müssen unter dem Schutz der Regeln über die culpa stehen, wenn nicht de contractliche Verkehr nach dieser Seite hin empfindlicher Weise bloßgestellt, jeder Contrahent der Gefahr Preis gegeben werden soll, das Opfer fremder Nachlässigkeit zu*

8. *Culpa in contrahendo* – The result of these two argumentative steps, (i) isolation of the residual *culpa* in the case of a void contract (*culpa*) and (ii) limiting this liability to the contract conclusion but not beyond (*in contrahendo*), is the *culpa in contrahendo*. More specifically, for Jhering, this *culpa* consists in concluding a contract without being certain of being able to furnish what has been agreed to. More pointily formulated:

> "whoever promises something, shall not err, he errs at his own expense, not at the expense of the other party."[29]

This is a rather strict and, as Jhering admits himself, abstract standard for the fault. It leaves no room for assessing the conduct of the party in question in as far as it departs from the position that the seller has to guarantee the validity of the sale. Jörg Benedict has been critical of the rigidity of this understanding of culpability in the first of two volumes dedicated to the *Culpa in Contrahendo*.[30] Like Benedict, many other scholars have critically analysed Jhering's construction. Yet my point here is not a critical evaluation of Jhering's construction. Instead, I want to focus on the *function* that Jhering wanted the *culpa in contrahendo* to be able to fulfil.

1.2. Function and means of the **culpa in contrahendo**

9. Function – Jhering is very open and straightforward about the aim he pursues when he states "Who does not feel that a claim for damages is needed here?"[31] What Jhering wants, i.e. the function his doctrine needs to serve, is to grant a claim for damages when "on the occasion of an intended contractual relationship, one party . . . has suffered damage by executing a contract proposed to him by others and which seemingly has come about according to the external course of events."[32] More succinctly expressed by Ulrike Babusiaux in her

---

werden." See on this also Küpper, *Das Scheitern von Vertragshandlugen als Fallgruppe der culpa in conrahendo*. p. 22.

29 Jhering, "Culpa in contrahendo oder Schadensersatz bei nichtigen oder nicht zur Perfection gelangten Verträgen." p. 39. Free translation. Original text: "*wer etwas verspricht, soll sich nicht irren, er irrt sich auf eigene, nicht auf Kosten der Gegenpartei.*"

30 Benedict, *Culpa in Contrahendo*, I. pp. 63–65.

31 Jhering, "Culpa in contrahendo oder Schadensersatz bei nichtigen oder nicht zur Perfection gelangten Verträgen." 5. Free translation. Original text: "Wer fühlt nicht, dass es hier einer Schadensersatzklage bedarf?"

32 Jhering, "Culpa in contrahendo oder Schadensersatz bei nichtigen oder nicht zur Perfection gelangten Verträgen." p. 7. Free translation. Original text: "*bei Gelegenheit eines intendirten Contractsverhältnisses, der eine Theil . . . dadurch in Schade gerathen [ist], dass er einen ihm von anderen proponierten und dem äußeren Hergang nach zu Stande gekommenen Vertrag ausführte.*" See also Reinhard Zimmermann, *Roman Law, Contemporary Law, European Law: The Civilian Tradition Today* (Oxford: Oxford University Press, 2001). p. 88.

contribution to Nils Jansen and Reinhard Zimmermann's *Commentaries on European Contract Laws*:

> "Jhering's (1861) main concern was to compensate the party who had relied on the void contract for the loss incurred."[33]

10. Means – The question then arises how this aim can be pursued. A first question in that regard is whether the existing legal framework already provides for this possibility. If it does, no further construction is necessary, but the question merely will be *how* the existing framework allows for such a claim. If, on the contrary, the existing legal framework does not allow to achieve the aimed-for purpose – as was the case for Jhering's *culpa in contrahendo* – the question arises as to what is *necessary* to allow for the function in question. These means were (i) a fault-based liability, (ii) allowing for the indemnification of pure economic loss, and (iii) applicable to the conclusion of the contract but not to the phase preceding the conclusion of the contract. These elements typify the *culpa in contrahendo* as developed by Jhering. This also means that the *culpa in contrahendo* covers another set of cases and can only, in a limited sense, be seen as the starting point to pre-contractual liability. This begs the question of the development of pre-contractual liability as understood today. Before dealing with this question, some brief terminological considerations.

11. Terminology: *Culpa in contrahendo* and positive and negative interest – As follows from the wording itself, the *culpa in contrahendo* is limited to the contractual realm and more specifically tailored to the case of a voided contract.[34] The understanding of positive and negative interest, hence, also stems from the scenario of a voided contract. By consequence, neither the *culpa in contrahendo* nor the notions of positive and negative interest were tailored or intended for the pre-contractual realm. Inevitably, these concepts are awkward to import to and apply in the pre-contractual context. That contemporary scholarship and court decisions stick to these concepts, probably due to an incorrect historical interpretation,[35] is troublesome, as it leads to a

33 Babusiaux, "Liability for Negotiations." p. 350, nr. 4.

34 Dieter Medicus and Stephan Lorenz, *Schuldrecht I Allgemeiner Teil* (München: C.H. Beck, 2021). p. 241, nr. 1; Nüsslein, *Die Integration der culpa in contrahendo in das BGB nach der Schuldrechtsrefomr*. p. 73; Stephan Lorenz, "Grundwissen – Zivilrecht: Culpa in contrahendo (§311 II, III BGB)," *Jus* (2015). p. 398. Contra Stoll, "Tatbestände und Funktionen der Haftung für culpa in contrahendo." p. 445. He argues that restricting the understanding of *culpa in contrahendo* to cases of voided contracts would depart from the erroneous assumption that it describes a single, well-delineated doctrine, though that is not the case. It is not constructive to, on the one hand, criticize that the doctrine of *culpa in contrahendo* covers various distinct questions which are dealt with in confusion while, on the other hand, defending a confusing use of terminology, hence condemning the *culpa in contrahendo* to an impossible conceptualization.

35 See in detail on this evolution Giaro, "Culpa in contrahendo: eine Geschichte der Wiederentdeckung." pp. 134–149.

conceptually awkward and unprecise reasoning.[36] To prevent such confusing (*infra* Chap. 4, nr. 3–6) terminology, I will not rely on it. When I refer to the *culpa in contrahendo* or the positive and negative interest, I do so in their technical and historically correct sense. Though this diverges from a common contemporary understanding,[37] I believe it to be more precise and to prevent unnecessary confusion.

2. Pre-contractual liability

2.1. From culpa in contrahendo *to pre-contractual liability*

12. "*Die ich rief, die Geister werd ich nun nicht los*"[38] – Jhering justified the fact that a voided contract can give rise to liability based on his *Rechtsgefühl*. More specifically, the fact that the actual contractual relation ("*Contractsverhältnisse*") parties had been in cannot be disregarded: if parties believed they were in a contractual relation in which one is liable for culpa, the *a posteriori* voidance of that contract should not arbitrarily do away with the protection against culpable conduct.[39] Claus-Wilhelm Canaris formulates this accurately about 100 years after Jhering:

> "It is obvious that this [nullity] only applies to the relationship of performance: only the performance is impossible, only to this extent is the consequence of nullity appropriate; it will be difficult to deny that a special relationship has arisen between the parties in all other respects."[40]

36 "In the case of unlawful acts, there can be no performance interest in the absence of a contractual promise of performance. It therefore makes little sense to speak of a 'negative interest'. In practice, however, damages for a tortious act are a 'negative interest' because the injured party is to be placed in the same position as if the tortious act had never occurred." Wolfgang Fikentscher and Andreas Heinemann, *Schuldrecht Allgemeiner und Besonderer Teil* (Leck: De Gruyter, 2022). p. 376, nr. 608. Free translation. Original text: "*Bei unerlaubten Handlungen kann es mangels eines vertraglichen Erfüllungsversprechens kein Erfüllungsinteresse geben. Auch von 'negativem Interesse' zu sprechen ist deshalb wenig sinnvoll. Praktisch ist aber der Schadensersatz aus unerlaubter Handlung ein 'negatives Interesse', weil der Geschädigte so zu stellen ist, als wäre die unerlaubte Handlung nie geschehen.*" See also MüKoBGB/Emmerich, 9. Aufl. 2022, BGB § 311 nr. 38.

37 See Babusiaux, "Liability for Negotiations." p. 360 who speaks about "a common understanding of *culpa in contrahendo*, as meaning the breaking off of negotiations contrary to good faith and fair dealing." See also for a discussion of different understandings of positive and negative interest Marcel R. Ruygvoorn, *Afgebroken onderhandelingen en het gebruik van voorbehouden*, Recht en Praktijk (Deventer: Kluwer, 2009). pp. 263–265.

38 J.W. von Goethe, *Der Zauberlehrling*.

39 See the analogy Jhering draws with the *bona fidei* possessor Jhering, "Culpa in contrahendo oder Schadensersatz bei nichtigen oder nicht zur Perfection gelangten Verträgen." p. 33.

40 Canaris, "Ansprüche wegen 'positiver Vertragsverletzung' und 'Schutzwirkung für Dritte' bei nichtigen Verträgen. Zugleich ein Beitrag zur Vereinheitlichung der Regeln über die Schutzpflichtverletzungen." 481. Free translation. Original text: "*Es liegt auf der Hand, dass dies [die Nichtigkeit] nur für das Leistungsverhältnis zutrifft: nur die Leistung ist unmöglich, nur insoweit ist daher die Nichtigkeitsfolge angebracht; dass im übrigen zwischen den Parteien eine Sonderbeziehung*

To the extent that this reasoning was underlying Jhering's *culpa in contrahendo*, it was unlikely that the duty to act diligently could be contained within the contractual realm. Indeed, when taking the reasoning of protecting the factual relation by the letter, a relation that is very much like a contractual one should – in that reasoning – also give rise to a duty to act diligently. This is the direction the evolution of the *culpa in contrahendo* has taken.[41] In this sense, Jhering's vision of the *culpa in contrahendo* – much like the broom to the magician's apprentice in Johann Wolfgang von Goethe's *Zauberlehrling* – was no longer under his own control and extended beyond Jhering's explicit aversion towards a fault-based liability in the pre-contractual context.

13. Pre-contractual phase – This extension to the pre-contractual phase is attributed to the Italian author Gabriele Faggella.[42] In his contribution, *Dei periodi precontrattuali e della loro vera ed esatta construzione scientifica*,[43] he points out the importance of the phase preceding the conclusion of a contract – *il periodo precontrattuale* – and the absence of its study in scholarship:

> "In the negotiation period two moments must be distinguished: the time when the parties discuss, pre-arrange, exchange ideas, design the contract, conceive and elaborate the clauses, pacts and conditions, analyse and synthesise them; and the decisive moment of the concrete proposal and acceptance. Romanists and civilists, in general, take into

---

entstanden ist, wird man schwerlich leugnen können." See also Benedict, *Culpa in Contrahendo*, I. p. 60. On the importance of Canaris in this context, see Medicus and Lorenz, *Schuldrecht I Allgemeiner Teil*. p. 238, nr. 6.

41 Orlandi, "Responsabilità precontrattuale." p. 1000, nr. 3; Giannina Kreutz, *Hypothetische Verträge im Rahmen des Schadensausgleichs* (Baden-Baden: Nomos, 2016). p. 18; Jansen, "Developing legal doctrine: fault in the German law of delict." p. 103; Zimmermann, *Roman Law, Contemporary Law, European Law: The Civilian Tradition Today*. pp. 89–90; Giaro, "Culpa in contrahendo: eine Geschichte der Wiederentdeckung." pp. 117–118 Küpper, *Das Scheitern von Vertragshandlugen als Fallgruppe der culpa in conrahendo*. pp. 23–24; Stoll, "Tatbestände und Funktionen der Haftung für culpa in contrahendo." p. 454.

42 "it is widely held that from the pre-contractual duty of good faith derives an obligation not to withdraw from negotiations without just cause. The thesis, alien to common law writers and Jhering himself, is linked to well-known studies by Faggella." Francesco Benatti, *La responsabilità precontrattuale* (Milano: Giuffrè, 1963). p. 51. Free translation. Original text: "*è opinione diffusa che dal dovere precontrattuale di buona fede discenda un obbligo di non recedere dalle trattative senza giusta causa. La tesi, estranea agli scrittori del diritto commune e allo stesso Jhering, siricollega a noti studi di Fagella.*" More recently Babusiaux, "Liability for Negotiations." p. 351, nr. 5.

43 Gabriele Faggella, "Dei Periodi Precontrattuali," in *Studi giuridici in onore di C. Fadda, III* (Napoli, 1906). pp. 269–342. The text got a second edition in 1918: Gabriele Faggella, *I periodi precontrattuali e la responsabilità precontrattuale* (Roma: Società Cartiere Centrali, 1918). 170 p. I have mostly relied on the first edition for the present analysis. Of course, I have, however, read the chapter on pre-contractual liability (Chapter 4) of the second edition as well. Unfortunately, in the version of the second edition I had access to, pages 40 and 41, which contain relevant parts for pre-contractual liability, were missing. However, as the text appears to be otherwise identical to the first edition and no other indication about Faggella changing his theory in this lapse of 12 years have come to my attention, I believe it reasonable to assume that the second edition remained identical to the first.

> consideration this second moment of the pre-contractual period, disregarding the first, as if the proposal arises suddenly and is separate from all the previous work that produced it."[44]

To structure this newly discovered phase, Faggella divides it into three sub-parts:[45]

> "In the first period, therefore, the purpose is that of negotiating, discussing, considering, and elaborating the proposal of the contract aimed at; in the second, it is that of formulating and concretising it; in the third, it is the choice of a given proposal already inwardly evaluated and elaborated."[46]

His ambition to structure the pre-contractual phase appears to a large part aimed at clarifying the relation between negotiations and the moment and the way in which a contract is concluded. That is necessary, as "the whole of the earlier period [pre-contractual phase], which has nothing compulsory, has remained almost foreign to legal studies, except for the case of extra-contractual fault."[47]

14. Pre-contractual liability – More importantly and innovatively,[48] Faggella argues for a liability in case of breaking-off of negotiations:

> "It seems to us that even in the early periods a responsibility is possible. It is certain, especially in the modern commercial world, that the most important contracts are preceded by extensive and laborious negotiations, projects, plans, studies, which often import not short time and not slight expense. In certain cases a liability of the withdrawing party is conceivable."[49]

44 Faggella, "Dei Periodi Precontrattuali." pp. 271–272. Free translation. Original text: "*Nel periodo delle trattative v'ha da distinguere due momenti: il tempo in cui le parti discutono, preordinano, si scambiano le idee, progettano il contratto, concepiscono ed elaborano le clausole, I patti e le condizioni, le analizzano e le sintetizzano; e il momento decisive della proposta concreta e dell'accettazione. I romanisti e i civilisti, in generale, prendono in considerazione questo secondo momento del periodo precontrattuale, senza tener conto del primo, quasi che la proposta sorga improvvisa e sia separata da tutto il precedente lavorio che l'abbia prodotta.*"

45 See also Babusiaux, "Liability for Negotiations." p. 351, nr. 5.

46 Faggella, "Dei Periodi Precontrattuali." p. 278. Free translation. Original text: "*Nel primo periodo, dunque, la volizione è quella di trattare, discutere, considerare, elaborare la proposta del contratto cui si tende; nel secondo è quella di formularla e concretarla; nel terzo, è volizione di una data proposta già interiormente valutata ed elaborata.*"

47 Faggella, "Dei Periodi Precontrattuali." pp. 273–274. Free translation. Original text: "*Tutto il period anteriore [periodo precontrattuale], che non presenta niente di obbligatorio, è rimasto quasi estraneo agli studi giuridici, tranne il caso di una colpa extra-contrattuale.*"

48 On the impact this early recognition of the possibility of culpably breaking-off of negotiations on Italian law see Tommaso Febbrajo, "Good Faith and Pre-Contractual Liability in Italy: Recent Developments in the Interpretation of Article 1337 of the Italian Civil Code," *Italian Law Journal* 2 (2016). p. 296.

49 Faggella, "Dei Periodi Precontrattuali." p. 298; Faggella, *I periodi precontrattuali e la responsabilità precontrattuale*. p. 34, nr. 30. Free translation. Original text: "*A noi sembra che anche nei primi*

The question then rises under which circumstances such a liability would be conceivable. Faggella argues that this would be the case where an authorization to work out a draft contract had been given. Though such an agreement is not a preliminary contract in his eyes, it nevertheless "generates a trust that the other party will persevere until either an agreement is reached or until, due to the exchange of ideas on contractual points and the outcome of the study and examination of the project, agreement is no longer possible. But the mere termination without reason is not right to be immune from liability."[50]

With this argumentation, a decisive move has been made towards our contemporary understanding of pre-contractual liability. Throughout the evolution from Faggella's writing in 1906 up until today, relatively little has changed. Though different authors have advanced different grounds to justify why the breaking-off of negotiations can become unlawful, the question as such has remained unchanged ever since.

15. LEGAL BASIS/CONDITIONS OF APPLICATION OF PRE-CONTRACTUAL LIABILITY – According to Faggella, the ground for pre-contractual liability is neither located in an obligation to contract nor in a fault of the party who withdraws from the negotiations, as he merely exercises his right to withdraw ('*il quale opera nella legittima sfera del suo diritto*').[51] Instead, he advances a double ground for liability:

> "The first consists in this: that he who consents to the other party's pre-contractual preparatory work or contributes to it, thereby assumes the obligation to compensate it for the expenses and the real cost of its work, when he untimely withdraws from it, although there is no obligation to contract. The second cause of action consists in the destruction of a value of others, i.e. of a patrimonial value of the renouncer to which it withdraws, represented by the expenses and work incurred for the creation of the contractual right, or by its concurrence in consideration of the consent to treat of the withdrawing party, and of the possibility or probability of the creation of that right."[52]

---

periodi una responsabilità sia possibile. È certo, specialmente nel mondo commerciale moderno, che i contratti più importanti sono preceduti da larghe e laboriose trattative, da progetti, da piani, da studi, che importano spesso tempo non breve e spese non lievi. In certi casi è concepibile una responsabilità del recedente."

50 Faggella, "Dei Periodi Precontrattuali." p. 299; Faggella, *I periodi precontrattuali e la responsabilità precontrattuale.* pp. 35–36, nr. 31. Free translation. Original text: "*Essa genera una fiducia che l'altra parte perseveri fino a che o intervenga l'accordo finché, per lo scambio delle idee sui punti contrattuali e pel risultato dello studio e dell'esame del progetto, l'accordo non sia più possibile. Ma il puro e semplice recesso sine causa non è giusto che sia immune da responsabilità.*"

51 Faggella, "Dei Periodi Precontrattuali." p. 302; Faggella, *I periodi precontrattuali e la responsabilità precontrattuale.* p. 41, nr. 35.

52 Faggella, "Dei Periodi Precontrattuali." pp. 302–303. Free translation. Original text: "*La prima consiste in questo: che chi consento verso l'altra parte un lavorio preparatorio antecontrattuale o il concorso in esso, assume con ciò stesso l'obbligazione a risarcirla delle spese e del costo reale del suo lavoro, quando intempestivamente vi receda, sebbene non esista un'obbligazione a trattare.*

Though Faggella speaks of the foundation ("*il fondamento*")[53] of his pre-contractual liability, it rather reads as two conditions of application necessary to entrench a liability in the pre-contractual period ("*responsabilità nel periodo ante-contrattualè*"). The first condition being the acceptation of the preparation of a contract, the second being that harm is inflicted by the breaking-off of negotiations.

16. SANCTIONS IN CASE OF PRE-CONTRACTUAL LIABILITY – Given that Faggella's pre-contractual liability follows from the combination of accepting the preparation of a contract and the suffering damage from the breaking-off of negotiations, the harm that would have to be compensated for covers costs made for the preparation of the contract and other preparatory work ('*spese e del costo del lavorio preparatorio consentito*'):[54]

> "Compensation is limited to the actual expenses and real cost of the pre-contractual preparatory work necessary to carry out the negotiations and the elaboration of the project, and up to the point where the consent of the withdrawing party has been obtained.
> Such is its content and such are its boundaries."[55]

17. BINDING FORCE OF OFFERS – Faggella also deals, and quite extensively so, with the question of the binding force of an offer.[56] Raymond Saleilles's writings from 1907, *La responsabilité précontractuelle: a propos d'une étude nouvelle sur la matière*,[57] on the pre-contractual phase must actually be located in that very context. As French law in his time did not consider an offer binding, he used the pre-contractual liability ("*responsabilité précontractuelle*") to explain why an offeror who retracted his offer was to be held liable. Rather incidentally, he clarifies that he did consider that the breaking-off of contractual negotiations could *not* lead to liability:

> "Withdrawing or breaking-off negotiations remains an absolute right for each party; it can never be, for any of them, an event constituting fault, still less could it be considered a risky event, even in a purely objective

---

La seconda causa consiste nella distruzione di un valore altrui, cioè di un valore patrimoniale del trattante verso cui se recede, rappresentato dalle spese e dall'opera sostenuta per la nascita del diritto contrattuale, o dal concorso di lui in considerazione del consenso a trattare del recedente, e dalla possibilità o dala probabilità del sorgere di quel diritto."

53 Faggella, "Dei Periodi Precontrattuali." p. 302; Faggella, *I periodi precontrattuali e la responsabilità precontrattuale*. p. 39, nr. 35.

54 Faggella, "Dei Periodi Precontrattuali." p. 303.

55 Faggella, "Dei Periodi Precontrattuali." p. 304. Free translation. Original text: "*Il risarcimento è limitato alle spese effettive e al costo reale del lavorio preparatorio antecontrattuale, necessario all'espletamento delle trattative e alla elaborazione del progetto, e fino al punto dove sia giunto il consenso del recedente. Tale è il suo contenuto e tali i suoi confini.*"

56 Faggella, "Dei Periodi Precontrattuali." pp. 308 *et seq*.

57 Raymond Saleilles, "De la responsabilité précontractuelle – A propos d'une étude nouvelle sur la matière," *RTD Civ.* VI (1907). pp. 697–751.

theory, which would eliminate any element of fault from the concept of quasi-fault. For, in such a case, the risks are necessarily shared; and each of the parties must expect the negotiations to be abandoned, since each remains absolutely free to withdraw."[58]

2.2. Historical function and means of pre-contractual liability

18. FUNCTION – The function that Faggella wants to see fulfilled is to allow to grant a liability claim in cases where negotiations are broken-off. The issue that Faggella faces in fulfilling this aim is that the breaking-off of negotiations is – as he himself clearly states (*supra* Chap. 1, nr. 15) – lawful. Clearly, such a function is distinct from the function of Jhering's *culpa in contrahendo* had to fulfil (*supra* Chap. 1, nr. 9).[59]

19. MEANS – The way Faggella explains that, in some circumstances, the breaking-off of negotiations can nevertheless be unlawful is by relying on the acceptation of the parties to get to a contract (*supra* Chap. 1, nrs. 14–15). Importantly, he does not answer that question with reference to the extra-contractual liability which, according to him, applies in the pre-contractual phase.[60] This results in a two-pronged structure: on the one hand, extra-contractual liability applies to the pre-contractual phase; on the other hand, a specific legal basis is needed to explain that the breaking-off of negotiations is wrongful.

20. TWO-PRONGED STRUCTURE – Indeed, for Faggella, it seems that the question of whether the breaking-off of negotiations is unlawful and that of the applicable liability in the pre-contractual phase are distinct: he does not rely on the latter to answer the former. Indeed, he recognizes that in the pre-contractual phase, one can be held extra-contractually liable (*supra* Chap. 1, nr. 13) but looks for another foundation for the liability that arises due to the breaking-off of negotiations

58 Saleilles, "De la responsabilité précontractuelle – A propos d'une étude nouvelle sur la matière." p. 700. Free translation. Original text: "*Le retrait ou la rupture des négociations reste pour chaque partie un droit absolu; il ne saurait jamais être, pour aucune d'elles, un fait constitutif de faute, encore moins pourrait-on y voir un fait risque, même dans une théorie purement objective, qui éliminerait tout élément de faute de la notion de quasi-délit. Car, en pareil cas, les risques sont forcément partagés; et chacun des parties doit s'attendre à l'abandon des négociations, puisque chacune reste absolument libre de se retirer.*"

59 Fagella also explicitly states that he is not trying to extend Jhering's *culpa in contrahendo*: "We do not intend to apply the Jeringian institute of *culpa in contrahendo* to the first periods when the offer has not yet been addressed, i.e. to extend *culpa in contrahendo* in the revocation of the offer to the mere withdrawal from negotiations." Faggella, "Dei Periodi Precontrattuali." p. 298. Free translation. Original text: "*Non intendiamo applicare l'istituto jheringhiano della culpa in contraendo ai primi periodi, in cui l'offerta non sia stata ancora indirizzata, estendere cioè la culpa in contrahendo nella revoca della proposta al semplice recesso dalle trattative.*"

60 "The entire earlier period, which presents nothing obligatory, has remained almost unknown to legal studies, except for the case of extra-contractual fault." Faggella, "Dei Periodi Precontrattuali." pp. 35–36. Free translation. Original text: "*Tutto il periodo anteriore, che non presenta niente di obbligatori, è rimasto quasi estraneo agli studi giuridici, tranne il caso di una colpa extra-contrattuale.*"

itself. This suggests a two-pronged structure for pre-contractual liability that underlies his thinking of that latter liability: on the one hand, a general liability to compensate loss suffered in the pre-contractual phase and, on the other hand, a specific ground for liability for the case of breaking-off of negotiations.

2.3. Contemporary approach to pre-contractual liability

21. TWO-PRONGED STRUCTURE IN CONTEMPORARY LITERATURE – If we fast forward to contemporary literature, we find a similar distinction between the liability applicable during the negotiation process and, distinct therefrom, the question of what makes the breaking-off of negotiations unlawful. The most recent and comprehensive study of the subject matter probably is Isabel Zuloaga's dissertation *Reliance in the Breaking-Off of Contractual Negotiations*,[61] which I'll use as an illustration of this two-pronged structure. She argues that the "higher concept"[62] behind pre-contractual liability is reliance. Within reliance, she distinguished a trust-oriented dimension and an expectation-based dimension. While the trust-oriented perspective explains a general liability applicable during the negotiation process, the expectation-oriented perspective justifies that the breaking-off of negotiations is unlawful. However, her line of argumentation is not as articulate; rather, it appears a little cryptic:

> "The second dimension of reliance is 'expectation-oriented'. Here, the focus is on a specific expectation of the future conclusion of the negotiated contract. Before analysing this dimension, it is necessary to establish the relationship between the two dimensions of reliance. The expectation dimension is a specific manifestation of the trust dimension, in that the expectation of the future conclusion of the contract presupposes the existence of trust between the negotiating parties. Therefore, expectation-based reliance emanates from trust-based reliance as a particular manifestation of it. *Because the trust dimension is of a more general nature, it can operate in different scenarios of precontractual liability, whereas the expectation dimension is specific to cases of broken negotiations*. Thus, it can be understood that in the selected jurisdictions, while mention of what is essentially trust-based reliance is sometimes made in breaking off cases, the key requirement for this liability to arise is expectation-based reliance."[63]

Zuloaga seems to suggest that within pre-contractual liability, two distinct functioning's of liability must be distinguished: a general trust-based one and a specific expectation-based one. She seems to criticize in the last sentence of the preceding citation that sometimes both are not clearly distinguished, to the

61 Zuloaga, *Reliance in the Breaking Off of Contractual Negotiations*. xxxviii+254 p.
62 Zuloaga, *Reliance in the Breaking Off of Contractual Negotiations*. p. 1.
63 Zuloaga, *Reliance in the Breaking Off of Contractual Negotiations*. p. 151.

extent that the reliance-based liability is used to explain why the breaking-off of negotiations would give rise to liability. Though her thinking in terms of trust-based reliance and expectation-based reliance seems rather difficult with existing liability law systems, the substance of her criticism shows a continuity between the way Faggella understands pre-contractual liability and the way Isabel Zuloaga, more than 100 years later, approaches that same issue.

Marcel Ruygvoorn, in his dissertation, *Afgebroken onderhandelingen en het gebruik van voorbehouden*,[64] also argues in favour of a two-pronged approach: at all times and independently of their freedom from contract, parties to negotiations can be held liable. On top of that general liability, parties can, under some circumstances, be under an obligation to negotiate or contract:

> "It [three-phases doctrine] may never have been intended that way by its creator, but wrongly creates the impression that each phase necessarily occurs in a negotiation process and it then wrongly creates the impression that the phases in question necessarily and irreversibly follow each other in time in all cases. In any event, I believe that the three-phase doctrine is frequently interpreted as such in practice while none of these impressions is correct as far as I am concerned. In what follows, it will be argued that only two situations can arise in the pre-contractual phase, namely: the situation in which both parties are still free to break-off negotiations, not liable for damages, and the situation in which (one of) the parties is no longer free to do so. In addition (and therefore not necessarily: successively), the situation may (but does not have to) arise in which an obligation to reimburse costs incurred in the context of the negotiations arises in the pre-contractual phase at any time during the period in which the negotiations can still be terminated unilaterally."[65]

A variant on this two-pronged structure is to say that liability can rise in the context of contract negotiations but that the breaking-off of negotiations or refusal to contract itself cannot give rise to liability. It is very prominent under

64 Ruygvoorn, *Afgebroken onderhandelingen en het gebruik van voorbehouden*. xvi+461.

65 Ruygvoorn, *Afgebroken onderhandelingen en het gebruik van voorbehouden*. p. 45. Free translation. Original version: "*Het is wellicht door de bedenker ervan nooit zo bedoeld, maar wekt ten onrechte de indruk dat iedere fase zich noodzakelijkerwijs in een onderhandelingstraject voordoet en het wekt vervolgens ten onrechte de indruk dat de betreffende fasen elkaar in alle gevallen noodzakelijkerwijs en onomkeerbaar in de tijd opvolgen. In elk geval meen ik dat de driefasenleer in de praktijk veelvuldig als zodanig wordt geïnterpreteerd terwijl geen van deze indrukken wat mij betreft juist is. In het hierna volgende zal worden betoogd dat zich in de precontractuele fase slechts twee situaties kunnen voordoen, te weten: de situatie waarin het beide partijen nog vrij staat om, niet-schadeplichtig, de onderhandelingen af te breken en de situatie waarin dit (één van) partijen niet langer vrij staat. Daarnaast (en dus niet noodzakelijkerwijs: opvolgend) kán (maar dit hoeft niet) zich de situatie voordoen dat er in de precontractuele fase op enig moment gedurende de periode dat de onderhandelingen nog eenzijdig, niet-schadeplichtig kunnen worden beëindigd, een verplichting ontstaat om kosten die in het kader van de onderhandelingen zijn gemaakt, te vergoeden.*"

French law[66] and also influential under Belgian law.[67] This way of reasoning rests on the same understanding as the two-pronged approach: a specific ground is needed to give rise to liability for the breaking-off or refusal itself. Yet it does not try to overcome this impossibility but accepts it for the sake of maintaining freedom from contract. The fault then lies in the circumstances surrounding the breaking-off or refusal, such as the abruptness, untimeliness, or other circumstances.[68] This position, based on the freedom from contract as an objection to any fault in the breaking-off or refusal, can be found under German law too. It has been a central argument in Thomas Krawitz's dissertation, *Schutz vorvertraglicher Investitionen*:

> "The main insurmountable objection here is that it is not compatible with the negative freedom of contract to regard the termination of negotiations without a valid reason as behaviour in breach of duty."[69]

From Faggella up until today, I observe a continuity in the underlying structuring of pre-contractual liability. Though this structure is always somewhat implicitly built upon without being clearly exposed, it is recognisable. This structure is composed of, on the one hand, duties of care applicable to contract negotiations and whose infringement can give rise to liability and, on the other hand, a specific legal basis/justification making the breaking-off of contract negotiations unlawful.

22. Monolithic structure in contemporary literature – To this two-pronged structure of pre-contractual liability, a monolithic structure can be opposed. Such a monolithic structure – as the name suggests – builds on a duty of care applicable to contract negotiations and related liability, while it also is the legal basis/justification rendering the breaking-off of negotiations unlawful. Essentially, the argument is (without much underlying reasoning) that the breaking-off of negotiations or refusal to contract *can* give rise to liability without the need for a specific explanation. Carla Sieburgh offers a telling illustration in the Dutch *Asser Serie*:

> "The rule that negotiating parties must let their conduct be determined in part by each other's legitimate interests may result in a party lacking the

66 See influentially Olivier Deshayes, "Le dommage précontractuel," *RTD Com.* (2004). pp. 187–204. Followed f.i. by Patrice Jourdain, "Préjudice consécutif à la rupture fautive des pourparlers," *RTD Civ.* (2006). p. 771. Also dealt with in Martijn W. Hesselink, *De redelijkheid en billijkheid in het Europese privaatrecht* (Den Haag: Kluwer, 1999). p. 72.

67 See f.i. Annick De Boeck, "Precontractuele aansprakelijkheid anno 2010," *Themis* (2010). p. 3, nr. 6; Isabelle Durant, "La rupture unilatérale des pourparlers ou l'exercice d'une liberté surveillée," in *La volonté unilatérale dans le contrat* (Bruxelles: Editions du jeune barreau de Bruxelles, 2008). p. 44, nr. 6.

68 Deshayes, "Le dommage précontractuel." pp. 195–196, nrs. 16–17. See the references there.

69 Thomas Krawitz, *Schutz vorvertraglicher Investitionen – Zur Haftung beim Scheitern von Vertragsverhandlungen* (Berlin: Duncker & Humblot, 2015). p. 88. Free translation. Original text: "*Der unüberwindbare Haupteinwand ist dabei, dass es nicht mit der negativen Vertragsfreiheit zu vereinbaren ist, den Verhandlungsabbruch ohne triftigen Grund als pflichtwidriges Verhalten anzusehen.*"

freedom to break off negotiations. If it nevertheless proceeds to do so, it may, in principle, be ordered to continue negotiations."[70]

Sieburgh explains that the breaking-off of negotiations is unlawful by relying on duties of care ("must let their conduct be determined in part by each other's legitimate interests"). That line of reasoning, for instance, can also be seen under German law, where following upon the BGH's approach,[71] it is generally accepted that the breaking-off of contract negotiations itself is wrongful if the expectation had been created that a contract would be concluded, provided no sufficient justification exists for the breaking-off.[72]

23. PLAN – Structurally, these two opposing approaches can be identified in contemporary scholarship.[73] The question will now be which one of those two convinces. To do so, I will first look at the legal context in which pre-contractual liability takes place in order to verify whether the function previously sketched out can be confirmed from a contemporary and more conceptual perspective (*infra* Chap. 1, nrs. 24–35). Then I will look at different types of liability law systems to assess which one of those allows to fulfil the functions needed for pre-contractual liability to provide remedies in the case of broken-off negotiations (*infra* Chap. 2, nrs. 1–14). Once I have established which kind of liability law system is needed to fulfil the identified functions, I will assess to what extent this is confirmed in the different systems I compare with (*infra* Chap. 2, nrs. 15–20). This should then allow me to test whether the isolated kind of liability law system allows to hold a party liable for the breaking-off of negotiations (*infra* Chap. 2, nrs. 25–37). If this is the case, and based on Ockham's razor principle,[74] such a monolithic understanding of

70 Asser/Sieburgh 6-III 2022/193. Free translation. Original text: "*De regel dat onderhandelende partijen hun gedrag mede moeten laten bepalen door elkaars gerechtvaardigde belangen, kan er voorts toe leiden dat een partij de vrijheid mist de onderhandelingen af te breken. Indien zij hiertoe niettemin overgaat, kan zij in beginsel tot voortzetting van de onderhandelingen worden veroordeeld.*" Another example is offered in John Cartwright and Martijn Hesselink, *Precontractual Liability in European Private Law* (Cambridge: Cambridge University Press, 2008). p. 451: "In its strongest form, and in its strongest statement within English law, we find a rejection of the duty to negotiate in good faith based on a rejection of the idea that one party, by entering into negotiations, has given up the freedom to change his mind."

71 BGH *NJW* 1996, 1884.

72 Staudinger/Feldmann (2018) BGB § 311, nr. 143.

73 Two-pronged: Zuloaga, *Reliance in the Breaking Off of Contractual Negotiations*. p. 151; Ruygvoorn, *Afgebroken onderhandelingen en het gebruik van voorbehouden*. p. 45; Deshayes, "Le dommage précontractuel." pp. 187–204. Followed f.i. by Jourdain, "Préjudice consécutif à la rupture fautive des pourparlers." p. 771. Monolithic: Asser/Sieburgh 6-III 2022/193. More generally, literature not thoroughly engaging with pre-contractual liability tend to rely on a monolithic approach.

74 "an underlying concern for ontological parsimony. This is summed up in the famous slogan known as 'Ockham's Razor,' often expressed as 'Don't multiply entities beyond necessity.' Although the sentiment is certainly Ockham's, that particular formulation is nowhere to be found in his texts. Moreover, as usually stated, it is a sentiment that virtually *all* philosophers, medieval or otherwise, would accept; no one wants a needlessly bloated ontology. The question, of course, is which entities are needed and which are not."

Stanford Encyclopaedia of Philosophy, URL: https://plato.stanford.edu/entries/ockham/#OckhRazo (consulted on 31 January 2024).

pre-contractual liability suffices to provide remedies in the case of broken-off negotiations. If, however, the identified liability law system does not allow a party that breaks off negotiations to be held liable, the monolithic approach does not convince. In that case, another additional explanation will be needed to give rise to a remedy for breaking off negotiations. By applying this test, it should be possible to identify the structure of pre-contractual liability.

3. Freedom from contract and the function of pre-contractual liability

3.1. Freedom of contract

24. FREEDOM OF CONTRACT – Liberal economies rest upon private autonomy, roughly speaking: individuals are free to pursue their own interests, and private law protects this pursuit – to the extent that the pursued interest is lawful.[75] The legal translation thereof is freedom of contract – namely, that individuals are free to conclude contracts, to decide their content and the contracting partner, and logically linked thereto, the freedom not to contract. In Nils Jansen and Reinhard Zimmermann's *Commentaries on European Contract Laws*, freedom of contract is defined as follows:

> "Everyone is free to contract or not to contract, to choose the person with whom to contract, and to determine the content of the contract."[76]

75 On this link Medicus and Lorenz, *Schuldrecht I Allgemeiner Teil*. pp. 29–30, nr. 10. More extensive discussion in Jan Busche, *Privatautonomie und Kontrahierungszwang*, Jus Privatium (Tübingen: Mohr Siebeck, 1999). pp. 13–45: "There is an interdependence between the private law system and the economic constitution, as both regulatory circles are grouped around the individual as the decision-maker. While the market activity of individual subjects of private law, carried out under private autonomy, is of system-forming importance in market-economy systems, the exchange processes in state-controlled economic systems take place in accordance with state interventionist guidelines. In contrast to economic constitutions characterised by a market economy, the primacy of individual control by individuals acting independently of one another does not apply; rather, these individuals must subordinate themselves to the execution of the state's will. Private autonomy can only be spoken of to a very limited extent, if at all." p. 45. Free translation. Original text: "*Zwischen der Privatrechtsordnung und der Wirtschaftsverfassung besteht eine Interdependenz, da sich beide Regelungskreise um das Individuum als Entscheidungsträger gruppieren. Während in marktwirtschaftlichen Ordnungen der in privatautonomer Verantwortung wahrgenommenen Marktbetätigung einzelner Privatrechtssubjekte systembildende Bedeutung zukommt, vollziehen sich die Austauschprozesse in staatlich gelenkten Wirtschaftsordnungen entsprechend staatsinterventionistischer Vorgaben. Im Unterschied zu marktwirtschaftlich geprägten Wirtschaftsverfassungen gilt nicht der Vorrang der Einzelsteuerung durch unabhängig voneinander handelnde Individuen, vielmehr haben sich diese der Exekution des staatlichen Willens unterzuordnen. Von Privatautonomie kann, wenn überhaupt, nur in sehr begrenztem Umfang gesprochen werden.*" See also for a more critical perspective Christoph Menke, *Kritk der Rechte*, Suhrkamp taschenbuch wissenschaft (Berlin: Suhrkamp, 2018). p. 77.

76 In Eike Hosemann, "Article 1:102: Freedom of Contract," in *Commentaries of European Contract Laws*, ed. Nils Jansen and Reinhard Zimmermann (Oxford: Oxford University Press, 2018). p. 51. Other definitions discussed in Busche, *Privatautonomie und Kontrahierungszwang*. p. 72 *et seq.*

Though not codified in all continental European codifications,[77] freedom of contract is the "'starting point' for all European systems of contract law."[78]

25. Freedom from contract – Logically necessary for a freedom to contract is a *freedom not to contract*: only where one is free not to contract is one also free to contract. Indeed, if one was *not* free not to contract, one would be forced to contract.[79] Hence, the freedom not to contract – which I will call *freedom from contract* ("*Abschlussfreiheit*")[80] but can also be designated as the negative aspect of the freedom of contract – is a necessary condition for freedom of contract. A significant consequence of freedom from contract is that the outcome of a no-contract scenario is lawful. This means that the refusal to contract and the breaking-off of negotiations – both exercises of the freedom from contract – is *a priori* lawful. It does not necessarily mean that it is under all circumstances lawful or could never be wrongful, but at least as a normative point of departure, the outcome of not contracting is lawful.

26. Freedom of negotiations – The outcome of not contracting could not be lawful if the breaking-off of negotiations would not be lawful itself. Otherwise, a party to negotiations could never leave negotiations and would be condemned to find an agreement. The freedom of and from contract would become illusory. In that sense, the freedom of and from negotiations is inherent to the freedom of and from contract. Another solution would be unplausible, if not impossible, to conceive. To the extent that the freedom of and from negotiations is inherent to the freedom of and from contract, it is generally not explicitly recognized as such. The French (article 1112 Fr. Civ. C.[81]) and Belgian

77 Especially older codifications tend not to have such a provision (the Napoleonic Civil Code of 1804, Austrian ABGB of 1810, German BGB of 1900 (but see art. 2 German constitution)) while more recent codifications tend to have one (see the recent re-codifications of France (article 1102 Be. Civ. C.) and Belgium (article 5.14 Be. Civ. C.)). The same is true for the harmonization model laws. Only the Dutch BW of 1992 contains no explicit provision on the freedom of contract, though relatively recent in date. See for an in-depth discussion of the possible reasons for the inclusion and non-inclusion of explicit provisions recognizing freedom of contract: Hosemann, "Article 1:102: Freedom of Contract." pp. 37 *et seq.*

78 Hosemann, "Article 1:102: Freedom of Contract." p. 31. Citations omitted.

79 Clearly expressed in MüKoBGB/Emmerich, 9. Aufl. 2022, BGB § 311, nr. 1; Busche, *Privatautonomie und Kontrahierungszwang*. p. 67.

80 Fikentscher and Heinemann, *Schuldrecht Allgemeiner und Besonderer Teil.* p. 71, nr. 93 and pp. 83–85, nrs. 112–113; Carsten Nickel, *Die Rechtsfolgen der culpa in contrahendo* (Berlin: Duncker & Humblot, 2004). p. 27.

81 "The commencement, continuation and breaking-off of precontractual negotiations are free from control. They must mandatorily satisfy the requirements of good faith." Original text: "*L'initiative, le déroulement et la rupture des négociations précontractuelles sont libres. Ils doivent impérativement satisfaire aux exigences de la bonne foi.*"

(article 5.15 Be. Civ. C.[82]) re-codification, however, probably for pedagogical reasons, do so:[83]

> "Art. 5.15. Freedom of negotiation
> The parties are free to initiate, conduct and break off pre-contractual negotiations.
> In that regard, they act in accordance with the requirements of good faith."

As the freedom of negotiations is implicit in the freedom from contract, I will understand freedom from contract to also contain freedom of and from negotiations.

3.2. Risk

27. Risk attribution – As a consequence of the lawfulness of the no-contract scenario, the risk of failing contract negotiations or conclusion remains with each party to the negotiations.[84] Would the outcome be unlawful, then such unlawfulness could trigger liability and justify that the costs would be leveraged onto another party. That, however, is not the case. Therefore, in case of failing negotiations, *the loss lies where it falls.*[85] Hence, freedom of contract has the

82 "Art. 5.15. Freedom of negotiation The parties are free to initiate, conduct and break-off pre-contractual negotiations. In that regard, they act in accordance with the requirements of good faith." Original text: "*Art. 5.15. Liberté de négocier Les parties sont libres d'entamer, de mener et de rompre des négociations précontractuelles. Elles agissent à cet égard conformément aux exigences de la bonne foi.*"/"*Art. 5.15. Onderhandelingsvrijheid De partijen zijn vrij precontractuele onderhandelingen aan te vatten, te voeren en af te breken. Ze handelen hierbij in overeenstemming met de eisen van de goede trouw.*"

83 On the reasons for codification by one of the drafters of the new law of obligations: Rafaël Jafferali, "La formation dynamique du contrat," in *La réforme du droit des obligations*, ed. T. Derval, Rafaël Jafferali, and Benoit Kohl (Bruxelles: Larcier, 2023). p. 172, nr. 2.

84 Clearly expressed in MüKoBGB/Emmerich, 9. Aufl. 2022, BGB § 311 nr. 193; Fikentscher and Heinemann, *Schuldrecht Allgemeiner und Besonderer Teil*. p. 71, nr. 93; Medicus and Lorenz, *Schuldrecht I Allgemeiner Teil*. p. 245, nr. 14; Busche, *Privatautonomie und Kontrahierungszwang*. p. 60.

85 A principled deviation from this risk attribution, such as defended by Thomas Krawitz, seems not convincing because the risk attribution follows from the freedom from contract: "The starting point of the considerations is that the affirmation of a claim for compensation deviates from the principle of 'casus sentit dominus'. In relation to the pre-contractual area, this principle is understood to mean that each party must bear the risk of frustration of its own expenses incurred in anticipation of the conclusion of a contract. However, it does not have any particular normative persuasive force, i.e. if a convincing justification for a different distribution of risk can be found, a deviation from the principle of 'casus sentit dominus' is possible without further ado." Krawitz, *Schutz vorvertraglicher Investitionen – Zur Haftung beim Scheitern von Vertragsverhandlungen*. pp. 113–114. Free translation. Original text: "*Ausgangspunkt der Überlegungen ist dabei, dass durch die Bejahung eines Ersatzanspruchs vom Grundsatz 'casus sentit dominus' abgewichen wird. Dieser Grundsatz wird in Bezug auf den vorvertraglichen Bereich so verstanden, dass jede Partei das Risiko der*

effect of operating a risk attribution, namely, that all costs a negotiator makes are made at his own risk. As early as 1907, this risk attribution is clearly seen by Raymond Saleilles:

> "For, in such a case [withdrawal from negotiations], the risks are necessarily shared; and each of the parties must expect the negotiations to be abandoned, since each remains absolutely free to withdraw. Undoubtedly, each of them may make enquiries, carry out research and prepare estimates for the proposed contract, which will constitute expenses. This is almost always the case when considerable financial undertakings or major orders are involved. But these are preparations that each party undertakes at its own risk, and because each party is willing to."[86]

28. Uncertainty and risk – Given the uncertainty of the outcome of the negotiation process, parties take a risk when entering negotiations. This risk lies, on the one hand, in the risk of making costs potentially at loss and, on the other hand, in not getting the contract that is negotiated. The former risk – costs made becoming a loss – explains why the damage suffered in no-contract law generally is pure economic loss (*infra* Chap. 1, nr. 29); the latter risk, in turn, is a thread to the freedom of contract of the party suffering the risk materialization (no-contract scenario) (*infra* Chap. 1, nr. 30).

29. Pure economic loss – As the outcome of contract negotiations is not certain, costs made in view of this outcome are at risk given the uncertain return on investment. If the outcome was to be guaranteed, then the costs would not be at risk, as it would be certain that they would serve their purpose (be it that the extent to which they would yield benefit would remain uncertain). As, however, this is not the case, the investment can potentially become a loss, as costs were made without a valuable counterpart. Hence, the materialization of the risk causes loss, which is purely economic,[87] i.e. pure economic

Frustrierung eigener, in Erwartung eines Vertragsschlusses getätigten Aufwendungen selbst zu tragen hat. Ihm kommt indes keine besondere normative Überzeugungskraft zu, d.h. wenn sich eine überzeugende Begründing für eine andersartige Risikoverteilung finden lässt, ist ein Abweichen vom Grundsatz des 'casus sentit dominus' ohne weiteres möglich." On this risk attribution in general see Nils Jansen, *The Structure of Tort Law* (Oxford: Oxford University Press, 2021). p. 71.

86 Saleilles, "De la responsabilité précontractuelle – A propos d'une étude nouvelle sur la matière." p. 700. Free translation. Original text: "*Car, en pareil cas* [abandon des négociations], *les risques sont forcément partagés; et chacune des parties doit s'attendre à l'abandon des négociations, puisque chacune reste absolument libre de se retirer. Sans doute, chacune d'elles peut faire, en vue du projet de contrat, des enquêtes, des recherches, des devis, qui constitueront des dépenses. Il en est presque toujours ainsi lorsqu'il s'agit d'entreprises financières considérables, ou de commandes importantes. Mais ce sont là des préparatifs que chacun entreprend à ses risques et périls, et parce que chaque partie le veut bien.*"

87 It can, of course, occur that people get hurt during contract negotiations. See on this Staudinger/Feldmann (2018) BGB § 311 nrs. 108–110. However, that is a matter for general delictual liability and does not pose the technical difficulties I deal with here.

loss. A pure economic loss is a loss that is immediately and solely suffered in the patrimony of the (legal) person in question. As Helmut Koziol puts it in *Compensation for Pure Economic Loss from a Continental Lawyer's Perspective*:

> "Pure economic loss is a harm not causally consequent upon an injury to the person (life, body, health, freedom or other rights to personality) or to property (tangible and intangible assets)."[88]

Mauro Bussani *et al.* point out that it is the word "pure" that is of crucial importance, as it marks the fact that the economic loss is not "consequential" to damage to person or property. Consequential economic loss, hence, "presupposes the existence of physical injuries, whereas pure economic loss strikes the victim's wallet and nothing else."[89]

30. Threat to freedom of contract – Besides the risk of vainly made costs, the absence of a contract puts pressure on the freedom of contract of the party which has no choice but to accept the absence of the contract in question. Someone exercising its freedom *from* contract annihilates someone else's freedom *to* contract. This is readily accepted by assuming that the harmed party could find another contract elsewhere. Yet it is by no means trivial. Indeed, it is crucial to understand that someone's freedom from contract always comes at the expense of someone else's freedom to contract. Indeed, if one refuses to contract, the other loses its possibility to contract in this very circumstance and thereby may lose access to certain goods, services, opportunities, status, recognition, *et cetera*. From this angle, protecting the freedom *to* contract of some requires limiting the freedom *from* contract of some others. How and when exactly this is done, fundamentally, is a political decision. An absence of a decision on this point is also a political statement, namely, a liberal one.

31. *Status quo* – Currently, the status quo is a liberal one, as Jan Busche explains in *Privatautonomie und Kontrahierungszwang*.[90] The result thereof is a perceived antinomy between freedom of contract and an obligation to contract.

88 Helmut Koziol, "Compensation for Pure Economic Loss from a Continental Lawyer's Perspective," in *Pure Economic Loss*, ed. W.H. van Boom, Helmut Koziol and Christian A. Witting (Wien: Springer, 2004). p. 141. See also on this notion Mauro Bussani and Vernon Valentine Palmer, "The Notion of Pure Economic Loss and Its Setting," in *Pure Economic Loss in Europe*, ed. Mauro Bussani and Vernon Valentine Palmer (Cambridge: Cambridge University Press, 2003). pp. 2–24.

89 Mauro Bussani, Anthony J. Sebok, and Marta Infantino, "Compensation for Pure Economic Loss," in *Common Law and Civil Law Perspectives on Tort Law*, ed. Mauro Bussani, Anthony J. Sebok, and Marta Infantino (Oxford: Oxford University Press, 2022). p. 145. See also in Gerhard Wagner, "Comparative Tort Law," in *The Oxford Handbook of Comparative Law*, ed. Mathias Reimann and Reinhard Zimmermann (Oxford: Oxford University Press, 2019). p. 1004.

90 Busche, *Privatautonomie und Kontrahierungszwang*. XXIV+722 p.

Bydlinski formulates this understanding quite strongly in 1980 in his *Zu den dogmatischen Grundfragen des Kontrahierungszwanges*:

> "However, the obligation to contract does not merely restrict freedom of contract; it virtually negates it."[91]

In a more contemporary and nuanced understanding, Busche clarifies that an obligation to contract is inherent in the freedom of contract and a system of private law. He thereby deconstructs the impression of an obligation to contract as a public law encroachment upon private law issues and points out that and how an obligation to contract inherently is a question of a well-functioning private law system:

> "Insofar as it is said that there is an antinomy between the idea of freedom of contract rooted in the BGB and the institution of the obligation to contract, this thesis cannot be substantiated by the present study, at least insofar as it concerns the consideration of the general obligation to contract. The contrary assumption of an insoluble contradiction between freedom of contract and coercion to contract corresponds to the view of liberalism at the end of the 19th century, in which the individual was only ever understood as the holder of legal positions. It was not recognised that the coexistence of individuals under a legal system also gives rise to immanent bonds of freedom rights or even duties towards other holders of rights. Rather, these were only ever seen as encroachments of public law into private law, from which the catchphrase 'socialisation of private law' quickly developed. This obscured the fact that the root of the general obligation to contract is to be found in private law and not in public law. It was overlooked that the principle of freedom of contract only follows the principle of private autonomy without fully reflecting it in legal reality. Freedom of contract does not mean freedom from all obligations in the sense of an isolated coexistence of individualistic freedom rights, but is only conceivable with regard to the integration of the individual into the social network with other individuals. This bond concretises the legal institution of the general obligation to contract. It therefore does not have an antinomic character, but rather reinforces the freedom-securing character of the contract law system."[92]

91 Franz Bydlinski, "Zu den dogmatischen Grundfragen des Kontrahierungszwanges," *AcP* (1980). p. 4. Free translation. Original text: "*Der Kontrahierungszwang beschränkt aber nicht bloß die Vertragsfreiheit; er negiert sie geradezu.*" In the same sense Iris S.J. Houben, *Contractdwang* (Deventer: Kluwer, 2005). p. 1.

92 Busche, *Privatautonomie und Kontrahierungszwang*. pp. 238–239. Citations omitted. Free translation. Original text: "*Soweit also gesagt wird, es bestehe eine Antinomie zwischen dem im BGB verwurzelten Gedanken der Vertragsfreiheit und dem Institut des Kontrahierungszwangs, so läßt sich diese These durch die hiesige Untersuchung jedenfalls insoweit nicht erhärten, als es um die Betrachtung des allgemeinen Kontrahierungszwangs geht. Die gegenteilige Annahme eines unlösbaren Widerspruchs zwischen Vertragsfreiheit und Kontrahierungszwang entspricht der Sichtweise des*

32. LIMIT OF FREEDOM FROM CONTRACT: FREEDOM TO CONTRACT – Quite simply put, the preceding rests on the understanding that the limit of freedom from contract should be someone else's freedom to contract: where the exercise of one's freedom from contract deprives another of its freedom to contract, freedom from contract actually hinders freedom to contract instead of making it possible. Franz Bydlinski, by way of nuancing his earlier statement, also expressed this idea:

> "It is necessary to examine whether the negative contractual decision was made in a sufficient assessment of the task of freedom of contract to ensure the adequate satisfaction of human needs, based on normal economic considerations, and if not, to correct it accordingly."[93]

Building forth on this, Jan Busche argues that with freedom of contract being based on the pre-supposition that both parties are free to contract, it must – for the institution of a contract to be sensibly applied – also provide for the means to have both parties being free to contract. Hence, to re-establish freedom of contract of one, the freedom from contract of the other needs to be limited, where the latter would deprive the prior of its ability of self-determination:

> "However, contractual self-determination also means legally bound self-determination, since the contract is not about the unilateral self-determination of an individual, but about self-determination in at least a bipolar relationship, which presupposes that all parties involved are enabled to realise their interests in a self-determined manner."[94]

Liberalismus ausgangs des 19. Jahrhunderts, in der das Individuum immer nur als Inhaber von Rechtsstellungen begriffen wurde. Nicht gesehen wurde, daß aus dem Zusammenleben der Individuen unter einer Rechtsordnung auch immanente Bindungen der Freiheitsrechte oder sogar Pflichten gegenüber anderen Trägern von Rechten entstehen. Diese wurden vielmehr immer nur als Übergriffe des öffentlichen Rechts in das Privatrecht aufgefaßt, woraus sich schnell das Schlag- wort von der "Sozialisierung des Privatrechts" entwickelte. Damit wurde der Blick darauf verstellt, daß die Wurzel des allgemeinen Kontrahierungszwangs im Privatrecht und nicht im öffentlichen Recht zu suchen ist. Übersehen wurde, daß der Grundsatz der Vertragsfreiheit nur dem Prinzip der Privatautonomie folgt, ohne es vollends in der Rechtswirklichkeit abzubilden. Vertragsfreiheit bedeutet nicht das Freisein von sämtlichen Bindungen im Sinne eines isolierten Nebeneinander individualistischer Freiheitsrechte, sondern ist nur denkbar im Hinblick auf die Einbindung des Individuums in den Sozialverbund mit anderen Individuen. Diese Bindung konkretisiert das Rechtsinstitut des allgemeinen Kontrahierungszwangs. Es hat damit keinen antinomischen Charakter, sondern verstärkt den freiheitssichernden Charakter der Vertragsrechtsordnung."

93 Bydlinski, "Zu den dogmatischen Grundfragen des Kontrahierungszwanges." p. 35. Free translation. Original text: "*Man hat zu prüfen, ob die negative Vertragsentscheidung in zureichender und mit normalen wirtschaftlichen Erwägungen verbundener Würdigung der Aufgabe der Rechtsgeschäftsordnung, die angemessene Befriedigung der menschlichen Bedürfnisse zu sichern, getroffen wurde und sie verneinendenfalls entschprechend zu korrigieren.*"

94 Busche, *Privatautonomie und Kontrahierungszwang*. p. 656. Free translation. Original text: "*Vertragliche Selbstbestimmung bedeutet jedoch zugleich auch rechtlich gebundene Selbstbestimmung, da es im Vertrag nicht um einseitige Selbstbestimmung eines Indlviduums geht, sondern um*

3.3. Function of pre-contractual liability

33. FUNCTION – With these two kinds of risks identified, the function ascribed to pre-contractual liability becomes clear: getting compensation in case one of these risks materializes. Roland Schwarze recognizes this ambivalence of the protected risks:

> "The more important field of application of the pre-contractual obligation is the protection of legal self-determination and property."[95]

Though this ambivalence is not always fully understood, it is important to realize that both risks are rather distinct in nature and that an adequate protection of them might require different approaches. While the pure economic loss can be made good and protected by granting compensation, freedom of contract of the counter party should, in principle, be protected by maintaining the possibility to contract. While the first can be done by any type of fault that gave rise to some loss, the second can only be done by considering the decision to break-off negotiations or not to contract *itself* to be wrongful.

34. CONTEXT: CONTRACT NEGOTIATIONS – The context within which these risks must be protected is that of contract negotiations. Negotiations being, as defined by Ekaterina Pannebakker in her dissertation, *Letter of intent in international contracting*,[96] "an interaction of two or more actors faced simultaneously with divergences and interdependences who voluntarily look for a mutually acceptable solution that allows them to create, maintain or develop a relationship."[97] For that purpose, it is important to clarify that parties to the negotiations 'look for a mutually acceptable solution'; *finding* such a solution is not necessarily part of negotiations.[98] Hence, the prospective outcome of

---

Selbstbestimmung im zumindest bipolaren Verhältnis, die voraussetzt, daß allen Beteiligten eine selbstbestimmte Interessenverwirklichung ermöglicht wird."

95 Roland Schwarze, *Das Recht der Leistungsstörung* (Berlin: De Gruyter, 2022). p. 480, nr. 3. Free translation. Original text: "*Das wichtigere Anwendungsfeld des vorvertraglichen Schuldverhältnisses ist der Schutz der rechtsgeschäftlichen Selbstbestimmung und des Vermögens.*" This is, however, not unanimously recognized: MüKoBGB/Emmerich, 9. Aufl. 2022, BGB § 311 nr. 64; Staudinger/Feldmann (2018) BGB § 311 nr. 100 limit the protection to the patrimony. This tendency to focus on the patrimonial protection only is a striking feature.

96 Ekaterina Pannebakker, *Letter of Intent in International Contracting*, Ius Commune Europaeum (Rotterdam: Erasmus University Rotterdam, 2016). 378+xiv p.

97 Pannebakker, *Letter of intent in international contracting*. p. 21.

98 Though it is not uncommon to see such understandings of pre-contractual liability (f.i. Guy Schrans, "Praecontractuele verhouding naar Belgisch recht," *Vereniging voor de vergelijkende studie van het recht van België en Nederland* (1968). pp. 229–230). Also, it should be borne in mind that negotiation strategy/technique literature may have another understanding of negotiations than legal literature should have. Indeed, according to negotiation literature, reaching an agreement is the aim of negotiations. Cassan and de Bailliencourt, for instance, suggest (among others) to understand negotiations as "a relation of interdependence meant to bring about an agreement between people which have at the same time common and opposed interests" and "intend to create rights and obligations between equal parties of free consent." (Hervé Cassan and Marie-Pierre de Bailliencourt, *Traité pratique de négociation* (Bruxelles: Larcier, 2019). p. 8. Free translation).

contract negotiations is *not* the conclusion of a contract but merely to assess whether a contract is desirable/possible/necessary to the parties to the negotiations.[99] This follows inherently from the freedom from contract according to which the outcome of no-contract is lawful.[100]

However trivial this may seem, it merits to be pointed out to the extent that it often seems as if when thinking about contract negotiations from a legal perspective, it is assumed that negotiations evolve in a linear trajectory from no agreement towards a full agreement. This could be observed in Faggella's understanding of contract negotiations (*supra* Chap. 1, nr. 13) and still finds a prominent expression in the Dutch way of conceiving pre-contractual liability: the *Hoge Raad* has established the so-called three-phases doctrine ("*driefasenleer*").[101] This doctrine pre-supposes a gradual evolution of negotiations, as it states that during a first phase, parties are free to break-off negotiations without legal consequences, a second phase in which they still are free to do so but have to

99 Asser/Sieburgh 6-III 2022/193.

100 For an illustration of the relevance of such *a priori* considerations, see Bussani, Sebok, and Infantino, "Compensation for Pure Economic Loss." pp. 162–163.

101 Established in HR 18 June 1982, *NJ* 1983, 723 (*Plas/Valburg*), ECLI:NL:HR:1982:AG4405, nrs. 3.4–3.5: "It cannot be excluded that negotiations on an agreement have reached such a stage that the very breaking-off of those negotiations under the given circumstances must be regarded as contrary to good faith, since the parties were entitled to expect that any contract would in any case result from the negotiations. In such a situation, there may also be room for an obligation to compensate for lost profit.

An obligation to do so [to reimburse costs incurred in the context of the preliminary negotiations] might even exist if the negotiations had not yet reached a stage where the municipality in good faith could no longer break-off those negotiations, but had already reached a stage where it would not have been free to do so in the given circumstances without bearing the costs incurred by Plas in whole or in part." Original text: "*Niet uitgesloten is dat onderhandelingen over een overeenkomst in een zodanig stadium zijn gekomen dat het afbreken zelf van die onderhandelingen onder de gegeven omstandigheden als in strijd met de goede trouw moet worden geacht, omdat pp. over en weer mochten vertrouwen dat enigerlei contract in ieder geval uit de onderhandelingen zou resulteren. In zo een situatie kan er ook plaats zijn voor een verplichting tot vergoeding van gederfde winst. . . . Een verplichting daartoe [tot vergoeding van in het kader van de vooraf-gaande onderhandelingen gemaakte kosten] zou zelfs kunnen bestaan, als de onderhandelingen nog niet in een zodanig stadium zouden zijn geraakt dat de gemeente te goeder trouw die onderhandelingen niet meer had mogen afbreken, maar reeds wel in een stadium dat zulk afbreken haar in de gegeven omstandigheden niet meer zou hebben vrijgestaan zonder de door Plas gemaakte kosten geheel of gedeeltelijk voor haar rekening te nemen.*" Confirmed in HR 12 August 2005, ECLI:NL:HR:2005:AT7337 (*CBB/JPO*), nr. 3.6: "The criterion for assessing the obligation to pay compensation in the event of the cessation of negotiations is that each of the negotiating parties – who are obliged to allow their conduct to be influenced by each other's legitimate interests – is free to break-off negotiations, unless this would be unacceptable on the basis of the other party's legitimate expectation that the agreement will be concluded or in view of the other circumstances of the case." Original text: "*als maatstaf voor de beoordeling van de schadevergoedingsplicht bij afgebroken onderhandelingen heeft te gelden dat ieder van de onderhandelende partijen – die verplicht zijn hun gedrag mede door elkaars gerechtvaardigde belangen te laten bepalen – vrij is de onderhandelingen af te breken, tenzij dit op grond van het gerechtvaardigd vertrouwen van de wederpartij in het totstandkomen van de overeenkomst of in verband met de andere omstandigheden van het geval onaanvaardbaar zou zijn.*"

indemnify the damage caused thereby, and a third phase in which breaking-off negotiations has become inacceptable.[102] This conception of the negotiation process as a sort of gradual evolution with no drawbacks is criticized in scholarship for being artificial,[103] and it has been debated whether with the *CBB/JPO* decision of 2005,[104] the *Hoge Raad* would not have opted for a two-phases doctrine.[105] Be that as it may, the *Hoge Raad* did not deviate from the idea that a negotiation process can be divided into different phases and that at some point during the negotiation process, parties no longer are free to break off those negotiations (for more nuance see *infra* Chap. 2, nr. 34).[106]

35. Means – In a situation of *a priori* lawfulness, the compensation of pure economic loss and the protection of freedom of contract must be possible. By defining the means that pre-contractual liability must be able to fulfil, the endless and generally fruitless discussion about the true nature of pre-contractual liability – extra-contractual, contractual, or a third type of liability – can be approached from an, in my opinion, more constructive angle. Namely, once the means that pre-contractual liability must offer are identified, it can be discussed which liability – extra-contractual, contractual, or a third type – allows to fulfil this function in the respective national system. Hence, what "nature" pre-contractual liability must have will always depend on the broader structure of the national liability law, specifically extra-contractual liability law. This insight is crucial: the organization of a national system of pre-contractual liability system always depends on the national system of extra-contractual liability, as the latter always will be the default system to go to, given that in the

102 For a description Ruygvoorn, *Afgebroken onderhandelingen en het gebruik van voorbehouden*. pp. 44–45.

103 See most notably Rieme-Jan L. Tjittes, *Commercieel Contractenrecht* (Den Haag: Boom Juridisch, 2018). p. 77; Ruygvoorn, *Afgebroken onderhandelingen en het gebruik van voorbehouden*. p. 57.

104 HR 12 August 2005, ECLI:NL:HR:2005:AT7337 (*CBB/JPO*), nr. 3.6: "The criterion for assessing the obligation to pay compensation in the event of the cessation of negotiations is that each of the negotiating parties – who are obliged to allow their conduct to be influenced by each other's legitimate interests – is free to break-off negotiations, unless this would be unacceptable on the basis of the other party's legitimate expectation that the agreement will be concluded or in view of the other circumstances of the case." Original text: "*als maatstaf voor de beoordeling van de schadevergoedingsplicht bij afgebroken onderhandelingen heeft te gelden dat ieder van de onderhandelende partijen – die verplicht zijn hun gedrag mede door elkaars gerechtvaardigde belangen te laten bepalen – vrij is de onderhandelingen af te breken, tenzij dit op grond van het gerechtvaardigd vertrouwen van de wederpartij in het totstandkomen van de overeenkomst of in verband met de andere omstandigheden van het geval onaanvaardbaar zou zijn*."

105 Mainly the article by Drion (C.E. Drion, "Ons onderhandelingsrecht onder handen," *NJB*, no. 34 (2005).) seems to have led to quite some debated. For an overview, see Ruygvoorn, *Afgebroken onderhandelingen en het gebruik van voorbehouden*. p. 118. See also critical perspective taken by Tjittes, *Commercieel Contractenrecht*. p. 76 *et seq*. and his own position on pp. 87–88. Recent case law seems to stick to a three-phases doctrine (f.i. Ger. Arnhem-Leeuwarden, 28 december 2021, 200.266.580, ECLI:NL:GHARL:2021:11869, nrs. 3.14 en 3.17.).

106 I have dealt with this in more detail in Tom Hick, "Aansprakelijkheid voor afgebroken onderhandelingen in België en Nederland: Op koers voor toenadering," *NTBR*, no. 29 (2022). pp. 245–246, nr. 9.

pre-contractual phase, no contract does yet exist. Only when extra-contractual liability does not offer the means necessary for pre-contractual liability will it be necessary to rely on another liability law system. In this sense, the legal basis for pre-contractual liability always is *relative* to the type of liability law of the respective national extra-contractual liability law system. In order to know which system of extra-contractual liability offers the means to fulfil the function of pre-contractual liability, it is necessary to assess which systems of extra-contractual liability are available. I will do so in the following title.

The idea that the organization of pre-contractual liability always depends on the organization of extra-contractual liability will be confirmed in what follows, with that nuance that some legal systems seem to go beyond what is *necessary* for a system of pre-contractual liability. Generally speaking, I would say that less is more in this regard and that a national system should stick to the necessary minimum, as all unnecessary extras run the risk of distorting or complicating matters. This will become clear throughout the remainder of this book.

2 Structure of pre-contractual liability

1. Structure of liability law

1.1. Liability law systems

1. Liability law – Before exploring the available liability law systems for pre-contractual liability, it may be worthwhile to clarify what I understand under "liability law" and "liability law system" (*infra* Chap. 2, nr. 2). Christian von Bar defines the law of delicts in his *The Common European Law of Torts*[1] as "the field of private law which determines whether a person who has a right to compensation (or where such damage is impending, to injunctive relief) even if the infliction of the damage forms the only legal bond between the two parties."[2] Central to his definition is the aspect of compensation of harm and "the fact that its operation requires no prior legal relationship between victim and tortfeasor."[3] In *The Structure of Tort Law*,[4] Nils Jansen defines "tort law" as "the law which sets out the requirements of a claim for damages which is not specifically based upon a contract"[5] and, more specifically, the *law of delicts* as " 'liability for wrongful conduct', which is here understood as co-extensive with the (albeit misleading) term, 'liability for fault'."[6]

More roughly, but sufficiently for the present purpose, I will simply speak of "liability law" in the sense of the elements common to both mentioned definitions: (i) a field of (private) law which defines the conditions under which compensation of damages can be granted (ii) without necessarily requiring a specific legal relationship. Within that context, I focus on personal liability, hence liability for own conduct and not for objects or other (legal) persons.

1 von Bar, *The Common European Law of Torts*, I. cxlv+661 p.

2 von Bar, *The Common European Law of Torts*, I. 2, nr. 1. Citations omitted.

3 von Bar, *The Common European Law of Torts*, I. 2–3, nr. 1.

4 Jansen, *The Structure of Tort Law*. 576 p. I have relied considerably on this book. Before discovering somewhere mid-2023 that this English translation exists, I have always relied on the German version from 2003 (Nils Jansen, *Die Struktur des Haftungsrechts* (Tübingen: Mohr Siebeck, 2003). xx+703 p.). Hence, the reader may still find some reference to the German version.

5 Jansen, *The Structure of Tort Law*. p. 24.

6 Jansen, *The Structure of Tort Law*. p. 24. Citations omitted.

DOI: 10.4324/9781003599166-4

2. LIABILITY LAW SYSTEMS – A *system of liability law* then is a way of approaching liability law, namely, an approach that focuses on the functioning of (personal) liability law. Approaching liability law from that angle allows me to argue at a more abstract level, overcoming national differences and subtleties which bar a more profound understanding of the functioning of liability law, much like what Peter Cane explains:

> "My claim is that organizing the law around the ideas of correlativity, protected interest, sanctioned conduct and sanctions provides a much deeper understanding of its inner logic than the traditional approach, and also a more satisfactory way of sorting out the relationship between tort law and other legal categories."[7]

With these preliminary clarifications, it is time to look at the available liability law systems. I have (*supra* Chap. 1, nr. 35) identified the means necessary for a system of pre-contractual liability. The next step then is to turn to the available liability law systems which could provide these means.

1.2. Possible personal liability law systems

3. EXPLANATIONS FOR LIABILITY – Liability law thus consists in holding someone responsible for some inflicted harm by obliging him to indemnify that harm. The follow-up question then is this: *Why* and *how* can a person be held liable? *Why* a party can be held liable indicates the justification or explanation that is given to explain that a party is held liable; *how* a party can be held liable concerns the question of the different conditions of application and their inner logic. Yet the reason why a party can be held liable will always impact the way how it is held liable. It is important to understand that the *why* will impact the *how*. Conceptually and historically, three relevant grounds (why) appear to exist which will trigger different systems of liability law (how).[8] *First*, one can be held liable because some specific prohibition has not been respected. The prohibition can either relate to some conduct or a specific outcome, and where it is the latter, the question arises whether that outcome alone suffices to give rise to liability (strict liability) or whether the conduct which leads to the prohibited outcome also must be reprehensible. *Second*, and as a specific instance of a prohibited outcome, the infringement of some identified rights can give rise to liability – again with the question of whether the adopted conduct is relevant or not for liability. *Third*, no requirement of a specific prohibition but committing some reprehensible conduct alone triggers liability.

Let me illustrate these different triggers for liability from a historical perspective and provide, *en passant*, a very brief overview of the evolution of liability law systems.

7 Peter Cane, *The Anatomy of Tort Law* (London: Hart Publishing, 1997). p. 2.
8 Liability based on risk will not be considered, as it is not seriously taken into consideration in the context of pre-contractual liability.

4. *Lex Aquilia*/SPECIFIC LEGAL PROHIBITION – The origin of personal liability law systems lies in the Roman *Lex Aquilia*, dating back to 287/286 BC.[9] It was composed of three chapters of which the first prohibited the *unlawful* ("*iniuria*") killing of slaves and of "four-footed beasts of the class of cattle."[10] The third chapter protects all goods in the patrimony of a person against damage done by *unlawful* ("*iniuria*") burning ("*urere*"), breaking ("*frangere*"), or mutilation ("*rumpere*"); the content of the second chapter remains somewhat unclear.[11] The *Lex Aquilia* itself thus states certain specific prohibitions, and the infringement of these specific prohibitions then triggers liability.

To give rise to liability, these infringements "had to be labelled 'iniuria'."[12] Essentially, *inuria* could mean two things in this context: there was no ground of justification for committing the infringement, or the infringement was made culpably. Ultimately, "inuria" came to mean that the infringement had been committed culpably:

> "As a result of these developments, one had overcome the archaic form of strict liability and had adopted a flexible and ethically more satisfactory approach that turned on the inquiry of whether or not the defendant had in fact behaved as he should have behaved."[13]

5. CONCEPTUAL ANALYSIS OF SPECIFIC PROHIBITION – From a conceptual point of view, and independently of how exactly the interpretation of the *Lex Aquilia* evolved, it becomes clear that the infringement of a specific legal norm itself can give rise to liability. Such a requirement of infringement of a specific legal norm can be adjusted via grounds of justification or a requirement to act culpably. In that latter case, the requirement of fault acts as a limitation of liability. Indeed, only in cases in which the prohibition has not been respected, *and* this has been done culpably, can liability arise.[14]

9 Jansen, *The Structure of Tort Law*. p. 153; Herbert Hausmaninger and Walter Selb, *Römisches Privatrecht* (Wien: Böhlau Verlag, 2001). p. 280. More extensive Zimmermann, *The Law of Obligations. Roman Foundations of the Civilian Tradition*. p. 955 *et seq.*

10 Zimmermann, *The Law of Obligations. Roman Foundations of the Civilian Tradition*. p. 957.

11 Steffen Schlinker, Hannes Ludyga, and Andreas Bergmann, *Privatrechtsgeschichte* (München: C.H. Beck, 2019). p. 171; Jansen, *The Structure of Tort Law*. p. 154; Hausmaninger and Selb, *Römisches Privatrecht*. pp. 280–281; Zimmermann, *The Law of Obligations. Roman Foundations of the Civilian Tradition*. p. 954.

12 Zimmermann, *The Law of Obligations. Roman Foundations of the Civilian Tradition*. p. 976.

13 Zimmermann, *The Law of Obligations. Roman Foundations of the Civilian Tradition*. p. 1006.

14 The origins of this ambivalence towards the notion of " 'fault' are easy to clarify. If the law protects a limited range of relatively well-defined interests against harmful conduct that the law describes in detail, the removal of casuistic descriptions of harmful conduct, or the expansion of the list of protected interests, achieves an expansion of delictual liability. The broad-brush approach of the civil codes enacted first in 1865 (Art. 1151) and then in 1942 (Art. 2043) is an eloquent testimony to this possibility. On the other hand, if the law provides that the mere invasion of protected interests triggers liability, then the interposition of the requirement of fault is rightly perceived as a factor limiting liability. Indeed, whenever lack of due care is difficult to establish in practice, the principle 'no liability without fault' works to exempt large numbers of potential defendants from liability."

6. Scholastics, natural law school, and Grotius/protected rights – Fast forward in time, the Scholastics have developed, via the notion of *dominion*, the concept of right ("*ius*").[15] With it comes the idea that rights merit protection, which entails the idea that an infringement of such a right can be a ground for liability. Indeed, once individual rights are recognized as worth of protection, the idea that the infringement of such a right triggers liability is almost self-evident.[16] This novel perspective, paired with the natural lawyer's tendency to work towards a general clause for liability, as opposed to the various, relatively narrowly delimitated, actions of the Roman law of delicts,[17] paved the way for Hugo Grotius's seminal[18] understanding of personal liability law. In his *De Jure Belli ac Pacis* of 1625, he conceived his law of delicts from the position of the subjective right, in which he distinguishes absolute subjective rights (life, body, freedom of act, honour, and property)[19] and relative subjective rights. Absolute subjective rights are protected *erga omnes*, relative subjective rights only in relation to some individuals (typically contractual rights protected against contracting parties).[20] Grotius's general clause coupled the idea of the infringement of a protected – absolute or relative – right with a requirement of culpable conduct.[21]
7. Conceptual analysis infringement of protected right – Much like the infringement of a specific legal prohibition, the infringement of a protected right itself could trigger liability. This means that only an infringement of certain protected rights can give rise to liability. As it is the infringement of the right which triggers liability – possibly coupled with a criterion of fault – only the infringement of certain absolute subjective rights can trigger liability.

Michele Graziadei, "Liability for Fault in Italian Law: The Development of Legal Doctrine from 1865 to the End of the Twentieth Century," in *The Development and Making of Legal Doctrine*, ed. Nils Jansen (Cambridge: Cambridge University Press, 2010). pp. 135–136. See also on this Jansen, *The Structure of Tort Law*. p. 227: "It follows then that on the conduct-based concept of unlawfulness, it must concretely be shown that the injurer has breached a duty of conduct for a successful claim, while with an outcome-based conception, an attributable loss suffices. Only a particular defense can then release the injurer from liability."

15 For a detailed discussion, see Jansen, *The Structure of Tort Law*. p. 235 *et seq*.

16 On this "idea," Jansen writes, "It is based on the idea that particular legal interests are assigned to individuals in such a way that everyone has to respect these interests of the other. This can, on the one hand, justify the duty not to conduct oneself in such a way that one infringes these interests; on the other, however, this idea can also directly lead to liability in the case of an infringement of a legal interest." Jansen, *The Structure of Tort Law*. p. 236.

17 In more detail Jansen, *The Structure of Tort Law*. pp. 221–223.

18 On this point Robert Feenstra, "Grotius' Doctrine of Liability for Negligence: Its Origin and Its Influence in Civil Law Countries Until Modern Codifications," in *Histoire du droit savant (13e–18e siecle) Doctrines et vulgarisation par incunables*, ed. Robert Feenstra (Aldershot: Variorum, 2005). pp. 129–171.

19 Jansen, *Die Struktur des Haftungsrechts*. p. 332.

20 See on the distinction between absolute and relative subjective rights Asser/Sieburgh 6-IV 2019/46.

21 Schlinker, Ludyga, and Bergmann, *Privatrechtsgeschichte*. p. 183; Jansen, *Die Struktur des Haftungsrechts*. p. 328.

Otherwise, the ensuing liability would be too broad. In line therewith, including the patrimony in general in that scope of protection would trigger liability in far too many cases – or at least that is what would be feared. The consequence of this policy consideration is that pure economic loss cannot be compensated for. Indeed, pure economic loss is loss suffered directly in the patrimony and not the consequence of harm to some other good or right (*supra* Chap. 1, nr. 29). Hence, if the patrimony is not counted among the protected absolute rights, pure economic loss cannot be protected or even trigger liability. Here lies the foundation of the "accident" that, according to James Gordley, is the exclusion of pure economic loss.[22]

8. Samuel Pufendorf/general duty of care – Samuel Pufendorf in *De iure naturae et gentium* of 1759 is strongly influenced by Grotius.[23] However, his focus is of much stronger moralistic nature. He conceives his delictual liability from the perspective of duties of conduct resting on individuals in society to act rightly.[24] By changing the focal point from protected subjective rights towards conduct, he also founds a general duty of care. Prior to such a general duty of care, the question of conduct only rose in relation to identified protected subjective rights. With Pufendorf, this understanding that people need to act according to certain standards is generalized to all of human interaction.

9. Conceptual analysis of fault – With this justification of a generalized duty of care, Pufendorf paved the way for a liability law system based on fault,[25] thus triggered by an assessment of conduct without any prior infringement of a specific prohibition or protected right. The role fault plays in such a context is different from the role it plays in a liability law system which is based on the infringement of a specific norm or a protected right (*supra* Chap. 2, nr. 5): Instead of limiting liability, fault triggers liability.

This conception will have a profound impact on personal liability law systems. It will inspire the drafters of the natural law–inspired codes – in chronological order: § 10, I, 6 of the *Allgemeines Landrecht für die Preussichen Staaten* of 1794, articles 1382 and 1383 of the Napoleonic *Code civil* of 1804,

22 James Gordley, "The Rule Against Recovery in Negligence for Pure Economic Loss: An Historical Accident?" in *Pure Economic Loss in Europe*, ed. Mauro Bussani and Vernon Valentine Palmer (Cambridge: Cambridge University Press, 2003). p. 25.

23 Feenstra, "Grotius' Doctrine of Liability for Negligence: Its Origin and Its Influence in Civil Law Countries Until Modern Codifications." pp. 160–162.

24 Jansen, *Die Struktur des Haftungsrechts*. p. 337; Jansen, "Gesetzliche Schuldverhältnisse Eine historische Strukturanalyse." p. 124, fn. 77. See also Olivier Descamps, "La responsabilité dans le Code civil," *Histoire de la justice* 19 (2009). p. 300.

25 Jansen, *Die Struktur des Haftungsrechts*. p. 342; Zimmermann, *The Law of Obligations. Roman Foundations of the Civilian Tradition*. pp. 1033–1034.

and § 1295 of the Austrian *Allgemeines bürgerliches Gesetzbuch* (ABGB) of 1811.

> § 10, I, 6 ALR: "A person who offends another intentionally or by gross negligence must grant him full pardon."[26]
>
> Articles 1382–1383 *Code civil*: "Any act of man which causes damage to others obliges the person by whose fault it was done to repair it. Each person is responsible for the damage he causes not only by his own act, but also by his negligence or imprudence."[27]
>
> § 1295 ABGB: "Every person shall be entitled to claim compensation from the damaging party for the damage which the latter has caused him through fault; the damage may have been caused by a breach of a contractual obligation or without reference to a contract."[28]

All three provisions rely on the tryptic conditions of application: harm that has been culpably – *i.e.* negligently or intentionally – caused gives rise to liability, i.e. an obligation of compensation.

10. Unlawfulness and conduct-based systems – Both the system of liability law based on specific legal prohibitions and the system based on protected rights require some form of *a priori* unlawfulness. Indeed, it requires that either specific outcomes or conduct be prohibited or that certain rights are identified to whom an infringement justifies liability. They can, for our purpose, be grouped under the heading as *unlawfulness-based* systems. A system that requires no specific *a priori* unlawfulness but merely is based on some *conduct* that is considered to be wrong can be designated as *conduct-based* or *fault-based*.[29]

11. Structure – The different starting points of a liability law system (why) translate into different structures of liability law systems (how). A conduct-based liability law system will rely on a general duty of care and translates into three conditions of application:

(i) Qualified conduct (fault)
(ii) Harm
(iii) Causal link between qualified conduct and harm

26 Free translation. Original text: "*Wer einen Andern aus Vorsatz oder grobem Versehen beleidigt, muß demselben vollständige Genugthuung leisten.*"

27 Free translation. Original text: "*Tout fait quelconque de l'homme, qui cause à autrui un dommage, oblige celui par la faute duquel il est arrive, à le réparer. Chacun est responsable du dommage, qu'il cause non seulement par son fait, mais encore par sa négligence ou par son imprudence.*"

28 Free translation. Original text: "*Jedermann ist berechtigt, von dem Beschädiger den Ersatz des Schadens, welchen dieser ihm aus Verschulden zugefügt hat, zu fordern; der Schaden mag durch Übertretung einer Vertragspflicht oder ohne Beziehung auf einen Vertrag verursacht worden sein.*"

29 Unlawfulness-based liability law systems can also have a fault requirement, but the liability is not based on fault (faut is not the conceptual starting point of the liability law system).

Such a system thus is in appearance relatively simple. However, given its simplicity, it needs some twists and tweaks in order to accommodate functions that need to also be fulfilled by liability law systems, namely, the infringement of specific legal norms, the limitation of legally protected interests, and causes of justification. As such, a liability law system does not provide the structural elements to explicitly deal with these questions. They need to be interpreted into the existing conditions of application.[30] The result is a deceptively simple system of liability law.

An unlawfulness-based liability law system precisely allows to overcome (at least some of) these limitations of a conduct-based liability law system. It does so by limiting duties of care to specific protected subjective rights. This comes, however, at the cost of a more complex structure, namely:

(i) Unlawfulness (infringement of protected subjective right/of a specific legal norm)
(ii) Conduct (fault)
(iii) Harm
(iv) Causal link between qualified conduct and unlawfulness
(v) Causal link between unlawfulness and harm

1.3. Relevant liability law system for pre-contractual liability

12. NECESSITY OF CONDUCT-BASED LIABILITY – These very abstract considerations on types of liability law systems matter to the extent that they have repercussions on the availability of pre-contractual liability under the non-contractual liability law. Based on the function and means defined *supra* (Chap. 1, nr. 35), only a conduct-based liability can fulfil the necessary functions for a system of pre-contractual liability. Indeed, given the *a priori* lawfulness in the context of pre-contractual negotiations, a liability law system only based on the infringement of specific legal norms will generally not allow to grant compensation.[31]

30 As explained by Gerhard Wagner: "Rather, legal responsibility is subject to various qualifications, elaborated upon later, which – and this is the crucial point – are not inherent in the application of these articles to the facts of an individual case but rather are extrinsic to them and must be sought in general legal principles or common sense notions about what civil liability is about. In the course of legal history, precedent and jurisprudence have worked together to implant numerous distinctions into the French law of delict which are invisible on the face of the Code itself. In this sense, Arts 1240 and 1241 *Code civil* do not supply the judge or attorney with rules capable of application, but instead with a guiding principle whose restriction by the operation of contrary principles is both possible in theory and common in practice." Wagner, "Comparative Tort Law." p. 999.

31 This point concerns the distinction between primary and secondary liability norms. Michele Graziadei speaks in this context of "first-order norm of liability" and a "second-order norm of liability": "The new approach to delictual liability developing in that period held that the maxim *alterum non laedere*, enshrined in Article 2043 of the Civil Code of 1942, established a first order-norm of liability. This norm could generate claims unconnected with the precise violation of other norms but. Based on the provision of Article 2043 itself." Graziadei, "Liability for Fault in Italian Law: The Development of Legal Doctrine from 1865 to the End of the Twentieth Century." p. 147. The point relates to how the infringement of specific legal norms is integrated into a liability law provision. A primary liability norm allows to base liability directly – hence, primarily – on this provision by providing for a standard of care, whose violation can give rise to liability. A secondary liability norm

The second reason explaining why only a conduct-based liability law system can accommodate for pre-contractual liability is that where an unlawfulness-based system relies on the infringement of a protected right, those generally do not comprise the patrimony as a protected right (*supra* Chap. 2, nr. 7). By consequence, pure economic loss will not be recoverable in such an unlawfulness-based liability law system.

That a conduct-based liability is the relevant liability law system for pre-contractual liability is particularly well illustrated in the context of German law. As one can read in Dieter Medicus and Stephan Lorenz *Schuldrecht I*:

> "If a party involved in contract negotiations is not injured in a legal interest protected by Section 823 I, but only in his patrimony, tortious liability under Section 823 I is out of the question. Such breaches of property exist, for example, if a party incurs expenses that prove to be useless due to the failure of the contract negotiations or due to the invalidity of the contract. It is also conceivable that a party has failed to conclude another profitable contract because it relied on the success of the – ultimately failed – contract negotiations. . . . In all these cases, tort law only grants claims for compensation if the damage was caused by a breach of a protective law protecting property (Section 823 II) or was intentional and immoral (Section 826). . . . However, this is usually not the case. If damages are to be owed here, the claim must therefore be based on a contractual obligation."[32]

13. Pre-contractual liability – If under German law pre-contractual liability must be brought under contractual liability, that is because contractual liability is a conduct-based liability under German law. This is done by § 311 BGB, which brings pre-contractual liability under contractual liability, much like Jhering did with the *culpa in contrahendo* (*supra* Chap. 1, nr. 3). Hence, for a personal

---

serves as a liability norm for more specific grounds of liability – hence, secondarily. A secondary liability norm serves, so to say, as a bridge between a liability norm and a specific legal ground. Put more briefly: a primary liability law norm suffices to itself to serve as a ground for liability (generally by providing a standard of care); a secondary liability norm merely regulates the liability aspects which are triggered by an element giving rise to liability set down in another norm.

32 Medicus and Lorenz, *Schuldrecht I Allgemeiner Teil*. p. 244, nr. 13. Free translation. Original text: "*Wird ein an Vertragsverhandlungen Beteiligter nicht an einem durch § 823 I geschützten Rechtsgut verletzt, sondern ausschließlich an seinem Vermögen, kommt eine deliktische Haftung nach § 823 I nicht in Betracht. Solche Vermögensverletzungen liegen etwa vor, wenn ein Beteiligter Aufwendungen macht, die sich wegen des Scheiterns der Vertragsverhandlungen oder wegen der Nichtigkeit des Vertrags als nutzlos erweisen. Denkbar ist auch, dass ein Beteiligter den Abschluss eines gewinnbringenden anderen Vertrags unterlassen hat, weil er sich auf den Erfolg der – dann schließlich doch gescheiterten – Vertragsverhandlungen verlassen hat. . . . In allen diesen Fällen gewährt das Deliktsrecht Ersatzansprüche nur, wenn die Schädigung durch den Verstoß gegen ein das Vermögen schützendes Schutzgesetz (§ 823 II) oder vorsätzlich und sittenwidrig (§ 826) erfolgt ist. . . . Daran fehlt es aber meist. Wenn hier Schadensersatz geschuldet sein soll, muss der Anspruch also aus einem Schuldverhältnis begründet werden.*" See also Stoll, "Tatbestände und Funktionen der Haftung für culpa in contrahendo." p. 439. From a comparative perspective: Wagner, "Comparative Tort Law." pp. 1004–1005.

liability law system to accommodate for pre-contractual liability (*supra* Chap. 1, nrs. 33–35), it must be a conduct-based liability law system.

As the German example illustrates clearly, in cases where the extra-contractual liability law is not conduct-based, there must either be a specific regime for pre-contractual liability or a provision or case law which attributes pre-contractual liability to a liability law system that is conduct-based.

This does, however, not mean that in systems that *do* have a conduct-based extra-contractual liability law, no specific provisions for pre-contractual liability exist;[33] it only means that they are, structurally speaking, not necessary in order to provide compensation for harm suffered in the context of contract negotiations.[34]

14. Hypothesis – I thus argue that a conduct-based liability law system is necessary in order to have a functioning system of pre-contractual liability and that liability for contract negotiations will be located in the respective conduct-based system, be that in the extra-contractual context (such as Belgium, France, and the Netherlands) or in the contractual context (such as Germany). By now, the basis for this hypothesis should have become clear and partly illustrated in the preceding paragraph. Now, I need to verify this hypothesis. As the organization of the system of pre-contractual liability always depends on the system of extra-contractual liability ("relativity of legal basis of pre-contractual liability" *supra* Chap. 1, nr. 35), testing the veracity of my hypothesis will require to look at the systems of extra-contractual liability in the analysed national legal systems and check how pre-contractual liability is dealt with in each of these systems. If systems that do have a conduct-based extra-contractual liability bring their pre-contractual liability under extra-contractual liability and those systems that have an unlawfulness-based extra-contractual liability need to bring their systems of pre-contractual liability under another liability law system, my hypothesis is confirmed.

For that purpose, I now will provide an evolutive overview of the systems of extra-contractual liability law in conjunction with the national system of pre-contractual liability.

1.4. Evolution of liability law in different national legal systems

> "Alles was ist, kann nur verstanden werden, wenn man weiß, wie es geworden ist."[35]

15. Napoleonic Civil Code and its realm of influence – As explained *supra* (Chap. 2, nr. 7), the Napoleonic Civil Code is the fruit of a strong natural law

33 As is the case under French (article 1112 Fr. Civ. C.) and Belgian (article 5.15 Be. Civ. C.) law.

34 Whether conduct-based liability law systems suffice to give rise to liability in the case of breaking-off of negotiations or refusal to contract still is another question.

35 Hähnchen, *Obliegenheiten und Nebenpflichten. eine Untersuchung dieser besonderen Verhaltensanforderungen im Privatversciherungsrecht und im allgemeinen Zivilrecht unter besonderer Berücksichtigung der Dogmengeschichte*. p. 3. Free translation: "Everything that is can only be understood if one knows how it has become."

tradition (*supra* Chap. 2, nr. 8).[36] It formulated very briefly the threefold conditions of application of fault, harm, and a causal link between both. In the course of the 19th century, French scholarship developed an understanding of the central notion of fault as meaning either the shortcoming of a general standard of care or the infringement of a specific statutory norm.[37] Some writers did also refer to the infringement of a right as constituting a fault, but the position seems to have gotten rather little drive and certainly less than in the German territories (*infra* nr. 60).[38] Somewhat inarticulately, the infringement of a specific statutory norm, of a right, and of a general duty of care all amounted to a fault. That way, the shortcomings of a conduct-based liability could be overcome, be it in a perhaps somewhat inarticulate manner.[39] Within the scope of articles 1382–1383 Nap. Civ. C., different systems of liability law had to co-exist.

When Belgium declared its independence in 1830, it took over the Napoleonic Civil Code without changes. Its Court of Cassation as well as scholarship remained for a long time generally faithful to the French example. Roughly from the late 1950s on, a movement towards a more autonomous Belgian scholarship is perceptible. Its increasing independence perhaps culminates in the re-codification movement which was launched in 2015 and is ongoing at the time of writing (on which *infra* Chap. 2, nr. 20).[40]

Similarly to the old Belgian, the Dutch codification of 1838 relied largely on the Napoleonic articles 1382 and 1383, respectively becoming articles 1401 and 1402 of the Dutch Civil Code. The only notable difference was the fact that the Dutch code focuses on an unlawful act ("*onrechtmatig daad*"), though the Napoleonic provisions focus on fault:

> "Article 1401: Every unlawful act, which causes damage to another person, places the person who caused the damage under an obligation to compensate.
>
> Article 1402: Everyone is responsible not only for the damage caused by his act, but also for that caused by his negligence or carelessness."[41]

36 Wagner, "Comparative Tort Law." p. 1000.

37 F.I. Paul Esmein, *Droit Civil Français*, Vol. 6, Aubry & Rau (Paris: Juris-classeurs, 1951). p. 425. For a general historical discussion see Geneviève Viney, *Introduction à la responsabilité*, ed. Jacques Ghestin, Traité de droit civil (Paris: LGDJ, 2019). nr. 16.

38 Jean-Louis Halpérin, "French Doctrinal Writing," in *The Development and Making of Legal Doctrine*, ed. Nils Jansen (Cambridge: Cambridge University Press, 2010). p. 82.

39 It seems as if all of these infringements, be it of a general duty of care, of a specific statutory provision, or of a subjective right, would amount to an unlawful act which was seen as the definition of "fault." (Halpérin, "French Doctrinal Writing." pp. 80–81). Overall, the impression one gets is that of a relatively unstructured understanding of the notion of "fault," which reportedly was one of the reasons pushing scholars in the German territories to come up with a more detailed understanding of the conditions for liability (Jansen, "Developing Legal Doctrine: Fault in the German Law of Delict." p. 100).

40 Act of 13 April 2019 creating a Civil Code and inserting into it Book 8 "Evidence" (*Loi du 13 avril 2019 portant création d'un Code civil et y insérant un livre 8 "La prevue," MB* 2019/12168/*Wet van 13 april 2019 tot invoering van een Burgerlijk Wetboek en tot invoeging van boek 8 "Bewijs" in dat Wetboek, BS* 2019/12168.)

41 Free translation. Original text: "Art. 1401 BW: *Elke onregtmatige daad, waardoor aan een ander schade wordt toegebragt, stelt dengenen door wiens schuld die schade veroorzaakt is in de verpligting om dezelve te vergoeden.*

As an inheritance of the *Lex Aquilia*, the notions of unlawful act and fault were used rather interchangeably at the time.[42]

A similar evolution can be observed under Italian law. After the unification of Italy in 1861, it promulgated its own *Codice civile* in 1865. The latter essentially was a translated version of the Napoleonic Civil Code and so were articles 1151 and 1152 *Codice civile:*[43]

> Article 1151: 'Every act whatever of man that causes damage to another, obliges him by whose fault it occurred to repair it.'
>
> Article 1152: 'We are responsible not only for the damage occasioned by our own act, but also by our own negligence or imprudence.'[44]

It comes as no surprise then that for Faggella, liability for contract negotiations could simply be dealt with under extra-contractual liability (*supra* Chap. 1, nr. 21) since pure economic loss could be indemnified or rather was not even a topic of discussion. That understanding, however, changed over time. Indeed, though articles 1151 and 1152 unambiguously codify a conduct-based liability, the understanding of this provision changed towards the end of the 19th century. A requirement of unlawfulness, understood as the infringement of a right or a specific norm, was read into the provision in order to limit liability.[45]

16. 19TH-CENTURY GERMAN TURN AWAY – The Italian move towards an unlawfulness-based liability had been influenced by the evolution German

---

Art. 1402 BW: *Een ieder is verantwoordelijk, niet aileen voor de schade welke hij door zijne daad, maar ook voor die welke hij door zijne nalatigheid of onvoorzigtigheid veroorzaakt heeft.*"

42 Antoine Hol, "Fault in Legal Doctrine in the Netherlands," in *The Development and Making of Legal Doctrine*, ed. Nils Jansen (Cambridge: Cambridge University Press, 2010). pp. 165–166. See also Asser/Sieburgh 6-IV 2019/38.

43 Nadia Coggiola, "The Influence of Foreign Legal Models on the Development of Italian Civil Liability Rules from the 1865 Civil Code to the Present Day," *Italian Law Journal*, no. 2 (2019). pp. 443–444. She illustrates: "In truth, the Italian 1865 Civil Code actually followed the French model so closely that most of the civil liability rules are actually a mere translation of the rules of the Code Napoléon, starting from the title of the book devoted to civil liability, which was literally translated from 'Des délits et des quasi-délits' in 'Dei delitti e dei quasi-delitti', that is to say 'Of Delicts and Quasi-Delicts'." See also Guido Alpa, "Unjust Damage and the Role of Negligence: Historical Profile," *Tulane European and Civil Law Forum* 9 (1994). p. 165.

44 Translation from Coggiola, "The Influence of Foreign Legal Models on the Development of Italian Civil Liability Rules from the 1865 Civil Code to the Present Day." p. 444. She in turn relies on the official translation from Legifrance, as the Italian text was a literal translation of the French text. Original text:

Art. 1151: "*Qualunque fatto dell'uomo che arreca danno ad altri, obbliga quello per colpa del quale è avvenuto, a risarcire il danno.*"

Art. 1152: "*Ognuno è responsabile del danno che ha cagionato non solamente per un fatto proprio, ma anche per propria negligenza o imprudenza.*"

45 Graziadei, "Liability for Fault in Italian Law: The Development of Legal Doctrine from 1865 to the End of the Twentieth Century." pp. 129–130; von Bar, *The Common European Law of Torts*, I. p. 24, nr. 15. For a more in-depth discussion, see Coggiola, "The Influence of Foreign Legal Models on the Development of Italian Civil Liability Rules from the 1865 Civil Code to the Present Day." pp. 446–448.

scholarship underwent. Indeed, in the beginning of the 19th century, German courts had generally applied a conduct-based liability. As Jansen explains in *Developing legal doctrine: fault in the German law of delict*, such a vague and unstructured approach was considered unsatisfactory to the Pandectists.[46] The result of these debates was codified in §§ 823 and 826 BGB:

§ 823 BGB

(1) "A person who, intentionally or negligently, unlawfully injures the life, limb, health, freedom, property or some other right of another person is liable to provide compensation to the other party for the damage arising therefrom.
(2) The same duty is incumbent on a person who commits a breach of a statute that is intended to protect another person. If, according to the contents of the statute, it is possible to violate it also without fault, then liability to compensation only exists in the case of fault".

§ 826 BGB

"A person who, in a manner offending common decency, intentionally inflicts damage on another person is liable to the other person to provide compensation for the damage".[47]

In § 823 BGB, unlawfulness has been placed at the central place of liability law.[48] Where in § 823 (1) BGB the infringement of a protected right generally[49] indicates an unlawfulness, in § 823 (2) BGB, it is the infringement of 'statute that is intended to protect another person' that indicates the unlawfulness.[50] Unlawfulness can be rebutted by invoking a ground of justification. On top of that, such unlawfulness must also be culpable, i.e. in breach of the relevant standard of care.[51] This novel way of structuring liability law led to a system which differs significantly from previous systems, with the notable

46 Jansen, "Developing Legal Doctrine: Fault in the German Law of Delict." pp. 100–101. See also Wagner, "Comparative Tort Law." p. 1000; Zimmermann, *The Law of Obligations. Roman Foundations of the Civilian Tradition*. p. 1036.

47 § 823 *(1) Wer vorsätzlich oder fahrlässig das Leben, den Körper, die Gesundheit, die Freiheit, das Eigentum oder ein sonstiges Recht eines anderen widerrechtlich verletzt, ist dem anderen zum Ersatz des daraus entstehenden Schadens verpflichtet.*

(2) Die gleiche Verpflichtung trifft denjenigen, welcher gegen ein den Schutz eines anderen bezweckendes Gesetz verstößt. Ist nach dem Inhalt des Gesetzes ein Verstoß gegen dieses auch ohne Verschulden möglich, so tritt die Ersatzpflicht nur im Falle des Verschuldens ein.

§ 823 BGB *Wer in einer gegen die guten Sitten verstoßenden Weise einem anderen vorsätzlich Schaden zufügt, ist dem anderen zum Ersatz des Schadens verpflichtet.*

48 Jansen, "Gesetzliche Schuldverhältnisse Eine historische Strukturanalyse." p. 126.

49 Except for so-called *Rahmenrecht*, being the right not explicitly recognized in § 823 (1) BGB but considered to fall under "other rights."

50 Hans-Jürgen Ahrens and Andreas Spickhoff, *Deliktsrecht*, Vols. XLVIII+723 (München: C.H. Beck, 2022). p. 85, nrs. 4–5. From a comparative perspective: von Bar, *The Common European Law of Torts*, I. p. 25, nr. 17.

51 Ahrens and Spickhoff, *Deliktsrecht*. p. 105, nr. 1.

consequence that pure economic loss cannot be indemnified (*supra* Chap. 2, nr. 7).[52] The only extra-contractual liability ground which allowed for the indemnification of pure economic loss is § 826 BGB. The latter, however, only covers instances of intentionally "offending common decency." Jansen reports that judges who wanted to circumvent the limited possibility to indemnify pure economic loss relied on a very loose interpretation to nevertheless grant liability.[53]

As the German system did not provide for the indemnification of pure economic loss, the discussion about the legal basis of pre-contractual liability were present early on from the inception; after all, another legal basis was *necessary*.[54] It was generally considered to be customary law that in the course of contract negotiations, parties were under duties of care whose infringement lead to the indemnification of pure economic loss, but the foundation and structure of this liability was subject of much scholarly debate.[55] Quite unsurprisingly, given that Jhering had already shown in 1861 that pure economic loss for wrongful conduct had to be brought under a contractual basis to give rise to liability, the contractual realm was a sensible alternative. In that context, good faith ("*Treu und Glaube*") was generally invoked as the legal basis for pre-contractual liability.[56] This move towards applying good faith in the pre-contractual realm gained traction in surrounding legal systems[57] to begin with under Italian law.

17. Italian and Dutch re-codification – The Italian re-codification of 1942 set forth the evolution that had started towards the end of the 19th century and beginning of the 20th century. Indeed, article 2043 of the Italian Civil Code (It. Civ. C.) provides:

> "Any intentional or negligent act which causes unlawful harm to another, obliges the person who committed the act to provide compensation."[58]

52 von Bar, *The Common European Law of Torts*, I. p. 26, nr. 18.

53 Historical perspective: Jansen, "Developing Legal Doctrine: Fault in the German Law of Delict." p. 107. For a more in-depth discussion, see Giaro, "Culpa in Contrahendo: eine Geschichte der Wiederentdeckung." pp. 130–134. Contemporary perspective: Fikentscher and Heinemann, *Schuldrecht Allgemeiner und Besonderer Teil.* p. 375, nr. 605. See also Bussani, Sebok, and Infantino, "Compensation for Pure Economic Loss." p. 157 and von Bar, *The Common European Law of Torts*, I. p. 26, nrs. 17–18 and p. 52, nr. 37.

54 Kreutz, *Hypothetische Verträge im Rahmen des Schadensausgleichs*. pp. 19–21; Giaro, "Culpa in Contrahendo: eine Geschichte der Wiederentdeckung." p. 129.

55 Staudinger/Feldmann (2018) BGB § 311 nr. 98; Kreutz, *Hypothetische Verträge im Rahmen des Schadensausgleichs*. p. 21.

56 Kurt Ballerstadt, "Zur Haftung für culpa in contrahendo bei Geschäftsabschluss durch Stellvertreter," *AcP* (1950/1951). p. 503.

57 For an overview of how widespread a requirement to act in good faith in the pre-contractual phase was in European private law around the change of the millennium, see Zuloaga, *Reliance in the Breaking Off of Contractual Negotiations*. pp. 158–163; Hesselink, *De redelijkheid en billijkheid in het Europese privaatrecht*. p. 67 *et seq*.

58 Translation by Graziadei, "Liability for Fault in Italian Law: The Development of Legal Doctrine from 1865 to the End of the Twentieth Century." p. 141. Nadia Coggiola also relies on this

Though this provision codifies mainly a French-style conduct-based liability system, it adds the requirement of *unlawful* harm ("*danno inguisto*"). As already under *Lex Aquila* (*supra* Chap. 2, nr. 4), the notion of unlawfulness often gives rise to considerable debates and difficulties in understanding. Allegedly, the drafters of the article intended to codify the possibility of grounds of justification by relying on the formulation of unlawful harm.[59] By locating this requirement at the level of harm, however, they did something different, namely, that the notion of unlawful harm translates the understanding of "unlawfulness" as infringement of a protected right akin to § 823 (1) BGB.[60] Only that damage which is unjust, thus damage to a protected right (rights *erga omnes*), can give rise to liability. Logically, the fate of compensation of pure economic loss became uncertain.

Though the sense in which the requirement of unlawful harm seems to have been *intended* does not require a specific provision on pre-contractual liability, a specific provision on pre-contractual liability appeared *necessary* in the later understanding of article 2043 It. Civ. C. This necessity for a specific provision was not problematic, as the Italian legislator of 1942 *had* already codified pre-contractual liability in article 1337 It. Civ. C.:

> "The parties, in the conduct of negotiations and the formation of the contract, shall behave according to good faith."[61]

Here, the influence of German law becomes apparent in the extension of the duty to act in good faith to the pre-contractual phase. The fact that the influence

---

translation. (Coggiola, "The Influence of Foreign Legal Models on the Development of Italian Civil Liability Rules from the 1865 Civil Code to the Present Day." p. 451.) Original text: "*Qualunque fatto doloso o colposo, che cagiona ad altri un danno ingiusto, obbliga colui che ha commesso il fatto a risarcire il danno.*" Alternative translation by Pietro Sirena: "Any action which deliberately or negligently causes an unlawful harm to another person, obliges the person who committed that action to compensate the harm." Pietro Sirena, "The Concepts of 'Harm' in the French and Italian Laws of Civil Liability," in *French Civil Liability in Comparative Perspective*, ed. Jean-Sébastien Borghetti and Simon Whittaker (Oxford: Hart Publishing, 2019). p. 207.

59 Graziadei, "Liability for Fault in Italian Law: The Development of Legal Doctrine from 1865 to the End of the Twentieth Century." p. 141; Francesco D. Busnelli and Giovanni Comandé, " 'Wrongfulness' in the Italian Legal System," in *Unification of Tort Law: Wrongfulness*, ed. Helmut Koziol (The Hague: Kluwer International, 1998). pp. 69–70; Alpa, "Unjust Damage and the Role of Negligence: Historical Profile." p. 176.

It should, however, be noted that to the extent such a reading would imply a conduct-based liability, grounds of justification need not specifically be located within the formulation.

60 Graziadei, "Liability for Fault in Italian Law: The Development of Legal Doctrine from 1865 to the End of the Twentieth Century." pp. 141–142; von Bar, *The Common European Law of Torts*, I. pp. 30–31, nr. 20.

61 Translation from Febbrajo, "Good Faith and Pre-Contractual Liability in Italy: Recent Developments in the Interpretation of Article 1337 of the Italian Civil Code." p. 292. Original text: "*Le parti, nello svolgimento delle trattative e nella formazione del contratto, devono comportarsi secondo buona fede.*" See also Hesselink, *De redelijkheid en billijkheid in het Europese privaatrecht*. p. 68.

of German law changed the intended understanding of article 2043 It. Civ. C. seems to have retroactively made article 1337 It. Civ. C. necessary.[62]

In any case, the understanding of *danno ingiusto* changed towards the end of the 20th century. From the infringement of a protected right, it now came to be understood as the infringement of a legally protected interest,[63] hence providing an opening for the indemnification of pure economic loss.[64] This consequence then was drawn by the Meroni decision of the *Corte di Cassazione* in 1971[65] in which a football club claimed compensation of lost benefits due to the decease of one of their players (called Meroni) in a car accident. The court granted the compensation of pure economic loss.[66]

The evolving and today still debated[67] fate of pure economic loss under Italian law has a notable impact on Italian pre-contractual liability law. On the one hand, an inherited focus on finding a damaged interest that could be perceived as an absolute right.[68] On the other hand, an ongoing difficulty to

62 For some explanations on the fascist past of the provision, see Febbrajo, "Good Faith and Pre-Contractual Liability in Italy: Recent Developments in the Interpretation of Article 1337 of the Italian Civil Code." pp. 295–296.

63 "Ultimately, for the purposes of the configurability of aquilian liability (*), the formal qualification of the legal position claimed by the subject is not decisive, since the protection of compensation is ensured only in relation to the injustice of the damage, which constitutes an autonomous case, marked by the injury of a legally relevant interest." Cass civ, sez un, 22 July 1999 no 500, p. 17. Free translation. Original text: "*In definitiva, ai fini della configurabilità della responsabilità acquiliana (*) non assume rilievo determinante la qualificazione formale della posizione giuridica vantata dal soggetto, poiché la tutela risarcitoria è assicurata solo in relazione alla ingiustizia del danno, che costituisce fattispecie autonoma, contrassegnata dalla lesione di un interesse giuridicamente rilevante.*" See on this point Sirena, "The Concepts of 'Harm' in the French and Italian Laws of Civil Liability." p. 213. See also Bussani, Sebok, and Infantino, "Compensation for Pure Economic Loss." pp. 154–155; Bussani and Palmer, "The Liability Regimes of Europe – Their Façades and Interiors." p. 134; von Bar, *The Common European Law of Torts*, I. p. 32, nr. 21.

64 Alberto Trabucchi, *Instituzioni di diritto civile* (Milano: Wolters Kluwer, 2022). p. 1420421bis. Graziadei, "Liability for Fault in Italian Law: The Development of Legal Doctrine from 1865 to the End of the Twentieth Century." pp. 148–149.

65 Cass. civ. 26 January 1971 no 174.

66 For a brief discussion of the case, see Bussani and Palmer, "The Liability Regimes of Europe – Their Façades and Interiors." pp. 134–135.

67 Trabucchi, *Instituzioni di diritto civile*. p. 1421, nr. 421bis and references there, particularly fn. 40; Cesare Salvi, *La responsabilità civile* (Milano: Giuffrè Francis Lefebvre, 2019). p. 111. Important critics: Carlo Castronovo, *Responsabilità civile* (Milano: Giuffrè, 2018). p. 75; Salvatore Mazzamuto, "Spunti in tema di danno ingiusto e di danno meramente patriomoniale," *Europea e diritto privato*, no. 2 (2008). pp. 349–400.

68 For instance: "The good protected by Art. 1337 is not only the traditional right not to suffer the effects of a termination of negotiations, having regard to their stage of development, but also the legitimate expectation that negotiations will take place on an equal footing, without the other party, out of malice or without seriousness of purpose, keeping the other party engaged, precluding it from other possibilities." Trabucchi, *Instituzioni di diritto civile*. p. 133, nr. 70. Free translation. Original text: "*Il bene tutelato dall'art. 1337 non è solo quello tradizionalemente considerato dal diritto a non subire gli effetti di un recesso dalle trattative, avuto riguardo al loro stadio evolutivo, ma anche la legittima aspettativa che le trattative si svolgano su un piano di parità, senza che la*

locate pre-contractual liability either in the extra-contractual or the contractual realm (*infra* Chap. 3, nr. 6).[69] This perfectly illustrates the interdependence between the extra-contractual liability system and pre-contractual liability. Uncertainty on the former translates into uncertainty on the latter.

The Dutch Civil Code of 1838 had been the first to focus on unlawfulness (*supra* Chap. 2, nr. 15). This had led to the understanding that only an unlawful act, understood to mean either the infringement of a protected right or a statutory provision, could give rise to liability.[70] However, this conception came to stand under pressure and was finally complemented in the *Lindenbaum* decision of 1919.[71] There, the *Hoge Raad* proclaimed that unlawfulness is understood as an overarching term which designates a wrongful act,[72] the infringement of a specific legal norm or the infringement of a right.[73] This has been clearly expressed in article 6:162 of the *Nieuw Burgerlijk Wetboek* (NBW) of 1992:[74]

> "1. A person who commits an unlawful act against another person that can be attributed to him, must repair the damage that this other person has suffered as a result thereof.
> 2. As an unlawful act is regarded a violation of someone else's right (entitlement) and an act or omission in violation of a duty imposed by law or of what according to unwritten law has to be regarded as proper social conduct, always as far as there was no justification for this behaviour."[75]

In 1992, the Dutch legislator considered introducing an article on pre-contractual liability (article 6.5.2.8a project-NBW[76]) but ultimately refrained from doing

controparte, per malizia o senza serietà di intenti, tenga impegnata l'altra parte, precludendole altre possibilità."

69 For an overview: Francesco Gazzoni, *Manuale di diritto privao* (Napoli: Edizioni Scientifiche Italiane, 2015). p. 883, nr. 1.

70 In more detail in Asser/Sieburgh 6-IV 2019/39–41.

71 HR 31 January 1919, (Lindenbaum/Cohen), *NJ* 1919, 418 ECLI:NL:HR:1919:AG1776. For a discussion Asser/Sieburgh 6-IV 2019/42.

72 Very clear in Asser/Sieburgh 6-IV 2019/37.

73 Asser/Sieburgh 6-IV 2019/39. See also von Bar, *The Common European Law of Torts*, I. p. 38, nr. 25. Von Bar interestingly points out that the legislator of 1992 shows considerable trust in the judiciary by placing judge-made duties of care on an equal level with statutory ones, thereby showing a different understanding from what was present at the drafting of the BGB, which limited the power of the judge considerably (p. 49, nr. 35).

74 Cees van Dam, *Aansprakelijkheidsrecht* (Den Haag: Boom Juridisch, 2023). p. 73; Asser/Sieburgh 6-IV 2019/43.

75 1. *Hij die jegens een ander een onrechtmatige daad pleegt, welke hem kan worden toegerekend, is verplicht de schade die de ander dientengevolge lijdt, te vergoeden.*

2. *Als onrechtmatige daad worden aangemerkt een inbreuk op een recht en een doen of nalaten in strijd met een wettelijke plicht of met hetgeen volgens ongeschreven recht in het maatschappelijk verkeer betaamt, een en ander behoudens de aanwezigheid van een rechtvaardigingsgrond.*

76 *Parl. Gesch. BW Boek 6* 1981, p. 878: "Negotiating parties are obliged to have their conduct determined partly by each other's legitimate interests. Each of them is free to break-off negotiations, unless this would be unacceptable on the basis of the other party's legitimate expectation of the conclusion of an agreement or in connection with the other circumstances of the case." Free translation.

so, as time was not considered ripe to do so.[77] Though not necessary from the present perspective (article 6:162 NBW sufficed to provide for pre-contractual liability), the *Hoge Raad* had recognized that duties of care based on good faith arose in pre-contractual relations as early as 1957 (*infra* Chap. 3, nr. 10).[78] In line with this early case law, the *Hoge Raad* stated in the *Plas/Valburg* decision[79] that pre-contractual liability is based on good faith and established the three-phases doctrine ("*driefasenleer*") (*supra* Chap. 1, nr. 34).

18. German *Schuldrechtsreform* – The German law of obligations was reformed in 2001 and entered into force in 2002. This reform did not have an impact on the structure of § 823 BGB, but it did bring along a codification of pre-contractual liability in § 311 (2) BGB. Roughly speaking, § 311 (2) BGB declares that in the context of contract negotiations, the duties of care of the contractual realm (§ 241 (2) BGB) apply. Interestingly, the German approach thus does not rely on good faith (§ 242 BGB).[80] In case of an infringement of such duties of care (fault), the party can be held liable according to § 280 (1) BGB, under which pure economic loss can also be compensable.[81] Compensation of harm then occurs according to § 249 BGB. Hence, as German extra-contractual liability does not allow to accommodate pre-contractual liability, contractual liability had to be mobilized to provide a means for pre-contractual liability – much like Jhering's *culpa in contrahendo* (*supra* nrs. 1–8) but extended to the pre-contractual phase.[82]

19. Harmonization models – The many European harmonization models contain provisions on pre-contractual liability, though they do not necessarily contain a system of extra-contractual liability. Hence, they must provide for a duty of care in the absence of an existing system of extra-contractual liability to fall back upon. In these cases, it makes perfect sense that they rely on good faith as a contractual conduct-based liability law system.[83] It must,

Original text: "*Onderhandelende partijen zijn verplicht hun gedrag mede door elkaars gerechtvaardigde belangen te laten bepalen. Ieder van hen is vrij de onderhandelingen af te breken, tenzij dit op grond van het gerechtvaardigde vertrouwen van de wederpartij in het tot stand komen van een overeenkomst of in verband met de andere omstandigheden van het geval onaanvaardbaar zou zijn.*" See for more information HR 23 oktober 1987, *NJ* 1988/1017 (VSH/Shell), nr. 3; Asser/Sieburgh 6-III 2022/194; and Ruygvoorn, *Afgebroken onderhandelingen en het gebruik van voorbehouden*. pp. 48–49.

77 Hesselink, *De redelijkheid en billijkheid in het Europese privaatrecht*. p. 68.

78 HR 15 November 1957, ECLI:NL:HR:1957:AG2023. For a discussion, see Ruygvoorn, *Afgebroken onderhandelingen en het gebruik van voorbehouden*. p. 41.

79 HR 18 June 1982, *NJ* 1983, 723 (*Plas/Valburg*), ECLI:NL:HR:1982:AG4405, nr. 3.4–3.5. For a discussion of the decision and its context Ruygvoorn, *Afgebroken onderhandelingen en het gebruik van voorbehouden*. p. 42.

80 Hesselink, *De redelijkheid en billijkheid in het Europese privaatrecht*. p. 69.

81 Medicus and Lorenz, *Schuldrecht I Allgemeiner Teil*. p. 242, nr. 4 and p. 244, nr. 13; Staudinger/Schwarze (2019) BGB § 280 nr. 38.

82 Kreutz, *Hypothetische Verträge im Rahmen des Schadensausgleichs*. p. 18.

83 See for a general discussion Zuloaga, *Reliance in the Breaking Off of Contractual Negotiations*. pp. 176–180.

however, be recognized that the insistence on good faith also is an expression of a divide between continental legal systems and the English common law and the ambition to overcome this divide.[84] The different provisions read as follows:

"DCFR II.-3:301

(1) A person is free to negotiate and is not liable for failure to reach an agreement.
(2) A person who is engaged in negotiations has a duty to negotiate in accordance with good faith and fair dealing and not to break off negotiations contrary to good faith and fair dealing. This duty may not be excluded or limited by contract.
(3) A person who is in breach of the duty is liable for any loss caused to the other party by the breach.
(4) It is contrary to good faith and fair dealing, in particular, for a person to enter into or continue negotiations with no real intention of reaching an agreement with the other party.

UPICC 2.1.15: Negotiations in bad faith

(1) A party is free to negotiate and is not liable for failure to reach an agreement.
(2) However, a party who negotiates or breaks off negotiations in bad faith is liable for the losses caused to the other party.
(3) It is bad faith, in particular, for a party to enter into or continue negotiations when intending not to reach an agreement with the other party.

PECL 2:301

(1) A party is free to negotiate and is not liable for failure to reach an agreement.
(2) However, a party who has negotiated or broken off negotiations contrary to good faith and fair dealing is liable for the losses caused to the other party.
(3) It is contrary to good faith and fair dealing, in particular, for a party to enter into or continue negotiations with the other party."

20. French and Belgian re-codifications – Respectively in 2016 and 2023, the French and the Belgian law of obligations have been reformed. At the time of writing, the reform of extra-contractual liability is still pending under French law and voted since February 2 in Belgium.[85] The Belgian reform does not

84 On the process see Babusiaux, "Liability for Negotiations." pp. 361–363, nrs. 3–7.
85 Expected entry into force in January 2025. Find the text on https://justitie.belgium.be/nl/bwcc.

fundamentally change the functioning of the type of liability law system. It still relies on a conduct-based liability (article 6.5. Be. Civ. C.):

> "Everyone is liable for the damage they cause to others through their own fault."[86]
>
> More importantly, the reform of contract law has led to a codification of pre-contractual liability in both systems. Given that the Belgian reform has been inspired by the French one,[87] the legistic approach chosen in both systems is quite similar. First, a specific duty of care applicable to contract negotiations is established to then provide for some specifics in case of an infringement of that duty of care.

Concerning the *duty of care*, both systems rely on a duty to act in good faith. Under French law, article 1112 Fr. Civ. C provides in its first alinea that "The commencement, continuation and breaking-off of precontractual negotiations are free from control. They must mandatorily satisfy the requirements of good faith."[88] The Belgian provision essentially is a copy of the French one, save for the explicit reference to its mandatory character:

> Article 5.15 Be. Civ. C. Freedom of negotiation
>
> "The parties are free to initiate, conduct and break off pre-contractual negotiations.
>
> In that regard, they act in accordance with the requirements of good faith."[89]

86 Free translation. Original text: "*Toute personne est responsable du dommage qu'elle cause à autrui par sa faute*."/"*Eenieder is aansprakelijk voor de schade die hij door zijn fout aan een ander veroorzaakt*."

See in this context also article 6.6 Be. Civ. C., which defines the notion of fault: "§ 1. Fault consists in a failure to comply with a legal rule imposing or prohibiting a certain conduct or with the general standard of prudence which must be observed in social relationships.

§ 2. the general standard of prudence requires that conduct be adopted which would have been adopted by a prudent and reasonable person in the same circumstances."

Free translation. Original text: "§ 1er. *La faute consiste dans un manquement à une règle légale imposant ou interdisant un comportement déterminé ou à la norme générale de prudence qui doit être respectée dans les rapports sociaux.* § 2. *La norme générale de prudence impose d'adopter un comportement conforme à celui qu'aurait adopté une personne prudente et raisonnable placée dans les mêmes circonstances*."/"§ 1. *De fout bestaat uit de schending van een wettelijke regel die een bepaald gedrag oplegt of verbiedt of van de algemene zorgvuldigheidsnorm die geldt in het maatschappelijk verkeer.* § 2. *De algemene zorgvuldigheidsnorm vereist een gedrag dat overeenkomt met dat van een voorzichtig en redelijk persoon in dezelfde omstandigheden geplaatst*."

87 Explanation to the law of 24 February 2021 containing Book 5 "Obligations" of the Civil Code, DOC 55 1806/001, pp. 25–26.

88 Original text: "*L'initiative, le déroulement et la rupture des négociations précontractuelles sont libres. Ils doivent impérativement satisfaire aux exigences de la bonne foi*."

89 Original text: "*Les parties sont libres d'entamer, de mener et de rompre des négociations précontractuelles. Elles agissent à cet égard conformément aux exigences de la bonne foi*."/"*De partijen zijn vrij precontractuele onderhandelingen aan te vatten, te voeren en af te breken. Ze handelen hierbij in overeenstemming met de eisen van de goede trouw*." The explanatory note confirms

It is interesting to observe that the Italian *Codice civile* already foresaw in a specific duty of care applicable to contract negotiations (*supra* Chap. 2, nr. 17) but did not provide for specific rules applying to the liability following from an infringement of the duty of care. The French second alinea of 1112 Fr. Civ. C., however, does so:

> "In case of fault committed during the negotiations, the reparation of the resulting loss is not calculated so as to compensate the loss of benefits which were expected from the contract that was not concluded."[90]

The Belgian provision (article 5.17 Be. Civ. C.) is even more detailed and specific:

> "The parties may incur extra-contractual liability to each other during the pre-contractual negotiations.
>
> In the case of wrongfully broken off negotiations, this liability entails reinstating the injured party to the situation in which it would have found itself had negotiations not taken place. If a legitimate expectation has been created that the contract would have been concluded without any doubt, this liability may include compensation for the loss of the expected net benefits from the contract not concluded.
>
> The breach of a duty to inform can lead not only to the pre-contractual liability, but also to the nullity of the contract if the requirements determined in article 5.33. are met."[91]

---

the French "inspiration" (Explanation to the law of 24 February 2021 containing Book 5 "Obligations" of the Civil Code, DOC 55 1806/001, p. 25).

90 Original text: "*En cas de faute commise dans les négociations, la réparation du préjudice qui en résulte ne peut avoir pour objet de compenser ni la perte des avantages attendus du contrat non conclu, ni la perte de chance d'obtenir ces avantages.*"

91 Original text: "*Les parties peuvent engager leur responsabilité extra-contractuelle l'une envers l'autre pendant les négociations précontractuelles.*

En cas de rupture fautive des négociations, cette responsabilité implique que la personne lésée soit remise dans la situation dans laquelle elle se serait trouvée s'il n'y avait pas eu de négociations. Lorsque la confiance légitime que le contrat serait sans aucun doute conclu a été suscitée, elle peut impliquer la réparation de la perte des avantages nets attendus du contrat non conclu.

Outre la responsabilité précontractuelle, la violation d'un devoir d'information peut conduire à la nullité du contrat s'il est satisfait aux exigences établies à l'article 5.33."/"*De partijen kunnen tijdens de precontractuele onderhandelingen jegens elkaar buitencontractuele aanspra- kelijkheid oplopen.*

Bij foutief afbreken van onderhandelingen houdt deze aansprakelijkheid in dat de benadeelde teruggeplaatst wordt in de situatie waarin hij zich zou hebben bevon- den indien er niet zou zijn onderhandeld. Wanneer het rechtmatig vertrouwen is gewekt dat het contract zonder enige twijfel gesloten zal worden, kan deze het herstel van het verlies van de verwachte netto-voordelen uit het niet gesloten contract inhouden.De schending van een informatieplicht kan niet enkel leiden tot de precontractuele aansprakelijkheid maar ook tot de nietigheid van het contract indien voldaan is aan de vereisten bepaald in artikel 5.33."

A duty of care specific to the pre-contractual phase does not appear necessary in systems which do undoubtedly rely on a conduct-based extra-contractual liability law system. That such a specific duty of care is redundant under French and Belgian law becomes obvious in article 5.17 Be. Civ. C., according to which pre-contractual liability is an application of extra-contractual liability: Given that French and Belgian extra-contractual liability do have a general standard of care, it appears perfectly superfluous to have a specific duty of care applying to the pre-contractual phase in the form of good faith (*infra* Chap. 3, nr. 11),[92] save where the specific duty of care would require a different level of care form the general one.

1.5. Means of pre-contractual liability

21. CONDUCT-BASED LIABILITY NECESSARY – The preceding analysis has corroborated the argument that a conduct-based liability law system, independent of whether that is extra-contractual or contractual liability, is necessary and sufficient to provide a remedy for pure economic loss in the context of contract negotiations. Indeed, in systems such as Belgian and French law, which have a clearly conduct-based extra-contractual liability, pre-contractual liability is in fact a mere application of extra-contractual liability. Dutch law, in turn, relies very clearly on good faith, but this ultimately appears to be identical to their extra-contractual liability, which is conduct-based. In Italy, where it is highly debated what type of liability law system their extra-contractual liability law system is, the legal basis for pre-contractual liability is also very unclear. German law, whose extra-contractual liability system is unlawfulness-based, has to deal with pre-contractual liability law under contractual liability law.

22. PERSISTENCE OF SPECIFIC PROVISIONS – It must be admitted that contemporary legislators seem to favour a specific provision for pre-contractual liability (generally based on good faith), even where that seems not to be strictly necessary. There seem to be two reasons for that tendency. First, the German discussions on the legal basis for pre-contractual liability seem to have been transposed into systems that need not have these discussions in the first place, as their national system of extra-contractual liability is conduct-based. Seemingly, and under influence of the common law–civil law divide, these considerations then also made their way into model laws, from where they, in turn, influenced contemporary legislation. As, without actually being necessary, these legal systems were already discussing specific provisions on pre-contractual liability, they appeared very keen to integrating specific provisions in this regard.

92 As I argued in Hick, "Aansprakelijkheid voor afgebroken onderhandelingen in België en Nederland: Op koers voor toenadering." p. 252, nr. 26. In another sense, see Sophie Stijns and S. De Rey, "Het nieuwe verbintenissenrecht in Boek 5 BW – Deel I," *RW*, no. 24 (2023). p. 932, nr. 22, fn. 81; Jafferali, "La formation dynamique du contrat." p. 172, nr. 2. From a comparative perspective: Zuloaga, *Reliance in the Breaking Off of Contractual Negotiations*. p. 65.

The recent Belgian codification provides a good example of this tendency. There, article 5.15 states that negotiators need to act according to the standard of good faith in the negotiation process, and article 5.17 Be. Civ. C. refers questions of pre-contractual liability to the general extra-contractual liability. Hence, article 5.15 Be. Civ. C. states a specific standard of care applicable in the course of contract negotiations which is sanctioned via general extra-contractual liability (articles 1382–1383 old Be. Civ. C. at the time of writing but under reform; as of January 2025 article 6.5 Be. Civ. C.). It is unclear whether there is a difference in the set standard of care, though it seems unlikely, and if so, it is doubtful whether it will be significant enough to change the outcome of a judicial decision. This suggests that relying on such a specific norm – where such is not necessary – is rather an intricate and superfluous approach.

Perhaps it is also considered to be clearer to explicitly provide that duties of care apply to the pre-contractual phase. In that case, the reason behind this tendency likely is of pedagogical nature and, as such, understandable. The risk that comes along with it, however, is that the specific provision deviates from the general liability regime. Where those deviations were intended, that is perfectly fine. Where, however, such deviations were not intended but occurred, the situation is more problematic (*infra* Chap. 4, nr. 4).

23. CONTRACTUAL/EXTRA-CONTRACTUAL – Thus, there is no metaphysical truth to the nature of pre-contractual liability. Where the extra-contractual liability law system is conduct-based, it suffices to provide sufficient ground for pre-contractual liability. Even if that is the case, a legislator may choose to provide a specific regime. The risk he takes by doing so is deviating from the rules of the extra-contractual liability regime. This can be intended and then in turn is necessary and structurally sound; where it is not intended, however, this is problematic.

Where, in turn, the extra-contractual liability law system is not conduct-based, a specific solution is necessary.

By consequence, what is relevant in that context is not whether the liability is of contractual or extra-contractual nature but that it is conduct-based and, hence, allows for the indemnification of pure economic loss. Still, whether one relies on a contractual or an extra-contractual basis *does matter* from a practical perspective, as prescription periods and other elements might and generally do differ depending on the applicable regime of liability. Yet these differences are *incidental* and are not inherently linked to pre-contractual liability. In the context of pre-contractual liability, the differences between both may thus possibly be arbitrary or difficult to justify, as they are made for other reasons.

24. TERMINOLOGY: PRE-CONTRACTUAL PHASE/LIABILITY – The terminology of pre-contractual liability refers to a necessarily extra-contractual liability, as it is explicit that it is a "not yet contractual" liability. This proves confusing under German law, possibly explaining why there, the liability regime is called – conceptually somewhat imprecisely – *culpa in contrahendo*.

Moreover, the reference to the pre-contractual legal basis is unhandy where preparatory contracts have been concluded, in which case one would be under a contractual liability in the pre-contractual phase. That is clumsy terminology.

Hence, and particularly from a comparative perspective, it seems preferable to abandon the terminology of pre-contractual liability which Paul Pitotet considered inconvenient ("*incommode*") already in 1963 in his *Culpa in contrahendo et responsabilité précontractuelle en droit privé suisse*.[93]

Instead, I suggest relying on an alternative terminology which in my opinion is more concise and less inconvenient, namely, "*contract negotiations*," or "*liability for contract negotiations*," where the liability is concerned. That terminology is detached from the contractual or extra-contractual context and thereby overcomes the clumsiness of the terminology of the pre-contractual related terminology. Making abstraction of the contractual/extra-contractual divide will prove more convenient in cases where negotiations are led under a negotiation agreement. Though that is, luckily so, rather a semantical issue than fundamentally problematic, and of course, I am aware of how engrained this terminology is in the legal mindset and cannot pretend to reverse the long evolution pre-contractual liability has gone through. Still, it appears preferable to rely on a clearer and more convenient ("*commode*") terminology which can be uniform throughout the different national systems.

For those reasons, as of now, I will refer to contract negotiations instead of pre-contractual negotiations/phase/realm, *et cetera*. When I refer to pre-contractual phase or liability, I do so in a technical and/or historical sense, meaning that I either use it in the context of Faggella's writings or more generally, academics, courts, or legislators presenting the questions related to contract negotiations in terms of pre-contractual phase and/or liability.

2. Liability for contract negotiations and pre-supposed obligation to contract

2.1. Liability for contract negotiations

25. CONDUCT-BASED LIABILITY SYSTEM ENOUGH? – *Supra* (Chap. 1, nr. 22), I have explained that essentially, two approaches to the structure of liability for contract negotiations can be observed: a monolithic one and a two-pronged one. The monolithic approach builds on a conduct-based liability to explain that not only faults committed in the context of contract negotiations can give rise to liability but also to explain that the breaking-off of contract negotiations and, for that matter, identical thereto, the refusal to contract can lead to liability. The two-pronged approach, on the contrary, argues that a conduct-based liability can give rise to liability for all kinds of faults committed during

93 Paul Pitotet, *Culpa in contrahendo et responsabilité précontractuelle en droit privé suisse* (Bern: Staempfli, 1963). p. 13.

contract negotiations, except for the breaking-off or refusal to contract itself. If that latter event should give rise to liability, something more specific is needed.

As I now have identified that a conduct-based liability is *necessary* to provide for remedies in case of faults committed in the context of contract negotiations, the follow-up question is whether such a conduct-based liability is also *sufficient* to give rise to liability where the breaking-off of contract negotiations or the refusal to contract is to be the invoked conduct. In other words, is the monolithic structure of liability for contract negotiations enough, or is a two-pronged structure necessary?

From the outset, it should be clear that a legal system must not necessarily provide a liability for the case of broken-off negotiations or the refusal to contract, but it appears as a relevant means to protect the freedom to contract of a party (*supra* Chap. 1, nr. 30). Provided the latter is intended, it should be possible to hold a party liable for the breaking-off or refusal itself.

26. Fault-based argument – This discussion on whether the breaking-off of negotiations or the refusal to contract itself can give rise to liability has, as far as I can see, so far been led on the level of the fault requirement.[94] Indeed, as Olivier Deshayes explains from a French perspective[95] in his *Le dommage précontractuel*,[96] essentially, two[97] approaches to liability for contract negotiations exist, whose disagreement lies at the conception of the invoked *fault*.[98] Some argue that the breaking-off of negotiations or refusal to contract can be a fault, giving rise to liability. According to another approach, the breaking-off of negotiations or the refusal to contract cannot be wrongful itself, as it consists in the exercise of the freedom from contract. According to this position, the exercise of the freedom from contract cannot lead to liability.

Yet it seems that no decisive argument can be found by looking at the question when addressed at the level of the fault requirement.[99] Instead, I suggest

94 For instance, Medicus and Lorenz, *Schuldrecht I Allgemeiner Teil*. p. 245, nr. 14.

95 But given that it deals with a conduct-based liability, the point is valid from a comparative perspective.

96 Deshayes, "Le dommage précontractuel." pp. 187–204. Also dealt with in Hesselink, *De redelijkheid en billijkheid in het Europese privaatrecht*. p. 72.

97 He distinguishes three positions, but they meaningfully boil down to two opposing positions.

98 Patrice Jourdain even argues that the French Court of Cassation is wrong to apply the argumentation it uses in this context in its case law on the level of causality instead of fault. Jourdain, "Préjudice consécutif à la rupture fautive des pourparlers." p. 771.

99 See, for instance, how fruitless the discussion is in Durant, "La rupture unilatérale des pourparlers ou l'exercice d'une liberté surveillée." p. 56, nr. 18: "No doubt the exercise of any freedom is presumed to be lawful on the part of its holder. However, this is only a presumption which will be rebutted whenever it is shown that the exercise of the liberty is the result of a quasi-delictual fault. There would therefore be many situations in which the breaking-off of talks, insofar as it constitutes the exercise of the freedom not to contract, could be qualified as wrongful where it shows, on the part of the negotiator who proceeds to do so, an incorrect conduct." Citations omitted. Free translation. Original version: "*Sans doute l'exercice de toute liberté est-il présumé licite dans le chef de son titulaire. Il ne s'agit toutefois que d'une présomption qui sera renversée chaque fois qu'il sera*

moving beyond the discussion on the level of *fault* towards the level of *causality* (*infra* Chap. 2, nr. 28).[100] For it is true that on the level of the fault, the argument in favour or against one or the other position is exhausted by saying the following: it is possible or not, given freedom from contract. From there, no fruitful ground for further discussion seems possible. If, however, we move from the question of fault to a question of causality, as I suggest, a meaningful debate can be had. As far as I can see, and except for Saleilles[101] mentioning it *en passant*, I have not found this argument in this form elsewhere. The argument I will make (which will again be addressed in more detail *infra* Chap. 3, nrs. 33–40) builds forth on the finding that all analysed legal systems rely on a conduct-based liability in the context of contract negotiations. It consists on testing whether in a conduct-based liability law system, a party breaking-off negotiations or refusing to contract can be held liable for the breaking-off or refusal itself. If that is the case, the monolithic structure suffices; if that is not the case, a two-pronged structure is necessary.

27. CONDUCT-BASED LIABILITY – I have *supra* (Chap. 2, nr. 11) explained that and how the starting point of a liability law system affects and determines the functioning of that system. In the case of a conduct-based system, the conditions of application are fault, harm, and causal link between both. Thus, to establish liability for contract negotiations, three conditions of application need to be fulfilled: a fault must have caused harm. I will deal extensively with each of these notions in Part 2 (*infra* Chap. 3, nr. 1- Chap. 5, nr. 5). For the time being, it suffices to state that the understanding of the required causal link always is at least a factual understanding of the causal link, the so-called *conditio sine qua non* test: Would the harm have occurred without the fault? If the answer is positive (yes), no causal link exists (the harm would exist absent the fault); if the answer is negative (no), a causal link exists (the harm would not exist absent the fault). More succinctly put with Patrice Jourdain:

> "the causal link will not be accepted if, without the fault, the damage would still have occurred."[102]

---

montré que l'exercice de la liberté procède d'une faute quasi-délictuelle. Il serait donc bien des situations dans lesquelles la rupture des pourparlers, en tant qu'elle constitue l'exercice de la liberté de ne pas contracter, pourrait être qualifié de fautive lorsqu'elle témoigne, dans le chef du négociateur qui y procède, d'une incorrection." This discussion cannot be led in productive terms: either one is in favour or opposed, but there is no conceptual or otherwise productive discussion to be had here.

100 Olivier Deshayes, in his article Deshayes, "Le dommage précontractuel." pp. 187–204 does rely on causality-based arguments but seems to always use them in a somewhat restricted way. I here present this argument in a much broader, and perhaps more fundamental, manner.

101 "if the other party withdraws, it is not liable. There is no legal causal link." Saleilles, "De la responsabilité précontractuelle – A propos d'une étude nouvelle sur la matière." p. 700. Free translation. Original text: "*et si cette autre se retire, sa responsabilité n'est pas engagée. Tout lien de causalité juridique fait défaut.*"

102 Patrice Jourdain, *Les principes de la responsabilité civile* (Paris: Dalloz, 2021). p. 67. Free translation. Original text: "*le lien de causalité ne sera pas retenu si, sans la faut, le dommage se serait quand même produit.*"

Some legal systems add a second causal link to this first, which serves to restrict the causal link in such a way as to reach legal-political desirable results.[103] While this second juridical causal link differs across the analysed systems, the factual one is identical to each of them.

28. CAUSAL UNCERTAINTY – Now, if we take the breaking-off of contract negotiations or the refusal to contract to be the culpable element, we need to establish whether harm following from that breaking-off or refusal would have been suffered in the absence of the fault. Here appears a peculiarity which follows from the freedom from contract. Given that *a priori* each party is always free to break-off negotiations, in the alternative course of action without the fault, the party could have broken-off negotiations and thereby have caused the same harm as long as that party is considered to enjoy its freedom from contract. It thus appears that due to and as long as freedom from contract is recognized, it is impossible to establish that absent the fault, the same harm would *not* have been suffered. In that sense, due to freedom from contract, a normative causal indeterminacy exists if the invoked fault is the breaking-off of negotiations or the refusal to contract itself.[104]

To formulate this in the *conditio sine qua non* test, the question is this: Would the harm have occurred without the fault of breaking-off of negotiations or refusal to contract? Due to freedom from contract, it is normatively impossible to affirm neither that "yes, absent the fault the harm would exist" (no causal link exists) nor that "no, absent the fault the harm would not exist" (a causal link exists).

29. THEORETICAL IMPOSSIBILITY – Essentially, two counterarguments appear possible to me. Yet they fail to convince. *The first* goes that indeed, there is a theoretical impossibility to prove a causal link between fault and harm but that – who knows – maybe it can still be proven in practice depending on the factual circumstances.[105] The argument is not rigorous but merely consists in shifting through one's own lack of stringent application of the law onto the practitioner, thereby leading to increased legal uncertainty.

A second argument, in my opinion, appears quite convincing at first glance, though ultimately, it is not. It provides, quite simply, that if the breaking-off of negotiations or the refusal to contract itself is the fault, the counter-factual

103 For a brief overview Eric Tjong Tjin Tai, *Tort Law a Comparative Introduction* (Celtenham: Edward Elgar, 2022). p. 113.

104 It "is right insofar as there can be no trust that a contract will be concluded in any case. This is opposed by the negative freedom of contract." Nickel, *Die Rechtsfolgen der culpa in contrahendo.* p. 144. Free translation. Original text: "*ist insoweit Recht zu geben, als es kein Vertrauen dahingehend geben kann, dass ein Vertrag auf jeden Fall zustande kommen werde. Dem steht die negative Abschlussfreiheit entgegen.*" However, Nickel does not seem to draw any consequences from this statement.

105 See for instance under German law (MüKoBGB/Emmerich, 9. Aufl. 2022, BGB § 311 nr. 220.) or Belgian law (Aloïs Van Oevelen, "Juridische verhouding en aansprakelijkheid bij onderhandelingen over (commerciële) contracten," *DAOR* (1990). p. 50, nr. 8.).

scenario would be that of continuing negotiations and not that of possibly breaking-off or refusing to contract. Put differently: if we think away the fault (the breaking-off or the refusal) *ceteris paribus*, the result is still being in negotiations. That is a fair, and at first sight, convincing point. Only does it, yet again, not take the *normative* indeterminacy following from the freedom from contract into account. We cannot establish, normatively, that in the scenario without the wrongful breaking-off or refusal, the negotiations would not have been broken-off or refused. That is the inevitable consequence of freedom from contract. Hence, if taken seriously, the normative indeterminacy of the counter-factual scenario always renders the suffered harm non-causal.

30. PRE-SUPPOSING OBLIGATION TO NEGOTIATE OR TO CONTRACT – To overcome this *normative* causal uncertainty, a *normative* hypothetical alternative course of action must be posited. This, and this is a central argument of this book, would require an obligation to contract or at least an obligation to continue negotiations (on the distinction between obligation to contract and to negotiate *infra* Chap. 7, nrs. 1–23): one can only be held liable for the breaking-off of contract negotiations or the refusal to contract if, and to the extent that, one is obliged to negotiate or to contract. Inversely put: if one is held liable for the breaking-off of negotiations or the refusal to contract *itself*, the reasoning underlying it *necessarily* pre-supposes an obligation to contract or to negotiate. Only in this case can the normative possible counter-factual scenario be turned into a *normative* counter-factual scenario in which liability can arise. Only so doing can the freedom from contract be put aside and the normative causal uncertainty be overcome. Olivier Deshayes tentatively argues in this sense:

> "It has been decided in the past that when talks are well advanced, the partners may only withdraw from them if they can demonstrate the existence of an obstacle relating to the negotiations themselves. If this is not the case, and in particular if the termination is justified by a reason that is 'internal' to one of the negotiators, a breach of contract is established. In other words, it seems that at a certain point in the negotiations, termination is no longer really permitted. The freedom to negotiate gives way to an obligation to continue negotiations and conclude the contract. Liability then logically changes its face: it allows compensation for the loss of the gain expected from the conclusion of the contract, and thus becomes a means of indirectly concluding the contract."[106]

106 Deshayes, "Le dommage précontractuel." p. 201, nr. 32. Citations omitted. Free translation. Original version "*Il a été en effet décidé par le passé que lorsque les pourparlers sont très avancés, les partenaires ne peuvent s'en dégager qu'à condition de rapporter l'existence d'un obstacle tenant aux négociations elles-mêmes. Si tel n'est pas le cas, et notamment si la rupture est justifiée par un motif 'interne' à l'un des négociateurs, une faute de rupture est constatée. C'est dire, semble-t-il, qu'à un certain point des négociations, la rupture n'est plus réellement permise. La liberté de*

Indeed, as long as it is not normatively determinable that in the alternative course of actions negotiations would not have been broken-off or the conclusion of a contract would not have been refused, liability cannot be established.

31. Illustration: article 1112, al. 2 Fr. C. Civ. – Very mindful of its wording, the French provision for the breaking-off of negotiations provides for a 'fault committed during the negotiations' ('*faute commise dans les négociations*') instead of the wrongful breaking-off of negotiations as does article 5.17, second sentence of the second al. of the Belgian civil Code ('the case of wrongfully broken off negotiations'). This careful choice of wording of the French legislator appears as the consecration of the *Manoukian* decision of the French Court of Cassation[107] (*infra* Chap. 3, nr. 20) and ensuing analysis within French scholarship.[108] Denis Mazeaud sums up the facts of the case as follows:

> "In this case, in the spring of 1997, Alain Manoukian entered into negotiations with the shareholders of another company concerning the sale of the shares making up the latter's share capital. Although the negotiations had lasted several months and several draft agreements had already been drawn up, the company learned on 24 November 1997 that its partners had, two weeks earlier, entered into a contract promising to sell the same shares to a third party. It therefore sought to hold the 'unfaithful' negotiator liable for wrongful termination of the talks and the third party with whom the contract under negotiation had finally been concluded."[109]

In the *Manoukian* case, the Court stated:

> "But whereas the circumstances constituting a fault committed in the exercise of the right to unilaterally terminate the pre-contractual talks are not the cause of the loss consisting in the loss of a chance to realise the gains that the conclusion of the contr.act allowed to be hoped for;
>
> Whereas the Court of Appeal rightly decided that, in the absence of a firm and definitive agreement, the loss suffered by Alain Manoukian

négocier cède la place à l'obligation de poursuivre les négociations et de conclure le contrat. La responsabilité change alors logiquement de visage: elle permet la réparation de la perte du gain attendu de la conclusion du contrat, et devient donc un moyen de conclure indirectement le contrat."

107 Cass.comm.fr., 26 November 2003, 00–10.243 00–10.949.

108 For an overview from a comparative perspective, see Zuloaga, *Reliance in the Breaking Off of Contractual Negotiations*. pp. 66–67.

109 Denis Mazeaud, "Rupture fautive des pourparlers," *Revue des contrats*, no. 2 (2004). p. 257. Free translation. Original text: "*En l'espèce, au printemps de l'année 1997, la société Alain Manoukian avait entrepris, avec les actionnaires d'une autre société, une négociation qui portait sur la cession des actions qui composaient le capital social de cette dernière. Alors que la négociation avait duré plusieurs mois et que plusieurs projets d'accords avaient déjà été établis, la société avait appris, le 24 novembre 1997, que ses partenaires avaient conclu, deux semaines plus tôt, un contrat de promesse de cession des mêmes actions avec un tiers à la négociation. Elle recherchait donc la responsabilité du négociateur 'infidèle', pour rupture fautive des pourparlers et du tiers avec lequel le contrat en cours de négociation avait finalement été conclu.*"

> included only the costs incurred by the negotiation and the preliminary studies that it had carried out and not the profits that it could, if the contract were concluded, hope to make from the operation of the business or even the loss of a chance to obtain such profits; whereas the plea in law is unfounded;"[110]

This somewhat cryptic statement concerning the unavailability of the benefits under the negotiated contract or the loss of the chance to these benefits has been interpreted as being the logical consequence of the fault not residing in the breaking-off itself but in the circumstances.[111] The argument, however, remains on the level of fault instead of being framed in terms of causality.

32. Conduct-based liability necessary but not sufficient – From the preceding follows the conclusion that in order to provide for remedies for wrongs committed in the context of contract negotiations, a conduct-based liability system is necessary. However, and provided a legal system should be able to provide a remedy in the case of breaking-off of negotiations or refusal to contract to protect the freedom to contract of the counterparty, a conduct-based liability law system alone does not suffice. Hence, a monolithic structure for liability for contract negotiations does not suffice. Instead, a two-pronged approach is necessary. The first part of this two-pronged structure is a conduct-based liability. Yet it remains to be clarified what the second element – that allows to give rise to liability in the case of breaking-off of negotiations or refusal to contract – is. In his dissertation *Schutz vorvertraglicher Investitionen*,[112] Thomas Krawitz argued for distinguishing two types of liabilities within *culpa in contrahendo* in the case of failed contract conclusion: one fault-based and one strict liability:

> "Now that it has been shown that the existing liability regime is not convincing when negotiations fail, an attempt will be made to develop a coherent liability concept that does justice to the interests of the parties. The central statement here is that strict liability under c.i.c. can only be considered if a party can be accused of a culpable breach of duty. In particular, such a breach of duty cannot be seen in the breaking-off of negotiations without good reason. Consequently, c.i.c. liability can be

110 Cass.fr., *Chambre commerciale*, 26 November 2003, 00–10.243 00–10.949. Free translation. Original text: "*Mais attendu que les circonstances constitutives d'une faute commise dans l'exercice du droit de rupture unilatérale des pourparlers précontractuels ne sont pas la cause du préjudice consistant dans la perte d'une chance de réaliser les gains que permettait d'espérer la conclusion du contrat;*

Attendu que la cour d'appel a décidé à bon droit qu'en l'absence d'accord ferme et définitif, le préjudice subi par la société Alain Manoukian n'incluait que les frais occasionnés par la négociation et les études préalables auxquelles elle avait fait procéder et non les gains qu'elle pouvait, en cas de conclusion du contrat, espérer tirer de l'exploitation du fonds de commerce ni même la perte d'une chance d'obtenir ces gains; que le moyen n'est pas fondé."

111 Deshayes, "Le dommage précontractuel." pp. 203–204, nr. 36.

112 Krawitz, *Schutz vorvertraglicher Investitionen – Zur Haftung beim Scheitern von Vertragsverhandlungen*. 233 p.

> assumed in significantly fewer cases than the case law has so far – at least potentially – done.
>
> However, in addition to fault-based liability, strict liability should also be recognised. It should be flexible and based less on aspects of the protection of legitimate expectations and more on a distribution of risk that takes into account the interests of the parties. This requires a further evolution of the law; this can be based on the principles of the frustration of contract."[113]

Whereas I do agree with the necessity to distinguish between a conduct-based liability and another type of liability, I do not want to go so far as to propose a new strict liability, which Krawitz, by the way, justifies based on some preliminary agreement[114] close to Faggella's position (*supra* Chap. 1, nr. 15). Though his suggestion is understandable, it lacks nuance and fails, therefore, to convince. Instead, I want to show on what reasoning scholars and courts in fact do rely on when they argue that the breaking-off of negotiations or the refusal to contract itself is considered wrongful. In other words, I will analyse what reasoning – be it unconsciously – parties in fact do rely on when trying to invoke that the breaking-off or refusal is wrongful (as explained *supra* in Chap. 2, nrs. 30 and 33). In my opinion, such an exercise of uncovering what is implicitly done

113 Krawitz, *Schutz vorvertraglicher Investitionen – Zur Haftung beim Scheitern von Vertragsverhandlungen*. p. 97. Free translation. Original text: "*Nachdem aufgezeigt worden ist, dass das bestehende Haftungsregime beim Scheitern von Verhandlungen nicht überzeugen kann, soll nun der Versuch unternommen werden, ein canarises Haftungskonzept zu entwickeln, das den Parteiinteressen gerecht wird. Die zentrale Aussage dabei ist, dass eine verschuldensunabhängige Haftung aus c.i.c. nur dann in Betracht kommt, wenn einer Partei eine schuldhafte Pflichtverletzung vorzuwerfen ist. Eine solche Pflichtverletzung kann insbesondere nicht im Verhandlungsabbruch ohne triftigen Grund gesehen werden. Folglich kann eine c.i.c.-Haftung in deutlich weniger Fällen angenommen werden als dies die Rechtsprechung bisher – zumindest potentiell – tut.*

Neben einer verschuldensabhängigien Haftung sollte aber auch eine verschuldensunabhängige Haftung anerkannt werden. Sie sollte flexibel ausgestaltet sein und weniger auf Gesichtspunkte des Vertrauensschutzes aufbauen, als vielmehr an einer den Parteiinteressen Rechnung tragenden Riskioverteilung orientiert sein. Dazu bedarf es einer gesetzesübersteigenden Rechtsfortbildung; diese kann sich an Grundsätzen des Wegfalls der Geschäftsgrundlage orientieren."

114 "The starting point and central prerequisite for liability, which enables a distribution of risk that does justice to the interests of the parties, should be the consent of the party not investing itself to the other party making the pre-contractual investment. If such consent – and not mere knowledge – exists, it can be inferred that the consenting party has an interest in the other party's investment. The consent to the investment against the background of the state of negotiations reached by the parties can be understood as the assumption of the risk." Krawitz, *Schutz vorvertraglicher Investitionen – Zur Haftung beim Scheitern von Vertragsverhandlungen*. p. 114. Free translation. Original text: "*Anknüpfungspunkt und zentrale Voraussetzung für eine Haftung, welche eine den Parteiinteressen gerecht werdende Risikoverteilung ermöglicht, sollte die Zustimmung der nicht selbst investierenden Partei zur Vornahme der vorvertraglichen Investition durch die andere Partei sein. Liegt eine solche Zustimmung – und nicht bloße Kenntnis – vor, so lässt sich daraus ein eigenes Interesse der zustimmenden Partei an der Investition der Gegenseite folgern. Die Zustimmung zur Investition vor dem Hintergrund des von den Parteien erreichten Verhandlungsstands kann als Übernahme des Risikos verstanden werden.*"

suffices to explain that and how liability can be incurred for the breaking-off of negotiations or the refusal to contract and prevents coming up with a novel conception of liability for contract negotiations. "New is always better," if it ever holds true, certainly does not hold true within the law of obligations.

33. Two-pronged structure – To provide a remedy in the case of breaking-off of negotiations or refusal to contract, an obligation to negotiate or to contract is necessary. Only by relying on an obligation to contract, or at least to negotiate, can the possibility of failing contract negotiations in the hypothetical alternative scenario be ruled out. Hence, only then can liability rise (*supra* Chap. 2, nrs. 30 and 33). Hence, liability for contract negotiations has a two-pronged structure: a general conduct-based liability for all kinds of faults that can be committed in the context of contract negotiations and, in some instances, an obligation to contract or to negotiate. The question remains: what this obligation is based on and what it contains. This will be dealt with in Part 3.

34. Illustration: Dutch *driefasenleer* – The Dutch three-phases doctrine (*supra* Chap. 1, nr. 34) provides the perfect illustration of the co-existence of, on the one hand, a conduct-based liability and, on the other hand, an obligation to contract or negotiate. As Marcel Ruygvorn describes it in his dissertation, *Afgebroken onderhandelingen en het gebruik van voorbehouden*:[115]

> "The thinking was the following. In the first phase, both parties would be free to break off negotiations at any time without being liable for reimbursement of costs incurred by the other in the course of the negotiations. The situation is different after entering the second phase. In the second phase, it was thought, the parties would still be free to break off negotiations unilaterally, but this does lead to liability for damages on the part of the party breaking off negotiations in respect of the costs incurred by the other party in the context of the negotiations. In principle, the terminating party could not be ordered to continue negotiations or to compensate for lost profits or losses (other than consisting of the aforementioned costs) in the second phase. In the third stage, the parties would no longer be free to break off negotiations unilaterally. Should the latter happen anyway, then, in that third phase, the other party could either claim further negotiations or the terminating party could be ordered to compensate the positive contract interest."[116]

115 Ruygvoorn, *Afgebroken onderhandelingen en het gebruik van voorbehouden*. xvi+461 p.

116 Ruygvoorn, *Afgebroken onderhandelingen en het gebruik van voorbehouden*. pp. 44–45. Free translation. Original text: "*De gedachte was de volgende. In de eerste fase zou het beide partijen vrij staan om de onderhandelingen op ieder gewenst moment af te breken zonder tot vergoeding van de door de ander in het kader van de onderhandeling gemaakte kosten te kunnen worden gehouden. Anders is dit na het intreden van de tweede fase. In de tweede fase, zo was de gedachte, zou het partijen weliswaar nog vrij staan om de onderhandelingen eenzijdig af te breken, maar leidt dit wel tot schadeplichtigheid van de afbrekende partij ter zake van de door de wederpartij in het kader van de onderhandelingen gemaakte kosten. Tot dooronderhandelen of tot vergoeding van gederfde winst of geleden verlies (anders dan bestaande uit de hiervoor bedoelde kosten) kon*

In the second phase, parties are still free to break-off negotiations but must compensate for the caused harm (conduct-based liability system); in the third phase, parties no longer are free to break-off negotiations and can be forced to contract or to continue negotiations (obligation to contract).[117] As already mentioned (*supra* Chap. 2, nr. 34), this overly formalistic understanding in terms of three phases is criticized in scholarship for being artificial. A more nuanced approach, suggested by Ruygvoorn, appears preferable and reflects even more clearly the need for, on the one hand, a conduct-based liability and, on the other hand, an obligation to contract:

> "It [three-phases doctrine] may never have been intended that way by its creator, but wrongly creates the impression that each phase necessarily occurs in a negotiation process, and it then wrongly creates the impression that the phases in question necessarily and irreversibly follow each other in time. In any event, I believe that the three-phase doctrine is frequently interpreted as such in practice while none of these impressions is correct as far as I am concerned. In what follows, it will be argued that only two situations can arise in the pre-contractual phase, namely: the situation in which both parties are still free to break off negotiations, not liable for damages, and the situation in which (one of) the parties is no longer free to do so. In addition (and therefore not necessarily: successively), the situation may (but does not have to) arise in which an obligation to reimburse costs incurred in the context of the negotiations arises

de afbrekende partij in de tweede fase in beginsel niet worden veroordeeld. In de derde fase zou het partijen niet meer vrij staan om de onderhandelingen eenzijdig af te breken. Zou dat laatste toch gebeuren, dan zou, in die derde fase, door de wederpartij ofwel dooronderhandelen gevorderd kunnen worden, ofwel zou de afbrekende partij kunnen worden veroordeeld om het positief contractbelang te vergoeden."

117 Same analysis also from a comparative perspective in Zuloaga, *Reliance in the Breaking Off of Contractual Negotiations*. p. 181 and Deshayes, "Le dommage précontractuel." p. 202, nr. 34. See also how Olivier Deshayes suggests, inspired by Dutch law, that French liability for contract negotiations needs to be understood as a two-pronged structure: "French law accepts two distinct definitions of fault in the breach of talks: the first definition, which sees fault solely in the circumstances external to the breach and to which the following two consequences are attached: a second definition, according to which the fault lies in the very fact of breaking-off, and to which two diametrically opposed consequences are attached: the control of the motives is fully applicable and the compensable damages must include all the consequences of the breaking-off (in particular the loss of chance to conclude the negotiated contract)." Olivier Deshayes, "La rupture des pourparlers," *Petites affiches* 203 (2008). p. 9. Free translation. Original text: "*le droit français admet deux définitions distinctes de la faute dans la rupture des pourparlers: une première définition, qui voit la faute dans les seules circonstances extérieures à la rupture et à laquelle sont attachées les deux conséquences suivantes: le contrôle des motifs n'a pas lieu d'être (ou ne peut servir qu'à présumer en fait la faute) et les préjudices réparables sont limités (aux frais et à la perte de chance de conclure un contrat avec un tiers); une seconde définition, suivant laquelle la faute résiderait dans le fait même de rompre, et à laquelle sont attachées deux conséquences diamétralement opposées: le contrôle des motifs joue à plein et les préjudices réparables doivent comprendre toutes les conséquences de la rupture (notamment la perte de chance de conclure le contrat négocié).*"

> in the pre-contractual phase at any time during the period in which the negotiations can still be terminated unilaterally."[118]

Ruygvoorn argues in favour of a two-pronged approach: at all times during negotiations, parties can be held liable, and on top of that general liability, parties can, under some circumstances, be under an obligation to negotiate or contract.

2.2. *Obligation to negotiate or to contract*

35. Obligation to contract – It has become clear that the breaking-off of negotiations and the refusal to contract as such cannot plausibly give rise to liability in a conduct-based system. The most convincing way of explaining the instances in which the breaking-off or refusal nevertheless gave rise to liability is to recognize that an obligation to negotiate or to contract has been pre-supposed. In my opinion, we find this reasoning in many legal systems but often in a very concealed way, covered under phrases such as "reaching a point of no-return" or "deceiving legitimate expectations." This suggests that a need for such an obligation is perceived but that it is unsoundly addressed, as generally, such obligation are not recognized. My approach is, at this stage, independent of whether one is in favour or against such an obligation. I merely want to point out that if it is done – which is the case in many legal systems – it needs to be done openly and accepting the implications thereof. Ultimately, this should clarify the understanding of liability for contract negotiations and allow to delimit the liability – both in terms of instances of application and of available remedies – more convincingly and coherently.

36. Overcoming causal uncertainty – However, some tricks to overcome the normative causal uncertainty have been relied upon, and I identify four of them. (i) A first and very pragmatic one is to rely on techniques to overcome such causal uncertainty by presenting the fault in different terms. Instead of saying that the breaking-off of negotiations is the fault, one locates the fault in the circumstances of the breaking-off. That is very prominent under French law, where the "abrupt" or "reckless" breaking-off of negotiations is often invoked. This changed description of the invoked fault, logically, will also alter

118 Ruygvoorn, *Afgebroken onderhandelingen en het gebruik van voorbehouden*. p. 45. Free translation. Original version: "*Het is wellicht door de bedenker ervan nooit zo bedoeld, maar wekt ten onrechte de indruk dat iedere fase zich noodzakelijkerwijs in een onderhandelingstraject voordoet en het wekt vervolgens ten onrechte de indruk dat de betreffende fasen elkaar in alle gevallen noodzakelijkerwijs en onomkeerbaar in de tijd opvolgen. In elk geval meen ik dat de driefasenleer in de praktijk veelvuldig als zodanig wordt geïnterpreteerd terwijl geen van deze indrukken wat mij betreft juist is. In het hierna volgende zal worden betoogd dat zich in de precontractuele fase slechts twee situaties kunnen voordoen, te weten: de situatie waarin het beide partijen nog vrij staat om, niet-schadeplichtig, de onderhandelingen af te breken en de situatie waarin dit (één van) partijen niet langer vrij staat. Daarnaast (en dus niet noodzakelijkerwijs: opvolgend) kán (maar dit hoeft niet) zich de situatie voordoen dat er in de precontractuele fase op enig moment gedurende de periode dat de onderhandelingen nog eenzijdig, niet-schadeplichtig kunnen worden beëindigd, een verplichting ontstaat om kosten die in het kader van de onderhandelingen zijn gemaakt, te vergoeden.*"

the compensable harm and thus lead to different outcomes. (ii) A second trick consists in trying to argue based on evidentiary law standards. Indeed, by saying that a given degree of certainty or likeliness must only be given to prove the causal link, one could try to overcome the causal uncertainty. Yet this does not take away the normative character of this uncertainty and, therefore, appears unsound. (iii) Third, the doctrine of loss of a chance. By relying on the loss of a chance doctrine, causal uncertainty can be overcome by framing the suffered harm in terms of chances. (iv) Lastly, doctrines that allow to declare a lawful act to be unlawful under certain circumstances – mainly the prohibition of abuse of rights doctrine – generally also allow to circumvent questions of causality.

37. Explaining and evaluating the means to overcome causal uncertainty – The foregoing ways of overcoming causal uncertainty call for many more clarifications. I will do so in Part 3. For that purpose, I will first explain and evaluate the different techniques to overcome causal certainty to then deal extensively with the obligation to negotiate or to contract which is pre-supposed in many cases. My ambition there is rather descriptive: I want to show what reasoning scholarship and case law rely on and show how these ways of reasoning become much more sensible and understandable once we look at them as cases of non-performance of an obligation.

3. Conclusion

38. The present part, the first substantive part of this book, has traced the history of no-contract law. Starting respectively with Jhering's *culpa in contrahendo* and Faggella's *responsabilità nel periodo ante-contrattualè,* I have found two distinct structural conceptions of liability for contract negotiations. A historically older one that still exists today and is two-pronged: a general liability and a specific ground that explains that the breaking-off of negotiations or refusal to contract is unlawful. Seemingly over time, this two-pronged approach has been rivalled by a monolithic understanding of liability for contract negotiations. This understanding explains both the unlawfulness of the rupture of contract negotiations or refusal to contract *and* all kinds of faults occurring in the context of contract negotiations as the result of a conduct-based liability. If the latter, monolithic, and more recent structure allows to explain both liability ensuing from breaking-off or refusing and other faults, it seems preferable, as it is a simpler structure.

39. Hence, I set out to assess what type of liability law system is needed in order to provide remedies in the context of contract negotiations. Based on a conceptual, comparative, and historical approach, I established that a conduct-based liability is necessary to grant remedies for wrongs committed in the context of contract negotiations. In a nutshell, a conduct-based liability is one that requires no *a priori* prohibition and can be actioned merely based on the finding that some reprehensible conduct has been committed and has caused some harm. This was subsequently confirmed throughout all analysed legal systems, be it that some legal systems have been willing to go beyond what is structurally necessary.

An important insight following therefrom is that the way liability for contract negotiations must be structured depends on the respective national system of extra-contractual liability law. In that sense, the legal basis for liability for contract negotiations is relative to the extra-contractual liability law system and can only be conceived and understood in relation to it.

40. Next, I assessed whether such a conduct-based liability could also give rise to liability when the breaking-off of contract negotiations or the refusal to contract are the invoked fault. This should allow me to verify whether the monolithic structure of liability for contract negotiations suffices. It turned out that it does not. That is not so much the case because the exercise of the freedom from contract, by breaking-off negotiations or refusing to contract, can never be a fault but due to a causal uncertainty following from freedom from contract. Normatively, and provided a party still is considered free from contract, no causal link can be established between the breaking-off or the refusal to contract and any kind of harm because in the hypothetical alternative scenario, a party still could have broken-off or refused to contract and thereby cause the same or greater harm.

41. By consequence, a two-pronged structure of liability for contract negotiations appears necessary. The first part of it is a conduct-based liability; the second some ground that justifies that the breaking-off of negotiations is unlawful. In my opinion, this second part is an obligation to contract or to negotiate. I think that this is, in fact, already what is done when the breaking-off is considered unlawful; it sufficiently and coherently explains what occurs, and it is an explanation which can draw on an existing body of law without requiring unnecessary novel solutions.

42. In a nutshell and as a general and fundamental insight, this leads us to the important finding that within what is monolithically addressed as pre-contractual liability or *culpa in contrahendo* in most contemporary scholarship, two distinct questions and necessarily two distinct answers co-exist and are too often dealt with in confusion: the question of whether the breaking-off of negotiations or refusal to contract itself can be unlawful is answered with reference to a conduct-based liability. Inevitably, trying to provide one answer to two distinct questions cannot lead to a convincing result, accounting probably for the ongoing and fundamental uncertainties within that field. Hence, I will hereafter deal distinctly with both questions: Part 2 will address in much detail liability for contract negotiations, as it can be observed in the analysed legal systems. Part 3 will explain how the issue of normative causal uncertainty is tried to be overcome in the different legal systems to then zoom in on the obligation to negotiate or contract, which is all too often pre-supposed in reasoning on no-contract law. Part 4 will build forth on the acknowledgement of the existence of this obligation and address the question of what such an obligation to negotiate or to contract should be based on in a contemporary European context.

Part II

Liability for contract negotiations

3 Structure and functioning of liability for contract negotiations

1. Conduct-based liability law system

1. CONDUCT-BASED LIABILITY – In Part 1, I've explained that liability for contract negotiations must be a conduct-based liability in order to accommodate for liability for contract negotiations. This finding will be confirmed in the present part. In each analysed legal system, the liability law system relied on for liability for contract negotiations will be conduct-based. I will thus, from a comparative perspective, explain how such a conduct-based liability law system for contract negotiations *should* be structured and function, based on the insights won in Part 1. In explaining how it *should* work, I will also explain how the analysed national legal systems actually *do* work and how, why, and to what extent some deviate from that structure and functioning.
2. METHODOLOGICAL CONSEQUENCES – In line with the aim I just defined, the used methodology will focus on establishing how liability for contract negotiations should be structured and functioning. From the finding that that all analysed legal systems rely on the same type of liability law system for liability for contract negotiations, it follows that, structurally speaking, the functioning of each of system is identical. This means that in general, insights that exist in one system are freely transposable from one to another. As some insights are only addressed in some systems but not in others, or are particularly well addressed in some systems, I extract these insights from the system in question to generalize them for all systems. In that sense, the following explanations will be highly conceptual and may appear at times somewhat detached from the positive law in the different analysed legal systems. I find this conceptual approach to be justified, as this way of proceeding allows to transpose transposable insights existing in one or more of the analysed systems to other systems. The insights highlighted under one legal system, so to say, serve as an illustration of a common functioning of the liability law systems.

DOI: 10.4324/9781003599166-6

2. Conditions of application

2.1. Legal basis

3. Relevance of legal basis – The legal basis on which liability for contract negotiations will be based will define the regime of liability law applicable to contract negotiations. That is to say that the conditions of application, remedies, and corresponding other consequences – such as prescription periods or evidentiary rules – of the respective liability law system will apply. I have established in the preceding part how the choice for one or another legal basis should be made, namely, based on the means that the liability law system in question offers. In this regard, I find it important to stress that in this context, it is helpful to opt for an already existing liability law system. This will guarantee, on the one hand, the compatibility and accessibility of the system of liability for contract negotiations and, on the other hand, allow to fall back on an existing system of liability law. By consequence, ascribing liability for contract negotiations to some sort of *sui generis* liability regime does not appear in any way a helpful approach: it does neither offer a practicable solution nor a meaningful clarification. Much rather, it appears to be a solution of convenience. I have thus refrained from such an approach.

4. Extra-contractual liability – Historically, and from the present perspective most sensibly, most systems deal with liability for contract negotiations under their extra-contractual liability. After all, no contract has been concluded and generally will not be concluded. Hence, in the dichotomy contractual/extra-contractual liability, extra-contractual liability appears as the most sensible option. In systems with an extra-contractual liability law system which provides for a conduct-based liability law system, the legal basis for liability for contract negotiations undoubtedly can and should be extra-contractual. As self-evident as this may presently seem, discussions on the legal basis of liability for contract negotiations have been long lasting, persistent, and surprisingly impactful. Indeed, though structurally speaking, relying on the general extra-contractual personal liability law system suffices to provide the necessary means for a system of liability for contract negotiations, recent codifications generally devote an article to duties of care in contract negotiations. That is the case under French law (article 1112 Fr. Civ. C.), Belgian law (article 5.15 Be. Civ. C.), and Italian law (article 1337 It. Civ. C.) (more nuances *infra* Chap. 3, nr. 6 on Italian law). Likewise, the *Hoge Raad* had already ruled in 1957 in *Baris/Riezenkamp*[1] that parties to contract negotiations need to act in good faith and

1 HR 15 November 1957 (*Baris/Riezenkamp*), ECLI:NL:HR:1957:AG2023, back then relying on the terminology of "good faith" instead of reasonableness and fairness: "that, by entering into negotiations on the conclusion of a contract, the parties enter into a special legal relationship governed by good faith, which implies that they must allow their conduct to be determined partly by the legitimate interests of the other party." Free translation. Original text: "*dat immers partijen, door in onderhandeling te treden over het sluiten van een overeenkomst, tot elkaar komen te staan in een bijzondere,*

has reaffirmed so in 2005 in the currently leading case for broken-off contract negotiations, *CBB/JPO*.[2] These systems provide for a specific duty to act according to good faith in contract negotiations on top of their general duty of care applicable in all non-contractual relations.

5. Contractual liability – Under German law, the discussion about the legal basis for liability for contract negotiations was necessary, given that their extra-contractual liability did not provide for a useful system for liability for contract negotiations (*supra* Chap. 2, nr. 16). Hence, since 2001, § 311 (2) BGB states that during contract negotiations (that is the commencement of contract negotiations, the initiation of a contract, and similar business contacts), the same duties of care apply as in the contractual realm (§ 241 (2) BGB). The full provision reads:

"Obligations created by legal transaction and obligations similar to legal transactions

(1) In order to create an obligation by legal transaction and to alter the contents of an obligation, a contract between the parties is required, unless otherwise provided by statute.

(2) An obligation with duties under section 241 (2) also comes into existence by

1. the commencement of contract negotiations
2. the initiation of a contract where one party, with regard to a potential contractual relationship, gives the other party the possibility of affecting its rights, legal interests and other interests, or entrusts these to the other party, or
3. similar business contacts.

(3) An obligation with duties under section 241 (2) may also come into existence in relation to persons who are not themselves intended to be contractual parties. Such an obligation comes into existence in particular if the third party, by laying claim to being given a particularly high degree of

---

door de goede trouw beheerste, rechtsverhouding, medebrengende, dat zij hun gedrag mede moeten laten bepalen door de gerechtvaardigde belangen van de wederpartij."

2 HR 12 August 2005 (*CBB/JPO*) ECLI:NL:HR:2005:AT7337, nr. 3.6: "the criterion for assessing the obligation to pay damages in the event of the breakdown of negotiations is that each of the negotiating parties – who are obliged to allow each other's legitimate interests to determine their conduct – is free to break-off negotiations." Free translation. Original text: "*als maatstaf voor de beoordeling van de schadevergoedingsplicht bij afgebroken onderhandelingen heeft te gelden dat ieder van de onderhandelende partijen – die verplicht zijn hun gedrag mede door elkaars gerechtvaardigde belangen te laten bepalen – vrij is de onderhandelingen af te breken.*" Recently for instance Ger. Arnhem-Leeuwarden, 23 November 2021, 200.272.141, ECLI:NL:GHARL:2021:10837, r.o. 4.52: "However, the compensation to be paid by FarmCamps does not relate to an agreement concluded between the parties, but to an obligation to reimburse costs, which has arisen on the basis of reasonableness and fairness." Free translation. Original texst: "*De door FarmCamps te betalen vergoeding heeft echter geen betrekking op een tussen partijen gesloten overeenkomst, maar op een verbintenis tot vergoeding van kosten, die is ontstaan op grond van de redelijkheid en billijkheid.*"

> trust, substantially influences the pre-contract negotiations or the conclusion of the contract."[3]

In case of a violation of these duties of care, parties are liable according to § 280 BGB. So doing, § 311 (2) 1. BGB provides that the contractual duties of care (§ 241 (2) BGB) and liability (§ 280 BGB) do apply to contract negotiations. Hence, with the *Schulrechtsreform* of 2001, the German legislator has "created" a conduct-based liability for contract negotiations.

6. UNDECIDED – An interesting case and perfect illustration of the necessity of a conduct-based liability law to accommodate a system of liability for contract negotiations is the Italian one. In 2016, the *Corte di Cassazione*[4] ruled that liability for contract negotiations is a contractual liability based on the qualified social contact parties come to stand in (*'responsabilità contrattuale da contatto sociale qualificato'*).[5] In 2019, however, the same court decided that the liability was of extra-contractual nature.[6] At the end of 2023, the *Corte di Cassazione* invoked the 2016 judgment as the authoritative one and turned back to the qualification as contractual liability.[7] It is striking how present the discussion on

3 Official translation. Original text:
"Rechtsgeschäftliche und rechtsgeschäftsähnliche Schuldverhältnisse

(1) Zur Begründung eines Schuldverhältnisses durch Rechtsgeschäft sowie zur Änderung des Inhalts eines Schuldverhältnisses ist ein Vertrag zwischen den Beteiligten erforderlich, soweit nicht das Gesetz ein anderes vorschreibt.
(2) Ein Schuldverhältnis mit Pflichten nach § 241 Abs. 2 entsteht auch durch

1. die Aufnahme von Vertragsverhandlungen,
2. die Anbahnung eines Vertrags, bei welcher der eine Teil im Hinblick auf eine etaige rechtsgeschäftliche Beziehung dem anderen Teil die Möglichkeit zur Einwirkung auf seine Rechte, Rechtsgüter und Interessen gewährt oder ihm diese anvertraut, oder
3. ähnliche geschäftliche Kontakte.

(3) Ein Schuldverhältnis mit Pflichten nach § 241 Abs. 2 kann auch zu Personen entstehen, die nicht selbst Vertragspartei werden sollen. Ein solches Schuldverhältnis entsteht insbesondere, wenn der Dritte in besonderem Maße Vertrauen für sich in Anspruch nimmt und dadurch die Vertragsverhandlungen oder den Vertragsschluss erheblich beeinflusst."

4 Corte di cassazione, 12 June 2016, n. 14188.

5 For some context, see Trabucchi, *Instituzioni di diritto civile*. p. 235, nr. 70.

6 Corte di cassazione 3 November 2019, nr. 24738: "7.1. It is, in fact, a well-established principle in this matter that pre-contractual liability arising from the breach of the rule of conduct, laid down by Art. 1337 of the Civil Code to protect the proper course of the transaction, constitutes a form of non-contractual liability." Free translation. Original text: "7.1. *Costituisce, infatti, principio consolidato in materia che la responsabilità precontrattuale derivante dalla violazione della regola di condotta, posta dall'art. 1337 c.c. a tutela del corretto dipanarsi dell'iter formativo del negozio, costituisce una forma di responsabilità extracontrattuale.*"

7 "In line with the most recent jurisprudential direction of legitimacy (see Cass. no. 14188/2016, Cass. no. 25644/2017, Cass. Sez. Un. 8236/2020), the district judge specified that the pre-contractual liability of the P.A. 'does not have an extra-contractual nature, but rather a contractual nature from "qualified social contact", understood as a fact capable of producing obligations pursuant to Article 1173 of the Italian Civil Code'." Corte di cassazione, 15 December 2023, nr. 35170. Free translation. Original text: "*In linea con il più recente indirizzo giurisprudenziale di legittimità (cfr. Cass. n. 14188/2016, Cass. n. 25644/2017, Cass. Sez. Un. 8236/2020), il giudice distrettuale ha precisato che la responsabilità*

the nature of liability for contract negotiations still is in Italy.[8] Alberto Trabucchi writes:

> "The nature of pre-contractual liability has for years been the subject of a stimulating doctrinal and jurisprudential debate, the topicality of which has been confirmed by recent – and conflicting – pronouncements of the *Corte di Cassazione*."[9]

As explained *supra* (Chap. 2, nr. 17), this great difficulty under Italian law must be understood against the background of a changing understanding of the very basic functioning of their extra-contractual liability law system which evolved from a conduct-based one towards an unlawfulness-based one to again evolve back towards a conduct-based one. This in turn impacted the possibility to indemnify pure economic loss. Though it seems recognized today that pure economic loss *can* be indemnified under extra-contractual liability (*supra* Chap. 2, nr. 17), the point still is not free from authoritative critique.[10]

Somewhat regardless of that critique and the ongoing uncertainties, extra-contractual liability appears to be sufficient to provide for liability for contract negotiations. This shows when looking at how this liability arising from qualified social contacts is delimited. Indeed, hardly any discussions are led on when such qualified social contacts are at stake, though that would seem very necessary to clarify if the specific ground for liability would in fact be necessary. This is shown in the German experience, where the field of application of the duty of care is delimitated with much greater care (*infra* Chap. 3, nr. 7).

7. Legitimate expectations – As already stated (*supra* Chap. 3, nr. 3), explaining liability for contract negotiations by some sort of *sui generis* approach generally is less helpful than it may appear. Indeed, as such, *sui generis* legal basis generally does (i) not exist and (ii) does not provide an overall regime; it only apparently serves as an explanation yet leaving most relevant aspects pending. By consequence, it is not helpful to explain liability for contract negotiations based on some *sui generis* ground of liability. Yet one of the *sui generis* approaches stands out, and I cannot let it go undiscussed, namely, liability

---

precontrattuale della P.A. 'non ha natura extracontrattuale, bensì contrattualeda "contatto sociale qualificato", inteso come fatto idoneo a produrre obbligazioni ai sensi dell'art. 1173 c.c.'."

8 See for instance recently still Orlandi, "Responsabilità precontrattuale." pp. 996–1031. For an overview, see Paolo Troiano, "Art. 1337 c.c. Trattative e responsabilità precontrattuale," in *Codici civile commentato online*, ed. Carlo Cicala (Kluwer, 2023). nr. 1; Giorgio Cian, *Commentario breve al Codice Civile* (Padova: Cedam, 2022). p. 1426, nr. 2; Salvi, *La responsabilità civile*. p. 16.

9 Trabucchi, *Instituzioni di diritto civile*. p. 235, nr. 70. Free translation. Original version: "*La natura della responsabilità precontrattuale è da anni oggeto di uno stimolante dibattito dottrinable e giurisprudenziale, la cui attualità trova conferma in recenti – e contrastanti – pronunce della Corte di Cassazione.*"

10 For some context Trabucchi, *Instituzioni di diritto civile*. p. 1421, nr. 421bis and the references in fn. 40. Critics: Castronovo, *Responsabilità Civile*. p. 75; Mazzamuto, "Spunti in tema di danno ingiusto e di danno meramente patriomoniale." pp. 349–400.

based on legitimate expectations. Across the analysed legal systems, attention to legitimate expectations in the future conclusion of a contract – not to be confused with legitimate expectations of an already concluded contract[11] – is omnipresent. That Isabel Zuloaga's dissertation, *Reliance in the Breaking-Off of Contractual Negotiations*,[12] is exclusively devoted to the subject matter testifies to this end. Though I consider such an expectation-based liability not helpful and rather suggest sticking to an existing legal basis, it must be admitted that an expectation-based liability can be tempting. A first and obvious reason for being convinced of its usefulness is that it can appear as intuitively just that acting in some way contrary to some legitimate expectations should give rise to liability. Yet to do so, one could perfectly rely on a fault-based liability and consider the conduct contrary to some legitimate expectations to be a fault (more nuance *infra* Chap. 3, nr. 21–25). Hence, a specific expectation-based liability appears superfluous, where a conduct-based liability law system exists. This, then, explains why such expectation-based liability law systems are biggest and most relevant in systems which precisely lack a general conduct-based liability law system. In other words: German law.[13] Indeed, absent a general conduct-based liability, there was much greater need for an expectation-based liability, and it is the merit of Claus-Wilhelm Canaris to have pushed this *Vertrauenshaftung* under German law.[14] The result is a liability law system which functionally and structurally is identical to a fault-based liability.[15] Indeed, a liability based on considerations of legitimate expectations allows to fulfil the function of a conduct-based liability without stating it explicitly: basing liability on the expectations of the harmed party is the equivalent of basing liability on fault yet looking at the facts from the perspective of the *harmed* party instead of that of the *harming* party (the latter is the case in a conduct-based).

But even considering the foregoing, the German legislator opted for a contractual liability for liability for contract negotiations (*supra* Chap. 2, nrs. 18 and Chap. 3, nr. 5) – hence, confirming the preference for existing systems of liability law.

11 Zuloaga, *Reliance in the Breaking Off of Contractual Negotiations*. p. 152.

12 Zuloaga, *Reliance in the Breaking Off of Contractual Negotiations*. xxxviii+254 p.

13 OLG Brandenburg 27 November 2008–12 U 228/07, nr. 23; Fikentscher and Heinemann, *Schuldrecht Allgemeiner und Besonderer Teil*. p. 71, nr. 93; Staudinger/Feldmann (2018) BGB § 311 nr. 143.

14 Canaris, "Ansprüche wegen 'positiver Vertragsverletzung' und 'Schutzwirkung für Dritte' bei nichtigen Verträgen. Zugleich ein Beitrag zur Vereinheitlichung der Regeln über die Schutzpflichtverletzungen." pp. 475–582 and Claus-Wilhelm Canaris, *Die Vertrauenshaftung im deutschen Privatrecht (unveränderter nachdruck 1981)*, ed. Grigoleit Hans Christoph and Neuner Jörg, Claus-Wilhelm Canaris, Gesammelte Schriften (De Gruyter, 1981). 567 p. https://doi.org/10.1515/9783110274035.1005.

15 At least, so it seems to me. In the current context, however, I cannot delve into this very vast domain of research.

The same reasoning animates Marc Ruygvoorn to argue in favour of an extra-contractual legal basis instead of good faith under Dutch law.[16]

8. Relative legal basis – A notable – though in this form currently not sufficiently recognized – insight is that the system of liability for contract negotiations will always depend on the system for extra-contractual liability. Hence, the legal basis for liability for contract negotiations is relative to the existing system of extra-contractual liability. Indeed, to know whether any specific legal basis for liability for contract negotiations is needed, one must first know which extra-contractual liability system is present in the legal system in question. This insight, as simple as it is, is key for prospective legislators, such as the Luxembourgian one.

2.2. ***Duties of care***

9. General and specific duties of care – A distinction can be drawn between systems with a general duty of care and systems with a specific duty of care applicable during contract negotiations: a general duty of care applies to all situations; a specific duty of care only within a given field of application. Where a general duty of care applies, a specific duty of care would only seem necessary if it would provide for a different standard of care from the general one. The standard of care required describes what kind of diligence is required of parties to whom it applies (normal care, greatest care, *et cetera*). Where the specific duty of care provides for a diverging standard of care than the general one, the prior must prime. If there is no deviance in standard of care between the general and the specific duty of care, the latter appears superfluous – at least from a structural perspective. It may be considered to have a clarifying merit.

16 "Breaking off negotiations in violation of reasonableness and fairness is then contrary to what is socially decent according to unwritten law and therefore leads to unlawful conduct within the meaning of art. 6:162 DCC. In this context, I believe that the standard 'social decency' of art 6:162 DCC is unquestionably interchangeable with the reasonableness and fairness that also governs pre-contractual relations. If one can accept this starting point, in my view it is hard to see why one would then not accept torts as a basis; I strongly prefer, from the point of view of legal certainty, to opt for the traditional sources of obligations when establishing bases for liability, especially when they are perfectly in line with the relevant factors developed in case law in terms of assessing a case based on allegedly unauthorised aborted negotiations." Ruygvoorn, *Afgebroken onderhandelingen en het gebruik van voorbehouden*. p. 311. Free translation. Original text: "*Het in strijd met de redelijkheid en billijkheid afbreken van de onderhandelingen is dan in strijd met hetgeen volgens ongeschreven recht in het maatschappelijk verkeer betaamt en leidt derhalve tot onrechtmatig handelen in de zin van art. 6:162 BW. Ik meen dat in dit verband de norm 'maatschappelijke betamelijkheid' van art. 6:162 BW zonder meer uitwisselbaar is met de redelijkheid en billijkheid die ook de precontractuele verhoudingen beheerst. Wanneer men dit uitgangspunt kan aanvaarden, valt mijns inzien niet in te zien waarom men dan niet onrechtmatige daad als grondslag zou aanvaarden; ik geef er sterk de voorkeur aan om, bij het vaststellen van grondslagen voor aansprakelijkheid, vanuit het oogpunt van de rechtszekerheid te kiezen voor de traditionele bronnen van verbintenissen, zeker wanneer die prima aansluiten bij de in de rechtspraak ontwikkelde relevante factoren voor wat betreft het beoordelen van een casus die is geënt op vermeend ongelegitimeerd afgebroken onderhandelingen.*"

10. General duties of care – Belgian, French, Dutch, and Italian law know a general duty of care in their extra-contractual liability law, thus also applicable to contract negotiations. The standard of care required is that of a normally diligent person in the same circumstances (*infra* Chap. 3, nr. 13). Nevertheless, recent codifications generally devote an article to duties of care in contract negotiations. That is the case under French law (article 1112 Fr. Civ. C.), Belgian law (article 5.15 Be. Civ. C.), and Italian law (article 1337 It. Civ. C.). Likewise, the *Hoge Raad* had already ruled in 1957 in *Baris/Riezenkamp*[17] that parties to contract negotiations need to act in good faith and has reaffirmed so in 2005 in the currently leading case for broken-off contract negotiations, *CBB/JPO*.[18] These systems provide for a specific duty to act according to good faith in contract negotiations on top of their general duty of care applicable in all non-contractual relations.

This leads to a somewhat irritating result of a double standard of care. Though this is not extensively dealt with, the required standard of care under both the general and specific duties of care are identical. Ludo Cornelis, for instance, had already argued in 1990 under Belgian law that adding a requirement to negotiate in good faith would provide no added value in the Belgian system.[19] By consequence, the existence of such a specific duty of care merely seems to fulfil a clarificatory function. That such a clarificatory function was considered necessary seems to find its root in some inconsiderate transplantation of German law (*supra* Chap. 2, nrs. 16 and 18) and the influence of

17 HR 15 November 1957 (*Baris/Riezenkamp*), ECLI:NL:HR:1957:AG2023, back then relying on the terminology of "good faith" instead of reasonableness and fairness: "that, by entering into negotiations on the conclusion of a contract, the parties enter into a special legal relationship governed by good faith, which implies that they must allow their conduct to be determined partly by the legitimate interests of the other party." Free translation. Original text: "*dat immers partijen, door in onderhandeling te treden over het sluiten van een overeenkomst, tot elkaar komen te staan in een bijzondere, door de goede trouw beheerste, rechtsverhouding, medebrengende, dat zij hun gedrag mede moeten laten bepalen door de gerechtvaardigde belangen van de wederpartij.*"

18 HR 12 August 2005 (*CBB/JPO*) ECLI:NL:HR:2005:AT7337, nr. 3.6: "the criterion for assessing the obligation to pay damages in the event of the breakdown of negotiations is that each of the negotiating parties – who are obliged to allow each other's legitimate interests to determine their conduct – is free to break-off negotiations." Free translation. Original text: "*als maatstaf voor de beoordeling van de schadevergoedingsplicht bij afgebroken onderhandelingen heeft te gelden dat ieder van de onderhandelende partijen – die verplicht zijn hun gedrag mede door elkaars gerechtvaardigde belangen te laten bepalen – vrij is de onderhandelingen af te breken.*" Recently for instance Ger. Arnhem-Leeuwarden, 23 november 2021, 200.272.141, ECLI:NL:GHARL:2021:10837, nr. 4.52: "However, the compensation to be paid by FarmCamps does not relate to an agreement concluded between the parties, but to an obligation to reimburse costs, which has arisen on the basis of reasonableness and fairness." Free translation. Original texst: "*De door FarmCamps te betalen vergoeding heeft echter geen betrekking op een tussen partijen gesloten overeenkomst, maar op een verbintenis tot vergoeding van kosten, die is ontstaan op grond van de redelijkheid en billijkheid.*" Asser/Sieburgh 6-III 2022/202.

19 Ludo Cornelis, "La responsabilité précontractuelle, conséquence éventuelle du processus précontractuel," *TBBR* 6 (1990). pp. 401–403. Followed by Durant, "La rupture unilatérale des pourparlers ou l'exercice d'une liberté surveillée." p. 61, nr. 25. See references there, specifically fns. 83 and 84. See also from a comparative perspective Zuloaga, *Reliance in the Breaking Off of Contractual Negotiations*. p. 169.

model laws (*supra* Chap. 2, nr. 19) on recent codifications. That besides some clarificatory function, no practical relevance is borne by those specific duties of care[20] can be seen quite clearly in how the field of application of these specific duties of care is delineated. Indeed, generally, stating that parties ought to negotiate according to the requirements of good faith will be considered sufficient.[21] This approach must be contrasted to the German approach in which great care is taken to delimit the specific duties of care, as they are the only ones to apply.

11. Specific duties of care – Indeed, under German law, which solely relies on specific duties of care, the question under which circumstances these specific duties of care arise matters. The German legislator has, in line with their practical relevance, tried to clarify those circumstances as much as possible in § 311 (2) BGB, namely, "1. the commencement of contract negotiations; 2. the initiation of a contract where one party, with regard to a potential contractual relationship, gives the other party the possibility of affecting its rights, legal interests and other interests, or entrusts these to the other party, or; 3. similar

20 In the similar sense Zuloaga, *Reliance in the Breaking Off of Contractual Negotiations*. pp. 165–170. Yet she potentially sees some three functions for good faith: "Nevertheless, one should not jump to the conclusion that good faith is completely irrelevant regarding precontractual liability for breaking off negotiations in the selected jurisdictions [Germany, France, Chile]. First, i twill always have the potential function, although in a somewhat indirect manner, of furthering the development of the doctrine. Secondly, it serves the function of providing additional validity to solutions that, although more directly based or entirely based on other legal provisions or on other doctrinal bases, can also be linked to the general good faith principle. Thirdly, in jurisdictions like the selected ones it is a commonplace to state that the objective standard of good faith gives rise to and defines the precontractual duties whose breach entails precontractual liability. Currently, this would be its most relevant and active role." (p. 168, citations omitted). Even for the latter function, as should be clear, there appears no necessity given the existence of conduct-based liability regimes in all systems.

21 See f.i. "Pre-contractual liability arises, therefore, from the violation of specific obligations (good faith, protection, information) that precede the obligations of performance that find their source in the contract, if and when it is concluded, not in the generic duty of the *neminem leadere*.

. . .

In other words, it is a contact from which a relationship arises that is characterised by legally relevant obligations that pre-exist with respect to the moment of the injury and that, as such, differs from the model of Aquilian liability, characterised by the generic duty of *neminem* that disregards a pre-existing relationship between the damaging party and the injured party." Trabucchi, *Instituzioni di diritto civile*. p. 235, nr. 70. Free translation. Original text "*La responsabilità precontrattuale deriva, dunque, dalla violazione di specifichi obblighi (buona fede, protezione, informazione) che precedono gli obblighi di prestazione che trovano la loro fonte nel contratto, se ed allorquando verrà concluso, non nel generico dovere del neminem leadere.*

. . .

Si tratta, cioè, di un contatto dal quale scaturisce un rapporto connotato da obblighi giuridicamente rilevanti che preesistono rispetto al momento della lesione e che, come tale, si discosta dal modello della responsabilità aquiliana, caratterizzato dal generico dovere del neminem cadere che prescinde da un preesistente rapporto tra il danneggiante e il danneggiato." Also illustrated under Dutch law in Asser/Sieburgh 6-III 2022/201–203.

business contacts."[22] As these categories appear to overlap,[23] differentiating between the different circumstances is less useful, as they all bring about the same legal consequences. Indeed, the commencement of contract negotiations (1.) is a sub-category of the initiation of a contract (2.) which in turn is rendered superfluous by the even broader category of similar business contacts (3.). By consequence, scenarios 1. and 2. always can fall under 3., making the prior categories technically speaking superfluous.[24] The main takeaway is that the contacts giving rise to duties of care must be "business contacts" to the exclusion of mere social contacts.[25] For the remaining part, this threefold extension of the realm of application leads to an overall broad field of application of duties of care in the negotiation's process.[26] The underlying justification is the close contact parties come to stand in during contract negotiations – much focus is put on the relation of trust between parties[27] – and the related risk of negatively impacting the other negotiator's patrimony:

> "The increased possibility of impact is balanced by a countervailing duty of care."[28]

If the negotiations fall within the scope of § 311 (2) BGB, parties to the negotiations come to stand in an obligatory relationship ("*Schuldverhältnisse*"),[29] "i.e. the right of a creditor to demand performance or forbearance from the debtor (§ 241 (1) BGB) or the duty of a party to take due care (§ 241 (2)

22 On the meaning of each of these categories in more detail: Staudinger/Feldmann (2018) BGB § 311 nrs. 107–117.

23 Fikentscher and Heinemann, *Schuldrecht Allgemeiner und Besonderer Teil.* p. 68, nr. 87.

24 MüKoBGB/Emmerich, 9. Aufl. 2022, BGB § 311 nr. 44. This is all the more the case, as the duties of conduct are identical for each of the three conditions (Staudinger/Feldmann (2018) BGB § 311 nr. 106). See also Schwarze, *Das Recht der Leistungsstörung.* p. 482, nr. 5.

25 Schwarze, *Das Recht der Leistungsstörung.* p. 482, nr. 5 and p. 484, nr. 8; Medicus and Lorenz, *Schuldrecht I Allgemeiner Teil.* p. 242, nrs. 3 and 6. In this context interesting to read how Hans Stoll explained that such a conduct-based liability could only be justified if applicable to all business contacts ("*geschäftlicher Kontakt*"). Stoll, "Tatbestände und Funktionen der Haftung für culpa in contrahendo." pp. 452–454. A somewhat insensible statement that can be read in this context (f.i. Medicus and Lorenz, *Schuldrecht I Allgemeiner Teil.* p. 242, nr. 6) is that if a party has outright no intention to contracting, it would not fall under the realm of application of § 311 BGB. This would lead to the outcome that a party who enters into negotiations knowing that it will certainly not conclude a contract would not be under a duty of care. This seems undesirable, and it appears unlikely that a court would interpret the scope of application of § 311 BGB in that sense.

26 MüKoBGB/Emmerich, 9. Aufl. 2022, BGB § 311 nr. 47.

27 Canaris, "Ansprüche wegen 'positiver Vertragsverletzung' und 'Schutzwirkung für Dritte' bei nichtigen Verträgen. Zugleich ein Beitrag zur Vereinheitlichung der Regeln über die Schutzpflichtverletzungen." p. 476.

28 Schwarze, *Das Recht der Leistungsstörung.* p. 479. Free translation. Original text: "*Die erhöhte Möglichkeit der Einwirkung wird durch eine gegenläufige Pflicht zur Rücksichtnahme ausgeglichen.*" See also Staudinger/Schwarze (2019) BGB § 280 nr. C38. See also Medicus and Lorenz, *Schuldrecht I Allgemeiner Teil.* p. 242, nr. 3; Kreutz, *Hypothetische Verträge im Rahmen des Schadensausgleichs.* pp. 26–27.

29 Staudinger/Bork (2020) Vorbemerkung zu §§ 145 ff nr. 48.

BGB)."[30] Hence, the duties of care applicable to all obligatory relationships under § 241 (2) BGB apply to contract negotiations:

"§ 241 Duties arising from an obligation

(1) By virtue of an obligation, an obligee is entitled to claim performance from the obligor. The performance may also consist of forbearance.
(2) By its contents, an obligation may oblige each party to take account of the rights, legal interests and other interests of the other party."[31]

As a result of the interplay between § 311 (2) and § 241 (2), a party to negotiations must take into account the 'rights, legal interests and other interests of the other party.'[32]

The existence of such duties of care does not entail that such duties would also give rise to a right to performance;[33] it merely justifies duties of care.[34] That is why the obligatory relation attached to contract negotiations is often described as 'obligatory relation without obligations' ('*Schuldverhältnis ohne (primäre) Leistungspflichten*')[35] or 'contract-like obligatory relation' ('*vertragsähnliches Schuldverhältnis*').[36]

> "The content of these duties is not to conclude a contract. Entering into a business relation does not bring about an obligation to enter into a

30 Staudinger/Schwarze (2019) BGB § 280 nr. B1. Free translation. Original text: "*dh das Recht eines Gläubigers, vom Schuldner eine Leistung oder ein Unterlassen zu fordern (§ 241 Abs 1 BGB) oder die Pflicht einer Partei zur Rücksicht (§ 241 Abs 2 BGB).*"

31 Official translation. German version: "*§ 241 Pflichten aus dem Schuldverhältnis*

(1) Kraft des Schuldverhältnisses ist der Gläubiger berechtigt, von dem Schuldner eine Leistung zu fordern. Die Leistung kann auch in einem Unterlassen bestehen.
(2) Das Schuldverhältnis kann nach seinem Inhalt jeden Teil zur Rücksicht auf die Rechte, Rechtsgüter und Interessen des anderen Teils verpflichten."

32 On which for context see Medicus and Lorenz, *Schuldrecht I Allgemeiner Teil*. p. 237, nr. 5. Under German law, the specific duties of care applicable to contract negotiations are not based on good faith. Indeed, the requirement to perform contracts in good faith is dealt with under § 242 BGB ("An obligor has a duty to perform according to the requirements of good faith, taking customary practice into consideration." (*"Der Schuldner ist verpflichtet, die Leistung so zu bewirken, wie Treu und Glauben mit Rücksicht auf die Verkehrssitte es erfordern."*)). Anecdotally, this is worth mentioning, as many legal systems seem to have drawn inspiration from German law founding the duties of care applicable to contract negotiations on good faith pre-*Schuldrechtsmodernisierung* (*supra* Chap. 2, nr. 16). However, the difference must not be overestimated, as it is recognized that both provisions do in fact formulate the same requirement (Staudinger/Schwarze (2019) BGB § 280 nr. C45.).

33 Staudinger/Feldmann (2018) BGB § 311 nr. 100.

34 Medicus and Lorenz, *Schuldrecht I Allgemeiner Teil*. p. 242, nr. 3; Staudinger/Schwarze (2019) BGB § 280 nr. B9 and nr. C54; Kreutz, *Hypothetische Verträge im Rahmen des Schadensausgleichs*. pp. 27–28.

35 F.i. Canaris, "Ansprüche wegen 'positiver Vertragsverletzung' und 'Schutzwirkung für Dritte' bei nichtigen Verträgen. Zugleich ein Beitrag zur Vereinheitlichung der Regeln über die Schutzpflichtverletzungen." p. 475. Can also be found under Italian law, useed by Carlo Castronovo (Carlo Castronovo, "The Italian Law of Obligations from the Civil Code of 1942 to today profiles of an evolution," *RFJ*, no. 9 (2021). p. 90.)

36 Fikentscher and Heinemann, *Schuldrecht Allgemeiner und Besonderer Teil*. p. 77, nr. 104.

contract. Rather, the parties are only obliged to behave loyally towards their negotiating partner and to take their interests into consideration."[37]

12. Parties to the negotiations – Another consequence of the absence of a general duty of care under German law is that the parties to which such a duty of care applies are in principle limited to the prospective contracting parties.[38] As that scope, however, may be too limited at times, a third alinea has been added to § 311 BGB:

> "(3) An obligation with duties under section 241 (2) may also come into existence in relation to persons who are not themselves intended to be contractual parties. Such an obligation comes into existence in particular if the third party, by laying claim to being given a particularly high degree of trust, substantially influences the pre-contract negotiations or the conclusion of the contract."

While the limits and the functioning of this duty of care remains somewhat vague (at least to me),[39] the underlying idea here is that those third parties can stand in a similar relation to the prospective contracting parties than the prospective contracting parties themselves. As there exists a form of proximity which creates a bigger risk of interfering with each other's interests,[40] a duty of care will also lie on the third party which is "given a particularly high degree of trust, substantially influences the pre-contract negotiations or the conclusion of the contract." This liability of third parties is an independent duty of care and related liability that exists next to the liability of the parties themselves.[41] It must not be confused with questions of agency, as it is not a question of one of the parties to the negotiations being held liable for someone else's conduct.[42]

Next to the duties of care applying to third parties, § 311 (3) BGB also implies a protection for third parties.[43] Roland Schwarze gives the example of a

37 Staudinger/Bork (2020) Vorbemerkung zu §§ 145 ff nr. 49. Free translation. Original text: "*Inhalt dieser Pflichten ist es nicht, einen Vertrag zu schließen. Der Eintritt in einen geschäftlichen Kontakt begründet keinen Kontrahierungszwang. Die Parteien sind vielmehr nur verpflichtet, sich gegenüber dem Verhandlungspartner loyal zu verhalten und auf seine Interessen Rücksicht zu nehmen.*"

38 Staudinger/Feldmann (2018) BGB § 311 nr. 118.

39 For instance, very difficult to grasp in Medicus and Lorenz, *Schuldrecht I Allgemeiner Teil*. p. 250, nr. 28.

40 Schwarze, *Das Recht der Leistungsstörung*. pp. 536–537, nrs. 59–60.

41 Schwarze, *Das Recht der Leistungsstörung*. p. 541, nr. 64; Medicus and Lorenz, *Schuldrecht I Allgemeiner Teil*. p. 250, nr. 29.

42 Fikentscher and Heinemann, *Schuldrecht Allgemeiner und Besonderer Teil*. p. 75, nr. 100.

43 Fikentscher and Heinemann, *Schuldrecht Allgemeiner und Besonderer Teil*. p. 75, nr. 99; Medicus and Lorenz, *Schuldrecht I Allgemeiner Teil*. p. 249, nrs. 26–27.

child going to a supermarket with its mother and slipping on a banana peel.[44] Though this kid is not a prospective party to the contract (its mother does the grocery shopping), it still is protected. To the extent that the kid is bodily injured, it could anyways rely on § 823 BGB but is granted the more advantageous protection of § 311 BGB.[45]

All in all, the extent to which the delimitation of the specific duties of care applicable to contract negotiations are proportionate to their relevance. Only because no general duty of care can be applicable must it be clear-cut where and when this specific duty of care applies. Where parties can, in any case, fall back upon a general duty of care, the specific duty of care is not needed and hence is rather symbolic than structurally necessary. By consequence, the delimitation of the specific duty of care becomes some sort of futile exercise.

2.3. Fault

13. STANDARD OF CARE – The fault is the infringement of the duty of care in question.[46] Whether the duty of care has been infringed depends on the standard against which the conduct ought to be assessed – the standard of care that parties need to live up to. From a comparative perspective, different phrasings of the standard of care exist. Under German law, for instance, the 'the care required in business dealings' ('*im Verkehr erforderliche Sorgfalt*') (§ 276 (2) BGB) is relevant,[47] under Belgian law, the required conduct is that of the 'prudent and reasonable person placed in the same circumstances' ('*personne prudente et raisonnable placée dans les mêmes circonstances*'/'*voorzichtig en redelijk persoon in dezelfde omstandigheden geplaatst*') (art. 5.73, first al., 1° Be. Civ. C.), under Dutch law, the 'act or omission in violation of . . . what according to unwritten law has to be regarded as proper social conduct' ('*doen of nalaten in strijd . . . met hetgeen volgens ongeschreven recht in het*

44 Schwarze, *Das Recht der Leistungsstörung*. p. 542, nr. 65. Inspired by the case of a kid slipping on a lettuce leaf in a supermarket, the so-called lettuce-leaf-case ("*Gemüseblattfall*"). BGHZ 66, 51. On this, see Medicus and Lorenz, *Schuldrecht I Allgemeiner Teil*. p. 249, nr. 27. On these types of cases in more detail Nüsslein, *Die Integration der culpa in contrahendo in das BGB nach der Schuldrechtsreform*. p. 28 *et seq*.

45 On the advantages of § 311 BGB, see Lorenz, "Grundwissen – Zivilrecht: Culpa in Contrahendo (§ 311 II, III BGB)." p. 401.

46 There may be discussions on national levels on how to exactly conceptualize a fault. Especially under French law, such discussions have a profound historical root (f.i. Philippe Brun, *Responsabilité civile extracontractuelle* (Paris: LexisNexis, 2023). pp. 205–207, nrs. 300–303). From a comparative perspective, however, the here presented approach seems warranted. As Zuloaga explains: even under French law, the diverging conceptions seem to boil down to an identical conception, namely, the one here presented (Zuloaga, *Reliance in the Breaking Off of Contractual Negotiations*. pp. 62–63. Especially for the current purpose, which is not to present an in-depth comparative study on the notion of fault, the brief address here given must suffice. See on this point Wagner, "Comparative Tort Law." pp. 1013–1014.

47 Staudinger/Schwarze (2019) BGB § 280 nr. C45.

maatschapelijk verkeer betaamt') (article 6:162 NBW), *et cetera*. Though it cannot be excluded that occasionally, based on the different wording of the relevant provisions, a different outcome is reserved to identical facts under the different legal systems, such variations are structurally speaking neglectable.[48] After all, these differences in outcome are also influenced by national, regional, or local socio-economic circumstances, moralistic conceptions, and many more factors which are somewhat unpredictable and perhaps ultimately unknowable. Even depending on the judge who adjudicates, different conclusions can be drawn. That is an inherent flaw of open norms.[49] Trying to distinguish too pointedly the different formulations would be Sisyphean work of very limited explanatory value. What matters is that there is some form of normative qualification ("required," "prudent and reasonable," "proper," *et cetera*) of conduct in order to have a normative or objective background against which conduct can be assessed.[50] So doing, a certain degree of abstraction of the specific character of the tortfeasor is reached. Whether such an objective fault then can be subjectively – hence, taking the character of the tortfeasor into account[51] – imputed to the person committing the wrong is another question which will be answered under the following section on attributability (*infra* Chap. 3, nrs. 27–29).[52]

A stricter standard of care is required under German law in case of negotiations for a formal contract. Stephan Lorenz explains:

> "In the case of formal contracts, however, liability for the termination of contract negotiations can only be affirmed in the event of an intentional breach of a duty of care by the party terminating the negotiations

48 Pierre Widmer, "Comparative Report on Fault as a Basis of Liability and Criterion of Imputation (Attribution)," in *Unification of Tort Law: Fault*, ed. Pierre Widmer (The Hague: Kluwer, 2005). p. 353.

49 Discussed mostly under German law (Staudinger/Schwarze (2019) BGB § 280 nr. C45 and nrs. D8-D9) and Italian law (Trabucchi, *Instituzioni di diritto civile*. p. 233, nr. 70; Febbrajo, "Good Faith and Pre-Contractual Liability in Italy: Recent Developments in the Interpretation of Article 1337 of the Italian Civil Code." p. 156). Maybe the greater attention to the risk of open norms is most present in these systems, as open norms were misused by their respective fascist regimes. One to criticize the use of open norms by the Nazis already in 1937 was Franz L. Neumann, "Der Funktionswandel des Gesetzes im Recht der bürgerlichen Gesellschaft," *Zeitschrift für Sozialforschung*, no. 6 (1937). pp. 542–596. How the Nazi regime and its lawyers and scholars relied on open norms to achieve their purposes in an apparent legality and continuity is a fascinating and important topic, which I cannot delve into in this context. Obviously, this point is also thematized, be it perhaps less in depth, in other systems. See for instance under French law Jourdain, *Les principes de la responsabilité civile*. p. 49.

50 Schwarze, *Das Recht der Leistungsstörung*. p. 556, nr. 18; Medicus and Lorenz, *Schuldrecht I Allgemeiner Teil*. p. 152, nr. 12; Ruygvoorn, *Afgebroken onderhandelingen en het gebruik van voorbehouden*. p. 53.

51 Wagner, "Comparative Tort Law." pp. 1017–1018. See also f.i. under national law Jourdain, *Les principes de la responsabilité civile*. p. 50.

52 On the relation between the objective and subjective understanding of fault, see Widmer, "Comparative Report on Fault as a Basis of Liability and Criterion of Imputation (Attribution)." pp. 347–349.

(e.g. fraudulent misrepresentation of a willingness to enter into a contract), because otherwise the protection against too hasty contracting intended by the formal requirement would be ineffective."[53]

53 Lorenz, "Grundwissen – Zivilrecht: Culpa in contrahendo (§ 311 II, III BGB)." p. 399. Free translation. Original text: "*Bei formgebundenen Verträgen kann eine Haftung wegen Abbruchs von Vertragsverhandlungen allerdings nur bei einer vorsätzlichen Treuepflichtverletzung des Abbrechenden (wie zB beim arglistigen Vorspiegeln einer tatsächlich nicht vorhandenen Abschlussbereitschaft) bejaht werden, weil sonst der durch die Formvorschrift intendierte Übereilungsschutz wirkungslos wäre.*" See also MüKoBGB/Emmerich, 9. Aufl. 2022, BGB § 311 nr. 196.

See for an application BGH 12 December 2012, *NJW* 2013, 928 nrs. 7–8: "a) Within the framework of private autonomy, each party has the right to withdraw from the envisaged contract until the contract is concluded. Expenditures made in anticipation of the conclusion of the contract are therefore generally at the party's own risk (BGH, NJW-RR 1989, 627 = ZIP 1989, 514 [515]; Emmerich, in: MünchKomm-BGB, 6th edition, § 311 para. 175). Only if the conclusion of the contract can be assumed to be certain after the negotiations between the parties and expenses are incurred for the execution of the contract prior to its conclusion in the confidence established by this can these be reimbursed by the negotiating party from the point of view of a breach of pre-contractual duties to protect if he later refuses to conclude the contract without good reason (BGH, WM 1969, 595 [597] = BeckRS 1969, 31169133; *NJW* 1975, 1774; BGHZ 76, 343 [349] = *NJW* 1980, 1683). The BerGer. still correctly assumes this.

b) However, it overlooked the fact that stricter requirements apply to the breach of pre-contractual duties of care in the case of a property purchase agreement. In the case of such a contract, the refusal of a negotiating partner to co-operate in the notarisation does not trigger claims for damages if there is no valid reason for this, but only if there is a particularly serious, usually intentional breach of fiduciary duty, as is the case, for example, when a willingness to conclude a contract is not actually present. If the lack of valid reasons for refusing to notarise a property purchase agreement already justified the liability of the negotiating party, this would mean indirect coercion to conclude the agreement. Such coercion would be contrary to the purpose of the formal requirement of § 311 b BGB, according to which, due to the objective nature of the subject matter of the contract, a commitment without compliance with the form should be prevented (Senate, *NJW* 1975, 43 [44]; *WM* 1982, 1436 [1437] = BeckRS 1982, 31073552 and *NJW* 1996, 1884 [1885]). So far, this has been decided for cases in which the negotiating partner has refused to participate in the notarisation. The situation here, where the negotiating party is represented at the notarisation by a representative without power of attorney and refuses to approve the contract, is no different. This is because, according to the provision of § 311 b BGB, a commitment should only arise if the party obliged under the contract has made the declarations required to bind it in the proper form, i.e. has authorised the contract in the proper form if it is concluded by a representative without power of attorney. The appellate court could therefore not stop at the finding that there were no valid reasons for refusing to approve the contract. Rather, it had to determine whether the defendant had committed a particularly serious breach of its fiduciary duties over and above the refusal of authorisation without good reason. This was not the case." Free translation. Original text: "*a) Im Rahmen der Privatautonomie hat jede Partei bis zum Vertragsabschluss das Recht, von dem in Aussicht genommenen Vertrag Abstand zu nehmen. Aufwendungen, die in Erwartung des Vertragsabschlusses gemacht werden, erfolgen daher grundsätzlich auf eigene Gefahr (BGH, NJW-RR 1989, 627 = ZIP 1989, 514 [515]; Emmerich, in: MünchKomm-BGB, 6. Aufl., § 311 Rdnr. 175). Nur wenn der Vertragsschluss nach den Verhandlungen zwischen den Parteien als sicher anzunehmen ist und in dem hierdurch begründeten Vertrauen Aufwendungen zur Durchführung des Vertrags vor dessen Abschluss gemacht werden, können diese vom Verhandlungspartner unter dem Gesichtspunkt der Verletzung vorvertraglicher Schutzpflichten zu erstatten sein, wenn er den Vertragsabschluss später ohne triftigen Grund ablehnt (BGH, WM 1969, 595 [597] = BeckRS 1969, 31169133; NJW 1975, 1774; BGHZ 76, 343 [349] = NJW 1980, 1683). Davon geht das BerGer. noch zutreffend aus.*

14. Classification – Fault designates that some conduct is contrary to the required standard of care. Patrice Jourdain defines the French *faute* as "transgression of a pre-existing duty."[54] The new Belgian article 6.6 Be. Civ. C. also illustrates this:

> "§ 1 Fault consists in a failure to comply with a legal rule imposing or prohibiting a specific behaviour or with the general standard of care that must be observed in social relations."[55]

By consequence, no specific acts are prohibited. Only if the harmed party can prove that, in the given circumstances, the conduct was contrary to the required standard of care is that conduct considered to be faulty. Certainly, some recurring types of conduct (*infra* Chap. 3, nr. 14–25) will more easily lead to liability, as they have already been found to be a fault in the past. Yet the fact that

---

b) Es hat aber übersehen, dass an die Verletzung vorvertraglicher Schutzpflichten bei einem Grundstückskaufvertrag strengere Anforderungen zu stellen sind. Bei einem solchen Vertrag löst die Verweigerung der Mitwirkung an der Beurkundung durch einen Verhandlungspartner nicht schon dann Schadensersatzansprüche aus, wenn es an einem triftigen Grund dafür fehlt, sondern nur, wenn eine besonders schwerwiegende, in der Regel vorsätzliche Treuepflichtverletzung vorliegt, wie sie beispielsweise beim Vorspiegeln einer tatsächlich nicht vorhandenen Abschlussbereitschaft gegeben ist. Begründete schon das Fehlen triftiger Gründe für die Verweigerung der Beurkundung eines Grundstückskaufvertrags die Haftung des Verhandlungspartners, bedeutete das nämlich einen indirekten Zwang zum Abschluss des Vertrags. Ein solcher Zwang liefe dem Zweck der Formvorschrift des § 311 b BGB zuwider, nach der wegen der objektiven Eigenart des Vertragsgegenstands eine Bindung ohne Einhaltung der Form verhindert werden soll (Senat, NJW 1975, 43 [44]; WM 1982, 1436 [1437] = BeckRS 1982, 31073552 und NJW 1996, 1884 [1885]). Entschieden ist das bisher für Fälle, in denen der Verhandlungspartner die Mitwirkung an der Beurkundung verweigert hat. Für die hier vorliegende Konstellation, dass der Verhandlungspartner bei der Beurkundung durch einen vollmachtlosen Vertreter vertreten wird und die Genehmigung des Vertrags verweigert, gilt nichts anderes. Denn nach der Vorschrift des § 311 b BGB soll eine Bindung erst und nur eintreten, wenn der aus dem Vertrag Verpflichtete die zu seiner Bindung erforderlichen Erklärungen formgerecht abgegeben, bei einem Abschluss durch vollmachtlosen Vertreter also den Vertrag formgerecht genehmigt hat. Das BerGer. durfte deshalb nicht bei der Feststellung stehen bleiben, triftige Gründe für die Verweigerung der Genehmigung des Vertrags lägen nicht vor. Es musste vielmehr feststellen, ob die Bekl. über die Verweigerung der Genehmigung ohne triftigen Grund hinaus ihre Treuepflichten besonders schwerwiegend verletzt hat. Daran fehlt es."

54 Jourdain, *Les principes de la responsabilité civile*. p. 46. Free translation. Original text: "*transgression d'un devoir préexistant.*"

55 The second paragraph defines the general standard of care: "§ 2 The general standard of prudence requires conduct which would have been adopted by a prudent and reasonable person in the same circumstances." Free translation. Original text: "*§ 1 La faute consiste dans un manquement à une règle légale imposant ou interdisant un comportement déterminé ou à la norme générale de prudence qui doit être respectée dans les rapports sociaux. § 2. La norme générale de prudence impose d'adopter un comportement conforme à celui qu'aurait adopté une personne prudente et raisonnable placée dans les mêmes circonstances.*"/"*§ 1 De fout bestaat uit de schending van een wettelijke regel die een bepaald gedrag oplegt of verbiedt of van de algemene zorgvuldigheidsnorm die geldt in het maatschappelijk verkeer. § 2. De algemene zorgvuldigheidsnorm vereist een gedrag dat overeenkomt met dat van een voorzichtig en redelijk persoon in dezelfde omstandigheden geplaatst.*"

they have been wrongful in the past does not *ipso facto* entail that they will be considered wrongful in another setting. In other words, a finding of fault will and should *always* depend on the concrete circumstances in a given case and their appreciation by the judge. By consequence, drawing an exhaustive list of prohibited conduct is as impossible as it is insensible.[56] Instead, I offer a brief overview and illustration of recurring faults in the context of contract negotiations. This overview draws inspiration from different legal systems and is presented somewhat interchangeably, as for the present purpose, the different kinds of reproached faults can be freely transposed from one legal system to another.

15. Breaking-off negotiations – It seems worthwhile to begin by stating what cannot be counted as a fault, namely, the breaking-off of negotiations or the refusal to contract itself, unless an obligation to contract or to negotiate exists (*infra* Chap. 3, nr. 35–37). I have already explained (*supra* Chap. 2, nr. 27–31) why that is the case, namely, due to the impossibility to establish a causal link between the breaking-off of negotiations/refusing to contract and suffered harm and will do so *infra* (Chap. 3, nr. 33–40) in more detail. In light thereof, the drafting chosen by the Belgian legislator in article 5.17, second al., first sentence Be. Civ. C. must be considered as unfortunate:

> "In the case of wrongfully broken off negotiations, this liability entails reinstating the injured party into the situation in which it would have found itself had negotiations not taken place."[57]

56 Even on a purely national level, such an endeavour appears doomed to fail as Marcel Ruygvoorn had to come to understand: "interpretation given in the lower courts to the wording used by the Supreme Court in the JPO/CBB judgment to the effect that, when assuming a legally relevant establishment trust, a 'strict standard requiring restraint must be applied'. How strict is strict and how restrained should the court be compared to the situation as it existed before the JPO/CBB judgment? An analysis of the (mainly lower) case law handed down after the JPO/CBB judgment shows that some courts are certainly more restrained and strict than others, making it, if possible, even more difficult than before for legal practice to assess on the legal merits a case involving aborted negotiations." Ruygvoorn, *Afgebroken onderhandelingen en het gebruik van voorbehouden*. pp. 302–303. Free translation. Original text: "*uitleg die in de lagere rechtspraak wordt gegeven aan de door de Hoge Raad in het arrest JPO/CBB gebruikte bewoordingen die erop neerkomen dat bij het aannemen van rechtens relevant totstandkomingsvertrouwen een 'strenge en tot terughoudendheid nopende maatstaf moet worden aangelegd'. Hoe streng is streng en hoe terughoudend moet de rechter zijn ten opzichte van de situatie zoals die bestond vóór het arrest JPO/CBB? Een analyse van de (voornamelijk lagere) jurisprudentie die is gewezen ná het arrest JPO/CBB leert dat de ene rechter bepaald terughoudender en strenger is dan de andere rechter en dat maakt dat het voor de rechtspraktijk zo mogelijk nog lastiger is dan voorheen om een casus waarin sprake is van afgebroken onderhandelingen, op de juridische merites te beoordelen.*"

57 "*En cas de rupture fautive des négociations, cette responsabilité implique que la personne lésée soit remise dans la situation dans laquelle elle se serait trouvée s'il n'y avait pas eu de négociations.*"/"*Bij foutief afbreken van onderhandelingen houdt deze aansprakelijkheid in dat de benadeelde teruggeplaatst wordt in de situatie waarin hij zich zou hebben bevon- den indien er niet zou zijn onderhandeld.*"

The provision seems to suggest that the breaking-off of contract negotiations itself can be a fault and lead to liability. Such a reading would be incompatible with the extra-contractual legal basis of the liability and its requirement of a causal link. Another reading, therefore, seems more coherent – namely, that the required "wrongfulness" indicates precisely that some element other than the breaking-off of negotiations must be present, such as a fault occurring in the context of broken-off negotiations, for example, an abrupt breaking-off. This other element must then clearly be indicated. This approach would be consistent with the conception of liability for contract negotiations preceding the reform, a proclaimed aim of the drafters.[58] Indeed, not only Belgian scholarship[59] but also case law[60] appeared aware – at least to some extent – of the impossibility of holding a person liable for the breaking-off of negotiations:

> "Since the basic principle is freedom of contract, the breaking-off of talks is not in itself wrongful, but only the circumstances of the breaking off and the behaviour of the person who broke off the talks may give rise to liability."[61]

Or:

> "It is not the breaking-off of negotiations per se that gives rise to liability, but rather the circumstances in which the breakdown intervenes, especially when the other party's reliance has been deceived."[62]

Under French law (*supra* Chap. 2, nr. 31), it is equally common not to find the fault in the breaking-off itself but in the circumstances. A case handed by the Court

58 Explanation to the law of 24 February 2021 containing Book 5 "Obligations" of the Civil Code, DOC 55 1806/001, p. 26.

59 For an overview, see Annick De Boeck, "De precontractuele fase als ontmoetingsplaats voor buitencontractuele en contractuele aansprakelijkheid: de schade ten gevolge van tekortkomingen tijdens de precontractuele fase nader geanalyseerd," in *Raakvlakken tussen de contractuele en buitencontractuele aansprakelijkheid*, ed. Sophie Stijns and Patrick Wéry (Brugge: Die Keure, 2008). pp. 152–153, nr. 30. I provide a more in-depth discussion in Annick De Boeck and Tom Hick, "Totstandkoming van contracten: het komend recht in de rechtspraak," in *Verbintenissenrecht Themis 2021–2022 nr. 120*, ed. Annick De Boeck and Sophie Stijns (Antwerpen: Intersentia, 2022). pp. 9–10, nr. 13.

60 F.i. Com. Tongeren 1 April 2020, *DAOR* 2021/3, (51); Liège, 31 October 2013, *DAOR* 2014 (271); Liège, 15 March 2012, *R.G.A.R.* 2012 (14909); Civil Court Brussels, 16 January 2012, *RW* 2014–15 (589). Contra: Antwerpen 4 maart 2020, *DAOR* 2020/4 (97).

61 Liège 15 March 2012, *R.G.A.R.* 2012 (14909) nr. 3. Free translation. Original text: "*Le principe de base étant la liberté contractuelle, la rupture de pourparlers n'est pas en soi fautive, seules les circonstances de la rupture et le comportement de son auteur pouvant donner lieu à responsabilité.*"

62 Com. Tongeren 1 April 2020, *DAOR* 2021/3 (51). p. 55. Free translation. Original text: "*Niet het verbreken van de onderhandelingen op zich doet de verantwoordelijkheid ontstaan, maar wel de omstandigheden waarin de verbreking tussenkomt, met name wanneer het vertrouwen van de tegenpartij werd verschalk.*" See for more examples the references in Durant, "La rupture unilatérale des pourparlers ou l'exercice d'une liberté surveillée." pp. 63–64, nr. 28.

of Appeal of Paris[63] illustrates this. In the case at hand, a municipality had broken-off negotiations for a rental agreement with a private party. The Court of Appeal rules:

> "It follows from the foregoing that the disputed talks were well advanced, so much so that all that was missing was the final signature of the lease agreement, the terms of which had been negotiated.
>
> At this stage, the local authority was aware of the steps taken to register a company specially set up for the purpose of this lease agreement, the steps taken to sublet part of the premises in order to sell products of Portuguese origin, and the purchase of equipment already stored on the premises; it would have been fair to approach Mr [M] in the event of any difficulties, rather than taking a unilateral decision. Thus, the very late nature of the termination on the one hand, and its abrupt nature on the other, constitute faults attributable to the municipality of Saint-Cyr sous Dourdan."[64]

Instead of finding that the breaking-off itself was culpable, the fault lies in the belatedness and abruptness of the breaking-off.

16. Abrupt breaking-off of negotiations – As just illustrated by the decision of the Court of Appeal of Paris, a typical instance of such fault in the circumstances of the breaking-off is the abruptness with which parties break-off negotiations. A decision of the Court of Appeal of Liège also illustrates this type of reasoning.[65] At issue is the sale of a residential home for the elderly. An agreement on the price can be reached, but it remained uncertain which party to the prospective sale would take care of the repair of some fire-retarding doors. Then the potential seller breaks off the negotiations. The Court of Appeal finds it to be wrongful to break-off negotiations given the advanced stage thereof and the unilateral and sudden end set to the negotiations. It was only because of the advanced stage of the negotiations and the abrupt character of the breaking-off that the court found a pre-contractual fault.

17. Adding unreasonable conditions at an advanced stage of negotiations – Negotiations do not only fail because the party adverse to the conclusion

63 Paris, 15 June 2022, n° 19/20114.

64 Paris, 15 June 2022, n° 19/20114. Free translation. Original text: "*Il résulte de ce qui précède que les pourparlers litigieux étaient très avancés, à tel point qu'il ne manquait que la signature définitive du contrat de bail dont les termes avaient été négociés.*

À ce stade, la commune avait connaissance des démarches entreprises pour l'immatriculation d'une société spécialement constituée pour ce contrat de bail, des démarches entreprises pour la sous-location partielle permettant la vente de produits d'origine portugaise, de l'achat de matériel déjà entreposé dans les lieux; une attitude loyale aurait consisté à se rapprocher de Monsieur [M], en cas de difficulté, plutôt que de prendre une décision unilatérale. Ainsi, le caractère très tardif de la rupture d'une part, et son caractère brusque d'autre part, constituent des fautes imputables à la commune de Saint-Cyr sous Dourdan."

65 Liège 27 March 2014, 2012/rg/1519, www.juportal.be.

of the contract breaks them off but also if the latter party sets unreasonable or unrealistic conditions. In that case, it would seem that the party did not act in any way suspiciously, as it did not break-off negotiations: the counter party did as it faces unreasonable or unrealistic conditions. To prevent that parties rely on this technique to circumvent possible liability claims, courts recognize that adding unreasonable or unrealistic conditions can also be seen as unrealistic conduct. A Belgian case delivered by the Court of Appeal of Antwerp in 2015 illustrates this point.[66] Essentially, the decision concerns a case of ongoing but relatively advanced negotiations for the sale of a pharmacy. At this stage, the seller of the pharmacy adds the condition of being employed in the pharmacy he is about to sell. The Court considers that adding such a condition and making it a decisive point of the negotiations is wrongful.[67] In a comparable decision from 1996, the BGH decided that it was wrongful to raise the negotiated price by one quarter (from 750.000 DM to 1 million DM), where parties merely had to finalize the formalities necessary to conclude a formal contract.[68]

18. Not taking the counterparties' interests sufficiently into account – A fairly comparable situation is that of a party to the negotiations which continuously adds new and unrealistic conditions to the negotiations. The case is illustrated in a decision of the Dutch Court of Appeal of Arnhem-Leeuwarden from 2021.[69] In that case, a company orders the development and production of luxury tents. Yet due to the fixation of an unrealistic price for the requested development and the changing requirements that the tent must fulfil, the tent will never be produced and negotiations will be broken-off, leading to the bankruptcy of the company developing the tent. The Court of Appeal of Arnhem-Leeuwarden considers that the ordering party no longer was free to break-off negotiations without the payment of damages.[70]

19. Parallel negotiations – The two preceding cases concern situations in which the way negotiations are led appear problematic. This may lead to the impression that parties have little leeway in how they negotiate. That is not true. An illustration of the leeway that parties to the negotiations maintain is that it is commonly accepted that leading parallel negotiations is both a recurrent and acceptable conduct.[71] Only where exclusive negotiations have been agreed upon or the impression was given that negotiations would be exclusive can parallel negotiations possibly be considered wrongful. Indeed, in the case where someone conducted parallel negotiations, it was not the fact to conduct these parallel negotiations that was wrongful but to let one of the parties conduct considerable costs and not telling about the parallel negotiations.[72]

66 Antwerp, 16 April 2015, *RABG* 2016/6 (436).
67 Antwerp, 16 April 2015, *RABG* 2016/6 (436). pp. 442–443, nr. 2.8.
68 BGH *NJW* 1996, 1884.
69 Ger. Arnhem-Leeuwarden, 23 November 2021, 200.272.141, ECLI:NL:GHARL:2021:10837.
70 Ger. Arnhem-Leeuwarden, 23 November 2021, 200.272.141, ECLI:NL:GHARL:2021:10837, nr. 4.43.
71 Hesselink, *De redelijkheid en billijkheid in het Europese privaatrecht*. p. 71.
72 Antwerpen 16 July 2018, *TBO* 2019, 1 (49).

20. STARTING NEGOTIATIONS WITHOUT ANY INTENTION OF CONCLUDING A CONTRACT – Negotiations not only fail because they have been broken-off or led in a manner which could not lead to a successful outcome but also because from their initiation on, it was impossible that the contract under negotiations would be concluded.[73] Articles II.-3:301 (4) DCFR, 2.1.15 UPICC, and 2:301 PECL even specifically mention this as a wrongful element (*supra* Chap. 2, nr. 19). Indeed, if there is no chance that a contract will be concluded, either because the party engaging or accepting to enter into negotiations is certain not to want to contract or is in some situation of impossibility of contracting, it is insensible to start negotiations or to accept them being started. Cases in which there was *little* chance that a contract could be concluded, but where there was still a minor chance that it would be, on the contrary, still appear sensible. Such a conduct appears acceptable, as this precisely is the purpose of contract negotiations: assessing the possibility and usefulness of concluding a contract.

A Belgian case of the Court of Appeal of Liège of 2013 illustrates this point.[74] In the case at hand, a couple intends to set up a hairdresser and contacts the agent of a brand producing hairdressing products to be the franchisee of the brand. The agent in question provides the couple with leaflets about the franchising options, recommends them to set up their hairdresser at another location than initially planned, and visits the new location with the couple. As, and the Court puts this explicitly, due to a clause of exclusivity in another franchising contract, it was "radically" ("*radicalement*") impossible to have a franchised hairdresser at the new location, the agent acted wrongfully:

> "the respondent's fault did not therefore consist in an abusive breach of negotiations that occurred on 8 June 2011, but rather in the fact that it had entered into talks that could in no way lead to the realisation of the appellants' project"[75]

Generally, in cases where negotiations have been started or accepted with the certainty of not contracting, the party that started or accepted the negotiations pursued some other purpose (such as gaining information it would otherwise not get or harming the counterparty by maintaining it in useless negotiations).[76] Though this suggests an intent to harm on behalf of the wrongful party, it seems to generally be accepted as negligent to start-up negotiations absent any

73 Hesselink, *De redelijkheid en billijkheid in het Europese privaatrecht*. p. 70; Gazzoni, *Manuale di diritto privao*. p. 881, nr. 1.

74 Liège, 31 October 2013, 2012/RG/1051, www.juportal.be.

75 Liège, 31 October 2013, 2012/RG/1051, www.juportal.be. Free translation. Original text: "*la faute de l'intimée ne consiste donc pas en une rupture abusive des négociations qui serait survenue le 8 juin 2011, mais bien dans le fait d'avoir engagé des pourparlers qui ne pouvaient en aucun cas aboutir à la concrétisation du projet des appelants*"

76 Hesselink, *De redelijkheid en billijkheid in het Europese privaatrecht*. p. 70. Under Italian law, see Gazzoni, *Manuale di diritto privao*. p. 881, nr. 1.

possibility to contract, hence not requiring the often difficult burden of proving intentional wrongdoing.[77]

21. Continuing negotiations without any intention of concluding a contract – Article 2.1.15 (3) UPICC (*supra* Chap. 2, nr. 19) provides that "It is bad faith, in particular, for a party to enter into or continue negotiations when intending not to reach an agreement with the other party." Indeed, related to the situation in which negotiations that cannot lead to the conclusion of a contract are initiated is that of negotiations that are maintained even though it has become clear to one of the parties that the contract under negotiations will not be concluded.[78] Here, again, it should be certain that no contract will possibly be concluded. The *Manoukian* decision of the French Court of Cassation[79] deals with a situation of that kind. *Manoukian* negotiates for the sale of parts of a company. After parties had agreed upon a preliminary agreement and while the sellers continued "to lead him [Manoukian] to believe that it was only the absence of the company's chartered accountant that was delaying the signing of the agreements,"[80] they in fact promised to sell their parts to another interested buyer. The Court of Cassation upheld the judgment of the Paris Court of Appeal, which had ruled that such conduct was wrongful.

The *Manoukian* decision also illustrates that many cases of failed contract negotiations may also be approached as cases of a breach of duties of information. Indeed, here (but see also for instance the decision of the Court of Appeal of Liège *infra* Chap. 3, nr. 24), the sellers should have informed *Manoukian* earlier about the impossibility of contracting. Denis Mazeaud, for instance, describes the fault in the *Manoukian* decision very much like a shortcoming in sharing relevant information:

> "In any event, nothing in the shareholders' conduct during the negotiations could have led Manoukian to believe that they wished to abandon the talks, especially not the fact that they had finally concluded a contract with a third party that had the same purpose as the negotiated contract. Given the circumstances and conditions in which the negotiations were broken off, it was therefore wrongful."[81]

77 On this Babusiaux, "Liability for Negotiations." p. 368, nr. 17.

78 Hesselink, *De redelijkheid en billijkheid in het Europese privaatrecht*. pp. 70–71.

79 Cass.fr., *Chambre commerciale*, 26 November 2003, 00–10.243 00–10.949.

80 Cass.fr., *Chambre commerciale*, 26 November 2003, 00–10.243 00–10.949. Free translation. Original text: "*tout en continuant à lui laisser croire que seule l'absence de l'expert-comptable de la société retardait la signature du protocole*"

81 Mazeaud, "Rupture fautive des pourparlers." p. 257. Free translation. Original text: "*Rien, en tout cas dans le comportement des actionnaires lors de la négociation, n'avait pu laisser penser à la société Manoukian qu'ils souhaitaient abandonner les pourparlers et surtout pas qu'ils avaient finalement conclu un contrat, ayant le même objet que le contrat négocié, avec un tiers. La rupture de la négociation était donc, en raison des circonstances et des conditions dans lesquelles elle s'était produite, fautive.*"

22. Legitimate expectations – An important element in the *Manoukian* decision was "that the parties had reached a draft agreement ironing out most of the difficulties and that Alain Manoukian was entitled to believe that the X . . . consorts were still prepared to sell it their shares".[82] This focus on legitimate expectations is widespread throughout all analysed legal systems.[83]

This is unsurprising, given how intuitively convincing and flexible this criterion is. A case of the BGH from 2001[84] illustrates this tellingly: the owner of some plot of land enters into negotiations for the construction of a building on that land. Yet the owner of the land sells his land in the course of the negotiations to another party but maintains negotiations ongoing for a year and eventually even reaches an agreement (which alone does not bring about the contract, as it concerned a formal contract). The BGH decides:

> "Only if the conclusion of the contract can be assumed to be certain after the negotiations between the parties and prior to the conclusion of the contract expenses for the execution are incurred in the confidence established by this, can these be reimbursed by the negotiating party under the aspect of fault in the contract negotiations if he later refuses to conclude the contract without good reason (BGHZ 76, 343, 349; BGH of 29 March 1996, V ZR 332/94, BGHR, BGB before § 1 – culpa in contrahendo, loss of confidence 9 with further references. N.). This applies all the more if the willingness to conclude a contract was only feigned from the outset (cf. Emmerich, in: MüKo, BGB 3rd ed. before § 275 para. 161 with further references) or if in the course of the negotiations the firm determination of the negotiating party to conclude the contract evaporates, but he continues to pretend his unconditional willingness to the other party and thus deceives it (cf. also BGH, of 10 January 1996, VIII ZR 327/94, WM 1996, 738, 740 with further references)."[85]

82 Cass.fr., *Chambre commerciale*, 26 November 2003, 00–10.243 00–10.949. Free translation. Original text: "*que les parties étaient parvenues à un projet d'accord aplanissant la plupart des difficultés et que la société Alain Manoukian était en droit de penser que les consorts X . . . étaient toujours disposés à lui céder leurs actions.*"

83 Bertrand De Coninck comes to this conclusion after having conducted a comparison of Belgian, French, German, and English and American Common Law: Bertrand De Coninck, "Le droit commun de la rupture des négotiations précontractuelles," in *Le processus de formation du contrat – Contributions comparatives et interdisciplinaires à l'harmonisation du droit européen*, ed. Marcel Fontaine (Bruxelles: Bruylant, 2002). p. 132, nr. 222. Alternatively illustrated under Belgian law in Durant, "La rupture unilatérale des pourparlers ou l'exercice d'une liberté surveillée." pp. 62–63, nr. 27.

84 BGH 15 January 2001 – II ZR 127/99, *DStR* 2001, 803. See for more cases Zuloaga, *Reliance in the Breaking Off of Contractual Negotiations*. p. 154, fns. 66–69.

85 BGH 15 January 2001 – II ZR 127/99, *DStR* 2001, 803, nr. 1. Free translation. Original text: "*Nur wenn der Vertragsschluss nach den Verhandlungen zwischen den Parteien als sicher anzunehmen ist und in dem hierdurch begründeten Vertrauen Aufwendungen zur Durchführung des Vertrages vor dessen Abschluss gemacht werden, können diese vom Verhandlungspartner unter dem Gesichtspunkt des Verschuldens bei den Vertragsverhandlungen zu erstatten sein, wenn er den Abschluss*

This is a typical instance of continuing negotiations without an intention of contracting (*supra* Chap. 3, nr. 20) but is approached as a case of legitimate expectations under German law,[86] testifying to the flexibility of this criterion.

However broad and flexible this approach may be, within it, two different variants of the argument can be singled out: the *deception* of legitimate expectations is the wrongful element, or the *creation* of legitimate expectations is the wrongful element. Distinguishing between both matters, as only the latter way of reasoning is sound.

23. Deceiving legitimate expectations – The issue with the reasoning in terms of *deceiving* legitimate expectations is that it relies on the premise that the creation of legitimate expectations was binding upon the party creating the expectations. Only if the creation of legitimate expectation is binding can the *deception* of these legitimate expectations be considered wrongful. Indeed, the deception of a legitimate expectation can only be considered to be faulty if one was bound by those legitimate expectations. In other words, "the party creating trust must act in accordance with this trust".[87]

In the context of broken-off negotiations, deciding that the breaking-off of negotiations or refusal to contract in violation of a legitimate expectation that the contract would be concluded, in fact, boils down to saying that the party that created these legitimate expectations was under an obligation to contract. In other words, the reasoning pre-supposes that a party did no longer enjoy its freedom from contract.[88]

My concern with this line of reasoning is that it introduces an obligation to negotiate or to contract without being explicit about it.[89] The case law of the BGH concerning the breaking-off of contract negotiations ("*Abbruch von Vertragsverhandlungen*") illustrates this patently. Though the formulation has slightly changed over time,[90] it seems (be it that the translation is not quite

---

des Vertrages später ohne triftigen Grund ablehnt (BGHZ 76, 343, 349; BGH v. 29. 3. 1996, V ZR 332/94, BGHR, BGB vor § 1 – Verschulden bei Vertragsschluss, Vertrauensschaden 9 m. w. N.). Dies gilt erst recht, wenn die Abschlussbereitschaft von vorneherein nur vorgetäuscht war (vgl. Emmerich, in: MüKo, BGB 3. Aufl. vor § 275 Rn. 161 m. w. N.) oder wenn sich im Laufe der Verhandlungen die feste Entschlossenheit des Verhandlungspartners, den Vertrag abzuschließen, verflüchtigt, er jedoch der Gegenseite weiterhin seine unbedingte Bereitschaft vorspiegelt und sie damit täuscht (vgl. auch BGH, v. 10. 1. 1996, VIII ZR 327/94, WM 1996, 738, 740 m. w. N.)."

86 The same analysis under French law in Deshayes, "Le dommage précontractuel." pp. 200–201, nr. 31. From a comparative perspective Zuloaga, *Reliance in the Breaking Off of Contractual Negotiations*. p. 155.

87 Staudinger/Schwarze (2019) BGB § 280 nr. C56. Free translation. Original text: "*Die Vertrauen hervorrufende Partei muss sich diesem Vertrauen entsprechend verhalten*"

88 Deshayes, "Le dommage précontractuel." p. 201, nr. 32.

89 Deshayes, "Le dommage précontractuel." p. 201, nr. 32.

90 1975: "The basis of liability for culpa in contrahendo is disappointed trust (BGHZ 60, 221, 226 = NJW 1973, 752 with further references). From this point of view, the unjustified termination of the contract negotiations also obliges the party breaking off the negotiations to pay compensation for the loss of confidence if the party breaking off the negotiations had previously aroused or nurtured the confidence through his behaviour that the contract would certainly be concluded (BGH, *NJW* 1957,

satisfying) that the BGH conceives wrongful breaking-off of contract negotiations in three steps: (i) a legitimate expectation must have been created, (ii) the party must have been subsequently deceived, and (iii) there must be no good reason for the break-off:

> "Within the framework of contractual freedom, each negotiating party has the fundamental right to refrain from the envisaged conclusion of the contract until the contract is concluded; for this reason, expenses incurred in anticipation of the conclusion of the contract are at the negotiating party's own risk. Only if the conclusion of the contract can be assumed to be certain after the negotiations between the parties and expenses are incurred to implement the contract prior to its conclusion in the confidence that this creates, can the negotiating party be required to reimburse these expenses under the aspect of fault in the contract negotiations if it later refuses to conclude the contract without good reason."[91]

---

746 = LM § 276[Fa]BGB no. 1; BGH, LM § 276 [Fa] BGB No. 11, 23 = *NJW* 1967, 2199; LM § 276 [Fa] BGB No. 28, 34 = *NJW* 1970, 1840; *NJW* 1975, 43, 44, in each case with further references.)." BGH, 12 June 1975 –, X ZR 25/73 (Hamm), *NJW* 1975, p. 1774. Free translation. Original text: "Grundlage der Haftung für Verschulden bei Vertragsverhandlungen ist enttäuschtes Vertrauen (BGHZ 60, 221, 226 = *NJW* 1973, 752 m.w. Nachw.). Unter diesem Gesichtspunkt verpflichtet auch der grundlose Abbruch der Vertragsverhandlungen zum Ersatz des Vertrauensschadens, wenn derjenige, der die Verhandlungen abbricht, zuvor durch sein Verhalten das Vertrauen geweckt oder genährt hatte, der Vertrag werde mit Sicherheit zustande kommen (BGH, *NJW* 1957, 746 = LM § 276[Fa]BGB Nr. 1; BGH, *LM* § 276 [Fa] BGB Nr. 11, 23 = *NJW* 1967, 2199; LM § 276 [Fa] BGB Nr. 28, 34 = *NJW* 1970, 1840; *NJW* 1975, 43, 44, jeweils m.w. Nachw.)."

1980: "Even during the negotiations on the conclusion of a contract, the negotiating party owes the other party reasonable consideration of its legitimate interests with regard to the contractual relationship of trust established by the negotiations. This also includes not breaking off the contract negotiations without good reason (for irrelevant considerations) if he has previously aroused the confidence of the other party that the contract will certainly be concluded. A culpable breach of this duty can lead to the obligation to compensate the negotiating partner for the loss of trust caused by this." BGH, 7 February 1980 – III ZR 23/78, *NJW* 1980 (1683). Free translation. Original text: "*Schon während der Verhandlungen über den Abschluß eines Vertrages schuldet der Verhandlungspartner dem anderen Teil im Hinblick auf das durch die Verhandlungen begründete vertragsähnliche Vertrauensverhältnis die zumutbare Rücksichtnahme auf dessen berechtigte Belange. Dazu gehört auch, daß er die Vertragsverhandlungen nicht grundlos (ohne triftigen Grund, aus sachfremden Erwägungen) abbricht, wenn er zuvor das Vertrauen des anderen Teils, der Vertrag werde mit Sicherheit Zustandekommen, erweckt hat. Ein schuldhafter Verstoß gegen diese Pflicht kann zu der Verpflichtung führen, dem Verhandlungspartner den dadurch verursachten Vertrauensschaden zu ersetzen.*" See also on the occurence of this line of arguing under French law Zuloaga, *Reliance in the Breaking Off of Contractual Negotiations*. pp. 71–74.

91 BGH 15 January 2001 – II ZR 127/99, *DStR* 2001, 803. Free translation. Original text: "*Im Rahmen der Vertragsfreiheit hat jeder Verhandlungspartner bis zum Vertragsabschluss grundsätzlich das Recht, von dem in Aussicht genommenen Vertragsschluss Abstand zu nehmen; aus diesem Grunde erfolgen Aufwendungen, die in Erwartung des Vertragsschlusses gemacht werden, auf eigene Gefahr. Nur wenn der Vertragsschluss nach den Verhandlungen zwischen den Parteien als sicher anzunehmen ist und in dem hierdurch begründeten Vertrauen Aufwendungen zur Durchführung des Vertrages vor dessen Abschluss gemacht werden, können diese vom Verhandlungspartner unter dem*

The argumentation seems to rely on a pre-supposed obligation to contract or to negotiate, but the point is not quite articulate. It is much clearer when the invoked fault lies in breaking-off negotiations, though a point of no-return has been reached. Olivier Deshayes rightly points out:

> "It has been decided in the past that when talks are well advanced, the partners may only withdraw from them if they can demonstrate the existence of an obstacle relating to the negotiations themselves. If this is not the case, and in particular if the termination is justified by a reason that is "internal" to one of the negotiators, a breach of contract is established. In other words, it seems that at a certain point in the negotiations, termination is no longer really permitted. The freedom to negotiate gives way to an obligation to continue negotiations and conclude the contract. Liability then logically changes its face: it allows compensation for the loss of the gain expected from the conclusion of the contract, and thus becomes a means of indirectly concluding the contract."[92]

24. Creating legitimate expectations – Contrary to reproaching the *deception* of legitimate expectations, the *creation* of legitimate expectations can perfectly be relied upon as a reproached fault:

> "Since and insofar as these expectations are not contractually secured, protection cannot take place through fulfilment of the expectation. Rather, the party concerned can only be placed in such a position as if it had not had the expectation; thus, it is only to be compensated for the loss of confidence. Accordingly, the misconduct of the liable opponent does not lie in the non-fulfilment of the expectation, but in the fact that the expectation was caused, nurtured, not prevented or that the expectation that arose was not removed from the world in good time."[93]

Gesichtspunkt des Verschuldens bei den Vertragsverhandlungen zu erstatten sein, wenn er den Abschluss des Vertrages später ohne triftigen Grund ablehnt." Same phrasing BGH 12 December 2012, NJW 2013, 928 nr. 7 or in LG Heidelberg 5 February 2010, NJW-RR 2010 (1469) 1469.

92 Deshayes, "Le dommage précontractuel." p. 201, nr. 32. Citations omitted. Free translation. Original version "*Il a été en effet décidé par le passé que lorsque les pourparlers sont très avancés, les partenaires ne peuvent s'en dégager qu'à condition de rapporter l'existence d'un obstacle tenant aux négociations elles-mêmes. Si tel n'est pas le cas, et notamment si la rupture est justifiée par un motif 'interne' à l'un des négociateurs, une faute de rupture est constatée. C'est dire, semble-t-il, qu'à un certain point des négociations, la rupture n'est plus réellement permise. La liberté de négocier cède la place à l'obligation de poursuivre les négociations et de conclure le contrat. La responsabilité change alors logiquement de visage: elle permet la réparation de la perte du gain attendu de la conclusion du contrat, et devient donc un moyen de conclure indirectement le contrat.*"

93 Schwarze, *Das Recht der Leistungsstörung*. p. 486, nr. 1. Free translation. Original text: "*Da und soweit diese Erwartungen nicht vertraglich abgesichert sind, kann der Schutz nicht durch Erfüllung der Erwartung stattfinden. Vielmehr kann die betreffende Partei nur so gestellt wer- den, als hätte sie die Erwartung nicht gehabt; zu ersetzen ist ihr also nur der Vertrauensschaden. Das Fehlverhalten*

When such an expectation has been created is a highly factual question which cannot be answered conclusively in the abstract. Duration, intensity, and the closeness to a final agreement are common elements mentioned in this context.[94] Those elements, but not limited thereto, will inform the question whether expectations were legitimate or reasonable for a mere subjective hope to conclude the contract is not sufficient; it must be corroborated by objective and verifiable elements.[95] In that sense, expectations must be legitimate or reasonable (used interchangeably): "a 'plain' expectation is not enough, only a 'legitimate' or 'reasonable' expectation will be protected."[96] Here, as for the conduct of the "reasonable" man, adding the requirement of *legitimate* or *reasonable* expectations allows to objectify the standard against which the conduct of the counterparty (the party whose conduct is assessed through the lens of the harmed party) is assessed. A decision of the Court of Appeal of Liège from 2008 offers an illustration. In the case at hand, one party wants to have built an apartment building and approaches the other party to realize the construction jointly. A notary is contacted to set up a contract for the collaboration. After somewhat less than a year of seemingly constructive negotiations, the party intending the construction of the apartment building voices some doubts about the feasibility of the project. One month later, the doubting party contracts with another party. The Court decides as follows:

> "It follows from all of these considerations that the trial judge was right to find that the respondent's legitimate expectations had been misled by the appellant's conduct, which, in the course of continuing negotiations, *wrongfully created* the appearance that the collaboration project had been completed.
>
> The appellant's fault lies in the fact that, after the draft agreement had been finalised by notary Angenot on 20 October 2005, it continued to work unreservedly with the respondent, waiting until 18 January 2006

des haftpflichtigen Gegners liegt dementsprechend nicht in der Nichterfüllung der Erwartung, sondern darin, die Erwartung verursacht, genährt, nicht verhindert oder die entstandene Erwartung nicht recht- zeitig aus der Welt geschafft zu haben." See also: "The 'circumstance requiring compensation' within the meaning of § 249 I in this group of cases is not the non-conclusion of the contract, but the arousal of disappointed trust in its conclusion." Lorenz, "Grundwissen – Zivilrecht: Culpa in contrahendo (§ 311 II, III BGB)." p. 399. Free translation. Original text: "*Der 'zum Ersatz verpflichtende Umstand' iSv § 249 I ist in dieser Fallgruppe nämlich nicht der Nichtabschluss des Vertrags, sondern die Erweckung von enttäuschtem Vertrauen auf dessen Zustandekommen.*" In the same sense also MüKoBGB/Emmerich, 9. Aufl. 2022, BGB § 311 nr. 193. Identical in Medicus and Lorenz, *Schuldrecht I Allgemeiner Teil*. p. 245, nr. 16. Krawitz, *Schutz vorvertraglicher Investitionen – Zur Haftung beim Scheitern von Vertragsverhandlungen*. p. 101. See also Hesselink, *De redelijkheid en billijkheid in het Europese privaatrecht*. p. 72.

94 A more in-depth discussion in Zuloaga, *Reliance in the Breaking Off of Contractual Negotiations*. p. 157.

95 Babusiaux, "Liability for Negotiations." p. 369, nr. 19.

96 Zuloaga, *Reliance in the Breaking Off of Contractual Negotiations*. pp. 156.

> and the numerous services it had provided to express its fears on two points of which it had been fully aware from the start of the negotiations, with regard to the question of the deadline for completion, and from the time of the intervention of architect Co."[97]

In a decision of the OLG Brandenburg, the OLG accepted that in a case where a party was told that if it would submit an offer that this offer would be accepted, a legitimate expectation of future contract conclusion had been created.[98] In the decision of the BGH from 2001 (*supra* Chap. 3, nr. 22), the defendant was found:

> "have 'most maliciously' continued to nurture confidence in the conclusion of the basic agreement for over a year after the sale had already taken place elsewhere and had deliberately and untruthfully led it to believe that the parties would still come together. This had manifested itself in numerous discussions between the parties, in telephone calls and fax letters, and finally in the solemn handshake agreement between the defendant and lawyer S on 25 March 1996, combined with the defendant's request to now arrange the notarisation appointment with the notary. Not only had the defendant concealed the sale to O-GmbH, which had long since taken place, but when she asked him about the the erection of the construction boards and then the excavation that she had noticed, he explained to be in ignorance and that the O-GmbH had acted upon unauthorised behaviour on the part of his father; he then continued to stall her and announced that he would obtain an injunction against O-GmbH."[99]

97 Liège, 26 June 2008, *J.L.M.B.* 2011 (442). p. 445. Free translation. Original text: "*Il résulte de l'ensemble de ces considérations que c'est à bon droit que le premier juge a estimé que la légitime confiance de l'intimée avait été trompée par le comportement de l'appelante qui, dans le cadre de la poursuite des négociations, a fautivement créé l'apparence de l'aboutissement du projet de collaboration.*

La faute de l'appelante consiste à avoir, après la finalisation du projet de convention par le notaire Angenot le 20 octobre 2005, poursuivi sans réserves sa collaboration avec l'intimée, attentant le 18 janvier 2006 et les nombreuses prestations accomplies pour faire part de craintes portant sur deux points dont elle avait parfaitement connaissance, dès le début des négociations en ce qui concerne la question du délai d'exécution, et dès l'intervention de l'architecte Co. qu'elle n'a pas critiquée, en ce qui concerne le risque de refus des plans modifiés. L'intimée a exposé une série de frais dont elle entend être indemnisée. En matière de négociations, les partenaires sont amenés à exposer, à leurs risques et périls, des frais qui entrent dans le cadre normal de la négociation."

98 OLG Brandenburg 27 November 2008–12 U 228/07, *BeckRS* 2009, 1224 nr. 2.

99 BGH 15 January 2001 –II ZR 127/99, *DStR* 2001, 803, nr. 2 b). Free translation. Original text: "*Die frühere Klin. hat in der Berufungsbegründung vorgetragen, der Bekl. habe 'höchst arglistig' das Vertrauen auf das Zustandekommen des Grundlagenvertrages über ein Jahr lang nach bereits erfolgtem anderweitigem Verkauf weitergenährt und sie bewusst wahrheitswidrig in dem Glauben gelassen, die Parteien würden noch zusammenkommen. Manifestiert habe sich dies durch zahlreiche Besprechungen zwischen den Parteien, in Telefonaten und Telefax-Schreiben, letztlich dann in der feierlichen Handschlagsvereinbarung zwischen dem Bekl. und Rechtsanwalt S am*

25. Combination of different wrongful elements – Thus far, I have presented different types of faults that are commonly invoked by parties, scholars, or judges to justify that some form of fault has been committed in the context of failing contract negotiations. However, presenting them in such an isolated manner next to each other provides a somewhat idealized state of affairs. It is, indeed, not uncommon that some sort of amalgam of different reproached faults is relied upon to explain that parties wrongfully broke-off negotiations or refused to contract. The Court of Appeal of Liège, for instance, combined the length of ongoing negotiations, the abruptness of the breaking-off, the absence of good reason for the breaking-off, and the continuation of negotiations, though they could no longer be successful:

> "Since the basic principle is freedom of contract, the breaking-off of talks is not in itself wrongful, but only the circumstances of the breaking off and the behaviour of the person who broke off the talks may give rise to liability. Liability may arise, for example, when a party abruptly and without valid reason breaks off negotiations that have been pursued to their final conclusion, by disloyally or recklessly giving the impression that the contract has been concluded, or by allowing a party to unnecessarily incur significant costs."[100]

It is understandable that to convince that the breaking-off of negotiations was in some way wrongful, one would multiply the criteria which indicate a wrongful way of breaking-off negotiations. However, this way of proceeding bears one problem: identifying the reproached fault becomes impossible, as too many different faults are invoked. This, in turn, will make the determination of the hypothetical alternative scenario absent the fault impossible. Hence, to allow for a clear application of liability for contract negotiations, it is important to single out one specific fault which is determinative.[101]

---

25. 3. 1996, verbunden mit der Aufforderung des Bekl., nun den Beurkundungstermin beim Notar zu vereinbaren. Nicht nur, dass der Bekl. den schon längst erfolgten Verkauf an die O- GmbH verschwiegen habe, habe er auch dann, als sie das Aufstellen der Bautafeln und sodann den Bauaushub bemerkt und ihn darauf angesprochen habe, dies mit Unkenntnis und eigenmächtigem Verhalten seines Vaters erklärt; er habe sie dann weiter hingehalten und angekündet, er werde eine einstweilige Verfügung gegen die O-GmbH erwirken."

100 Liège 15 March 2012, *R.G.A.R.* 2012 (14909) nr. 3. Free translation. Original text: "*Le principe de base étant la liberté contractuelle, la rupture de pourparlers n'est pas en soi fautive, seules les circonstances de la rupture et le comportement de son auteur pouvant donner lieu à responsabilité. Celle-ci peut être engagée notamment lorsqu'une partie rompt brutalement et sans motif valable des négociations poursuivies jusqu'à leur terme final en laissant croire par déloyauté ou par imprudence que le contrat serait conclu ou en laissant une partie exposer inutilement des frais importants.*"

101 In the same sense Ruygvoorn, *Afgebroken onderhandelingen en het gebruik van voorbehouden*. p. 302: "First of all, I note that in many cases the courts of fact, when they have to rule on a case of aborted negotiations, simply refer to the facts in their considerations as to whether or not reliance

From the perspective of a sound application of liability law rules, and importantly for being able to delimit liability claims sensibly and coherently, it is important to opt for one single reproached fault. It must, however, be admitted that it often appears that it rather is a concurrence of circumstances which makes the failure of negotiations wrongful. That may be so, but legally speaking, it matters which element exactly is the invoked fault, as it will affect the causally linked harm. In this regard, it is important to bear in mind that parties are virtually free to present any kind of conduct as wrongful element, as long as it convinces the judge. They can use this to frame the invoked fault in such a way as to maximise the compensation they can claim. Judges and legislators, however, may only accept such reasonings which do not pre-suppose an obligation to contract or to negotiate. Parties, of course, are always free to give them a try, as they may yield are better outcome. For indeed, parties ought to be mindful that depending on how they frame the reproached fault, the hypothetical alternative scenario will differ and, with it, the causal harm. Strategically aiming at the best outcome for a harmed party thus begins with a mindful presentation of the invoked fault.

26. Importance of attention to detail – In line with the preceding, the reader may have felt that the different types of invoked faults are overly detailed and unsuitable for practice. That is a justified criticism. Jacques Ghestin considers such approaches to be "artificial" ("*artificiel*").[102] Yet this is how liability law works, and this is why it is so important to minutely define the specific invoked fault.[103] If one does not, and only broadly argues that negotiations have been wrongfully broken-off, it will torpedo the proper application of the other conditions of application: harm and a causal link. Indeed, since no causal link can be established between that fault and any kind of harm, indemnifiable harm cannot be meaningfully delimited. Perhaps this explains why relying on the distinction between positive and negative interest is so common (*infra* Chap. 4, nr. 3):

---

on the formation of trust is legally relevant, but in many cases fail to indicate in concrete terms which facts and circumstances exactly contributed to the reliance on the formation being honoured or not being honoured in the case in question. Legal practice would therefore benefit if case law argued this point more extensively by indicating more concretely which facts and circumstances exactly contributed to the establishment trust (or the absence of legally relevant establishment trust) and to what extent this should be given importance." Free translation. Original text: "*In eerste instantie stel ik vast dat de feitenrechters, wanneer zij hebben te oordelen over een geval van afgebroken onderhandelingen, in veel gevallen in hun overwegingen om totstandkomingsvertrouwen al dan niet rechtens relevant te achten, eenvoudigweg verwijzen naar de feiten, maar in veel gevallen nalaten concreet aan te geven welke feiten en omstandigheden er nu precies toe hebben bijgedragen dat in het betreffende geval totstandkomingsvertrouwen wel of niet gehonoreerd wordt. De rechtspraktijk zou er dan ook mee gediend zijn indien de rechtspraak dit punt uitvoeriger zou beargumenteren door meer concreet aan te geven welke feiten en omstandigheden nu precies tot het totstandkomingsvertrouwen (of het ontbreken van rechtens relevant totstandkomingsvertrouwen) hebben bijgedragen en in welke mate daaraan belang moet worden gehecht.*"

102 Ghestin, "La responsabilité délictuelle pour rupture abusive des pourparlers." p. 18, nr. 16.

103 As argued by Nils Jansen: pragmatic difficulties do not justify to improperly apply the law. Nils Jansen, "The Idea of a Lost Chance," *Oxford Journal of Legal Studies* 1, no. 2 (1999). p. 293.

because harm cannot be meaningfully delimited if a fault is invoked that leads to no causal harm. Instead, one then relies on the very approximate distinction between positive and negative interest, a distinction which, when assessed closely, is hardly useful (*infra* Chap. 4, nr. 3–5). Hence, however revolting the nit-picking distinction of invoked faults may appear, a sound and coherent application of liability law requires to do so.

2.4. *Attributability*

27. Individualization of objective standard – The question that is dealt with as a matter of fault is, very roughly put, whether objectively, the conduct is reprehensible in comparison to the expected standard of care. However, such an objective – that is, more or less independently of the personal traits, weaknesses, *et cetera* of the tortfeasor – is insufficient. Some degree of individualization of the tortfeasor is considered desirable.[104] This concerns the question whether an objective wrongdoing can be *attributed* to the tortfeasor. How and to what extent such individualization is considered implemented is as tricky as it is interesting a question. That is because, depending on the type of liability law system, the criterion (for instance, culpability under German law) relied upon to achieve this degree of individualization differs,[105] which complicates the comparative study of the matter. Yet this is an interesting but *unspecific* question in the current context.[106] I will thus not delve into it. Only some brief remarks on agency (*infra* Chap. 3, nr. 28) and the presumption of attributability (*infra* Chap. 3, nr. 29) will be formulated.

28. Agency – A second question dealt with in the context of attributability is whether a person acted on his own behalf and in his own interest or on behalf or in the interest of another person. In the latter case, we speak of agency. If that is the case, again very roughly, it is the person on behalf of whom a person acted that should be held liable instead of the person acting (the agent). Though very common in practice,[107] it does not follow from the scholarship and case law consulted in researching for this project that questions of attributability require – from a comparative perspective[108] – specific attention. Henceforth, I will not address the issue.[109]

104 Wagner, "Comparative Tort Law." pp. 1016–1017.

105 See on this diversity Helmut Koziol, "Conclusions," in *Unificatio of Tort Law: Wrongfulness*, ed. Helmut Koziol (The Hague: Kluwer International, 1998). pp. 129–130.

106 For an overview Widmer, "Comparative Report on Fault as a Basis of Liability and Criterion of Imputation (Attribution)." pp. 344–347.

107 Lukas Radermacher, "Authority of agents," in *Commentaries on European Contract Laws*, ed. Nils Jansen and Reinhard Zimmermann (Oxford: Oxford University Press, 2018). pp. 587–588, nr. 1.

108 Under German law, attributability is presumed in the contractual context (§ 278 BGB) which also applies to contract negotiations. Schwarze, *Das Recht der Leistungsstörung*. p. 535, nr. 58; Staudinger/Feldmann (2018) BGB § 311 nrs. 168–171.

109 See for a historical and comparative overview Radermacher, "Authority of Agents." pp. 587–648.

29. Presumption of attributability – As a starting point, it is the claimant who has to prove that he has a claim. Inversely, it will be on the defendant to prove that the claimant does not have a claim. Yet the attributability is generally presumed. The defendant can invoke a lack of attributability to discharge himself of his liability. Under German law, for instance, this follows from the wording of § 280 (1) second sentence BGB and is considered as one of the advantages of the *culpa in contrahendo* as opposed to the extra-contractual liability under § 823 BGB. Under French law, the same line of argumentation has been relied on in some court decisions as is reported by Olivier Deshayes.[110] Under Dutch law, it is reported that attributability is generally assumed as well.[111] The Belgian legislator went one step further by not only presuming attributability but also not requiring it anymore at all. Under Belgian law, attributability used to be dealt with under a subjective element of the fault (as opposed to an objective element (infringement of duty of conduct)), but this subjective element has been abandoned in the new definition of the notion of fault (article 6.6 Be. Civ. C.). Only some specific grounds of non-attributability are maintained, such as being a minor (article 6.9 Be. Civ. C.).

2.5. Harm

30. Consequence of the infringement of an interest – Ulrich Magnus defines damage from a comparative perspective as "any negative modification in the injured party's legally protected sphere."[112] For the present purpose, damage or harm (which I use as synonyms) is understood as the negative consequence of the infringement of a legally protected interest.[113] Indeed, the Belgian reform literally defines harm in article 6.24 Be. Civ. C. as "the economic or non-economic repercussions of an infringement of a legally protected personal interest."[114] This distinction between, on the one hand, the infringed right or interest and, on the other hand, the ensuing harm is common to all ana-

110 Deshayes, "Le dommage précontractuel." p. 201, nr. 32.

111 Asser/Sieburgh 6-IV 2019/107.

112 Ulrich Magnus, "Comparative Report on the Law of Damages" in *Unification of Tort Law: Damages*, ed. Ulrich Magnus (The Hague: Kluwer Law, 2001). p. 191, nr. 38.

113 This understanding of interest must not be confused with the notion of interest as in "positive interest."

114 Free adaptation from the translation in Bernard Dubuisson, "The Projet de Réforme du Code Civil Belge and the Reform of the French Civil Code – A Comparison of Selected Topics," in *French Civil Liability in Comparative Perspective*, ed. Jean-Sébastien Borghetti and Simon Whittaker (Oxford: Hart Publishing, 2019). p. 416. I needed to add "personal" to accommodate the change in phrasing that occurred in the finally adopted text. Its original text reads: "Le dommage consiste dans les conséquences écono- miques ou non économiques d'une atteinte à un intérêt personnel juridiquement protégé."/"Schade bestaat uit de economische en niet-econo- mische gevolgen van de aantasting van een juridisch beschermd persoonlijk belang." See also for a perspective of the pre-reform project perspective Hubert Bocken, Ingrid Boone, and Marc Kruithof, *Inleiding tot het schadevergoedingsrecht* (Brugge: Die Keure, 2014). p. 46, nr. 70.

lysed legal systems, as von Bar explains.[115] Under Italian law, the distinction is expressed by distinguishing between *danno-evento* (the harmed interest) and *danno-conseguenza* (harm).[116] Under French law, the same distinction is foreseen in the reform project, be it that the terminology is somewhat confusing.[117] Indeed, a distinction is drawn between harm ("*dommage*") (corresponding to the Belgian legitimate interest) and prejudice ("*préjudice*") (corresponding to the Belgian harm).[118] Be that as it may, in the cases presently dealt with, that interest is the patrimony of the harmed party, and the consequence of this infringement consists in pure economic loss. Obviously, other interests can also be infringed in the context of contract negotiations – such as bodily integrity – but those types of harm raise distinct questions from those I deal with and essentially consist in a regular application of delictual liability.[119] Hence, those types of harm do not require special attention in the present context.

31. Loss – Harm/damage being the 'the negative consequence of the infringement of a legally protected interest' (*supra* Chap. 3, nr. 30), the "negative consequence" is loss. Indeed, the infringement of an interest must have had a negative consequence; it must have led to a loss. Such a loss can either consist in a decrease of the patrimony (*damnum emergens*) or in the missing out of certain advantages (*lucrum cessans*).[120] In the context of failed contract negotiations, this quite simple distinction leads to conceptual difficulties when the *lucrum cessans* is understood to designate the expected benefits under the negotiated contract. Though tempting, this is conceptually not right: the *lucrum cessans* designates

115 Christian Von Bar, *The Common European Law of Torts*, Vol. II (Oxford: Clarencon Press, 2000). p. 9, nr. 5. Very prominent under German law (Fikentscher and Heinemann, *Schuldrecht Allgemeiner und Besonderer Teil*. p. 373, nr. 600; Kreutz, *Hypothetische Verträge im Rahmen des Schadensausgleichs*. p. 22.) and interestingly under Belgian law (Bocken, Boone and Kruithof, *Inleiding tot het schadevergoedingsrecht*. p. 46, nr. 70. For a, in my opinion, slightly confusing contribution dealing with the French and Belgian reform project from a German/Swiss perspective, see Olivier Berg, "Le dommage dans les projets de réforme français et belge. Perspectives d'Outre-Rhin," in *La réforme du droit de la responsabilité en France et en Belgique*, ed. Bernard Dubuisson (Bruxelles: Bruylant, 2020). pp. 445–452.

116 Sirena, "The Concepts of 'Harm' in the French and Italian Laws of Civil Liability". p. 207; Bussani, Sebok, and Infantino, "Compensation for Pure Economic Loss." pp. 154–156; Bussani and Palmer, "The Liability Regimes of Europe – Their Façades and Interiors." pp. 133–135.

117 For the comparatist, the choice of terminology can only be deplored, as it is highly confusing that the requirement of "harm" takes a different significance in both systems, though they introduce the same distinction.

118 The distinction between prejudice and harm today is most prominently drawn by Philippe le Tourneau in Philippe le Tourneau et al., *Droit de la responsabilité et des contrats* (Paris: Dalloz, 2023). pp. 583 *et seq*. See Brun, *Responsabilité civile extracontractuelle*. pp. 123–125, nrs. 178–180 and Jourdain, *Les principes de la responsabilité civile*. pp. 131–132 for a discussion.

119 Under German law, they are dealt with under the *culpa in contrahendo*, though they can also be dealt with under § 823 BGB. That is so as the conditions of application of the *culpa in contrahendo* are more lenient than those of § 823 BGB.

120 Magnus, "Comparative Report on the Law of Damages." p. 193, nr. 44. Specifically under French law (Brun, *Responsabilité civile extracontractuelle*. pp. 149–150, nr. 215; Jourdain, *Les principes de la responsabilité civile*. p. 132.) and Dutch law (Asser/Sieburgh 6-II 2021/25).

any kind of lost advantages and is compensable provided its causally linked to the invoked fault. It may, for instance, concern the lost advantages under a contract with a third party, where there had been an offer to conclude the contract with the third party. What seems to happen, though, is that to explain that the compensation of the expected benefits under the negotiated contract cannot be granted, it is said that the *lucrum cessans* is not compensable. The problem that arises if the *lucrum cessans*, without any further nuance, is described as the expected benefit under the negotiated contract and, therefore, excluded from compensation is that it also excludes *a fortiori* the loss of a chance of the benefits under the contract with the third party, even though this could be considered an indemnifiable loss. Hence, arguing that the *lucrum cessans* is excluded *ipso facto* certainly stems from a right intuition (the benefits under the concluded contract are not causal harm) but explains this along the wrong vector, namely, the definition of harm instead of causality (I will thus deal again with this point *infra* Chap. 4, nr. 6). It seems to me that this type of reasoning is perceptible in article 1112 Fr. Civ. C. ("In the event of negligence in the negotiations, compensation for the resulting loss cannot be intended to compensate for the loss of benefits expected from the contract that was not concluded, or for the loss of a chance to obtain such benefits.")[121] The assimilation of the loss of a chance to conclude the contract with the actual benefit – though in the outcome largely identical – is problematic, as the compensability of both types of damage rests on a totally different reasoning (*infra* Chap. 6, nrs. 12–16).[122] That this is so can be seen quite nicely in the annual report of the French Court

121 Original text: "*En cas de faute commise dans les négociations, la réparation du préjudice qui en résulte ne peut avoir pour objet de compenser ni la perte des avantages attendus du contrat non conclu, ni la perte de chance d'obtenir ces avantages.*"

122 The Court of Appeal of Gent explains this very clearly: "However, a distinction must be made between compensation of the positive contract interest and compensation for the loss of a chance.

Compensation of the positive contract interest amounts to compensating the injured party as if an actual contract had been concluded, i.e. the profit foregone from the designed but lost contract or its equivalent. In this case, one assumes that contracting was a certainty for the injured party.

However, loss of an opportunity occurs in situations where a person has a real possibility but not the certainty to gain an advantage or avoid a disadvantage where this possibility is nullified by the mistake of a third party. This real possibility but not certainty is the 'opportunity'." Gent, 3 December 2014, *TBBR* 2018/1 (47) p. 51. Free translation. Original text: "*Er moet echter een onderscheid gemaakt worden tussen een vergoeding van het positief contractbelang en een vergoeding voor het verlies van een kans.*

Een vergoeding van het positief contractbelang komt er op neer dat de schadelijder een vergoeding ontvangt alsof er een daadwerkelijk contract werd gesloten, m.a.w. de ge- derfde winst van het ontworpen maar misgelopen contract of het equivalent ervan. In dit geval gaat men ervan dat de contractsluiting voor de schadelijdende partij een zekerheid was.

Het verlies van een kans komt echter voor in situaties waar iemand een reële mogelijkheid maar niet de zekerheid heeft om een voordeel te verwerven of een nadeel te vermijden waarbij deze mogelijkheid tenietgaat door de fout van een derde. Deze reële mogelijkheid maar geen zekerheid is de 'kans'."

of Cassation of 2006 in which the Court explains the evolution in its case law as follows:

> "As regards the wrongful unilateral termination of pre-contractual talks, the case law traditionally excluded full compensation for the benefits that the victim could have expected to derive from the envisaged contract but allowed compensation for loss of opportunity to realise them (Com. 2 November 1993, Bull. no. 380; 3e Civ. 12 November 2003, Appeal no. 02–10.352).
>
> In a decision of 26 November 2003 (Bull. no. 186), the Commercial Chamber, reversing this case law, held that 'the circumstances constituting a fault committed in the exercise of the right to unilaterally terminate contractual talks are not the cause of the loss consisting in the loss of a chance to realise the gains that could be expected from the conclusion of the contract'."[123]

This change in the French Court of Cassation's case law, in my opinion, is the result of an overly simplified understanding of *lucrum cessans* and seems based on an erroneous assimilation of all kinds of benefits under the expected contract with the *lucrum cessans*. *Dans la foulée*, the loss of a chance, is excluded from compensation. This reasoning, if my interpretation is correct, lacks nuance because the *lucrum cessans* can be subject to indemnification (to the extent it is causally linked to the invoked fault), and therefore, the loss of a chance of the benefits under the negotiated contracts is not *ipso facto* excluded, as it now is the law (article 1112 Fr. Civ. C.). In this sense, the exclusion of the loss of a chance to the benefits under the negotiated contract under French law does not stand on a technically sound basis, though there may be other arguments to do exclude the loss of a chance to the benefits under the negotiated contract which I will discuss *infra* (Chap. 6, nr. 20).

32. Loss and later benefit – Another specific question in the context of contract negotiations then is whether the fact that the harmed party later on concludes a more advantageous contract than the initial one excludes that this party has suffered harm. In my opinion, the argument lacks nuance. It is not because a party

123 La Cour de Cassation et la construction juridique européenne, *Rapport Annuel* 2006. p. 400. Free translation. Original text: "*S'agissant de la rupture unilatérale fautive de pourparlers précontractuels, la jurisprudence excluait traditionnellement la réparation intégrale des bénéfices que la victime aurait pu escompter du contrat envisagé, mais admettait l'indemnisation d'une perte de chance de les réaliser (Com. 2 novembre 1993, Bull. no 380; 3e Civ. 12 novembre 2003, pourvoi no 02–10.352).*

Par un arrêt du 26 novembre 2003 (Bull. no 186) la chambre commerciale, revenant sur cette jurisprudence, avait retenu que 'les circonstances constitutives d'une faute commise dans l'exercice du droit de rupture unilatérale des pourparlers contractuels ne sont pas la cause du préjudice consistant dans la perte d'une chance de réaliser les gains que permettait d'espérer la conclusion du contrat'."

has later concluded a more advantageous contract that *all* costs that were made in the negotiation process where not lost. The fact that later on, another contract has been concluded does not *ipso facto* swallow the prior losses. If one can, however, prove that the costs made during the former negotiations were reused in the latter negotiations, those specific costs, indeed, seem not to have been made as a loss. Ultimately, a nuanced case-by-case analysis is required. A decision of the Court of Appeal of Liège of 2013 provides a telling application of this nuanced reasoning.[124] The case concerned the intended, but actually impossible, franchising of a hairdresser (facts in more detail *supra* Chap. 3, nr. 14). In that case, the costs that had been made to prepare the hairdresser in order to be in conformity with the franchising rules of the intended franchise were considered to be subject to compensation. Costs that served the opening of the hairdresser under another franchise contract, however, were not subject to compensation.

2.6. Causal link

33. CAUSAL HARM – Not only must harm exist to give rise to liability but the harm must also have been *caused* by the reproached fault. The causal link must exist between the wrongful conduct and the suffered harm and *only if and to the extent that* such a causal link does exist can liability arise.[125] Under German law, the situation is somewhat confusing. Indeed, in the contractual realm (since liability for contract negotiations is a contractual liability), causality is only required under § 249 (1) BGB,[126] the provision dealing with the compensation of harm. It seems thus, as if causality merely is a matter of measuring the extent of harm and not a condition of application.[127] Practically speaking, however, this little

124 Liège, 31 October 2013, 2012/RG/1051, www.juportal.be.

125 Comparative law overview in Jaap Spier and Olav A. Haazen, "Comparative Conclusions on Causation," in *Unification of Tort Law: Causation*, ed. J. Spier (The Hague: Kluwer International, 2000). p. 127.

126 "A person who is liable in damages is to restore the position that would exist if the circumstance obliging them to pay damages had not occurred." Original text: "*Wer zum Schadensersatz verpflichtet ist, hat den Zustand herzustellen, der bestehen würde, wenn der zum Ersatz verpflichtende Umstand nicht eingetreten wäre.*"

127 "Unlike French and Belgian law, proof of damage caused by an infringement of one of the interests protected by law is not one of the conditions for civil liability. The existence and extent of the damage are assessed only after the liability of the person who infringed a protected interest has been established, in order to determine the extent of the compensation due. This means that, in the absence of damage resulting from an infringement of one of the interests referred to in section 823 (1) of the BGB or from a breach of contract, the tortfeasor's liability is certainly established, but the legal effect referred to in section 249 (1) of the BGB ('to restore the state of affairs that would have existed if the event giving rise to the obligation to make reparation had not occurred') cannot operate." Jonas Knetsch, "Les effets de la responsabilité et la réparation des dommages. unité ou diversité des formes de réparation dans les projets français et belge. Point de vue du droit allemand," in *La réforme du droit de la responsabilité en France et en Belgique*, ed. Bernard Dubuisson (Bruxelles: Bruylant, 2020). p. 536. Free translation. Original text: "*À la différence des droits français et belge, la preuve d'un préjudice causé par l'atteinte à l'un des intérêts protégés*

peculiarity – which follows from the structural role of § 249 BGB, which is the relevant provision for compensation both in the contractual and extra-contractual context – rather is irritating than problematic. Indeed, to the extent that if liability could be established but no causal harm be proven, the liability claim would lead nowhere. Ultimately, causal harm must exist in order to give rise to a *meaningful* liability claim.[128] So generally speaking, causal harm is a condition of application of a liability claim and not merely a matter of indemnification.

34. Factual causal link – Essentially, to establish whether a causal link exists, one must establish whether the harm would not have risen without the wrongful conduct *ceteris paribus*.[129] This is a factual causal link, the so-called *conditio sine qua non* test: Would the harm anyway have risen in the absence of the fault? If the answer is positive (the harm would have been suffered absent the fault), no causal link exists; if the answer is negative (the harm would not have been suffered absent the fault), a causal link exists to *that very* harm in question.[130] The Belgian article 6.18 Be. Civ. C. codifies this test as follows:

> "An event giving rise to liability is the cause of damage if it is a necessary condition of the damage. An event is a necessary condition of the damage if, without that event, the damage would not have occurred as it did in the concrete circumstances present at the time of the event giving rise to the damage."[131]

---

par la loi ne fait pas partie des conditions de la responsabilité civile. L'existence et la consistance du préjudice ne sont appréciées qu'après avoir établi la responsabilité de l'auteur de l'atteinte à un intérêt protégé, afin de connaître l'étendue de la réparation due. Cela signifie qu'en l'absence de préjudice consécutif à une atteinte à l'un des intérêts visés par le paragraphe 823, alinéa 1er, du BGB ou à une inexécution contractuelle, la responsabilité de l'auteur est certes constituée, mais l'effet juridique indiqué au paragraphe 249, alinéa 1er, du BGB ('rétablir l'état des choses qui aurait existé si le fait d'où résulte l'obligation de réparer n'était pas survenu') ne pourra s'opérer."

128 That this legistic approach is confusing also becomes clear when looking at scholarship. While most authors would count causality among the conditions of application (f.i. Philipp Scholz, "Haftungsbegründende und haftungsausfüllende Kausalität im Zivil- und Zivilprozessrecht," *JuS* (2021). p. 915; Staudinger/Schwarze (2019) BGB § 280 nr. E1;: Hermann Lange and Gottfried Schiemann, *Schadensersatz* (Tübingen: Mohr Siebeck, 2003). p. 75.), some do not. In Schulze, Bürgerliches Gesetzbuch, 11. Auflage 2021 nrs. 7–15, for instance, causal harm is not mentioned as a condition of application.

129 On causality in general: Luidiger Röckrath, *Kausalität, Wahrscheinlichkeit und Haftung – Rechtliche und ökonomische Analyse* (München: C.H. Beck, 2004). p. 8 and Lange and Schiemann, *Schadensersatz*. pp. 79–80. Belgium: article 5.18 Be. Civ. C. France: Brun, *Responsabilité civile extracontractuelle*. p. 166, nr. 238; Jourdain, *Les principes de la responsabilité civile*. pp. 63–63. Germany: Fikentscher and Heinemann, *Schuldrecht Allgemeiner und Besonderer Teil*. pp. 382–383, nrs. 622–624; Medicus and Lorenz, *Schuldrecht I Allgemeiner Teil*. p. 316, nr. 3; Kreutz, *Hypothetische Verträge im Rahmen des Schadensausgleichs*. p. 121; Lange and Schiemann, *Schadensersatz*. pp. 79–80. Italy: Salvi, *La responsabilità civile*. p. 235. Netherlands: Asser/Sieburgh 6-II 2021/31.

130 Spier and Haazen, "Comparative Conclusions on Causation." p. 127.

131 Free translation. Original text: "*Un fait générateur de responsabilité est la cause d'un dommage s'il est une condition nécessaire de ce dernier. Un fait est une condition nécessaire du dommage si, sans ce fait, le dommage ne se serait pas produit tel qu'il s'est produit dans les circonstances*

To further limit the legally relevant harm,[132] this factual causal link is topped with a juridical or normative causal link in most legal systems.[133] That is the case for German law, which relies, on top of the factual causal link, on an adequate causal link ('*Adäquanztheorie*') ('Does the wrongful conduct in the normal course of circumstances cause such a harm?') and the scope of protection of the infringed norm ('*Schutzzwecktheorie*' or comparable terminology with slight variances) ('Is the harm suffered such harm as the infringed norm aims to protect from?').[134] Under French law, an adequate causal link must be established, though reportedly, the practice of French courts is rather diffuse.[135] Italian law seems to follow the French example closely,[136] and under Dutch law, an additional causal link similar to the adequate causal link is required under article 6:98 NBW,[137] namely, a *reasonable attribution.*[138] In the reform

concrètes présentes lors de l'événement dommageable."/"*Een tot aansprakelijkheid leidend feit is oorzaak van de schade indien het een noodzakelijke voorwaarde is voor deze laatste. Een feit is een noodzakelijke voor- waarde voor de schade indien de schade zich zonder dit feit, in de concrete omstandigheden die bestonden ten tijde van het schadegeval, niet zou hebben voorgedaan zoals deze zich heeft voorgedaan.*"

132 Von Bar, *The Common European Law of Torts*, II. pp. 29–30, nr. 24; Spier and Haazen, "Comparative Conclusions on Causation." p. 130.

133 Belgium used to be the only system relying merely on a factual causal link until its recent reform: Spier and Haazen, "Comparative Conclusions on Causation." p. 130.

134 Fikentscher and Heinemann, *Schuldrecht Allgemeiner und Besonderer Teil.* pp. 384–386, nrs. 625–629; Medicus and Lorenz, *Schuldrecht I Allgemeiner Teil.* pp. 317–319, nrs. 6–12; Staudinger/Höpfner (2021) BGB § 249 nrs. 13–34. For an in-depth discussion, Lange and Schiemann, *Schadensersatz.* pp. 81–128.

135 Brun, *Responsabilité civile extracontractuelle.* p. 173, nr. 249; Jourdain, *Les principes de la responsabilité civile.* p. 68. From a comparative perspective Spier and Haazen, "Comparative Conclusions on Causation." p. 132.

136 Francesco D. Busnelli and Giovanni Comandé, "Causation under Italian Law," in *Unification of Tort Law: Causation*, ed. J. Spier (The Hague: Kluwer, 2000). p. 82.

137 "Article 6:98 Causal relation and attribution

Only damage that is connected in such a way to the event that made the debtor liable, that it, in regard of the nature of his liability and of the damage caused, can be attributed to him as a consequence of this event, is eligible for compensation."

Original version: "*Voor vergoeding komt slechts in aanmerking schade die in zodanig verband staat met de gebeurtenis waarop de aansprakelijkheid van de schuldenaar berust, dat zij hem, mede gezien de aard van de aansprakelijkheid en van de schade, als een gevolg van deze gebeurtenis kan worden toegerekend.*"

Attribution as a criterion is not quite meaningful if it is not stated according to which criterion damage can be attributed.

138 As becomes clear under Dutch law (Asser/Sieburgh 6-II 2021/14.) but also recognized under German law ("In the almost unanimous opinion, however, these endeavours are normative moments of attribution that should not be included in the concepts of cause and effect." Lange and Schiemann, *Schadensersatz.* p. 81. Free translation. Original text: "*Nach nahezu einhelliger Ansicht handelt es sich bei diesen Bemühungen jedoch um normative Zurechnungsmomente, die in die Begriffe Ursache und Wirkung nicht hineingelegt werden sollten.*"), these juridical causal links, in fact, formulate criteria to determine the attribution of harm rather than a requirement of a causal link.

project, Belgian law now also implements a juridical causal link, based on the probability of the occurrence of that harm.[139]

Be that as it may, in all legal systems, *at least* a factual causal link is required (only if a factual causal link can be shown to exist does the question of a juridical causal link arise).[140] It will be the factual causal link which will prove relevant in the present cases; the juridical causal link generally does not present specific issues in the context of no-contract law (as far as I can see).

35. COUNTER-FACTUAL SCENARIO – To know whether harm is causal, the so-called "difference-theory" ("*Differenztheorie*"), attributed to Friedrich Mommsen,[141][142] is applied. Essentially, the counter-factual scenario without the wrongful event must be constructed to assess whether in that counter-factual scenario, the invoked harm would rise too. This counter-factual scenario is constructed by tracing how things would have evolved absent the fact giving rise to liability.[143] This exercise is somewhat constructive in as far as the counter-factual scenario always is a hypothetical scenario which entails some degree of uncertainty as to how things would have gone without the fault:[144]

> "This analysis, which is sometimes referred to as hypothetical reconstruction, necessarily involves a degree of guesswork, as no one really knows what would have happened in the absence of the wrongful act."[145]

139 Article 6.18, § 2 Be. Civ. C.: "However, there shall be no liability if the link between the event giving rise to liability and the loss or damage is so remote that it would be manifestly unreasonable to attribute the loss or damage to the person claimed to be liable. In this assessment, account is taken, in particular, of the unlikely nature of the damage in the light of the normal consequences of the event giving rise to liability and of the fact that that event did not contribute significantly to the occurrence of the damage." Free translation. Original text: "*Toutefois, il n'y a pas de responsabilité si le lien entre le fait générateur de responsabilité et le dommage est à ce point distendu qu'il serait manifestement déraisonnable d'imputer ce dommage à la personne dont la responsabilité est invoquée. Dans cette appréciation, il est tenu compte, en particulier, du caractère improbable du dommage au regard des conséquences normales du fait générateur de responsabilité et de la circonstance que ce fait n'a pas contribué de manière significative à la survenance du dommage.*"/"*Er is evenwel geen aansprakelijkheid indien het verband tussen het tot aansprakelijkheid leidende feit en de schade dermate verwijderd is dat het kennelijk onredelijk zou zijn de schade toe te rekenen aan de persoon die wordt aangesproken. Bij deze beoorde- ling wordt in het bijzonder rekening gehouden met het onwaarschijnlijke karakter van de schade in het licht van de normale gevolgen van het tot aansprakelijkheid leidende feit en met de omstandigheid dat dit feit niet op betekenisvolle wijze heeft bijgedragen tot het ontstaan van de schade.*"

140 France: Brun, *Responsabilité civile extracontractuelle*. p. 174, nr. 251. Germany: Staudinger/Höpfner (2021) BGB § 249 nr. 9. Italy: Busnelli and Comandé, "Causation under Italian Law." pp. 79–81. Netherlands: Asser/Sieburgh 6-II 2021/14. No sources on this under Belgian law yet.

141 Mommsen, *Beiträge zum Obligationenrecht II: Zur Lehre von dem Interesse*. XIII+301 p.

142 Magnus, "Comparative Report on the Law of Damages." p. 191, nr. 37. Staudinger/Höpfner (2021) BGB § 249 nr. 5.

143 Belgium: Durant, "La rupture unilatérale des pourparlers ou l'exercice d'une liberté surveillée." p. 67, nr. 35.

144 As explained, for instance, under Dutch law in Asser/Sieburgh 6-II 2021/40.

145 Bernard Dubuisson, "Les mystères de l'alternative légitime," *RGAR*, no. 9 (2021). p. 15820. Free translation. Original text: "*Cette analyse qu'on appelle parfois la reconstruction hypothétique*

To overcome this ontological (relating to its existence) uncertainty, the *normal* course of action, according to the *best available science and experience*, will have to be constructed.[146] Graphically, this can be represented as follows:[147]

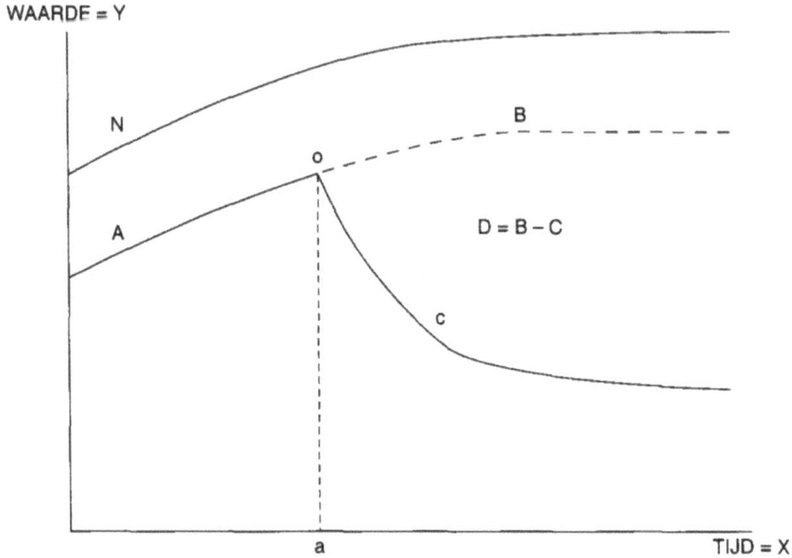

Figuur 1

Figure 3.1 Causality test

Y axis indicating value; X axis indicating time. A indicates the course of action, O indicates the fault, and B indicates the hypothetical course of action without the fault. C in turn indicates how things have evolved pursuant to the fault, making D the harm that has been caused by that fault. The alternative course of action (B), though potentially subject to discussion, can at least, with some degree of certainty, be predicted. But this uncertainty is ontological, as it pertains to some degree of uncertainty about how things would be in the counter-factual scenario. N indicates the normal value but need not interest us here and will be left out in the following graphs.

36. Counter-factual scenario and freedom of contract – The uncertainty of the alternative course of action in the case of broken-off negotiations or refusal to contract, however, is of a different kind. In those cases, the counter-factual scenario is *normatively unknowable*. The point here is not so much that

emporte nécessairement une part de supputations car nul ne sait véritablement ce qu'il serait advenu en l'absence du fait illicite."

146 Spier and Haazen, "Comparative Conclusions on Causation." p. 127.

147 Taken from Dries Simoens, *Schade en schadeloosstelling*, Beginselen van Belgisch Privaatrecht, (Antwerpen: E. Story-Scientia, 1999). p. 26, nr. 12.

ontologically, the alternative course of things remains unknowable but rather that different courses of action remain free for the tortfeasor. Indeed, as long as a party still is considered to enjoy freedom of contract, the party is normatively free to contract, continue negotiations, or not to contract in the hypothetical alternative scenario. Graphically, I've tried to express this as follows:

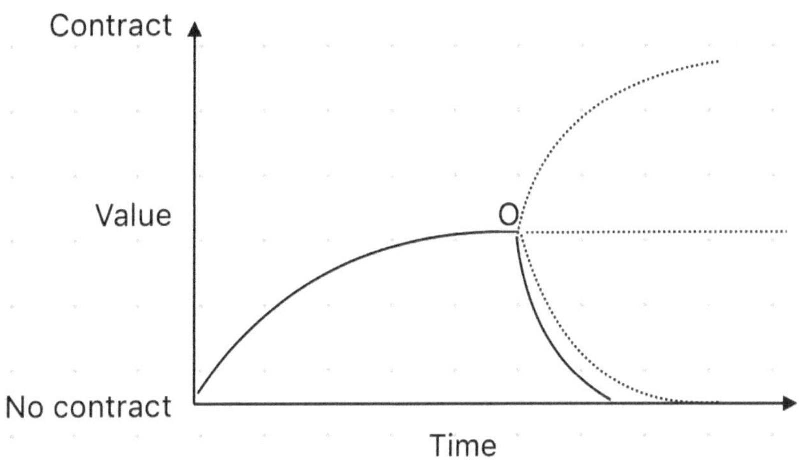

Figure 3.2 Causality for broken-off negotiations

As this graph aims to show, the alternative course of action after the breaking-off is not one line but multiple different lines representing the situation in which either a contract would be concluded, negotiations would go on, or no contract would be concluded. Indeed, as from the moment that negotiations are broken-off (O), the alternative course of action is uncertain. A "normal" course of action does, normatively speaking, not exist.

37. Normative uncertainty and causal harm – This normative causal uncertainty of the hypothetical alternative course of action is the reason for the impossibility of establishing causal harm. Indeed, and that is quite generally speaking, if normatively speaking, no alternative course of action can be established, it is impossible to assess whether causal harm in fact does exist, as in the alternative course of action, the same harm could arise absent the fault.

38. Normative certain alternative course of action – This means that to find liability, the normative causal uncertainty needs to be overcome. Logically, that must be done by *normatively* creating a certain alternative course of action. In other words, legally, a course of action that parties have to abide by must be created, i.e. a party must be considered to be under an obligation to either contract or to negotiate. In that case, the possibility of the no-contract scenario in the alternative course of action is normatively excluded, hence making the existence of causal harm and pursuant of liability possible. Graphically, I try to visualize this as follows:

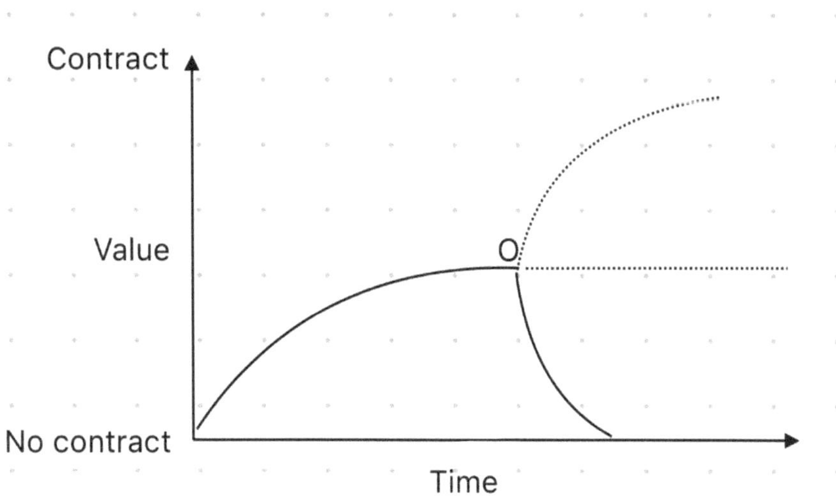

Figure 3.3 Causality for broken-off negotiations with obligation to contract or to negotiate

In this graph, the alternative course of action of failed negotiations has been ruled out, and only the continuation or conclusion of the contract have been retained. In that case, there can be causal harm and hence liability.

39. Pre-supposed obligation to contract – This finding has considerable consequences for how we see pre-contractual liability: each time the breaking-off of negotiations to contract or the refusal to contract is considered a fault giving rise to liability, an obligation to contract or to negotiate must have been pre-supposed. This also means that each time that this reasoning has been followed, the indemnification would have to put the party in the position it had been in had the negotiations continued or the contract concluded, in other words: performance of the respective pre-supposed obligation. Where performance is *not* granted, the underlying reasoning is incoherent. This becomes clear in cases where due to wrongful breaking-off of negotiations or refusing to contract, the wronged party claims the *vainly* made costs.

40. The incoherence of vainly made costs – Semantically, there is a difference between framing harm either as costs that would not have been made absent the fault and costs that have become vain due to the fault. Yet it does generally not seem to matter in practice. Indeed, if, for instance, one says that costs that would not have been made without the fault (for instance, maintaining negotiations longer than necessary) are the relevant harm, this means that only the costs that were made during the additional time of negotiating will be causal harm; if one says that costs that would not have become vain without the fault (maintaining negotiations longer than necessary), the formulation is perhaps somewhat less clear but does not seem to change the extent of the compensable harm. Yet reasoning in terms of vainly made costs can potentially be problematic, namely, when the invoked fault is the breaking-off or refusal itself. Indeed, framing the suffered harm as vainly made costs allows to, on the one hand, state that the breaking-off of negotiations or refusal to contract itself would be wrongful, leading to the hypothetical alternative course of action of still remaining in negotiations or concluding a contract (given that freedom from contract *has* be negated in that case) and, on the other hand, state that this has led the made costs come to be harm, as they have become vain. Two antagonistic counter-factual positions are so doing assimilated: continuing negotiations/contracting and not having started negotiations at all. The artifice and inadmissibility of such a reasoning is patent.[148] With the words of Olivier Deshayes: "One has to make a choice between these two approaches, because it seems impossible to combine them."[149] Such insensible application of liability law rules inevitably leads to an unmanageable body of liability law, thereby confirming the common criticism of arbitrariness of pre-contractual liability ("*Billigkeitsrechtsprechung*").[150]

Nevertheless, the Belgian legislator seems to have relied on such a reasoning in the first sentence of the second alinea of article 5.17 Be. Civ. C.:

> "In the case of wrongfully broken off negotiations, this liability entails reinstating the injured party to the situation in which it would have found itself had negotiations not taken place."[151]

148 As argued rightly by Krawitz, *Schutz vorvertraglicher Investitionen – Zur Haftung beim Scheitern von Vertragsverhandlungen*. pp. 92–93 under German law and by Deshayes, "Le dommage précontractuel." p. 198, nr. 24 under French law. I've argued in this sense under Belgian law De Boeck and Hick, "Totstandkoming van contracten: het komend recht in de rechtspraak." pp. 12–13, nr. 15; Hick, "Aansprakelijkheid voor afgebroken onderhandelingen in België en Nederland: Op koers voor toenadering." p. 251, nr. 22. It had already been argued under Belgian law prior to the reform in Durant, "La rupture unilatérale des pourparlers ou l'exercice d'une liberté surveillée." p. 68, nr. 36.

149 Deshayes, "Le dommage précontractuel." p. 194, nr. 13. Free translation. Original text: "*Entre ces deux optiques il faut bien choisir car le cumul paraît impossible.*"

150 Strongly expressed in Stoll, "Tatbestände und Funktionen der Haftung für culpa in contrahendo." p. 436. More recently for instance in Medicus and Petersen, *Grundwissen zum Bürgerlichen Recht*. p. 91, nr. 2.

151 "*En cas de rupture fautive des négociations, cette responsabilité implique que la personne lésée soit remise dans la situation dans laquelle elle se serait trouvée s'il n'y avait pas eu de négociations.*"/"*Bij foutief afbreken van onderhandelingen houdt deze aansprakelijkheid in dat de benadeelde teruggeplaatst wordt in de situatie waarin hij zich zou hebben bevonden indien er niet zou zijn onderhandeld.*" See one of the drafters of the reform explaining the provision in this sense Rafaël Jafferali, "La réforme du droit des contrats – Les principales nouveautés," *JT* (2023). p. 26, nr. 14, nbp. 80: "If negotiations begin in the normal way, and one party incurs legal fees to advise it in the negotiations, and at the last moment the other party culpably breaks off the negotiations, rendering the legal fees incurred up to that point worthless, can it really be considered that these legal fees are not causally linked to the fault? On the contrary, it seems to me that the effect of the fault was to deprive the lawyers' fees previously incurred of any usefulness, and therefore of any value, and that it is this damage that constitutes the negative interest for which compensation is sought (see, in the same vein, I. CLAEYS et T. TANGHE, Algemeen contractenrecht. Handboek voor nu en straks, 2e éd., Anvers, Intersentia, 2022; PEDC, art. 2:301, comm., VII, p. 152 and the reference to illustration 3;

This can be contrasted with a much more nuanced wording in the case law of the BGH:

> "Only if the conclusion of the contract can be assumed to be certain and expenses are incurred to implement the contract prior to its conclusion in the created confidence, can the negotiating party be required to reimburse these expenses under the aspect of fault in the contract negotiations if it later refuses to conclude the contract without good reason."[152]

By stating that only 'these expenses' – being the 'expenses . . . incurred to implement the contract prior to its conclusion in the created confidence' that 'the conclusion of the contract can be assumed to be certain' – the BGH declares the costs made relying on *created* legitimate expectations compensable (*supra* Chap. 3, nr. 24).

3. Negotiation agreements

3.1. Modifying liability

41. Facilitating or limiting liability – After having exposed the different conditions of application of the liability for contract negotiations, it is necessary to briefly add that parties can – to some extent – modify these conditions of application. Parties generally try to limit their own liability to facilitate their possibilities of holding the counterparty liable, or both at the same time. This is done by what can broadly be framed as negotiation agreements. Annick De

---

DCFR, art. II. – 3:301, comm, H, p. 243 and the reference to illustration 3; Unidroit Principles 2016, art. 2.1.15, comment, no. 4, pp. 65 et seq.) In any event, this is the solution adopted by the text of art. 5.17, para. 2, in the event of a culpable breach of negotiations (a breach that must not be confused with that of negotiations without intent to contract)." Free translation. Original text: "*Si les négociations commencent normalement, que dans ce cadre une partie expose des frais d'avocat pour la conseiller dans cette négociation et qu'au dernier moment l'autre partie rompt fautivement les négociations, rendant vains les frais d'avocat exposés jusqu'alors, peut-on vraiment considérer que ceux-ci ne seraient pas en lien causal avec la faute? Il me semble au contraire que la faute a eu pour effet de priver de toute utilité, et donc de toute valeur, les frais d'avocats exposés antérieurement, et que c'est ce dommage qui constitue l'intérêt négatif dont la réparation est demandée (voy. dans le même sens I. CLAEYS et T. TANGHE, Algemeen contractenrecht, op. cit., no 59, p. 68; PEDC, art. 2:301, comm., VII, p. 152 et le renvoi à l'illustration 3; DCFR, art. II. – 3:301, comm., H, p. 243 et le renvoi à l'illustration 3; Principes d'Unidroit 2016, art. 2.1.15, commentaire, no 4, pp. 65 et s.). Telle est en tout cas la solution retenue par le texte de l'art. 5.17, al. 2, en cas de rupture fautive des négociations (faute qui ne doit pas être confondue avec celle consistant à entamer ou poursuivre des négociations sans intention de contracter).*"

152 BGH 15 January 2001 – II ZR 127/99, *DStR* 2001, 803. Free translation. Original text: "*Nur wenn der Vertragsschluss nach den Verhandlungen zwischen den Parteien als sicher anzunehmen ist und in dem hierdurch begründeten Vertrauen Aufwendungen zur Durchführung des Vertrages vor dessen Abschluss gemacht werden, können diese vom Verhandlungspartner unter dem Gesichtspunkt des Verschuldens bei den Vertragsverhandlungen zu erstatten sein, wenn er den Abschluss des Vertrages später ohne triftigen Grund ablehnt.*" Same phrasing BGH 12 December 2012, *NJW* 2013, 928 nr. 7.

Boeck describes negotiation agreements ("*onderhandelingsafspraken*")[153] as agreements on the "rights and obligations of the negotiating parties during the negotiation and often also for the hypothesis of their failure (temporary study agreement, meeting calendar arrangements, settlement of futile expenses, exoneration clauses, damages clauses, confidentiality, exclusivity, etc.) and should thus be clearly distinguished from the ultimately envisaged agreement under negotiation."[154]

42. Types of negotiation agreements – A common endeavour in relation with negotiation agreements is to classify them in order to be able to provide a clearer account of existing negotiation agreements. In essence, it comes down to dogmatically defining different types of negotiation agreements. Denominations such as letter of intent (LoI) or memorandum of understanding sound familiar in this context.[155] A good example is how a gentlemen's agreement is described under Belgian law. It is characterized by its legally non-binding nature. These agreements bind their issuer only as a matter of honesty. As a consequence, gentlemen's agreements are not enforceable.[156] Nevertheless, a gentlemen's agreement is not bereft of any legal relevance; it is considered a legal fact.[157] Legally speaking, however, this tendency to create a taxonomy of existing negotiation agreement relies on an arbitrary definition of these agreements. The legal consequences ascribed to a gentlemen's agreement do not follow from its denomination or classification but from its content.[158] That is so because the question that, legally speaking, is relevant is not what type of agreement parties have concluded and even less what name it has been given but *what types of legal effects parties wanted to create* and *what legal effects they did create*. In other words, what did parties want to obligate themselves or

153 Annick De Boeck, "Onderhandelen met de rem op: het gebruik van voorbehoudmechanismen in de precontractuele fase," *TBBR* 1 (2018). p. 5.

154 De Boeck, "Onderhandelen met de rem op: het gebruik van voorbehoudmechanismen in de precontractuele fase." p. 5. Free translation. Original text: "*rechten en plichten van de onderhandelende partijen tijdens de onderhandeling en vaak ook voor de hypothese dat die mislukken (tijdelijke studieovereenkomst, vergaderkalenderafspraken, regeling voor de nutteloos gemaakte kosten, exoneratiebedingen, schadebedingen, geheimhouding, exclusiviteit, enz.) en moet dus duidelijk worden onderscheiden van de uiteindelijk beoogde overeenkomst waarover de onderhandeling loopt.*"

155 As illustrated in Yves Lequette et al., *Droit civil Les Obligations* (Paris: Dalloz, 2022). p. 266, nr. 249.

156 Kurt Willems, "Gentlemen's agreements," in *Gemeenrechtelijke clausules, Vol. I en II*, Contractuele Clausules (Mortsel: Intersentia, 2013). pp. 46–47; Eric Dirix, "Gentlemen's Agreements en adnere afspraken met onzekere rechtsgevolgen," *RW* (1985–1986). pp. 2135–2136, nr. 22.

157 De Boeck, "Onderhandelen met de rem op: het gebruik van voorbehoudmechanismen in de precontractuele fase." p. 7; Dirix, "Gentlemen's Agreements en adnere afspraken met onzekere rechtsgevolgen." pp. 2131–2132, nr. 18.

158 As Annick De Boeck rightly points out: "mere designation is not decisive but rather the true intention of the parties." De Boeck, "Onderhandelen met de rem op: het gebruik van voorbehoudmechanismen in de precontractuele fase." p. 8. Free translation. Original text: "*loutere benaming is niet doorslaggevend doch wel de ware bedoeling der partijen.*"

their counterpart to, and are they bound to it? The relevant question thus is not what type of agreement they have concluded but what type of obligations they have taken on or charged their counterparty with; classification on the level of the type of agreement thus inevitably lacks pertinence.

Alternatively, more functional typologies exist. In his comparative study of pre-contractual liability, Bertrand De Coninck, for instance, provides a tripartite functional approach.[159] First, accessory preparatory contracts. Those comprise contracts which regulate exclusivity, secrecy, or set a calendar for negotiations. They are accessory to the preparation of the final contract, as they direct the negotiation process procedurally but not content-wise. Second, and complementary to the first category, are partial contracts. Those lay down on which parts of the final contract the parties were able to reach an agreement content-wise. These contracts can get very close to the final contract, depending on whether the essential and/or substantial elements of the final contract are agreed upon in that partial contract. Third, agreements to negotiate. Such an agreement entails an obligation to negotiate and thus does not oblige the negotiators to conclude the main contract. Alternatively, Ekaterina Pannebakker draws a dual distinction between so-called dynamic constituents and substantive constituents.[160] The substantive constituent is the content of the prospective contract, its price, object, and modalities. The dynamic constituent focuses on the process of bringing about that prospective contract, meaning the planning, timing, and structuring of negotiations. Of course, often an agreement will comprise parts of both these elements. Though such functional approaches appear more useful than a dogmatic approach, they remain mainly relevant for pedagogical purposes. From a legal perspective, the only relevant distinction is whether an obligation to contract or to negotiate has been agreed upon or not. Since this question relates to an obligation to contract or to negotiate, I will address it *infra* (Chap. 3, nr. 16–20).

43. BINDING CHARACTER AND CONTENT – Instead of trying to somewhat arbitrarily attribute certain characteristics to some – legally speaking – interchangeable notions, it appears more fruitful to discuss the two distinct questions which matter in the context of negotiation agreements. First, the question of the binding character of such negotiation agreements (*infra* Chap. 3, nrs. 44–45); second, the question of the possible content of those negotiation agreements (*infra* Chap. 3, nrs. 46–47). Though both questions in practice often are interrelated (the content defines the binding character), they should be discussed separately for the sake of conceptual clarity.

159 De Coninck, "Le droit commun de la rupture des négotiations précontractuelles." pp. 40–47, nr. 32–40.

160 Pannebakker, *Letter of intent in international contracting*. pp. 20–21; Ekaterina Pannebakker, "Offer and Acceptance and the Dynamics of Negotiations: Arguments for Contract Theory from Negotiation Studies," *Erasmus Law Review* 6, no. 2 (2013). pp. 135–136.

3.2. Binding character

44. CONTRACT LAW – The question of the binding character of negotiation agreements as such is rather unspecific. Essentially, the question boils down to one of how in the respective legal system, binding agreements are made. That is nothing else than a question of valid contract conclusion.[161] If a valid contract has been concluded in the negotiation phase, that contract is binding; if no valid contract has been concluded, there is no contract which could be binding.[162]

To the extent that a valid contract has been formed, the legal basis of the related liability claim should be contractual. In systems which can base their liability for contract negotiations on an extra-contractual liability, this implies a difference in legal basis, which may have consequences on prescription periods and other incidental elements.[163]

45. LIABILITY LAW – If a negotiation agreement is not a binding contract, the statements made can still lead to liability claims under general liability for contract negotiations. Indeed, statements that have been made carelessly and have caused harm to the counterparty can lead to liability if the conditions of application are fulfilled. Whether these statements can lead to liability and with what consequences will depend on the concrete circumstances, of which the content of the agreement is an important part.

3.3. Content

46. VALID CONTRACT CONCLUSION – The limit to the content of a negotiation agreement is formed by the limit of a valid contract conclusion.[164] As briefly mentioned (*supra* Chap. 3, nr. 42), this seems to only require special attention regarding the validity of an obligation to contract and to negotiate (on which *infra* Chap. 3, nr. 16–20).[165] Here, I will only briefly illustrate some type of contents that serve to organize the negotiation process (the dynamic constituent in Pannebakker's typology (*supra* Chap. 3, nr. 42)).

47. ILLUSTRATIONS – There is, for the present purpose, no need and no point in providing an exhaustive list; freedom of contract allows parties to agree on what seems best to them. Hence, some illustrations should suffice. For instance, so-called subject-to-contract clauses clarify that though an agreement has been reached on certain points, they still need to be confirmed in a final (generally written) contract to prevent the parties from being prematurely bound;[166]

161 As clearly stated under German law (Staudinger/Bork (2020) Vorbemerkung zu §§ 145 ff nr. 51.) and French law (Brun, *Responsabilité civile extracontractuelle*. p. 83, nr. 121.)

162 Clearly expressed in Staudinger/Bork (2020) Vorbemerkung zu §§ 145 ff nr. 3.

163 As is the case under French law Brun, *Responsabilité civile extracontractuelle*. p. 83, nr. 121.

164 For more examples, see Lequette et al., *Droit civil Les Obligations*. p. 267, nr. 249.

165 Discussed, for instance, in Staudinger/Bork (2020) Vorbemerkung zu §§ 145 ff nr. 57.

166 De Boeck, "Onderhandelen met de rem op: het gebruik van voorbehoudmechanismen in de precontractuele fase." p. 8.

non-disclosure agreements (NDAs) stipulate that identified information that is exchanged in the process of negotiations cannot be disclosed to persons outside the negotiations; or exclusivity clauses stipulate that parties do not conduct parallel negotiations with other parties. Such a clause is, generally speaking, necessary, as parties, generally speaking, are free to conduct parallel negotiations (*supra* Chap. 3, nr. 19).

Specific attention should go to exoneration clauses. Parties cannot exclude the applicability of conduct-based liability systems in its entirety; doing so would, of course, deplete these conduct-based liability law systems from their purpose. That is what one can read in article 1112 Fr. Civ. C. Indeed, it specifies that parties mandatorily must act in accordance with good faith during the negotiation process. Interestingly, the Belgian provision which otherwise is a perfect copy and paste of the French one left out the "mandatorily." The explanatory note does not explain this deviation from article 1112 Fr. Civ. C., but it may well be that this has been done to prevent the redundance of the French provision, as article 1104 Fr. Civ. C. already provides that the requirement to act in good faith is of public order ("*ordre public*"). For indeed, article 5.73 Be. Civ. C. states that parties need to perform contract in good faith and that each deviation from this principle will be void. As a deviation from the requirement to act in good faith during negotiation process will have to be contractually stipulated, both the French and the Belgian systems do not allow to contractually deviate from the requirement to act in good faith.

The extent of this prohibition is uncertain: it could either mean that no exoneration of liability for contract negotiations is possible or merely that the liability cannot be excluded in its entirety. French doctrine does not seem to deal with the question in detail, leaving some *flou artistique* as to how to understand it:

> "the text [of article 1112 Fr. Civ. C.] leaves the door open to contractual arrangements to govern the effects of a fault committed during the negotiation period. Adjustments of all kinds are therefore possible, except on one point: the negotiators will not be able to deviate the requirements of good faith that are 'imperatively' imposed, i.e. without any possible derogation. As we already knew from article 1104, paragraph 2."[167]

In my opinion, it seems most plausible that parties cannot discard the duty to act in good faith during contract negotiations in its entirety. That would, as already said, deplete the conduct-based liability of its purpose. This should,

167 Dalloz Commentaire du Code civil (16 avril 2024). Free translation. Original text: "*le texte* [*de l'article 1112 C. civ. Fr.*] *laisse ouverte la porte aux aménagements contractuels propres à régir les effets d'une faute commise lors de la période des négociations. Des aménagements de toutes sortes sont donc possibles, sauf sur un point: les négociateurs ne pourront revenir sur les exigences de bonne foi qui s'imposent 'impérativement', c'est-à-dire sans dérogation possible. Ce qu'on savait déjà à la lecture de l'article 1104, alinéa 2.*"

however, not prevent parties from providing contractually that they are exonerated from certain types of damages or for certain kinds of faults. As the exoneration will generally be interpreted restrictively, only the conduct or damage for which a party has provided can be subject to exoneration.[168] Hence, a general exoneration for all types of faults or damages cannot be considered sufficiently precise in order to be a valid exoneration, but specific exoneration clauses should generally be valid, except where they undermine the negotiation agreement that has been agreed to.

Yet even if one would be inclined to consider that no specific exoneration from the duty to act in good faith would be possible, I would argue that this leaves untouched the specific ground for finding the breaking-off or refusal to contract faulty. Hence, parties could still contractually modify for the extent to which they can be bound to contract in a two-pronged structure of liability for contract negotiations.

168 Clearly explained in W. FIKENTSCHER and A. HEINEMANN, *Schuldrecht Allgemeiner und Besonderer Teil*, Leck, De Gruyter, 2022, p. 315, nr. 516.

4 Sanctions

1. Extent of compensation

1. Full compensation – Compensation must place the party that suffered the harm as close as possible in the situation without the harmful event.[1] In other words, compensation or indemnification – which I use as synonyms – must make good the causal harm. More specifically, it must make good all the harm and nothing but the harm. That is what is designated as *full* compensation of harm,[2] or as Geneviève Viney tellingly formulates it: 'the principle of equivalence between harm and compensation' (*'principe d'équivalence entre dommage et réparation'*).[3] How much that harm is depends on each case specifically and can only be determined for each case specifically. In that sense, the extent of the available compensation will always depend on the harm that is caused. The extent of the caused harm in turn will depend on how the fault has been framed. By way of illustration, here are some examples of sound applications of full compensation in the context of contract negotiations:

(i) In a case in which it is claimed that a party has not voiced concerns on the feasibility of a negotiated project, the wronged party is entitled to get compensation of all the costs engaged as of the moment at which the other party should have voiced its concerns.[4]

(ii) Where a party accepted to enter negotiations of a contract which it could not conclude due to a clause of exclusivity, it must pay damages for the

1 Magnus, "Comparative Report on the Law of Damages." p. 188, nrs. 21–22. For a comparative perspective on Belgian, French, and German law, see Knetsch, "Les effets de la responsabilité et la réparation des dommages. unité ou diversité des formes de réparation dans les projets français et belge. Point de vue du droit allemand." pp. 537–538. Germany: § 249 BGB, Medicus and Lorenz, *Schuldrecht I Allgemeiner Teil*. p. 310, nr. 5. Netherlands: art. 6:103 NBW, Asser/Sieburgh 6-II 2021/21 an 31.

2 Germany: § 249 BGB, Medicus and Lorenz, *Schuldrecht I Allgemeiner Teil*. p. 310, nr. 5. Netherlands: Asser/Sieburgh 6-II 2021/14.

3 Geneviève Viney, "L'appréciation du préjudice," *Petites affiches*, no. 99 (2005). p. 90. Also in Jourdain, *Les principes de la responsabilité civile*. pp. 152–153.

4 Liège, 26 June 2008, *J.L.M.B.* 2011 (442) p. 445.

DOI: 10.4324/9781003599166-7

costs vainly made in preparation of the conclusion of the contract under negotiations. Costs that still had been useful to the conclusion of another contract could not be subject to indemnification.[5]

(iii) Costs made to install a telephone line as required by the negotiating party are compensable harm; costs made subsequently to the breaking-off of negotiations are not compensable.[6]

(iv) Where a party broke-off negotiations very shortly before a planned event for which the harmed party was going to be the caterer, the lost contract with a third party can, in principle, be indemnifiable.[7] However, the proof the court requires in that context is questionable: "However, an award of such damages requires that concrete contract opportunities with third parties were lost at the time of the negotiations, and the court found insufficient evidence of this. Indeed, [plaintiff] did not mention any concrete lost contracts."[8] Requiring actual proof of a concrete lost contract and not merely of the likeliness of an alternative contract appears very restrictive, as, where a party believes that it will be contractually bound, it will not look for an alternative contract.

(v) Costs made after the moment at which the party that ultimately broke-off negotiations should have voiced their discontent about the offered goods and ensuing unlikeliness of contract conclusion are subject to compensation.[9]

More generally speaking, as Patrice Jourdain illustrates, the "costs unnecessarily incurred by the victim of the breaking-off are generally considered to be a certain damage resulting from the fault. These are expenses incurred purely for waste, such as such as study costs, travel expenses, the cost of hiring third-party advisers, experts or consultants, to which should be added the loss of time caused or the loss of working hours of staff who took part in the negotiations."[10]

2. Dependent on fault – That the compensable harm is the causal harm and thus dependent on the fault, as such, is a common place and an almost laconic statement. Olivier Deshayes put it elegantly as follows: "damage is only the shadow

5 Liège, 31 October 2013, 2012/RG/1051, www.juportal.be.

6 Court of Appeal of Paris, 15 June 2022, n° 19/20114.

7 Eerste aanleg Oost Brabant, 12 February 2020, ECLI:NL:RBOBR:2020:1003, nr. 2.6.

8 Eerste aanleg Oost Brabant, 12 February 2020, ECLI:NL:RBOBR:2020:1003, nr. 2.6. Free translation. Original text: "*Voor toewijzing van dergelijke schade is echter wel vereist dat concrete contractsmogelijkheden met derden zijn misgelopen ten tijde van het onderhandelen en daarvan is de rechtbank onvoldoende gebleken. [eiseres] heeft namelijk geen concrete misgelopen contracten genoemd.*"

9 Ger. Arnhem-Leeuwarden, 23 november 2021, 200.272.141, ECLI:NL:GHARL:2021:10837, nr. 4.48.

10 Jourdain, "Préjudice consécutif à la rupture fautive des pourparlers." p. 771. Free translation. Original text: "*les 'frais occasionnés par la négociation et les études préalables'. Ces frais inutilement exposés par la victime de la rupture sont généralement considérés comme un préjudice certain résultant de la faute. Il s'agira des dépenses exposées en pure perte, telles que frais d'études, de déplacement, coût d'intervention de tiers conseils, experts ou consultants, auquel il faudrait ajouter la perte du temps occasionnée ou la perte d'heures de travail du personnel ayant participé aux négociations.*"

of the fault, carried by causality".[11] The German § 249 BGB ("A person who is liable in damages is to restore the position that would exist if the circumstance obliging them to pay damages had not occurred.") or Belgian article 6.31, § 1 Be. Civ. C. ("The aim of compensation for patrimonial loss is to put the injured party in the position he or she would have been in had the event giving rise to liability not occurred.")[12] express this very aptly as well.

This understanding which depends on the invoked fault also lies at the root of the notion of "interest." Indeed, as Friedrich Mommsen explained influentially ("*Differenzhypothese*" *supra* Chap. 3, nr. 36) in 1855,[13] the interest is "the difference between the amount of a person's patrimony as it is at a given time and the amount which this patrimony would have had at the time in question without the intervening occurrence of a certain damaging event."[14] The fault then is the "certain damaging event." However, and for historical reasons (*supra* Chap. 1, nr. 6), this simple and essential rule appears to be often disregarded in the context of contract negotiations. That is the case because harm is commonly framed in terms of positive and negative interest. Inevitably, framing and understanding harm in terms of positive and negative interest must lead to conflicting results with a conduct-based approach. Indeed, differentiating between positive and negative interest departs from two preconceived wrongful elements ("certain damaging event"), the non-performance of a contractual obligation for the positive interest and the conclusion of a void contract for the negative interest, respectively.[15] Relying on these preconceived wrongful elements may be a sensible shortcut in reasoning when applied in the context of a voided contract (as was the case for Jhering) (*supra* Chap. 1, nr. 6) or to organise damages pursuant

11 Deshayes, "Le dommage précontractuel." p. 195, nr. 15. Free translation. Original text: "*Le dommage n'étant que l'ombre de la faute, portée par la causalité.*" In the same sense Durant, "La rupture unilatérale des pourparlers ou l'exercice d'une liberté surveillée." p. 69, nr. 36 and p. 70, nr. 38.

12 Free translation. Original text: "*La réparation du dommage patrimonial vise à placer la personne lésée dans la situation où elle se serait trouvée si le fait générateur de responsabilité ne s'était pas produit.*"/"*Schadeloosstelling voor patrimoniale schade strekt ertoe de benadeelde te plaatsen in de toestand waarin hij zich zou hebben bevonden indien het tot aansprake- lijkheid leidende feit zich niet zou hebben voorgedaan.*"

13 Mommsen, *Beiträge zum Obligationenrecht II: Zur Lehre von dem Interesse.* XIII+301 p.

14 Mommsen, *Beiträge zum Obligationenrecht II: Zur Lehre von dem Interesse.* p. 3. Free translation. Original text: "*die Differenz zwischen dem Betrage des Vermögens einer Person, wie derselbe in einem gegebenen Zeitpunkte ist, und dem Betrage, welchen dieses Vermögen ohne die Dazwischenkunft eines bestimmten beschädigenden Ereignisses in dem zur Frage stehenden Zeitpunkte haben würde.*"

15 Ulrich Magnus states this clearly and from a comparative perspective: "But the assessment of damage in tort and contract is also concerned insofar as in contract, the loss is usually measured by what the creditor would have had, had the contract been properly performed (the expectation or 'positives Interesse'), while in tort the normal measure is the difference to the situation which would have existed had the tort not been committed (the integrity interest or 'negatives Interesse'). The point of reference – the hypothetical situation with which the actual situation is compared in order to assess whether there is a negative difference – therefore varies between tort and contract damage." Magnus, "Comparative Report on the Law of Damages." p. 192, nr. 41. Citations omitted.

non- or bad-performance but does not work outside of that context. Hence, when applied in a different context, as I argued *supra* (Chap. 1, nr. 11), these notions become meaningless and actually are as confusing as unnecessary.

3. Positive and negative interest – A telling example of how unfortunate the framing of positive and negative interest is in the context of contract negotiations is Carsten Nickel's dissertation, *Die Rechtsfolgen der culpa in contrahendo*,[16] in which he insists that compensable harm can always only be defined in relation to the invoked fault.[17] To be able to reconcile this starting point with the thinking in terms of positive and negative interest, he either has to give up on the understanding of causal harm or on any kind of distinctive meaning of positive and negative interest.[18] He does the latter:

> "In this respect, the positive interest is merely a particular manifestation of the damage resulting from the particular damaging event."[19]

> "However, the concept of negative interest is not characterised by a particular manifestation of the negative interest, such as useless expenditure, but by the damaging event. It is therefore not a question of whether compensation for the damage in the individual case is made by cancelling the contract or by reimbursing useless expenses, but rather of what the circumstance obliging compensation is to be seen."[20]

If invoking the notions of positive and negative interest can only lead to actually paddle back to the notion of causal harm, it is unclear why it is relevant to invoke in in the first place. With Francesco Gazzoni:

> "Compensation according to the traditional thesis would concern the so-called negative interest (i.e. not to commence negotiations) and would be limited by the positive interest, in the sense that the *quantum debeatur* could never be higher than what would have been paid if the contract had been concluded and the breach subsequently occurred, but the solution to the problem depends both on the various possible types of breach of good faith and on a correct framing of the interests of the parties at stake."[21]

16 Nickel, *Die Rechtsfolgen der culpa in contrahendo*. 277 p.

17 Nickel, *Die Rechtsfolgen der culpa in contrahendo*. p. 36.

18 Nickel, *Die Rechtsfolgen der culpa in contrahendo*. pp. 37–41.

19 Nickel, *Die Rechtsfolgen der culpa in contrahendo*. p. 40. Free translation. Original text: "*Das positive interesse ist insoweit lediglich eine besondere Erscheinungsform des Schadens, die sich aufgrund des besonderen schädigenden Ereignisses ergibt.*"

20 Nickel, *Die Rechtsfolgen der culpa in contrahendo*. p. 43. Free translation. Original text: "*Der Begriff des negativen Interesses wird jedoch nicht durch eine bestimmte Erscheinungsform des negativen Interesses, wie beispielsweise nutzlose Aufwendungen, geprägt, sondern durch das schädigende Ereignis. Es kommt also nicht darauf an, ob der Ersatz des Schadens im Einzelfall durch Vertragsaufhebung oder durch Ersatz nutzloser Aufwendungen erfolgt, sondern darauf, worin der zum Ersatz verpflichtende Umstand zu sehen ist.*"

21 Gazzoni, *Manuale di diritto privao*. p. 883, nr. 1. Free translation. Original text: "*Il risarcimento secondo la tesi tradizionale riguarerebbe il c.d. interesse negativo (a non iniziare, cioè, la trattative)*

4. Rule-exception relation – That in the context of contract negotiations, the reasoning in terms of negative and positive interest is not helpful (or rather only helpful at first glance) is further sustained by the unhelpful rule-exception relation that the indemnification of, respectively, the negative and positive interest is described in.[22] Indeed, stating that "generally" or "most of the time" the negative interest will be compensated and only in very rare or exceptional cases the positive interest can be compensated does neither allow to clarify *when* nor *what harm* can be compensated. Such a lapidary formula does also not allow to understand what the compensability of either of those interest depends on. Again, this is unsurprising, as harm is not framed in terms of rule-exception relation but based on considerations of causality. That the explanatory note to the reform of the Belgian law of obligations relies on such a rule-exception explanation to dissipate concerns about the principled compensability of the positive interest[23] seems in this light not convincing and certainly not helpful to adjudicators and concerned parties. Indeed, the Belgian legislator has relied on an understanding of compensable harm in terms of the distinction between positive and negative interest in codifying pre-contractual liability in article 5.17 Be. Civ. C. The second alinea reads as follows:

> "In the case of wrongfully broken off negotiations, this liability entails reinstating the injured party to the situation in which it would have found itself had negotiations not taken place. If a legitimate expectation has been created that the contract would have been concluded without any doubt, this liability may include compensation for the loss of the expected net benefits from the contract not concluded."

The text clearly departs from two distinctive fault moments and ties them to two distinctive ways of framing the damage. The first sentence starts from the wrongful breaking-off of negotiations to grant the negative interest; the second

---

e incontrerebbe il limite consituito dall'interesse positivo, nel senso che il quantum debeatur non potrebbe mai essere superiore a quello che sarebbe stato corrisposto in caso di conclusione del contratto e successivo inadempimento, ma la soluzione del problema dipende sia dai vari possibili tipi di violazione della buona fede, sia da un corretto inquadramento degli interessi delle parti in giuoco."

22 In the same sense Nickel, *Die Rechtsfolgen der culpa in contrahendo*. pp. 21–22.

23 "In response to the observations of the *Conseil d'État*, it seems useful to specify that this will only be done in exceptional cases." Explanation to the law of 24 February 2021 containing Book 5 "Obligations" of the Civil code, DOC 55 1806/001, p. 26. Free translation. Original text: "*En réponse aux observations du Conseil d'État, il semble utile de préciser que ceci n'aura lieu que dans des cas exceptionnels.*"/"*In antwoord op de opmerkingen van de Raad van State lijkt het nuttig te preciseren dat dit slechts in uitzonderlijke omstandigheden zal kunnen plaatsvinden.*" See Sophie Stijns, *Verbintenissenrecht Boek 1* (Brugge: die Keure, 2024). nr. 102. Conceptualizing harm in the context of failed negotiations in terms of positive and negative interest is very common under Belgian law. See for instance Brecht Verkempinck, *Schadevergoeding wegens wanprestatie in Europese perspectief* (Brugge: die Keure, 2017). p. 101, nr. 305; Annick De Boeck, "De tussenkomst van de rechter in de precontractuele fase: mogelijkheden en grenzen," in *Le juge et le contrat – De rol van de rechter in het contract*, ed. Sophie Stijns and Patrick Wéry (Brugge: die Keure, 2014). p. 230, nr. 24.

sentence starts from the legitimate expectations of contract conclusion to grant the positive interest.[24] Beside the fact that the first sentence seems to invoke the breaking-off of negotiations itself as fault to then grant the position in which no negotiations would have taken place altogether (*supra* Chap. 3, nr. 15 on the incoherence of such a reasoning), it also seems to grant compensation for all costs made during the negotiation process (*supra* Chap. 3, nr. 40 on the incoherence of such a reasoning). Hence, the general structure of this provision is unfortunate, as it does not allow to assess the specific harm which would be causal to a specific reproached fault, though the explanatory note states that this is what ought to be done.[25] This illustrates that the reasoning in terms of positive and negative interest not only is frustratingly confusing and unhelpful but can actually lead to incoherent legislation.

5. MEANINGLESS TERMINOLOGY – It could, however, be opposed to this criticism that conceptualizing harm in terms of positive and negative interest would be helpful from a pedagogical perspective to the extent that it describes two directions the indemnification of harm can take. However, this argument only holds true on a very superficial level. As soon as one tries to delineate more stringently what exactly the positive or the negative interest might be in a specific case, it becomes very unclear where the positive and the negative interest begins and ends.[26] That, again, is unsurprising, as they have no strict legal meaning; they merely are pedagogical terms which generalize an underlying legal reasoning.[27]

24 Explanation to the law of 24 February 2021 containing Book 5 "Obligations" of the Civil Code, DOC 55 1806/001, p. 26.

25 "Only damages that have a causal link with the culpable breach of negotiations are taken into account for compensation purposes. For example, compensation for negative interest includes expenses incurred that have become unnecessary and the loss of the opportunity to conclude a contract with a third party. On the other hand, expenses that would have been incurred in any event are not eligible for compensation." Explanation to the law of 24 February 2021 containing Book 5 "Obligations" of the Civil Code, DOC 55 1806/001, p. 26. Free translation. Original versions: "*Seuls les dommages ayant un lien de causalité avec la rupture fautive des négociations entrent en considération pour l'indemnisation. Par exemple, la réparation de l'intérêt négatif inclut les frais engagés devenus inutiles et la perte de l'opportunité de conclure un contrat avec un tiers. En revanche, des dépenses qui auraient été exposées en toute hypothèse n'entrent pas en ligne de compte pour l'indemnisation.*"/"*Enkel schade die in oorzakelijk verband staat met het foutief afbreken van de onderhandelingen komt voor vergoeding in aanmerking. Het herstel van het negatief contractbelang omvat bijvoorbeeld de gemaakte kosten die nutteloos geworden zijn en het verlies van een kans op een contract met een derde. Uitgaven die men sowieso gemaakt zou hebben, komen daarentegen niet voor vergoeding in aanmerking.*"

26 As deplored by Deshayes, "Le dommage précontractuel." p. 189.

27 The same is true for the notion of reliance interest, generally taken to be a synonym of the negative interest, as Giannina Kreutz states in her dissertation, *Hypothetische Verträge im Rahmen des Schadensausgleichs*: "Since culpa in contrahendo is generally based on aspects of trust, trust in the contractual partner and his information or in the conclusion of the contract is also disappointed in this respect. The damage resulting from the breach of trust must be compensated. The synonymy of these two terms can be understood from this point of view. However, the concept of trust is not very meaningful and has no contours, as the damage can also be based on aspects of trust when positive interest is granted." Kreutz, *Hypothetische Verträge im Rahmen des Schadensausgleichs*. p. 42. Free translation. Original text: "*Da*

Ultimately, it is unclear why a classification in terms of negative and positive interest matters at all, to the extent that the relevant test for assessing which harm is indemnifiable is never dependent on whether suffered harm can be labelled as negative or positive interest but on whether it has been *caused* by the reproached fault. With Gianna Kreutz:

> "Irrespective of trying to classify possible compensation, one must be guided by the wording of the law, according to which the injuring party must restore the condition that would exist if the circumstance obliging compensation had not occurred. A variety of legal consequences are conceivable. The categorisation into positive, negative interest or reliance damage is of secondary importance."[28]

Or with Stephan Lorenz:

> "For the fulfilment of liability under §§ 280 I, 311 II, 241 II [*culpa in contrahendo*], it is regularly stated that this is directed towards compensation for the negative interest, i.e. the reliance harm. This is entirely correct in the vast majority of cases but can be confusing as a rule in some groups of cases in which liability for the positive interest, i.e. the performance interest, is also recognised. It is better to simply apply the difference hypothesis of § 249 I: The injured party is to be placed in the position he would have been in if the damaging event had not occurred."[29]

---

die culpa in contrahendo generell auf Vertrauensgesichtspunkten beruht, wird insoweit auch jeweils Vertrauen in den Vertragspartner und seine Informationen btw. in den Vertragsschluss enttäuscht. Der Schade, der aus der Verletzung des Vertrauens resultiert, muss ersetzt werden. Unter diesem Gesichtspunkt versteht sich die Synonymie dieser beiden Begriffe. Jedoch ist der Begriff des Vertrauens wenig aussagekräftig und konturenlos, da auch bei der Gewährung des positiven Interesses der Schaden auf Vertrauensgesichtspunkten beruhen kann." As her dissertation deals with the questions of detrimentally concluded contracts and not failed contract conclusion, it is understandable that the notions of negative and positive interest are more sensible to her.

28 Kreutz, *Hypothetische Verträge im Rahmen des Schadensausgleichs*. p. 44. Free translation. Original version: "*Unabhängig von der Klassifizierung eines möglichen Schadensersatzes muss man sich an den Wortlaut des Gesetzes orientieren, wonach der Schädigen den Zustand herzustellen hat, der bestehen würde, wenn der zum Ersatz verpflichtende Umstand nicht eingetreten wäre. Hierbei ist eine Vielzahl von Rechtsfolgen denkbar. Die Einordnung in positives, negatives Interesse oder Vertrauensschaden hat dabei nachrangige Bedeutung.*"

29 Lorenz, "Grundwissen – Zivilrecht: Culpa in contrahendo (§ 311 II, III BGB)." pp. 398–399. Free translation. Original text: "*Für die Ausfüllung der Haftung aus §§ 280 I, 311 II, 241 II [culpa in contrahendo] wird regelmäßig dargelegt, dass diese auf Ersatz des negativen Interesses, dh des Vertrauensschadens gerichtet ist. Das ist in der großen Mehrzahl der Fälle durchaus zutreffend, kann aber in manchen Fallgruppen, in welchen auch eine Haftung auf das positive Interesse, dh das Erfüllungsinteresse anerkannt ist, als Regel verwirrend sein. Besser ist es, schlicht auf die Differenzhypothese des § 249 I abzustellen: Der Geschädigte ist so zu stellen, wie er stünde, wenn das schädigende Ereignis nicht eingetreten wäre.*" Identical in Medicus and Lorenz, *Schuldrecht I Allgemeiner Teil*. p. 243, nr. 9: "For the content of liability in the event of a breach of a pre-contractual obligation under § 280 I, § 311 II, III, idem II, it is regularly stated that this is aimed at compensation for the negative interest,

6. *DAMNUM EMERGENS* AND *LUCRUM CESSANS* AND POSITIVE AND NEGATIVE INTEREST – A last misunderstanding resulting from thinking in terms of positive and negative interest is to understand the distinction between *damnum emergens* and *lucrum cessans* (*supra* Chap. 3, nr. 31) to coincide with the distinction between, respectively, negative and positive interest:

> "The use of the 'negative interest' assessment method was first proposed in Germany in relation to the consequences of the wrongful termination of contractual negotiations, but it subsequently developed in England, the United States and many other countries, not only in this particular area, but also in relation to the calculation of compensation due following the termination or cancellation of a contract attributable to the fault of one of the partners. This method leads to the denial of compensation for the profits that the victim could have hoped to obtain from the proper performance of the contract that was not performed."[30]

Yet this assimilation is an oversimplification and, by the way, rests on an erroneous understanding of the origin of the notion of negative interest (*supra* Chap. 1, nr. 6). Indeed, the positive and negative interest describe a certain pre-fixed understanding of how to frame damage, while the distinction between *damnum emergens* and *lucrum cessans* merely clarifies that loss consists not only in actual loss but also in lost advantages. Carla Sieburgh illustrates this:

> "The distinction between incurred loss and lost profit does not coincide with that between negative and positive interest. In principle, the

i.e. the loss of confidence. This is quite correct in the vast majority of cases, but can be confusing as a rule in some groups of cases in which liability for the positive interest, i.e. the interest in performance, is also recognised. It is better to simply apply the difference hypothesis of idem I: The injured party is to be placed in the position he would have been in if the damaging event had not occurred." Free translation. Original text: "*Für den Inhalt der Haftung bei der Verletzung einer vorvertraglichen Pflicht aus idem I, § 311 II, III, § 241 II wird regelmäßig dargelegt, dass diese auf Ersatz des negativen Interesses, d.h. des Vertrauensschadens gerichtet ist. Das ist in der großen Mehrzahl der Fälle durchaus zutreffend, kann aber in manchen Fallgruppen, in welchen auch eine Haftung auf das positive Interesse, d.h. das Erfüllungsinteresse anerkannt ist, als Regel verwirrend sein. Besser ist es, schlicht auf die Differenzhypothese des idem I abzustellen: Der Geschädigte ist so zu stellen, wie er stünde, wenn das schädigende Ereignis nicht eingetreten wäre.*"

30 Viney, "L'appréciation du préjudice." p. 89. Free translation. Original text: "*l'utilisation de la méthode d'appréciation en fonction de l'intérêt dit 'négatif' a été proposée d'abord en Allemagne à propos des conséquences de la rupture fautive de pourparlers contractuels, mais elle s'est ensuite développée en Angleterre, aux États-Unis et dans beaucoup d'autres pays non seulement dans ce domaine particulier, mais aussi à propos du calcul des indemnités dues à la suite de la résolution ou de l'annulation d'un contrat imputable à la faute de l'un des partenaires. Or cette méthode conduit à refuser la compensation des profits que la victime pouvait espérer obtenir de l'exécution correcte du contrat qui n'a pas été exécuté.*" See for other illustrations of such a confused overlap of positive and negative interest and *damnum emergens* and *lucrum cessans* in case law in Cass.civ.it., 15 December 2023, nr. 35170 or in scholarship in Durant, "La rupture unilatérale des pourparlers ou l'exercice d'une liberté surveillée." pp. 69 *et seq*, nrs. 37 *et seq*.; Viney, "L'appréciation du préjudice." pp. 99–100; or Deshayes, "Le dommage précontractuel." p. 189 *et seq*., nrs. 2 *et seq*.

former distinction is relevant for any form of liability, the latter especially for contractual liability. In case of breach of contract, the debtor is obliged to compensate the so-called positive contractual interest, i.e. the creditor must be put in the position by the compensation as if the contract had been properly performed. Indeed, his entire loss should be compensated. . . . If the creditor has lost profit due to the non-performance (which need not be the case; see the examples given above), then he must be compensated. The negative contractual interest is the damage suffered by the creditor compared to the situation he would have been in if no contract had been concluded; one thinks of the case where the contract is void or annulled ab initio, while the debtor is liable in tort in respect thereof. . . . In this case, there will usually only be loss, but loss of profit is not excluded, albeit not loss of profit due to non-performance of the contract, but loss of profit due to an act or omission connected with the conclusion of the contract. Consider the case where, in connection with the conclusion of the void or subsequently annulled contract, the creditor did not conclude another contract that would have yielded him a profit, or where he collected the goods purchased in time, or stored them in warehouses, which he could otherwise have used profitably;"[31]

2. Means of compensation

7. Priority – Different legal systems give priority to different means of compensation. In most systems (France, the Netherlands (article 6:103 NBW), Italy), monetary compensation is the principle, while compensation in kind is the exception. In Belgium and Germany (§§ 249 and 251 BGB), it is the other way

31 Asser/Sieburgh 6-II 2021/26. Free translation. Original text: "*De onderscheiding tussen geleden verlies en gederfde winst valt niet samen met die tussen negatief en positief belang. De eerstgenoemde onderscheiding is in beginsel relevant voor iedere vorm van aansprakelijkheid, de laatstgenoemde vooral voor contractuele aansprakelijkheid. In geval van wanprestatie is de schuldenaar verplicht tot vergoeding van het zogenoemde positive contractsbelang, dat wil zeggen de schuldeiser moet door de schadevergoeding in de positie worden gebracht alsof het contract behoorlijk was nagekomen. Zijn gehele schade dient immers te worden vergoed; . . . Heeft de schuldeiser door de niet-nakoming winst gederfd (hetgeen niet het geval behoeft te zijn; zie de boven gegeven voorbeelden), dan moet deze hem worden vergoed. Negatief contractsbelang is de schade die de schuldeiser lijdt ten opzichte van de situatie waarin hij zou hebben verkeerd als geen overeenkomst zou zijn gesloten; men denke aan het geval dat de overeenkomst ab initio nietig is of vernietigd wordt, terwijl de schuldenaar ter zake daarvan uit onrechtmatige daad aansprakelijk is. . . . In dit geval zal doorgaans slechts sprake zijn van geleden verlies, doch gederfde winst is niet uitgesloten, zij het dan dat hierbij niet moet worden gedacht aan het derven van winst ten gevolge van het niet-nakomen van de overeenkomst, doch ten gevolge van een handelen of nalaten dat met het sluiten van de overeenkomst samenhangt. Men denke aan het geval dat de schuldeiser in verband met het sluiten van de nietige of later vernietigde overeenkomst een andere overeenkomst die hem winst zou hebben opgeleverd, niet heeft gesloten, of dat hij de gekochte goederen heeft opgehaald in tijd, of opgeslagen in opslagruimte, die hij anders winstgevend had kunnen benutten.*"

round.[32] Though their starting points differ, the outcomes are said to be relatively identical insofar as systems prioritizing monetary compensation allow for compensation in kind, while – inversely – compensation in kind will be discarded where it is impossible or abusive under systems prioritizing compensation in kind.[33] Be that as it may, whether the outcomes are distinct or identical depending on which system one choses does not matter much for the present purpose. As a matter of fact, compensating pure economic loss will always be done by way of monetary compensation. Hence, all compensation of harm suffered in the contract negotiations will be monetary.

Given the focus on pure economic loss (*supra* Chap. 3, nr. 30), the means to compensate other types of harm does not need to be addressed.

32 Magnus, "Comparative Report on the Law of Damages." p. 188, nr. 25. For a comparative view on the Belgian and French reform projects from a German perspective, see Knetsch, "Les effets de la responsabilité et la réparation des dommages. unité ou diversité des formes de réparation dans les projets français et belge. Point de vue du droit allemand." pp. 538–540.

33 Sébastien De Rey, *Herstel in Natura. Rechtsvergelijkende studie in het contractenrecht met buitencontractuele invalshoek* (Brugge: die Keure, 2019). p. 5, nr. 5; Magnus, "Comparative Report on the Law of Damages." p. 189, nr. 26.

5 Findings

1. The structure of liability for contract negotiations, common to all analysed legal systems, is that of a conduct-based liability, i.e. a threefold requirement of fault, harm, and a causal link between fault and harm. In this sense, liability for contract negotiations is a plain and simple application of either contractual or extra-contractual liability – relative to the type of extra-contractual liability a legal system knows. This latter finding – that the legal basis of liability for contract negotiations depends on the respective national extra-contractual liability law system – is important both for scholars in order to better understand liability for contract negotiations and for legislators to better conceive liability for contract negotiations.
2. The fact that liability for contract negotiations is such a plain and simple application of the respective conduct-based liability law brings about an important finding: the breaking-off of contract negotiations or the refusal to contract itself as fault cannot give rise to liability. However, the explanation for the impossibility of the breaking-off or refusal giving rise to liability lies not in the fact that the breaking-off or refusal itself is the exercise of freedom from contract and, therefore, cannot be wrongful. Instead, it is the normative causal uncertainty that explains this impossibility: given the principled freedom from contract, suffered harm cannot causally be linked to the breaking-off or the refusal to contract.
3. Other than this important insight, which, in fact, is merely the application of the principles of conduct-based liability law systems, liability for contract negotiations calls for no other specifications. A rigorous and clean application of the principles of conduct-based liability law systems should prove sufficient to delineate liability and compensation convincingly and coherently. This also means that the understanding of recoverable harm as, in principle, being the negative interest and, in exceptional cases, the positive interest can and should be abandoned (*supra* nrs. Chap. 4, nrs. 2–5). Both notions are taken out of their original context and lead to more confusion than clarification. This is sadly proven by the recently codified article 5.17 of the Belgian Civil Code. Had its first alinea – which states that pre-contractual liability is an application of extra-contractual liability – been codified, the system would have been much clearer and more coherent. The addition of the second alinea mainly brings

DOI: 10.4324/9781003599166-8

about confusion and incoherencies. They can be resolved by interpreting the provision, as much as possible, as a mere illustration of the first alinea, as seemingly intended by the drafting committee.

4. This preceding point is of particularly great practical and conceptual importance. It is, in fact, quite exasperating to see to what extent the delimitation of compensable harm is ill guided in many legal systems. Often, the laudable aim of excluding from compensation the expected benefit under the negotiated contract is done along the wrong vectors or variables, namely, the understanding of harm. That is done by excluding the *lucrum cessans* from compensation, though it should not be (*supra* Chap. 3, nr. 31), or by restricting harm to the negative interest, a notion which really does not make much sense in the context of failed contract negotiations (*supra* Chap. 4, nrs. 3–5). In a plain application of conduct-liability law, this delimitation is performed in a very concise and relatively objectifiable manner based on causality. My hypothesis for explaining this bizarre disregard for causality to delimit compensable harm is that this means of delimitation cannot work properly where the breaking-off itself is invoked as a wrongful element. Hence, judges and scholars turn to these approximative explanations based on *lucrum cessans* or positive/negative interest. Once it is established that it is not the breaking-off or refusal to contract which can give rise to liability, causality can be reinstated in fulfilling – and much more convincingly so – the compensable harm. It may at times be a bit of a brain breaker to exactly single out the harm that is causally linked to the invoked fault but offers a very case-related and convincing delimitation of compensable harm.
5. In light of the functions of liability for contract negotiations, it perfectly allows to protect the financial interests of a party suffering the failure of contract negotiations, as pure economic loss can be indemnified. However, liability for contract negotiations falls short to protect the freedom of contract of the party suffering the failure of negotiations, as it cannot be based on the breaking-off of contract negotiations or the refusal to contract itself. Henceforth, it cannot provide any remedies which allow to counter the exercise of the freedom from contract. Given how politically and socio-economically important this question is, this may be perceived as a shortcoming of liability for contract negotiations. In the following part, I will, therefore, deal with some tricks used to overcome the normative causal uncertainty (*infra* Chap. 6, nrs. 1–32), which precisely stands in the way of declaring the breaking-off or refusing itself as fault giving rise to liability. To a certain extent, these tricks may help to lessen this potential flaw. More importantly, I will deal with a way of addressing the issue upfront and convincingly overcoming this potential flaw, namely, by recognizing an obligation to contract (*infra* nrs. Chap. 6, nr. 36-Chap. 7, nr. 27).

Part III

Obligation to negotiate or to contract

6 Circumventing causal uncertainty

1. Hiding causal uncertainty

1.1. Overview of existing approaches

1. Overview – The preceding part of this book has shown that the breaking-off of negotiations or the refusal to contract itself cannot give rise to liability in a conduct-based liability law. That is so due to the normative causal uncertainty flowing from freedom from contract. As this can be perceived as impractical, out of touch with reality, and generally unsatisfactory, ways of overcoming this technical – yet inevitable – impediment have been developed in the different legal systems. All of these approaches must allow to overcome or circumvent this causal uncertainty but do not necessarily do so by directly acting on the causal link; they can also rely on a different understanding of the invoked fault or harm.

I will first present some little hacks, so to say, which require no extensive introduction, namely, tweaking the construction of the fault (*infra* Chap. 6, nrs. 4–7), the standardization of the compensable harm (*infra* Chap. 6, nrs. 8–9), and relying on the degree of certainty necessary for evidentiary law (*infra* Chap. 6, nr. 10–11). Then I will discuss two approaches which require some more conceptual explanation: the loss of a chance (*infra* Chap. 6, nr. 12–24) and the prohibition of abuse of rights (*infra* Chap. 6, nrs. 25–35).

2. *De lege lata* – These approaches consist in tweaks or tricks within the respective legal system or some specific doctrines which primarily (loss of a chance) or incidentally (abuse of rights) make it possible to overcome causal uncertainty. Me discussing these tricks is meant to be descriptive of the existing (*de lege lata*) practice and placing them in context. This should allow to understand them in light of the function they fulfil – overcoming causal uncertainty – while also indicating that a more open and transparent approach (an obligation, or even better, *Obliegenheit*, to contract) is preferable.

3. Necessity to protect freedom of contract – It seems important, at this point, to clarify that I am not opposed to holding a party liable for the breaking-off of negotiations or the refusal to contract. I merely point out that to be able to do so, a conduct-based liability law system alone does not suffice.

DOI: 10.4324/9781003599166-10

Instead, it would be soundest and most coherent to recognize that in some cases, an obligation to contract exists. Doing so would allow to open the debate on which grounds such an obligation to contract should be recognized.

1.2. Construction of fault

4. TWO APPROACHES – In light of the impossibility of having the breaking-off or the refusal itself be the wrongful element giving rise to liability, two alternatives exist: either choosing another wrongful element than the breaking-off or refusal itself or implying an obligation to contract or negotiate. I have dealt with both *supra* (Chap. 3, nr. 15–16) and only will briefly analyse them in the present context.
5. FAULT IN THE CIRCUMSTANCES – A common approach, and a perfectly acceptable one, is to locate the fault not in the breaking-off or refusal itself but in its circumstances. In finding and establishing alternative faults, parties are virtually free if they can convince the judge. Importantly, however, the way parties frame the fault will affect the compensable harm.
6. LEGITIMATE EXPECTATIONS – The liberty parties enjoy in framing the fault should stop, however, where it implies an obligation which does not stem from one of the accepted sources of obligations within the legal system in question. That is typically the case, where the *deception* of legitimate expectations is relied upon as fault. By framing the fault in this way, parties overcome causal uncertainty, as the whole reasoning pre-supposes that parties no longer were free to break-off negotiations – as is clearly stated under Dutch law (*supra* Chap. 2, nr. 34). A reasoning that relies on legitimate expectations, provided it is clearly admitted as a source of obligations, is acceptable. Where however, it is hidden away, such a reasoning is inacceptable, as it conceals the creation of an obligation *ex nihilo*.
7. CONCLUSION OF THE CONTRACT – Building forth on the fault of deceiving legitimate expectations, as is the case under Dutch law (*supra* Chap. 2, nr. 34), framing the fault as the deception of legitimate expectations should have as remedy the conclusion of the negotiated contract, either in kind or by way of damages. However, that is generally considered as too far reaching and, therefore, must be artificially limited by explaining that compensable harm is limited to the negative interest.

1.3. Standardization of compensable harm

8. THINKING IN POSITIVE AND NEGATIVE INTEREST – Interestingly, thinking in terms of positive and negative interest appears as another way of circumventing causal uncertainty. The reasoning in terms of positive and negative interest, as already explained (*supra* Chap. 1, nrs. 6 and 11 and Chap. 4, nr. 2), departs from a fixed fault from which the harm causal to that fixed wrongful element is described by the positive or negative interest. If then, as is for instance stated in article 5.17 Be. Civ. C. ("In the case of wrongfully broken off negotiations, this liability entails reinstating the injured party to the situation in which it would have found itself had negotiations not

taken place."[1]), that the consequence of wrongfully breaking-off is the compensation of the negative interest, parties no longer *need* to establish a causal link, as the fault of breaking-off suffices to give rise to the described legal consequences.

9. PRE-EMPTIVE ASSESSMENT OF CAUSAL HARM – Strikingly, the just-described approach side-lines to a large extent the general requirements of liability law. Whether such a deviation from liability law is acceptable, seems doubtful. Of course, if it is statutorily provided for as is the case under Belgian law, this seems to be acceptable. Under German law, this practice may possibly also be somewhat easier to get through since, in the contractual realm, causality is not a matter of the existence of a claim, but merely of the extent of the compensation (*supra* Chap. 3, nrs. 33–34). Hence, it may be less obvious that by framing harm in terms of positive and negative interest, the requirement of causality is side-lined.

1.4. Standard of proof

10. JURIDICAL CERTAINTY – The framing of the fault and the standardization of compensable harm both conceal the causal uncertainty. A different approach lies in admitting causal issues but trying to overcome them by referring to the applicable standard of proof. Indeed, an argument occasionally invoked[2] is that causality must never be proven with scientific certainty but only as a legal certainty and the according standard of proof (reasonable certainty or

1 "*En cas de rupture fautive des négociations, cette responsabilité implique que la personne lésée soit remise dans la situation dans laquelle elle se serait trouvée s'il n'y avait pas eu de négociations.*"/"*Bij foutief afbreken van onderhandelingen houdt deze aansprakelijkheid in dat de benadeelde teruggeplaatst wordt in de situatie waarin hij zich zou hebben bevonden indien er niet zou zijn onderhandeld.*"

2 Isabel Durant provides a quite unprecise and confusing, but in essence, representative, example of such an argumentation: "Despite this, some authors do not exclude the idea of lucrum cessans compensation if the circumstances were to lead the court to decide that the contract would indeed have been concluded if there had been no breakdown in negotiations, given that the parties had reached a point of no return at the time of the breakdown. In absolute terms, we can follow them, as we know that judicial certainty is never absolute certainty. Rather, it is a certainty that, given the specific facts of the case, excludes doubt; it can be likened to a high degree of probability or even to a very high degree of likelihood." Durant, "La rupture unilatérale des pourparlers ou l'exercice d'une liberté surveillée." p. 75, nr. 43. Citations omitted. Free translation. Original text: "*Malgré tout, certains auteurs n'excluent pas l'idée d'une réparation du lucrum cessons si les circonstances devaient amener le juge à décider que le contrat aurait bel et bien été conclu s'il n'y avait pas eu de rupture des négociations, compte tenu de ce que les parties auraient atteint, au moment où celle-ci intervint, un point de non-retour. Dans l'absolu, on peut les suivre, la certitude judiciaire, on le sait, n'est en effet jamais une certitude absolue. Il s'agit plutôt d'une certitude qui, compte tenu des données propres à l'espèce, exclut le doute; elle peut-être assimilée à un haut degré de probabilité ou encore à une très forte vraisemblance.*" She confuses *lucrum cessans* with the positive interest and brings in a point of no-return, which, in fact, must be seen as working with an obligation to contract, in which case, the causal alternative scenario is fixed, making the question of the actual hypothetical alternative scenario moot anyways.

something comparable). Hence, as long as it can be made reasonably certain that absent the breaking-off of negotiations, a contract would have been concluded, a causal link would be established.

11. NORMATIVE UNCERTAINTY – This argument is fallacious: precisely because a legal causal link must be established, and because a normatively uncertain causal link bares liability in the case of the breaking-off of negotiations or refusal to contract, liability for contract negotiations fails to protect the freedom of contract of the party suffering the failure of contract conclusion. Hence, the indication that merely judicial causal certainty is required does not, by any means, solve the issue.

2. Loss of a chance

2.1. The doctrine

12. LOSING A CHANCE – The "idea," as Nils Jansen puts it,[3] of loss of a chance is that someone's harm lies not in what he *actually* has lost but in having lost a *chance* not to have suffered that loss. Loss being either missing a benefit or incurring a disadvantage (*supra* Chap. 3, nr. 31), the loss of a chance designates the loss of a chance either to some form of benefit or not to incur a disadvantage. A typical example is the owner of a stable who, due to some fault, could not have one of his horses participate in a race. He lost a chance of his horse winning the race. This shift of focus from the actual harm to a lost chance is debatable[4] and thus – quite unsurprisingly so – not commonly accepted.[5] Relevantly for the present purpose, loss of a chance is accepted as harm in Belgium, France, Italy, and the Netherlands but not under German law.[6] The Belgian reform actually codified the loss of a chance in article 6.22 Be. Civ. C.:

> "Where it is not certain that the fault committed by the person claimed to be liable is a necessary condition of the damage, because the damage

3 Jansen, "The Idea of a Lost Chance." pp. 271–296.

4 Clear under Dutch law (Asser/Sieburgh 6-II 2021/79.) or under French law (Brun, *Responsabilité civile extracontractuelle*. pp. 131–132, nr. 190.). See f.i. the recent disserations on the subject under French law (Laura Vitale, *La Perte de Chances en Droit Privé* (Paris: LGDJ, 2020). XVI+581p.) and Belgian law (Céline Joisten, *L'incertitude causale en droit de la responsabilité civile* (Bruxelles: Larcier-Intersentia, 2024). 823 p.).

5 Comparative overview in Deshayes, "Le dommage précontractuel." p. 192, nr. 8.

6 German extra-contractual liability law relies on an unlawfulness-based liability law system. Along with this unlawfulness-based system comes a double requirement for a causal link: a first one to establish liability ("*haftungsbegründende Kausalität*") between the culpable conduct and the infringed protected absolute right and a second to establish the extent of liability ("*haftungsausfüllende Kausalität*") between the infringed right and the actual harm. (Lange and Schiemann, *Schadensersatz*. p. 77.) For a brief overview: Scholz, "Haftungsbegründende und haftungsausfüllende Kausalität im Zivil- und Zivilprozessrecht." pp. 914–917. In this regard, Nils Jansen considers the question to be "whether a lost chance in itself could be a harm generating recovery (*Haftungsbegründung*). In

> could also have occurred if that person had behaved lawfully rather than committing a fault, the injured party is entitled to partial compensation in proportion to the probability that the fault caused the damage."[7]

Without going into much detail, I will briefly explain how framing harm as the loss of a chance functions (*infra* Chap. 6, nr. 13–17) to then discuss how it could apply in the context of failed contract negotiations or conclusion (*infra* Chap. 6, nrs. 18–22).

German legal terms, our question is whether a lost potential benefit or the lost chance of avoiding a final injury or damage constitute a legally acknowledged harm." (Jansen, "The Idea of a Lost Chance." p. 291. In much detail discussed in Vitale, *La Perte de Chances en Droit Privé*. p. 308 *et seq.*, nrs. 579 *et seq.*) This perspective seems also to have been the one the Swiss Federal Supreme Court took (*supra* Chap. 6, nr. 5). Yet I think that the answer to this question is negative precisely because of the required double causal link. A lost chance, in and of itself, does not seem to be a protected right under § 823 (1) BGB; only the actual harm towards which the lost chance is a causal extension *can* – conceptually speaking – constitute an infringement of a protected right. Take, for instance, the case of the horse unable to participate in a horse race. The infringed right here is the patrimony (be it that the patrimony itself is not a protected right under German law). The whole point of the loss of a chance idea is to distinguish the chance from the actual harm. (Holger Fleischer, "Schadensersatz für verlorene Chancen im Vertrags- und Deliktsrecht," *JZ* 54, no. 15/16 (1999). p. 769.) Where this implies to establish a causal link with the infringed right before establishing a causal link with the harm, the trick turns against itself: if, and to the extent that, a causal link must be established between the conduct and the infringement of the protected right, this can never be done by interposing a lost chance. By consequence, and even independently of the normative question about the value of a chance, sneaking in a lost chance cannot do the trick, where a distinct causal link is required between the conduct and the infringed absolute right. The same argument goes *a fortiori*, where a distinct causal link would be required between the conduct and the infringement of an interest.

As far as I can see, this structural argument is not made in the consulted relevant scholarship, which should induce scepticism about it. However, in my understanding, it appears plausible.

An important consequence of understanding that, and how, the loss of a chance idea is structurally unimplementable in German law allows to nuance this impossibility. Indeed, if it is – at least from a structural perspective and thus leaving aside policy consideration – due to the requirement of a double causal link that the loss of a chance doctrine cannot be implemented, then this is only valid for the liability under § 823 and, it seems to me, even only to § 823 (1) BGB. (Seems confirmed in Lange and Schiemann, *Schadensersatz*. p. 77.) By consequence, it would not apply under contractual liability (a development on how loss of a chance would apply in the contractual context under German law in Gerald Mäsch, *Chance und Schaden* (Tübingen: Mohr Siebeck, 2004). p. 239 *et seq.*) – a conduct-based liability which merely requires a single causal link (Scholz, "Haftungsbegründende und haftungsausfüllende Kausalität im Zivil- und Zivilprozessrecht." p. 915.) – and thus also in the context of contract negotiations. Hence, structurally, the loss of a chance of a future contract could be invoked in the context of failed contract conclusion.

7 Free translation. Original text: "*Lorsqu'il n'est pas certain que la faute commise par la personne dont la responsabilité est invoquée est une condition nécessaire du dommage parce que le dommage aurait pu se produire également si cette personne s'était comportée de manière licite plutôt que de commettre une faute, la personne lésée a droit à une réparation partielle en proportion de la probabilité que cette faute ait causé le dommage.*"/"*Wanneer het onzeker is of de fout van de persoon die wordt aangesproken een noodzakelijke voorwaarde is voor de schade omdat de schade zich ook kon hebben voorgedaan indien deze persoon zich rechtmatig had gedragen eerder dan een fout te begaan, heeft de be- nadeelde recht op een gedeeltelijke schadeloosstelling voor de schade in verhouding tot de waarschijnlijkheid waarmee de fout de schade heeft veroorzaakt.*"

13. Two components: loss and chance – To lose a chance, one must have had a chance.[8] Hence, a person must have had a chance which he subsequently lost. To be able to delimit the loss of a chance doctrine, it then matters to know more specifically *what a chance is* and when it can be considered to having been lost. This is subject to much scholarly debate, and I need not go in detail into it.[9] What matters for the present purpose is to understand how the "idea" of a loss of a chance functions, namely, in two times: first, by interposing a chance and, second, by considering that chance as valuable.

14. The trick: interposing a chance – The loss of a chance doctrine can be relevant/useful whenever a party is unable to establish a causal link between the wrongful element and the harm – lost benefits in the case of the race of the horse. Then instead of framing its harm in terms of the lost benefit, one can do so in terms of losing a chance to those benefits. By interposing a lost chance as harm, where no causal link can be established between the fault and the actual harm that has been suffered, the unanswerable question of whether the "actual" harm was causal can be left aside.[10] Importantly, this lost chance, as damage itself, is distinct from the "actual" damage.[11]

15. and considering it valuable – This trick, however, only works to the extent that a chance is considered valuable. Indeed, only if a chance had a value, can losing it be considered a loss (*supra* Chap. 3, nr. 31). The Swiss Federal Supreme Court, for instance, considered that chances are no valuable patrimonial assets and could thus not constitute harm.[12] To overcome such difficulties, scholars argue that a chance is a right[13] or, in general, indicate that chances can be

8 W. Thijmen Nuninga, "Het recht op een kans," *NTBR*, no. 8 (2019). p. 45.

9 I just refer to one take on the issue, as it is comparative in nature, recent in date, and may prove a useful starting point to the reader who wants to deepen his understanding. Nuninga et al. state that "for the doctrine of loss of a chance to logically apply," it "is required that (i) the claimant has a chance of improving his or her position and (ii) the claimant must have been prevented from exercising that chance." (W. Thijmen Nuninga et al., "Chances as Legally Protected Assets," *ERPL* (2020). p. 400, nr. 47.) A chance, in this context, supposes an uncertainty relating to how things would have gone; "'Having a chance' requires that there is some uncertainty as to whether the position of the relevant individual will improve or not. There must be some ex ante uncertainty in the outcome even in the absence of the wrongful act" (Nuninga et al., "Chances as Legally Protected Assets." p. 396, nr. 39.).

10 Jansen, "The Idea of a Lost Chance." p. 283. Followed by Christoph Müller, *La perte d'une chance* (Bern: Staempfli editions, 2002). p. 240, nr. 340.

11 Belgian law: Bocken, Boone, and Kruithof, *Inleiding tot het schadevergoedingsrecht*. p. 48, nr. 73. Dutch law: Asser/Sieburgh 6-II 2021/80a; Nuninga, "Het recht op een kans." p. 43. French law: Brun, *Responsabilité civile extracontractuelle*. p. 131, nr. 188. German law: Mäsch, *Chance und Schaden*. p. 248; Fleischer, "Schadensersatz für verlorene Chancen im Vertrags- und Deliktsrecht." p. 769. Italy: Daniela M. Frenda, "Il danno da mancata realizzazione di un risultato atteso: ai confini tra la perdita di chances e il lucro cessante?" *Danno e responsabilità* no. 1 (2024). p. 16.

12 BGE 133 III 462 p. 471.

13 "Its [the loss of a chance] significance is to establish chances of avoiding a final injury or of obtaining a final gain *as personal rights*. . . . English and German law should both acknowledge the loss of a chance as a harm giving rise to a tort law claim." Jansen, "The Idea of a Lost Chance." p. 296. Own italics. A discussion of his article in Mäsch, *Chance und Schaden*. p. 230. Why a chance must be considered as a right, however, is not made explicit. Without reference to Jansen, the idea of chances

valuable.[14] Ultimately, as Nils Jansen stresses, that is a normative question: "People apparently do think that chances are important things to be legally protected."[15]

So systems that do allow for the loss of a chance doctrine – as is the case under Belgian, French, Italian, and Dutch law – consider chances to be valuable. More precisely, the chance is given the value of the percentage of the chance to have prevented the occurrence of the "actual" harm. In the case of the horse not participating in a race, the chance for the horse to win the race, had it participated, was, for instance, of 30%. The lost chance to win the race is valued at 30% of the scenario of winning the race. By interposing a chance as harm *and* by quantifying the chance in function to the actual harm that cannot be causally linked, at least the percentage of likeliness of the chance can be compensated.

16. Function – Relying on a lost chance as suffered harm, instead of the actual suffered harm, allows to shorten the causal chain of events that must be established and thereby overcome the issue of proving the causal chain of events where this is impossible or very difficult. Nils Jansen formulates this very precisely:

> "This is the causal relevance of the idea of a lost chance as a harm. The idea makes it possible to hold firm to the fundamental requirement of a *conditio sine qua non* in cases which – without this idea – seem to be causally problematic."[16]

This is done by interposing a valuable chance in the causal chain to link the fault to a percentage of the "actual" harm while respecting the requirement of a *conditio sine qua non* causal link. Again, as Jansen explains:

> "a new kind of harm is accepted, and causation has to be shown in relation to this harm. A's loss of a chance to regain her health or to gain a benefit is in itself regarded as legally constituting a harm which generates recovery even though the loss is neither in itself physical damage nor necessarily results in financial loss. The basis for none the less acknowledging such a harm is to be found in people's interest in the protection of such chances."[17]

as rights can also be found recently under Dutch law. Nuninga, "Het recht op een kans." p. 47. His argumentation, however, does not convince: he seems to argue that a chance is a right because it can be considered as damage and thus must be a right. Such post factum reasoning does not convince. A proper reasoning would be the following: it is a right; hence, it can be damage.

14 Christoph Müller, "La perte d'une chance n'a pas perdu sa chance en droit suisse (Commentaire de l'ATF 133 III 462)," *Responsabilité et Assurances* (2008). p. 59.

15 Jansen, "The Idea of a Lost Chance." p. 281.

16 Jansen, "The Idea of a Lost Chance." p. 283; Bocken, Boone, and Kruithof, *Inleiding tot het schadevergoedingsrecht*. p. 48, nr. 73.

17 Jansen, "The Idea of a Lost Chance." p. 274. Helge Großerichter provides a very, perhaps more, lucid explanation. However, as it relies on much specific German legal terminology, the translation is rather unsatisfactory. It reads as follows: "For the consideration of the liability offence based

17. Proportional liability – Importantly, interposing a lost chance makes it possible to overcome causal uncertainty without altering the understanding of causality as *conditio sine qua non.*[18] This distinguishes the loss of chance from proportional liability, an approach to causal uncertainty mostly known under Dutch law but now also codified under Belgian law,[19] which occasionally and mistakenly is taken to be identical to the loss of a chance.[20] Proportional liability, instead of looking at how things *would* have gone (*ex ante* uncertainty), looks at how things did go (*ex post* uncertainty). Where, due to the state of scientific knowledge, it is impossible to say which of multiple possible causes is the actual cause for the suffered

on the requirement of *dommage certain*, it is first of all important in these cases that no already existing part of the property has been destroyed and thus there is no present or fixed loss, but only a hoped-for property benefit lying in a hypothetical future is in question. Against this background, the 'damage' is not seen in the real success (e.g.: loss of the lawsuit due to incrimination of the legal remedy), but only in the 'advantage', which is synonymous with the interest of the injured party that was at stake in the situation in question." Helge Großerichter, *Hypothetischer Geschehensverlauf und Schadensfeststellung – Eine rechtsvergleichende Untersuchung vor dem Hintergrund der perte d'une chance*, ed. Claus-Wilhelm Canaris, Münchener Universitätsschriften (München: C.H. Beck, 2001). p. 157. Footnotes omitted. Free translation. Original text: "*Für die vom Erfordernis des* dommage certain *ausgehende Betrachtung des Haftungstatbestandes ist in diesen Fällen zunächst von Bedeutung, dass kein bereits vorhandener Bestandteil des Vermögens vernichtet worden ist und damit keine gegenwärtige oder feststehende Einbuße vorliegt, sondern lediglich ein erhoffter, in einer hypothetischen Zukunft liegender Vermögensvorteil in Frage steht. Der 'Schaden' wird vor diesem Hintergrund nicht im realen Erfolg (z.B.: Verlust des Prozesses infolge Verkrustung des Rechtsmittels), sondern erst in dem 'Vorteil' gesehen, der gleichbedeutend ist mit dem Interesse des Geschädigten, des in der fraglichen Situation auf dem Spiel stand.*" His presentation of the subject matter is particularly lucid; p. 158 and 159 are very instructive.

18 Jansen, "The Idea of a Lost Chance." p. 283.

19 Article 6.23: "If several similar events for which different persons are liable have exposed the injured party to the risk of the damage occurring, without it being possible to prove which of these events caused the damage, each of these persons is liable in proportion to the probability that the event for which he is liable caused the damage. However, a person who proves that the event for which he is liable did not cause the damage is not liable." Free translation. Original text: "*Si plusieurs faits similaires dont sont responsables des personnes différentes ont exposé la personne lésée au risque de survenance du dommage qui s'est produit, sans qu'il soit possible de démontrer lequel de ces faits a causé le dommage, chacune de ces personnes est responsable en proportion de la probabilité que le fait dont elle répond ait causé le dommage. Celle qui prouve que le fait dont elle répond n'est pas une cause du dommage n'est toutefois pas responsable.*"/"*Indien meerdere soortgelijke feiten waarvoor ver- schillende personen aansprakelijk zijn de benadeelde hebben blootgesteld aan het risico op het ontstaan van de schade die zich heeft voorgedaan, maar niet kan wor- den aangetoond welk van deze feiten de schade heeft veroorzaakt, is elk van deze personen aansprakelijk in verhouding tot de waarschijnlijkheid waarmee het feit waarvoor hij instaat de schade heeft veroorzaakt. Wie bewijst dat het feit waarvoor hij instaat geen oorzaak is van de schade, is evenwel niet aansprakelijk.*"

20 The mistake, however, can have considerable consequences. The Swiss Federal Supreme Court seems to have mixed up the two concepts and partially relied on that confusion to justify its decision declaring that the loss of a chance is not recoverable under Swiss law. BGE 133 III 462 p. 471. In this sense Laurent Bieri, "Perte d'une chance vs responsabilité précontractuelle à la probabilité de la causalité," *Jusletter* (2007). and Müller, "La perte d'une chance n'a pas perdu sa chance en droit suisse (Commentaire de l'ATF 133 III 462)." pp. 55–60.

harm, proportional liability can be used to temper the "all-or-nothing" approach by granting liability in proportion to the likeliness that one of the given causes was the cause for suffered harm. A telling example is the Dutch case, where a heavy smoker had been exposed to asbestos during his working hours. When he was diagnosed with lung cancer, the *Hoge Raad* ruled that the employer should be held liable in proportion to the likeliness with which of the exposition to asbestos had caused his lung cancer.[21] Quite clearly, proportional liability is distinct from the idea of loss of a chance. The former overcomes a causal uncertainty by using a different understanding of the *conditio sine qua non* test, while the latter maintains the *conditio sine qua non* condition to evaluate the existence of a causal link but relies on a different damage to overcome the lacking causal link.[22]

Though conceptually speaking, both approaches are clearly distinct; it is totally conceivable that both approaches can be applied to an identical case – yet with different conditions and different outcomes. In the context of failed contract negotiations or conclusion, however, only the loss of a chance doctrine is relevant, as it concerns a case of uncertainty about how things would have evolved absent the fault, not cases about which of multiple events was the cause of some harm (proportional liability). The latter, in fact, is a mere question of law of evidence.[23]

2.2. In the context of failed contract conclusion

18. Chance of concluding the contract under negotiations – The risk of failing contract conclusion (*supra* Chap. 1, nr. 28) is mirrored by the chance of contract conclusion.[24] By consequence, relying on a lost chance as a type of damage in the context of failed contract negotiations or conclusion appears as a plausible way of overcoming (partially) the causal uncertainty. A difference is drawn

21 HR 21 December 2012, ECLI:NL:HR:2012:BX7491, NJ 2013/237, m.nt. S.D. Lindenbergh (Deloitte/Hassink), nr. 3.5.2. A discussion of the decision in Asser/Sieburgh 6-II 2021/81.

22 Nuninga, "Het recht op een kans." pp. 43–45; Eric Tjong Tjin Tai, "Schadebegroting, verlies van een kans en proportionele aansprakelijkheid," *NJB*, no. 31 (2016). p. 2243.

23 "Thus a chance always entails a necessarily hypothetical expectation. Clearly, chances and risks cease to exist in retrospect. They materialize into what will here be called a *final gain* or a *final damage* or *loss*. But, before it materializes, a chance always presupposes a genuine, unavoidable uncertainty, relative, to standards of scientific knowledge. This means that the usual uncertainty problem of later evidence, where in principle, certainty is possible, does not constitute a chance." Jansen, "The Idea of a Lost Chance." p. 279. Find the same point also in Nuninga et al., "Chances as Legally Protected Assets." p. 396, nr. 36; Müller, *La perte d'une chance*. p. 241, nr. 342. Critical on this distinction: Mäsch, *Chance und Schaden*. pp. 259–264.

24 "Put simply, a chance is the possibility of gaining a certain benefit or avoiding a possible harm or injury. It constitutes a good and can be understood as the opposite to the concept of a risk, which constitutes an evil. A chance to avoid an injury mirrors the risk that this injury might materialize, and the chance to gain a benefit is mirrored by the risk of not obtaining it." Jansen, "The Idea of a Lost Chance." p. 279. Citations omitted. Critical of such an understanding Brun, *Responsabilité Civile Extracontractuelle*. p. 129, nr. 186.

between the loss of a chance to conclude the contract under negotiations (*infra* Chap. 6, nrs. 18–21) and the loss of a chance to conclude a contract with a third party (*infra* Chap. 6, nrs. 22–23).

19. Unavailable under French law – Reportedly, relying on the "idea" of loss of chance of concluding the contract under negotiations was common in French and Belgian case law and scholarship.[25] As for French law, however, the *Cour de cassation* decided otherwise in the 2003 *Manoukian* decision.[26] In this case (continuing negotiations though the conclusion of the contract had already become impossible (*supra* Chap. 3, nr. 21)), the Court declared that the loss of a chance of concluding the contract under negotiations could not be causally linked to the fault of breaking-off negotiations:

> "But whereas the circumstances constituting a fault committed in the exercise of the right to unilaterally terminate the pre-contractual talks are not the cause of the loss consisting in the loss of a chance to realise the gains that the conclusion of the contract allowed to be hoped for;
>
> Whereas the Court of Appeal rightly decided that, in the absence of a firm and definitive agreement, the loss suffered by Alain Manoukian included only the costs incurred by the negotiation and the preliminary studies that it had carried out and not the profits that it could, if the contract were concluded, hope to make from the operation of the business or even the loss of a chance to obtain such profits; whereas the plea in law is unfounded;"[27]

The Court reconfirmed its decision in 2006[28] and recently in 2021:

> "Having regard to article 1382, now 1240, of the Civil Code:
>
> 6. It follows from this text that the circumstances constituting a fault committed in the exercise of the right to unilaterally terminate pre-contractual discussions are not the cause of the loss consisting in the loss of a chance

25 Belgian law: Durant, "La rupture unilatérale des pourparlers ou l'exercice d'une liberté surveillée." p. 81, nr. 47. French law: Deshayes, "Le dommage précontractuel." p. 188, nr. 1.

26 Cass.comm.fr., 26 November 2003, 00–10.243 00–10.949.

27 Cass.comm.fr., 26 November 2003, 00–10.243 00–10.949. Free translation. Original text: "*Mais attendu que les circonstances constitutives d'une faute commise dans l'exercice du droit de rupture unilatérale des pourparlers précontractuels ne sont pas la cause du préjudice consistant dans la perte d'une chance de réaliser les gains que permettait d'espérer la conclusion du contrat;*

Attendu que la cour d'appel a décidé à bon droit qu'en l'absence d'accord ferme et définitif, le préjudice subi par la société Alain Manoukian n'incluait que les frais occasionnés par la négociation et les études préalables auxquelles elle avait fait procéder et non les gains qu'elle pouvait, en cas de conclusion du contrat, espérer tirer de l'exploitation du fonds de commerce ni même la perte d'une chance d'obtenir ces gains; que le moyen n'est pas fondé;"

28 Cass.civ.fr. 28 June 2006, 04–20.040: "That in so ruling, when a fault committed in the exercise of the right to unilaterally terminate pre-contractual discussions is not the cause of the loss consisting in the loss of an opportunity to realise the gains that were to be expected from the conclusion of the contract, the Court of Appeal violated the aforementioned text." Free translation. Original text: "*Qu'en statuant ainsi, alors qu'une faute commise dans l'exercice du droit de rupture unilatérale des pourparlers pré-contractuels n'est pas la cause du préjudice consistant dans la perte d'une chance de réaliser les gains que permettait d'espérer la conclusion du contrat, la cour d'appel a violé le texte susvisé.*"

to realise the gains which the conclusion of the contract allowed to be hoped for."[29]

20. CAUSAL LINK – In its annual report of 2006,[30] the French Court of Cassation (merely) explained that no causal link can exist between the breaking-off of negotiations itself and advantages under the negotiated contract:

> "This leads it to exclude any causal relationship between the loss of the advantages attached to the conclusion of the contract and the conditions of the breach, which alone are the culpable element."[31]

In the meantime, this case law has already been codified in article 1112 Fr. Civ. C.[32] The actual reasoning relied upon, in this context, however, remains unclear: From the present perspective, it appears obvious that not only can there be no causal link between the breaking-off and expected advantages under the negotiated contract but there can also be no causal harm at all. Olivier Deshayes, however, restricts the lacking causal link argument to the advantages under the expected contract in his *Le dommage précontractuel*:

> "Let's continue by analysing the damage corresponding to the loss of the chance to conclude the aborted contract. Such damage should not be compensated. If the fault is not the breaking-off of the talks but simply the circumstances surrounding that breaking off, the situation in which the victim would have found himself in the absence of fault (and in which we must try to put him back) is as follows: the negotiations would still have been broken-off, but without any additional circumstances capable of establishing fault. This establishes that the loss of the gain expected from the contract is not linked to fault. Such a loss should not therefore be compensated, as there is no causal link. As we know, this is the conclusion that the Commercial Division of the Cour de cassation has just reached in its decision of 26 November 2003."[33]

29 Cass.comm.fr. 31 March 2021, n° 19–14.533. Free translation. Original text: "*Vu l'article 1382, devenu 1240, du code civil:*

> *6. Il résulte de ce texte que les circonstances constitutives d'une faute commise dans l'exercice du droit de rupture unilatérale des pourparlers précontractuels ne sont pas la cause du préjudice consistant dans la perte d'une chance de réaliser les gains que permettait d'espérer la conclusion du contrat.*"

30 La Cour de Cassation et la construction juridique européenne, *Rapport Annuel* 2006. p. 400.

31 La Cour de Cassation et la construction juridique européenne, *Rapport Annuel* 2006. p. 400. Free translation. Original text: "*Ceci la conduit à exclure toute relation de cause à effet entre la perte des avantages attachés à la conclusion du contrat et les conditions de la rupture qui seules sont fautives.*"

32 "In case of fault committed during the negotiations, the reparation of the resulting loss is not calculated so as to compensate the loss of benefits which were expected from the contract that was not concluded." Original text: "*En cas de faute commise dans les négociations, la réparation du préjudice qui en résulte ne peut avoir pour objet de compenser ni la perte des avantages attendus du contrat non conclu, ni la perte de chance d'obtenir ces avantages.*"

33 Deshayes, "Le dommage précontractuel." p. 197, nr. 18. "*Poursuivons par l'analyse du préjudice correspondant à la perte de chance de conclure le contrat avorté. Un tel dommage ne doit pas être*

Seemingly, the Court of Cassation followed his reasoning in its decision of 2006 and its annual report of the same year and, hence, ultimately, the French legislator. Though I agree that between the breaking-off itself and the advantages under a contract no causal link can exist – as much as there can also be no causal link with any other harm – it seems to me that the loss of a chance doctrine precisely allows to overcome this issue of causality by framing the harm in terms of losing a chance. I am, thus, not so sure about the argument made by Deshayes. Instead, the argument appears to be based on an erroneous understanding of the *lucrum cessans* in the context of contract negotiations, as I explained *supra* (Chap. 3, nr. 31).[34]

21. Unavailable under Belgian law – A very recent Belgian decision of the Court of Appeal of Liège[35] offers another explanation. In the case at hand, two parties negotiate the sale of a plot of land. As the soil had been spoiled, parties agree during the negotiation process that the seller would take the required works at his expense up to 500.000 €, and if the actual costs would be higher, parties would work out how to divide the remaining costs. When a first expertise estimates costs to be as high as 800.000 €, the seller offers to pay the whole 800.000 €. The buyer, in turn, is not satisfied with this option and requires a second expertise to get a more reliable estimation of the possible expenses. The seller responds that as it offers to pay up until 800.000 € of the required works, it sees no need in requiring a second expertise and urges to sign the sale agreement. To this, the buyer responds that, given the disagreement on how to divide costs for the depollution works, it would not proceed to signing the sales agreement. Throughout various Belgian instances, all the way up to the Court of Cassation, the buyer is considered

réparé. Car si la faute n'est pas la rupture des pourparlers mais simplement les circonstances accompagnant cette rupture, la situation dans laquelle se serait trouvée la victime en l'absence de faute (et dans laquelle il faut chercher à la replacer) est la suivante: les négociations auraient tout de même été rompues, mais sans aucune circonstance supplémentaire propre à établir une faute. Par là, on établit que la perte du gain attendu du contrat n'est pas liée à la faute. Un tel préjudice ne doit donc pas être réparé, faute de lien de causalité. C'est d'ailleurs, nous le savons, la conclusion à laquelle vient de se rallier la chambre commerciale de la Cour de cassation dans son arrêt du 26 novembre 2003." In the same sense Jourdain, "Préjudice consécutif à la rupture fautive des pourparlers." pp. 770–771.

34 Denis Mazeaud also appears to be critical of this solution, while at the same time perfectly illustrating the association of expected benefit under the negotiated contract and lucrum cessans: "Unless we are mistaken, it would seem that by stating very clearly that there is no causal link between the culpable breach of the talks and the loss resulting from 'the loss of an opportunity to realise the gains that could have been expected from the conclusion of the contract', the Commercial Chamber is vindicating those who claim that this lost opportunity does not constitute a compensable loss." Mazeaud, "Rupture fautive des pourparlers." p. 258. Free translation. Original text: "*Sauf à se tromper, il semble bien qu'en affirmant très nettement qu'il n'existe pas de lien de causalité entre la rupture fautive des pourparlers et le préjudice résidant dans 'la perte d'une chance de réaliser des gains que permettait d'espérer la conclusion du contrat', la Chambre commerciale donne raison à ceux qui prétendent que ce gain manqué ne constitue pas un préjudice réparable.*"

35 Liège, 27 June 2023, 2022/RG/206.

to wrongfully have broken-off negotiations. The Brussels Court of Appeal, charged with the case before going to the Court of Cassation, found that the seller lost the chance to conclude the contract with the buyer in question. The Court of Cassation, however, broke that decision: it is contradictory to, on the one hand, accept that a party was not willing to contract and to, on the other hand, state that there was a certain chance of concluding the contract under negotiations.[36] In other words, at the moment of breaking-off negotiations, no chance to conclude the contract under negotiations existed any more (as the decision of breaking-off had already been made); hence, this chance could not be lost, as there was no chance anymore. The case was handed back to the Court of Appeal of Liège, which found that a chance had been lost to contract with a *third party*.

22. Chance of concluding a contract with a third party – As controversial as the loss of a chance to conclude the contract under negations appears to be, the loss of a chance to conclude a contract with a third party seems to be generally indemnifiable, provided – of course – that in the case at hand, such a chance existed and that its loss was caused by the reproached wrong.[37] Olivier Deshaye concludes: "here do not appear to be any theoretical difficulties preventing such compensation."[38]

Carlos Bollen however argues that since there is – except if otherwise agreed – no obligation to negotiate exclusively with one party, leading negotiations with one party does not cause the loss of a chance to negotiate with a third party as one could have continued negotiations with the third party.[39] It is true that negotiating with one party does not preclude a party also to negotiate with another party. This does, however, not necessarily mean that the reproached fault did not make the harmed party lose the chance to contract with a third party. If, for instance, a party keeps negotiations ongoing while knowing that it will not conclude the contract while the counter party, awaiting the contract conclusion with that party, refuses a timely available alternative, it lost its chance to conclude that contract with a third party due to the wrongful continuation of negotiations. Hence, Bollen's argument should be read as a reminder to not grant this loss of a chance systematically, but it does not mean that, occasionally, it could not be the case.

36 I was unable to get access to the actual decision of the Court of Cassation and could only rely on the cited parts in Liège, 27 June 2023, 2022/RG/206. This position had already been defended under Belgian law by Sander Baeyens, "De theorie van het verlies van een kans: een rechtsvergelijkende analyse toegepast op de zuivere vermogensschade," *RW* (2016). p. 368, nr. 15; Jean-Luc Fagnart, *La causalité* (Waterloo: Kluwer, 2009). p. 140, nr. 274.

37 As clarified by Deshayes, "Le dommage précontractuel." p. 197, nr. 20. Under Belgian law Stijns, *Verbintenissenrecht Boek 1*. nr. 102. From a comparative perspective, see Zuloaga, *Reliance in the Breaking Off of Contractual Negotiations*. p. 174.

38 Deshayes, "Le dommage précontractuel." p. 193, nr. 11. Free translation. Original text: "*Aucune difficulté d'ordre théorique ne semble s'oppposer à une telle compensation*."

39 C. Bollen, "Precontractuele aansprakelijkheid voor het afspringen van onderhandelingen, in het bijzondere m.b.t. een acquisiteovereenkomst," *TBBR* (2003). p. 157, nr. 66.

23. CERTAINTY OF CONCLUDING A CONTRACT WITH A THIRD PARTY – The Italian *Corte di Cassazione* recently recognized that the advantage lost in not concluding a contract with a third party can also amount to indemnifiable damage:

> "The (Omissis) in l.c.a. therefore wrongly complains that the Court of Latium wrongly excluded the possibility of compensation for loss of profit consisting in the loss of the economic profit that it could have made if the negotiations conducted with I.N.A.I.L. had resulted in the conclusion of the sale and purchase contract on which it had relied.
>
> The applicant claims, in fact, to obtain compensation for the damage caused by the impairment of the positive interest in the performance of the contract not concluded, that is to say, pecuniary loss which cannot be compensated where the liability alleged in the case is based on failure to comply with the duty to act in good faith at the pre-contractual negotiation stage.
>
> On the other hand, if it is true that the damage that can be compensated within the limits of negative interest also includes the loss of profit represented by the loss of the economic advantage that the party could have obtained if, instead of being involved in a negotiation that turned out to be useless, it had devoted itself to other negotiations, it is nevertheless true that this is not the prejudice of which the appellant complains that the district court did not recognise.
>
> In the light of this, the alleged infringement of the rules of law referred to in the heading of the pleas in law under examination cannot, therefore, be held to exist."[40]

This is quite remarkable, as the reasoning does not appear to be based on a lost chance of contracting with a third party but instead on some certainty of contracting with a third party. The validity of such a decision is somewhat doubtful, unless it can be established that the other party was under an obligation to contract (for instance, because the party missing the opportunity to contract with a third party had received an offer from that third party).

40 Cass.civ.it. 15 December 2023, n. 35170. Free translation. Original version: "*A torto, dunque, l' (Omissis) in l.c.a. addebita alla Corte laziale di aver erroneamente escluso la risarcibilità del danno da mancato guadagno consistito nella perdita dell'utile economico da essa conseguibile qualora le trattative condotte con l'I.N.A.I.L. fossero sfociate nella stipula del contratto di compravendita in cui aveva fatto affidamento.*

La ricorrente pretenderebbe, infatti, di ottenere il risarcimento del danno da lesione dell'interesse positivo all'esecuzione del contratto non concluso, cioè di un detrimento patrimoniale insuscettibile di ristoro ove la responsabilità dedotta in causa sia fondata sull' inosservanza del dovere di comportarsi secondo buona fede nella fase delle trattative precontrattuali.

D'altro canto, se è pur vero che il danno risarcibile nei limiti dell' interesse negativo comprende anche il lucro cessante rappresentato dalla perdita del vantaggio economico che la parte avrebbe potuto conseguire se, invece di essere coinvolta in una trattativa rivelatasi inutile, si fosse dedicata ad altre contrattazioni, è nondimeno vero chenon è questo il pregiudizio di cui l'impugnante lamenta il mancato riconoscimento ad opera del giudice distrettuale.

Alla luce di ciò, non può, dunque, ritenersi configurabile la denunciata violazione delle norme di legge evocate nella rubrica dei motivi in disamina."

24. Loss of chance and no-contract scenario – It seems uncontested that the lost chance to conclude a contract with a third party can be compensable harm in the legal systems allowing for the loss of chance. Of course, there must have been a chance that has been lost, which needs to be proven in each and every case.

The discussion on the availability of the loss of the chance to conclude the contract under negotiation appears more difficult. Unfortunately, it appears to be largely based on an erroneous assimilation of the *lucrum cessans* and the positive interest (*supra* Chap. 3, nr. 31). Instead, it seems to me that the loss of a chance doctrine precisely allows to overcome the normative causal uncertainty: in the alternative scenario to the wrongful breaking-off of negotiations, negotiations could have continued, leading to a contract, or to no contract. Hence, there was at least a chance to conclude the contract.

Invoking, as is done under Belgian law, that at the moment of breaking-off there was already no more chance to conclude the contract, however, appears as a more refined argument. It asks the question whether it was the decision to break-off *itself* which was wrongful or the communication thereof. If it was the former, the fault must be left out in the hypothetical alternative course of action and the chance to conclude the contract has been lost by that very decision. If the communication of the decision is considered to be the wrongful element, the chance had indeed already been lost. I would think that, where the breaking-off of negotiations or the refusal to contract *itself* is considered wrongful, it is the decision that is considered wrongful. Hence, the argument invoked under Belgian law would not hold good. Again, it is crucial how the invoked fault is described and must be done with great care.

3. Abuse of rights

3.1. The doctrine

25. Rabbit hole – Though having been codified in some legal systems,[41] the prohibition of the abuse of rights remains somewhat of a doctrinal rabbit hole.[42] It is a perplexing legal issue, in which an act appears to be lawful and unlawful at the same time. This "paradox" – as Roman Guski recently put it[43] – has led, ever since the beginning of the 19th century, to long-lasting attempts of conceptualization and delimitation. Great scholars have put much time and

41 Art. 3:13 NBW, art. 1.10 Be. Civ. C. For a general perspective on the state of recognition, see Laura Melusine Baudenbacher, *Vom gemeineuropäischen zum europäischen Rechtsmissbrauchsverbot* (Baden-Baden: Nomos, 2016). pp. 26–50.

42 Asser/Sieburgh 6-IV 2019/86 opens the discussion of the subject in a similar manner and provides equally a very brief sketch of the different theories.

43 Roman Guski, *Rechtsmissbrauch als Paradoxie – Negative Selbstreferenz und widersprüchliches Handeln im Recht* (Tübigen: Mohr Siebeck, 2019). XXVI+753 p.

energy in presenting their understanding of the prohibition of abuse of rights. Marcel Planiol's[44] so-called "critique of form" ("*critique de forme*") is but one example of those efforts. Planiol argued that the idea of an abuse of rights is a false concept: the right stops where the abuse begins ('*le droit cesse où l'abus commence*'),[45] he famously proclaimed. Hence, an abuse of right is inconceivable. Another, more recent, conception is that of Jacques Ghestin, who distinguishes between the internal and external limits of subjective rights ('*les limites "externes" et "internes" des droits subjectifs*').[46] Transgressing these internal limits, which seem to pertain to the way in which the right is exercised, leads to an abuse of rights,[47] *et cetera*.[48]

Be that as it may, quite frankly, I fail to see how – except for different degrees of plasticity – such descriptions provide a better understanding of the prohibition of abuse of rights.[49] Instead, and as an alternative to the existing explanations, I provide a functional and structural approach, which builds on the structure of the liability law systems I have presented *supra* (Chap. 2, nrs. 3–11).

26. Lawfulness – Thinking back to the possible liability law systems (*supra* Chap. 2, nrs. 3–11), the prohibition of abuse of rights is in some way the mirror of an unlawfulness-based liability. The unlawfulness-based liability is triggered by an unlawfulness (infringement of a specific legal norm/protected right or interest) and limited by a requirement of fault. By consequence, lawful acts (acts which are permitted) do not give rise to liability. The abuse of rights doctrine is a correction of this consequence:[50] a lawfulness (act allowed by a specific legal norm/protected right or interest) can still be done wrongfully (conduct).

44 Which can also be found in Germany, as argued by Wolfgang Siebert: "The *critique de forme* is therefore right: abuse of rights is in fact acting without rights." Wolfgang Siebert, *Verwirkung und Unzulässigkeit der Rechtsausübung* (Marburg in Hessen: Elwert'sche Verlagsbuchhandlung, 1934). p. 90. Free translation. Original text: "*Die* critique de forme *hat also Recht: Rechtsmissbrauch ist in Wahrheit ein Handeln ohne Recht.*" For a discussion, see Philipp Eichenhofer, *Rechtsmissbrauch Zu Geschichte und Theorie einer Figur des Europäischen Privatrechts* (Tübingen: Mohr Siebeck, 2019). p. 131.

45 Marcel Planiol, *Traité élémentaire de droit civil*, Vol. 2 (Paris: LGDJ, 1949). pp. 336–337, nr. 978. On the discussion Eichenhofer, *Rechtsmissbrauch Zu Geschichte und Theorie einer Figur des Europäischen Privatrechts*. p. 64.

46 Jacques Ghestin, "L'abus dans les contrats," *Gazette du Palais* 2 (1981). p. 379. More recently: Jacques Ghestin and Hugo Barbier, *Introduction générale Tome II – Droit de la preuve, Abus de droit, fraude et apparence* (Paris: LGDJ, 2020). p. 467, nr. 621.

47 Ghestin, "L'abus dans les contrats." p. 379. More recently: Ghestin and Barbier, *Introduction générale Tome II – Droit de la preuve, Abus de droit, fraude et apparence*. p. 467, nr. 621.

48 For a comparative discussion of these different approaches, see Holger Fleischer, "Der Rechtsmissbrauch zwischen Gemeineuropäischem Privatrecht und Gemeinschaftsprivatrecht," *JZ*, no. 18 (2003). pp. 865–874.

49 For a thorough and in-depth historical and comparative discussion and description of the doctrine, I refer the reader to Eichenhofer, *Rechtsmissbrauch Zu Geschichte und Theorie einer Figur des Europäischen Privatrechts*. XVII+272 p. or Baudenbacher, *Vom gemeineuropäischen zum europäischen Rechtsmissbrauchsverbot*. p. 26 *et seq.* for a broader array of discussed systems.

50 Very clearly expressed by Ghestin and Barbier, *Introduction générale Tome II – Droit de la preuve, Abus de droit, fraude et apparence*. p. 459, nr. 616.

Yet to overrule the lawfulness, the fault must be qualified. Philipp Eichenhofer formulates this convincingly when he discusses the role of the abuse of rights doctrine under French law:

> "In any case, when a right was abused, prima facie a right was exercised, and therefore an additional argument was needed to eliminate the right in this specific situation. The significance of the abus de droit was therefore that it provided such arguments. This argumentative effort was not required in the typical tort law constellation."[51]

The function of the prohibition of abuse of rights doctrine thus is to allow to hold a legal subject liable, even though the act committed is lawful.[52]

27. Conduct-based liability – Hence, the abuse of rights doctrine appears as a correction of the *a priori* lawfulness of the exercise of a right or any other type of prerogative giving rise to an *a priori* lawfulness. It does so, based merely on the assessment of the conduct of a party in the circumstances of the exercise of its right/prerogative. Yet given that the exercise of a right or prerogative is *a priori* lawful, it must be very clear that the conduct in question should nevertheless give rise to liability. Hence, the requirement that the conduct be excessively or manifestly wrongful in the given circumstances. Ultimately, the abuse of rights doctrine appears as a mere application of a conduct-based liability but applied in the context of a more specific *a priori* lawfulness. This, then, also explains why under French law – and by extension, systems with a conduct-based liability, such as Belgian law – the abuse of rights doctrine could be conceptualized as part of liability law,[53] leading to issues of delineation between general personal liability law and the abuse of rights doctrine.[54]

51 Eichenhofer, *Rechtsmissbrauch Zu Geschichte und Theorie einer Figur des Europäischen Privatrechts*. p. 68. Free translation. Original text: "*Beim Missbrauch eines Rechts wurde jedenfalls prima facie ein Recht ausgeübt, und deshalb war ein zusätzliches Argument erforderlich, um das Recht in dieser konkreten Situation auszuschalten. Die Bedeutung des abus de droit lag also darin, dass sie solche Argumente zur Verfügung stellte. Dieser argumentative Aufwand war in der typischen deliktsrechtlichen Konstellation nicht erforderlich.*" See also Baudenbacher, *Vom gemeineuropäischen zum europäischen Rechtsmissbrauchsverbot*. p. 44, where she refers to a Swiss judgment expressing the same idea.

52 Eichenhofer, *Rechtsmissbrauch Zu Geschichte und Theorie einer Figur des Europäischen Privatrechts*. pp. 67, 126, and 247.

53 "Thus, from the beginning, a conception of tort law dominated in France, which understood the abuse of rights as a damaging event requiring compensation." Eichenhofer, *Rechtsmissbrauch Zu Geschichte und Theorie einer Figur des Europäischen Privatrechts*. p. 235. Free translation. Original text: "*So dominierte in Frankreich von Beginn an eine deliktsrechtliche Konzeption, die den Rechtsmissbrauch als schädigendes, kompensationsbedürftiges Ereignis verstand.*" As opposed to a German unlawfulness-based conception: "The idea of distributing risks arising from lawful activities seems flatly to contradict the BGB's conception of delictual liability, which makes compensation dependent upon 'unlawful' causation of loss, and whose section in the code is entitled 'Unlawful Conduct'." Jansen, *The Structure of Tort Law*. p. 5.

54 See for an illustration thereof Ghestin and Barbier, *Introduction générale Tome II – Droit de la preuve, Abus de droit, fraude et apparence*. pp. 468–469, nr. 624. The malaise which comes along

28. ABUSE OF FREEDOMS? – This question of delimitation of the abuse of rights doctrine relates to a discussion about the applicability of the prohibition to freedoms. The point being that if the abuse of rights doctrine was to be applicable to freedoms, it would also apply to the general freedom of individuals to come and go as they please and would thus apply to the general realm of extra-contractual liability.[55] A question would then rise, namely, whether a qualified fault (criterion of abuse of right) or a "simple" fault (extra-contractual fault) would be required. The result being the "ominous" ("*ominös*")[56] question of whether *freedoms* could be subject to the abuse of *rights* doctrine.[57] From a functional perspective, my answer clearly is yes. Indeed, the qualified fault is necessary to explain that even in light of the *a priori* lawfulness, the conduct was such that it trumps the *a priori* lawfulness and leads to liability.[58] In the case of the exercise of a freedom, the conduct is *a priori* lawful and thus requires a qualified fault. From that perspective, it also becomes clear why the degree of qualified fault is proportional to the precision of the lawfulness: the clearer the lawfulness, the "more" qualified the fault must be.[59] Depending on the freedom in question, this *a priori* lawfulness may be more or less clear (the exercise of the freedom from contract is very clearly *a priori* lawful, the general freedom to come and go much less).

29. CRITERIA OF ABUSE OF RIGHTS – The consequence of these type of discussions and related conceptual unclarity is that no underlying common ground exists from where to explain the criteria of application of the abuse of right. This translates into an array of criteria which can be more or less consistent with potential underlying conceptions of the prohibition of the abuse of rights.[60] From

---

with these efforts of justification is palpable. Under Belgian law, see importantly Sophie Stijns, "Abus, mais de quel(s) droit(s)?" *JT* (1990). p. 40, 3.2.4. In the same sense Durant, "La rupture unilatérale des pourparlers ou l'exercice d'une liberté surveillée." 54, nr. 17 and Elke Swaenepoel, *Toetsing van het contractuele evenwicht* (Antwerpen: Intersentia, 2011). nr. 625, 370 en nr. 630, 372.

55 F.i. in Lequette et al., *Droit civil Les Obligations*. p. 1089, nr. 966.

56 As it is called in Eichenhofer, *Rechtsmissbrauch Zu Geschichte und Theorie einer Figur des Europäischen Privatrechts*. p. 91.

57 Eichenhofer, *Rechtsmissbrauch Zu Geschichte und Theorie einer Figur des Europäischen Privatrechts*. pp. 57 and 73 for a description and general discussion. On the question Stijns, "Abus, mais de quel(s) droit(s)?" p. 40, 3.2.4. See also interestingly Nils Jansen, who conceptualizes freedom of contract as "Freedom of contract is itself composed of a bundle of rights, which, among other things, contain freedom from claims not to conclude a contract or forbear from concluding a contract, and the legal competence effectively to create legal rights by means of a contract." Jansen, *The Structure of Tort Law*. p. 47, fn. 96.

58 Read from that perspective the discussion in Ghestin, "La responsabilité délictuelle pour rupture abusive des pourparlers." p. 16, nrs. 4–10.

59 As defended, f.i., in Ghestin and Barbier, *Introduction générale Tome II – Droit de la preuve, Abus de droit, fraude et apparence*. pp. 469–470, nr. 625. Relied on in Lequette et al., *Droit civil Les Obligations*. pp. 1091–1092, nr. 968.

Eichenhofer, *Rechtsmissbrauch Zu Geschichte und Theorie einer Figur des Europäischen Privatrechts*. pp. 70, 72, and 247 for a discussion and references.

60 As explained in Lequette et al., *Droit civil Les Obligations*. pp. 1092–1093, nrs. 969–970.

a comparative perspective, it, therefore, seems doomed to fail to normatively determine which criteria are *the* relevant criteria to look at. Structurally speaking, it also does not matter, as long as they make it acceptable that an *a priori* lawfulness can still give rise to liability. This becomes quite clear in the Belgian structure of the criteria of abuse of rights. It departs from an overarching criterium that "One who uses one's right in a manner that manifestly exceeds the limits of the normal exercise of that right by a prudent and reasonable person in the same circumstances abuses the right"[61] (article 1.10 Be. Civ. C.). Under this general criterion, different sub-criteria can be subsumed. They, however, only serve the closer identification of why the exercise of the right was manifestly unreasonable; the fulfilment of the general criterion suffices. This makes sense, as the qualification as "manifestly unreasonable" clearly expresses that a qualified fault is required and the further sub-criteria merely help in understanding when such a manifestly unreasonable exercise of a right is at stake.

30. Sanction – That so much effort has been put into conceptualizing the prohibition of abuse rights stands in a bizarre contrast with the little consideration that is given to the sanction of an abuse of right.[62] Ultimately, it is on this level that the prohibition of abuse of rights is truly fascinating. Though being an instance of conduct-based liability in the context of the exercise of a right/prerogative, its sanction not only lies in compensation of harm (which would be logical) but also and primarily in a moderation of the exercise of a right. Such a moderation consists in the judge deciding that the right or prerogative had been exercised abusively and has to be *moderated* to its normal exercise. Philipppe Stoffel-Munck, in his dissertation, *L'abus dans le contrat*,[63] speaks of the ineffectiveness ("*inefficacité*") of the abusive exercise of a right[64] or the reduction ("*réduction*"/"*matiging*") as it is framed under Belgian law (article 1.10 Be. Civ. C).[65] This latter sanction is, in fact, quite amazing. The fact that, and how, it is justified that a judge, *ex post* and *ex nihilo*, dictates the conduct a

61 Original text: "*Commet un abus de droit celui qui l'exerce d'une manière qui dépasse manifestement les limites de l'exercice normal de ce droit par une personne prudente et raisonnable placée dans les mêmes circonstances.*"/"*Wie zijn recht uitoefent op een wijze die kennelijk de grenzen te buiten gaat van de normale uitoefening van dat recht door een voorzichtig en redelijk persoon in dezelfde omstandigheden geplaatst, maakt misbruik van zijn recht.*"

62 As pointed out by Philippe Stoffel-Munck, *L'abus dans le contrat – Essai d'une théorie*, ed. Jacques Ghestin, Bibliothèque de droit privé, (Paris: L.D.D.J., 2000). p. 236, nr. 272.

63 Stoffel-Munck, *L'abus dans le contrat – Essai d'une théorie*. VIII+649 p. Under Belgian law influentially Stijns, "Abus, mais de quel(s) droit(s)?" p. 40, nr. 3.2.4.

64 Stoffel-Munck, *L'abus dans le contrat – Essai d'une théorie*. p. 266, nr. 313.

65 "The sanction for such abuse is the reduction of the right to its normal use, without prejudice to the reparation of the damage caused by the abuse." Original text: "*La sanction d'un tel abus consiste en la réduction du droit à son usage normal, sans préjudice de la réparation du dommage que l'abus a causé.*"/"*De sanctie voor een dergelijk misbruik bestaat in de matiging van het recht tot zijn normale rechtsuitoefening, onverminderd het herstel van de schade die het misbruik heeft berokkend.*"

See in more detail in Sophie Stijns and Françoise Auvray, "L'abus de droit dans le Livre 1er du Code civil," in *Le Livre 1er du Code civil: dispositions générales*, ed. Patrick Wéry and Eric Dirix (Bruxelles: Larcier, 2024). nr. 17.

party had to adopt in the exercise of its right, truly challenges very fundamental principles of the law of obligations. Yet it is commonly accepted and will thus be taken as a premise for my further analysis.

31. FUNCTION – As said *supra* (Chap. 6, nr. 26), I approach the abuse of rights doctrine from a functional perspective and understanding, namely, that the abuse of rights doctrine allows to sanction a lawful act and overcome issues of causality by the "ineffectiveness" of the wrongful conduct. Under Belgian and French law, the abuse of rights doctrine is the doctrine to rely on for this function. In other systems, which have been somewhat less strongly focused on the abuse of rights doctrine,[66] such as German law and Italian law, other doctrines seem to be more commonly invoked, namely, it is also assumed by other legal institutes – such as *venire contra factum proprium* (v.c.f.p.) or, more specifically, forfeiture of rights ("*Verwirkung*") (a sub-category of v.c.f.p.). That is, the prohibition to act contrarily to previous acts:

> "A right . . . is forfeited if the entitled party does not assert it over a longer period of time, although he would be able to do so ("moment of time"), and the obligated party could and did expect that the entitled party would not assert his right in the future either, taking into account the entire behaviour of the entitled party."[67]

I deal with the abuse of rights doctrine, as it seems more readily invoked under French and Belgian law in the context of failed contract conclusion, while forfeiture of rights today seems to be not commonly invoked in the context of failed contract negotiations in German or Italian law. Hence, I will focus on French and Belgian law in this context. Given their common function, however, applying these doctrines to overcome the issue of causal uncertainty may be an interesting option to consider. Since Dutch law has an obligation to contract since the *Plas/Valburg* decision (*supra* Chap. 2, nr. 34 and *infra* Chap. 7. nr. 5), there appears to be no need to fall back onto the prohibition of abuse of rights, and indeed, Marcel Ruygvoorn does not even consider it among the different potential sources in his dissertation, *Afgebroken onderhandelingen en het gebruik van voorbehouden*.[68]

3.2. In the context of failed contract conclusion

32. ABUSE OF FREEDOM TO BREAK-OFF NEGOTIATIONS OR REFUSAL TO CONTRACT – Presently, the question will be whether the abuse of rights doctrine can be

66 See for a description of the evolution under German law Eichenhofer, *Rechtsmissbrauch Zu Geschichte und Theorie einer Figur des Europäischen Privatrechts*. pp. 99–173. For a contemporary overview, see Baudenbacher, *Vom gemeineuropäischen zum europäischen Rechtsmissbrauchsverbot*. pp. 33–38 for German law and pp. 39–41 for Italian law.

67 Jauernig/Mansel, 19. Aufl. 2023, BGB § 242 nr. 54. Free translation. Original text: "*Ein Recht . . . ist verwirkt, wenn es der Berechtigte über einen längeren Zeitraum hinweg nicht geltend macht, obwohl er dazu in der Lage wäre ('Zeitmoment'), und der Verpflichtete sich mit Rücksicht auf das gesamte Verhalten des Berechtigten darauf einrichten durfte und eingerichtet hat, dass dieser sein Recht auch in Zukunft nicht geltend machen werde.*"

68 Ruygvoorn, *Afgebroken onderhandelingen en het gebruik van voorbehouden*. pp. 231–252.

applied to instances of broken-off negotiations or the refusal to contract. Among scholars, the question is – and perhaps surprisingly – strongly debated.[69] The discussion seems to be related to the uncertain understanding of the abuse of rights doctrine (*supra* Chap. 6, nr. 25) in general[70] and to revolve mostly around the notion of right (*supra* Chap. 6, nrs. 27–28).[71] Philippe Stoffel-Munck in his dissertation under French law, *L'abus dans le contract*,[72] for instance, argues that breaking-off negotiations would not amount to the exercise of a right.[73] The focus of this argument lies on a the understanding of the notion of right and whether the exercise of a freedom can amount to the exercise of a right.[74] Jacques Ghestin, in turn, strongly argues in favour of the application of the prohibition of abuse of rights to cases of broken-off negotiations.[75] He argues that, independent of whether one wants to call the possibility not to contract a right or a freedom, it is still a sufficiently well-delineated lawful act for it to be subject to the more stringent criterion of a qualified fault. Without aiming to resolve this debate, it appears to me that when functionally looking at the prohibition of abuse of rights, it perfectly suits the purpose: it allows to overcome the issue of an *a priori* lawfulness of the refusal to contract or breaking-off of negotiations. More importantly, yet less recognized, it is particularly the very flexible sanction of moderation of the exercise of a right that

69 For an overview of French and Belgian law, see Durant, "La rupture unilatérale des pourparlers ou l'exercice d'une liberté surveillée." pp. 46–50, nrs. 10–13. For a merely French perspective, see Ghestin, "La responsabilité délictuelle pour rupture abusive des pourparlers." p. 16, nrs. 4–16.

70 "The supposed renaissance of the *abus de droit* in contract law thus proves, on closer inspection, to be a desperate attempt by the doctrine to once again suggest a uniform concept of abuse. However, these efforts have so far been unsuccessful. Contributing to this impression is the fact that in many cases the case law vacillates between the terms 'abus' and 'bonne foi' without being guided by recognisable principles." Eichenhofer, *Rechtsmissbrauch Zu Geschichte und Theorie einer Figur des Europäischen Privatrechts*. p. 98. Free translation. Original text: "*Die vermeintliche Renaissance des abus de droit im Vertragsrecht erweist sich also bei näherer Betrachtung als verzweifelter Versuch der doctrine, erneut einen einheitlichen Missbrauchs-Begriff zu suggerieren. Diese Bemühungen sind bisher allerdings erfolglos geblieben. Zu diesem Eindruck trägt bei, dass die Rechtsprechung in vielen Fällen zwischen den Ausdrücken 'abus' und 'bonne foi' hin- und herschwankt, ohne sich an erkennbaren Grundsätzen zu orientieren.*"

71 See for an overview Ghestin, "La responsabilité délictuelle pour rupture abusive des pourparlers." p. 16, nrs. 4–10.

72 Stoffel-Munck, *L'abus dans le contrat – Essai d'une théorie*. VIII+649 p. Under Belgian law influentially Stijns, "Abus, mais de quel(s) droit(s)?" p. 40, nr. 3.2.4.

73 Stoffel-Munck, *L'abus dans le contrat – Essai d'une théorie*. pp. 111–112, nr. 121. See also.

74 The discussion serves to delimit the area of application between the abuse of rights doctrine and general liability law. The prohibition to abuse one's right would only apply to rights; general liability law would apply to freedoms. The delineation appears difficult (see, for instance, the laborious attempt in Ghestin and Barbier, *Introduction générale Tome II – Droit de la preuve, Abus de droit, fraude et apparence.*, p. 473, nr. 627, and the much more laborious attempt in Thierry Léonard, "L'abus de la liberté de ne pas contracter: une application excessive de la théorie de l'abus de droit (note sous Cass. 11 october 2011)," *R.C.J.B.* (2013). pp. 542–593. Thierry Léonard, *Conflits entre droits subjectifs, libertés civiles et intérêts légitimes. Un modèle de résolution basé sur l'opposabilité et la responsabilité civile* (Bruxelles: Larcier, 2005). 894 p.). From the *a priori* lawfulness approach here adopted, the issue does not seem problematic.

75 Ghestin, "La responsabilité délictuelle pour rupture abusive des pourparlers." pp. 17–18, nrs. 11–18.

allows one to sidetrack questions of causality which otherwise would hinder a liability claim. The abuse of rights doctrine thus makes it possible to overcome the causality issues. From this functional perspective, the application of the abuse of rights doctrine in the context of broken-off negotiations appears sensible and convincing.

33. Courts apply abuse of rights to failed contract negotiations – By consequence, it seems coherent and pertinent to apply the abuse of rights doctrine to cases of failed contract negotiations or conclusion. That French and Belgian case law disregards the consistent criticism of scholars must thus be welcomed. Recently, the Court of Appeal of Rennes[76] found that a party did not commit an abuse of right in breaking-off negotiations for putting motorcycles at auction, even though the auction in question had to go through less than two weeks from the moment of breaking-off, given that the party breaking-off the negotiations clearly had expressed its doubt and dissatisfaction with the course of the negotiations. On similar grounds, the Court of Appeal of Versailles[77] ruled that, even though negotiations had been ongoing for 18 months about the installation of photovoltaics, it still had been clear that parties were not yet close to a final agreement and that, hence, there was no abusive breaking-off of contract negotiations.

The Belgian Court of Cassation, as well, has ruled two times that the refusal to contract can amount to an abuse of rights. In 2011 the Belgian Court of Cassation stated most explicitly that the refusal to contract can amount to an abuse of rights:

> "Refusal to contract may constitute an abuse of rights where the freedom not to contract is exercised in a manner that manifestly exceeds the limits of the normal exercise of that freedom by a prudent and diligent person."[78]

The case concerned a doctor who, in the process of a merger of two hospitals, was promised a specific position in the new merged hospital, be it under the condition of approval by that hospital. When he asked to get promoted to that position, his request was refused. The Court of Appeal withheld the argument of the doctor that the hospital was abusing its right to refuse to contract. The Court of Cassation did not overrule the decision of the Court of Appeal and explicitly recognized that one can abuse its right to refuse to contract. Though the decision had been received with mixed feelings,[79] the Court clearly reaffirmed its

76 Rennes, 14 September 2022, n° 19/02235.

77 Versailles, 13 October 2022, n° 21/00432.

78 Cass.be. 7 Oktober 2011, C. 10.0227.F. Free translation. Original text: "*Le refus de contracter peut constituer un abus de droit lorsque l'usage de la liberté de ne pas contracter est exercé d'une manière qui excède manifestement les limites de l'exercice normal de cette liberté par une personne prudente et diligente.*"

79 Léonard, "L'abus de la liberté de ne pas contracter: une application excessive de la théorie de l'abus de droit (note sous Cass. 11 october 2011)." pp. 542–593; Sanne Jansen and S. Stijns, "Contractweigering kan rechtsmisbruik uitmaken (noot onder Cass. 7 oktober 2011)," *RW* (2012–13). pp. 1182–1186.

decision – be it in somewhat less strong wording[80] – in 2020.[81] This time, a person bought a camper that was attached to the ground on some camping site. Because the person running the camping site was side-lined in the process of selling that camper and, therefore, missed a commission on the sale, it then refused to rent the spot on which the camper was located to the acquirers of it. The refusal of the person running the camping site was considered abusive, as it merely was motivated by the latter's frustration of having missed some commission on the sale of the camper. Again, the Court of Cassation did not break the decision. In the meantime, the re-codification of the Belgian Civil Code has recognized the general applicability of the abuse of rights doctrine by codifying it in its general part (Book 1 of the Belgian Civil Code) (article 1.10 Be.Civ. C.).[82]

34. Sanction: ineffectiveness – As the sanction of an abuse of rights is the ineffectiveness of the exercise of that right, or its moderation as it is called under Belgian law, the sanction consists in not enforcing the abusive exercise of a right and thereby imposing a reasonable exercise of the right. Alternatively, damages can be granted. If the refusal to contract or the breaking-off of negotiations is the exercise of a right or freedom for that matter, the reasonable exercise of that right or freedom would consist in forced contract conclusion or, at least, negotiations. Sébastien De Rey argued in this sense in his dissertation *Herstel in natura*:

> "However, the refusal to contract could also be seen as the non-exercise of the power to contract. This can be changed by the court by imposing exactly the exercise of the power to contract. . . . In either line of reasoning, the court can turn the exercise of power not to contract into contracting. To do so, the court can substitute itself in the unwilling party to give the required consent with its ruling with a view to making that contract (ruling replaces negotium). This is what is called contract coercion or forced contracting."[83]

80 "The appellate court thus considered the benefits of the contract refusal for the plaintiff in its judgment and could consequently rule as a matter of law that these are disproportionate to the detriment of the defendants, who were forced to sell their caravan at a loss so that the refusal of contract is abusive. The plea cannot be accepted." Cass.be., 27 April 2020, C. 19.0423.N. Free translation. Original text: "*De appelrechter betrekt aldus de voordelen van de contractweigering voor de eiseres in zijn oordeel en kon bijgevolg naar recht oordelen dat deze buiten verhouding staan tot het nadeel van de verweerders die zich genoodzaakt zagen hun caravan met verlies te verkopen zodat de contractweigering abusief is. Het middel kan niet worden aangenomen.*"

81 Cass.be., 27 April 2020, C. 19.0423.N, case note T. HICK en F. VAN DEN ABEELE, *TBBR* 2021, 155, noot S. JANSEN en S. STIJNS, and *T.Not.* 2021, 368, noot M. MEIRLAEN.

82 On the applicability of the prohibition of abuse of rights to the refusal to contract in light of the recent case law and re-codification see Stijns and Auvray, "L'abus de droit dans le Livre 1er du Code civil." nr. 2. See also on the impact of the re-codification Thierry Léonard, "L'interdiction de l'abus de droit dans le nouveau Code civil: requiem pour un principe général de droit?" in *Les principes généraux du droit privé*, ed. J. Van Meerbeeck and Y. Ninane (Limal: Anthemis, 2023). pp. 67–113.

83 De Rey, *Herstel in Natura. Rechtsvergelijkende studie in het contractenrecht met buitencontractuele invalshoek*. p. 784, nr. 922. Free translation. Orginal text: "*De contractweigering zou echter ook kunnen worden gezien als de niet-uitoefening van de bevoegdheid om te contracteren. Dit kan de rechter beteugelen door de bevoegdheidsuitoefening precies wel op te leggen. . . . Hoe dan ook, in*

De Rey consequently observes that if the refusal to contract was considered abusive, the party that refused to contract no longer was considered free not to contract. Hence, imposing an obligation to contract appears as the logical consequence.[84] This is as true as revealing: De Rey, without stating it explicitly, observes that, in fact, via the abuse of rights doctrine, an obligation to contract is imposed.

35. Abuse of rights and no-contract scenario – Relying on the abuse of rights appears as a structurally sound approach to overcome the normative causal uncertainty. The discussions on the applicability of the prohibition of abuse of rights to the exercise of the freedom from contract do not appear warranted, at the very least not when approached from a structural perspective. It comes, thus, as no surprise how frequently the prohibition of abuse of rights is relied on in the context of no-contract law. Though often not sufficiently highlighted, it is mostly the specific sanction of the reduction of the exercise of a right or inefficacy that explains the functional strength of the prohibition of the abuse of rights: it allows to enforce an obligation under the veil of reduction. This strength is also its weakness, as indeed, this is a challenge to the general structure of private law systems. Hence, I would argue that, in the short run, relying on the prohibition of abuse of rights is a, if not the, most sensible approach to overcome the issue of normative causal uncertainty. In the long run, however, it appears preferable to face what is actually happening and recognize the existence of an obligation to contract or to negotiate.

4. Beating around the bush

36. Underlying obligation – I have discussed different techniques to circumvent or overcome, depending on how one sees it, the problem of the normative causal uncertainty following from freedom from contract. Some of those techniques rely on tweaked understanding of one of the conditions of application (fault (*supra* Chap. 6, nrs. 4–7), harm (*supra* Chap. 6, nr. 8–9) or the degree of certainty of the causal link (*supra* Chap. 6, nrs. 10–11)). Especially for the understanding that pre-supposes an obligation and standardized harm, this deviance from general liability law has repercussions on the application of the other conditions of application and might in turn explain some resulting incoherencies. Aside from these little tricks, the "idea" of loss of a chance (*supra* Chap. 6, nr. 12–24) provides a means to overcome causal uncertainty by invoking another harm – the lost chance – and the abuse of rights (*supra* Chap. 6, nrs. 25–35) doctrine allows for side-lining considerations of causality in favour of a judge-made obligation to

beide redeneringen kan de rechter de bevoegdheidsuitoefening om niet te contracteren ombuigen tot wel contracteren. Daarvoor kan de rechter zich in de onwillige partij kunnen substitueren om met zijn uitspraak de vereiste toestemming te geven met oog op totstandkoming van dat contract (uitspraak vervangt negotium). Dat is wat men noemt contractdwang of gedwongen contractsluiting."

84 De Rey, *Herstel in Natura. Rechtsvergelijkende studie in het contractenrecht met buitencontractuele invalshoek*. p. 787, nr. 923.

exercise one's right as would have been reasonable in the given circumstances. Thus, where reasonings in terms of "deceiving legitimate expectations" or "reaching a point of no-return" conceal an obligation to contract in the fault (but often not enforcing it and artificially limiting the compensable harm to the negative interest), the prohibition of the abuse of rights enforces an obligation to negotiate or to contract by way of moderation of the exercise of a right (or freedom) – be it in kind or in damages. Indeed, while the pre-supposed obligation is hidden in the characterization of the fault in the first case, it is enforced in the second one of abuse of rights: the judge decides how a party should have exercised its freedom (i.e. creates an obligation) and holds the party to it (i.e. enforces the obligation).[85]

37. ESCAPISM – These ways of circumventing the causal uncertainty are – in a way – techniques to beat around the bush. They do, some more convincingly than others, allow to overcome or make less apparent the underlying causal uncertainty. Yet they always remain just that, a way to escape the actual point of causal uncertainty. Invoking the prohibition to abuse one's rights appears to me as the most convincing way of arguing, but ultimately, this also remains a technique that allows to conceal a judge-made obligation to negotiate or to contract. Hence, all of these techniques are a matter of escapism, not one of solving the issue. Such approaches can be useful in a first instance, when scholarship and case law struggle to accommodate a desired legal outcome. Figures such as the prohibition of the abuse of rights or invoking legitimate expectations are very useful in such cases, but they ideally remain temporary solutions:

> "Equity is precisely the ignoring of categorically useful characteristics, indeed the refraining from general conflict situations and their just general regulation in favour of the *hic et nunc* just decision. Modern jurisprudence should neutralise and absorb such unica. They do not belong in the collection of case law, but rather the new formations that should and may apply in principle to cases of a similar nature. We can speak here of programmatic legal development, which is also often born out of emotional considerations of fairness and yet seeks and asserts a firm normative and systematic position."[86]

85 In the same sense Krawitz, *Schutz vorvertraglicher Investitionen – Zur Haftung beim Scheitern von Vertragsverhandlungen*. p. 95. See references there.

86 As explained in Josef Esser, "Wandlung von Billigkeit und Billigkeitsrechtsprechung im modernen Privatrecht," in *Summum Ius Summa Iniuria; Individualgerechtigkeit und Schutz allgemeiner Werte im Rechtsleben* (Tübingen: Mohr Siebeck, 1963). p. 39. Free translation. Original text: "*Billigkeit ist eben das Übergehen van kategorische brauchbaren Merkmalen, ja das Absehen von generellen Konfliktslagen und ihrer gerechten allgemeinen Reglung zugunsten der hic et nunc gerechten Entscheidung. Die moderne Jurisprudenz sollte solche Unica neutralisieren und absorbieren. Nicht sie gehören in die Judikatursammlung, sondern die Neubildungen, die für Fälle Ähnlicher Art grundsätzlich gelten sollen und dürfen. Wir können hier von programmatischer Rechtsfortbildung sprechen, die gleichfalls oft aus emotionalen Billigkeitserwägungen geboren und doch festen dormatischen und systematischen Stand sucht und behauptet.*"

A more mature legal system should be able to provide a more convincing and coherent solution. As a matter of fact, that is exactly what Jan Busche argues in the context of German law based on § 826 BGB (liability for immoral conduct). He argues that using § 826 BGB as a legal basis for an obligation to contract is some sort of compromise but not as a mature solution for the underlying question of when an obligation to contract should arise.[87]

38. Obligation to negotiate or to contract – In my opinion, the only truly convincing and coherent argument lies in recognizing that judges do, on more or less of a legal basis, pre-suppose an obligation to negotiate or to contract in their reasoning. To the extent that this is, technically speaking, true, the two main questions that arise in this context are (i) whether there is a legal basis for that obligation and, if so, which one and (ii) what its extent is, thereby also defining, to a large extent, the remedy in case of non-respect of that obligation. The aim of the following title will precisely be to uncover and describe this obligation. Yet as these obligations to negotiate or to contract are generally merely implied or pre-supposed, their regime is not yet quite clear. Only occasional manifestations of their functioning are described in scholarship or appear in case law. Those "occasional manifestations" are most common under Dutch and German law, which explains why I rely so much on Dutch and German scholarship in this context.

87 "In this respect, he accepts that he sometimes robs the general clauses of their actual thematic roots and transplants them into a foreign environment. Nothing else happens with § 826 BGB when the provision is misappropriated to protect the freedom of contract just because the contract law of the BGB does not recognise a provision that supports the obligation to contract and thus leaves the freedom of contract unprotected at its most sensitive flank, namely the freedom of contract.

In this context, the provision of § 826 BGB, as a normative proxy, only provides the formal-dogmatic basis for a legal application process, in that an abuse of the freedom to form a contract is interpreted as behaviour that is (also) relevant under tort law. The tort law norm is merely the instrument for introducing contract law judgments into the application of the law. This is also shown by the handling of § 826 BGB in legal practice, which usually does not even bother to justify the immorality of the refusal to contract in detail. On closer inspection, the derivation of the general obligation to contract has completely replaced § 826 BGB over the course of time." Busche, *Privatautonomie und Kontrahierungszwang*. pp. 651–652. Free translation. Original text: "*Er nimmt insoweit in Kauf, daß er dabei zuweilen die Generalklauseln ihrer eigentlichen thematischen Wurzeln beraubt und sie in eine ihnen fremde Umgebung verpflanzt. Nichts anderes geschieht mit § 826 BGB, wenn die Vorschrift zum Schutze der Vertragsbegründungsfreiheit zweckentfremdet wird, einzig aus dem Grunde, weil das Vertragsrecht des BGB eine den Kontrahierungszwang tragende Be- stimmung nicht kennt und damit die Vertragsfreiheit an ihrer empfindlichsten Flanke, eben der Vertragsbegründungsfreiheit, ungeschützt läßt.*

Die Vorschrift des § 826 BGB gibt in diesem Zusammenhang als normativer Stellvertreter nur den formal-dogmatischen Aufhänger für einen Rechtsanwen- dungsvorgang ab, indem ein Mißbrauch der Vertragsbegründungsfreiheit als ein (auch) deliktsrechtlich relevantes Verhalten gedeutet wird. Die deliktsrechtliche Norm ist lediglich das Instrumentarium, um vertragsrechtliche Wertungen in den Rechtsanwendungsvorgang einführen zu können. Das zeigt auch der Umgang mit § 826 BGB in der Rechtspraxis, die sich zumeist nicht einmal mehr der Mühe unterzieht, die Sittenwidrigkeit der Vertragsverweigerung im einzelnen zu begrün- den. Bei näherer Betrachtung hat sich die Herleitung des allgemeinen Kontrahierungszwangs im Laufe der Zeit vollständig von § 826 BGB abgelöst."

7 The obligation to negotiate or to contract

1. Obligations to negotiate or to contract

1.1. Legal basis

1.1.1. Conventional sources of obligations

1. Sources of obligations – In a liberal system of private law, parties can only be under an obligation if a more or less identified source for such an obligation exists. Classically, such sources are the will of the party under an obligation, the law, and torts. More sources for obligations may exist in the respective legal system, but it is not so much the point here to provide a comparative inventory of sources of obligations. I merely want to point out that obligations can, in principle, only be enforced, provided a valid source for such an obligation exists. Faced with the necessity to explain the existence of an obligation absent a fitting source for that obligation, some substitute sources of obligations are invoked by scholars and courts to overcome the absence of classical source of obligations. The case of broken-off negotiations is a clear example of such implied sources of obligations, relying on sources of obligations such as implicit agreements (*infra* Chap. 7, nr. 4), legitimate expectations (*infra* Chap. 7, nr. 5), or reaching a point of no-return (*infra* Chap. 7, nr. 6). Besides such alternative sources of obligations, there, of course, is a very classical source of obligations which can also occur, namely, the negotiation agreement. I will first briefly deal with this latter question to then address the different implicit sources of obligations. I will not deal with specific statutory obligations to contract, as they always are targeted at solving a specific issue and should not serve as a basis for a general obligation to contract.[1]

2. Negotiation agreement and risk modulation – Essentially, what parties aim for by concluding a negotiation agreement is to modify the default risk attribution. They will do so either by improving their rights in case they suffer the failure of contract conclusion or, inversely, by limiting their own liability in that

1 Busche, *Privatautonomie und Kontrahierungszwang*. pp. 647–648.

DOI: 10.4324/9781003599166-11

same case. To improve their rights in the case of failed contract conclusion, the party will want to stipulate an obligation to contract or to negotiate. So doing and depending on how exactly it frames this obligation (on which *infra* Chap. 7, nrs. 9–13), they will strengthen their position in order to hold their counterparty liable. To this end, different formulations and techniques exist, and I cannot deal with them comprehensively, but they all boil down to clarifying that the outcome the parties aim for is the conclusion of a contract. To limit their risk of being held liable, the opposite will be done: clarifying that no agreement is yet in sight and that the aim is not at this stage to conclude a contract but to explore the possibility of contracting. Though this should be the default situation, clarifying it by way of a negotiation agreement certainly eases the burden (of proof) of discharging oneself of liability.

3. Defining conduct or harm – Another way of anticipating possible liability claims is to specify what can and what cannot give rise to liability, on the one hand, and/or, on the other hand, specify the consequences of liability. In terms of specifying the conditions for liability, parties may want to define certain conduct that can give, or precisely not give, rise to liability – depending on the aim a party pursues via its negotiation agreement. Concerning the consequences of liability, parties may want to circumscribe – more or less extensively depending on their aim – the harm that has to be indemnified and provide for the way it needs to be indemnified if that appears appropriate.

1.1.2. Implied sources of obligations

4. Implied agreement – An almost intuitive reaction is to justify the existence of an obligation to negotiate or to contract based on some kind of implied agreement. Indeed, the will of parties is a very convenient source of an obligation which can, with relatively great ease, be relied on if it is considered to be implied in some form of conduct of one or both parties. Whether such implied consent actually exists or only has been found to exist *ex post* for the sake of a convenient explanation is a tricky question. Remaining critical of such explanations, however, seems warranted.

Much of French-speaking scholarship, for instance, explains that Jhering's *culpa in contrahendo* was based on contractual liability because Jhering relied on some form of implied agreement.[2] That is, of course, not true (*supra* Chap. 1, nr. 3). Rather, it was Faggella who relied on some form of implied agreement – that parties had agreed to work out a final contract (*supra* Chap. 1, nr. 15) – to justify that the breaking-off of negotiations was prohibited.

In a more contemporary context, relying on an implicit agreement takes different forms in different national legal systems.[3] Under Dutch law, more

2 Some illustrations Lequette et al., *Droit civil Les Obligations*. p. 265, nr. 248; Durant, "La rupture unilatérale des pourparlers ou l'exercice d'une liberté surveillée." p. 42, nr. 3; Ghestin, "La responsabilité délictuelle pour rupture abusive des pourparlers." p. 15, nr. 3.

3 By way of caveat, of course, it is important to remind the reader that these different dogmatic ways of defining different types of negotiation agreements fail to have any legal relevance and merely have

attention goes to the so-called trunk-agreement ("*rompovereenkomst*"), designating that essential parts of the contract under negotiation have already been agreed upon without the contract being actually concluded. Marcel Ruygvoorn describes the trunk-agreement in his dissertation, *Afgebroken onderhandelingen en het gebruik van voorbehouden*,[4] as "an agreement which is not yet 'perfect' in law, which still has gaps, which still need to be filled in."[5] Different from the meaning it has under French law (*infra* Chap. 7, nr. 10),[6] the Belgian understanding of a heads of agreement or, more literally translated, an agreement on the principle of contracting ("*accord de principe*"/"*beginselakkoord*") resembles to that of the Dutch *rompovereenkomst*. This is an agreement on the principle *that* parties want to contract, without however agreeing exactly on the terms of the contract at this stage.[7] This technique can be observed in a decision of the Belgian Court of Appeal of Antwerp from 1994.[8] In that case, a travel agency had gotten the request to prepare a business trip to Indonesia. The travel agency did so: it organized a scouting trip, ordered goodies for the travellers, *et cetera*. Shortly before the planned departure, the party who had requested the preparation of the business trip states that they will rely on another travel agency. The Court of Appeal rules that in the case at hand, an agreement on the principle of contracting had been concluded and that, therefore, the party no longer had been free to break-off negotiations and had to compensate the lost benefit of the travel agency. The Court reasoned as follows:

> "Considering it cannot be assumed that in February-March 1989 the parties were still in the legally non-binding negotiation phase; considering that phase had already been left much earlier; considering, in view of the above, it has been established that in any event – and already at an early stage – an agreement in principle on the trip had been reached that, by changing mind a few weeks before departure by entering into business with a competitor on the ground that the latter would offer more

---

a pedagogical function. Whether this pedagogical function is beneficial, however, is doubtful and particularly so from a comparative perspective, as the different dogmatic typologies differ in meaning across different national systems but often also within a single national system.

4 In particular relied on by Ruygvoorn, *Afgebroken onderhandelingen en het gebruik van voorbehouden*. 461+xvi p.

5 Ruygvoorn, *Afgebroken onderhandelingen en het gebruik van voorbehouden*. p. 31. Free translation. Original text: "*Het betreft een overeenkomst die rechtens nog niet 'perfect' is, die nog lacunes bevat, die nog moeten worden ingevuld.*"

6 Brun, *Responsabilité civile extracontractuelle*. p. 83, nr. 121.

7 Critical about this the value of such an agreement: "The agreement in principle does not oblige the parties to conclude the final contract, and either party may break-off negotiations provided it has complied with the obligation to negotiate in good faith." De Coninck, "Le droit commun de la rupture des négotiations précontractuelles." p. 44, nr. 37. Free translation. Original text: "*L'accord de principe n'oblige pas à conclure le contrat définitif, chacune des parties pouvant rompre les négociations pour autant qu'elle ait respecté l'obligation de négocier de bonne foi.*" Stijns, *Verbintenissenrecht Boek 1*. nr. 103.

8 Antwerp, 22 March 1994, *RW* 1994–1995 (296).

favourable conditions, while the appellant's prices had been known from the outset and by allowing the appellant to continue working on the preparations for the trip for several months, and furthermore in such a way as to give the appellant a legitimate expectation that the contract could no longer slip away, the respondent acted negligently and breached its pre-contractual liability;

Whereas, by way of compensation for the damage caused by that error, the appellant claims in the first place its intermediation percentage of 13% of the total travel expenses, i.e. 716 430 francs; whereas that percentage is appropriate compensation for the work done and efforts made and for the loss of profit which it was entitled to expect from the performance of the contract; whereas the loss of profit (positive contractual interest) is the same as the loss of profit caused by the error that that percentage is appropriate compensation for the work and effort expended and for the loss of profit which the appellant could legitimately expect from the performance of the contract; that the loss of profit (positive contractual interest) in the case of pre-contractual liability is eligible for compensation if, as in the present case, the other party had been led to believe that a contract would be concluded;"[9]

5. Legitimate expectations – The other argument that is brought up by the Court of Appeal in the cited passage is the existence of legitimate expectations of a future contract conclusion. This is not the expectation that a contract *had* already been concluded but *would* anyways be concluded. The exact value that is attached to such legitimate expectations is often somewhat unclear in national systems. It will generally not be recognized as a general source of obligations but, within the context of breaking-off of contract negotiations, does fulfil that function. That is quite explicitly the case under (i) Belgian law, (ii) Dutch law,

9 Antwerp, 22 March 1994, *RW* 1994–1995 (296). pp. 297–298. Free translation. Original text: "*Overwegende dat niet aangenomen kan worden dat par-tijen zich in februari-maart 1989 nog in de rechtens vrijblijvende onderhandelingsfase bevonden; dat die fase reeds veel eerder was verlaten; dat gelet op de vorenstaande elementen is komen vast te staan dat in ieder geval – en reeds in een vroeg stadium – een beginselakkoord over de reis tot stand was gekomen; dat, door enkele weken voor het vertrek het geweer van schouder te veranderen door met een concurrent in zee te gaan om reden dat deze gunstigere voorwaarden zou anbieden, terwijl de prijzen van appellante reeds van aanvang aan bekend waren en men appellante geduren-de maanden an de voorbereiding van de reis verder liet werken, zulks bovendien op een wijze die bij haar het gewettigd vertrouwen mocht doen ontstaan dat de opdracht haar niet meer kon ontglippen, geintimeerde onzorgvuldig handelde en tekort is geschoten in haar precontractuele aansprakelijkheid; Overwegende dat ter vergoeding van de schade die door deze fout werd veroorzaakt, appellante in de erste plaats aanspraak maakt op haar bemiddelingspercentage ten belope van 13% op de totale reiskosten, te weten 716.430 fr.; dat dit percentage en passende vergoeding is voor de geleverde werkzaambeden en inspanningen en voor de gederfde winst die zij wit de uitvoering van de overeenkomst mocht verwachten; dat de gederfde winst (positief contractsbelang) bij precontractuele aansprakelijkheid voor vergoeding in aanmerking komt indien, zoals in casu, bij de wederpartij het vertrouwen was gewekt dat een overeenkomst zou worden gesloten.*"

and in some way, (iii) German law.[10] Under French law, neither the Court of Cassation nor the legislator recognizes such an obligation to contract.

(i) Belgian article 5.17, second alinea, second sentence Be. Civ. C.: "If a legitimate expectation has been created that without any doubt the contract would have been concluded, this liability may include compensation for the loss of the expected net benefits from the contract not concluded."[11] By introducing this second sentence, the legislator has – at least in my opinion[12] – codified an obligation to contract, or at least a variant thereof, without saying it in the text itself.[13] However, in the explanatory note, the legitimate expectations about the future contract conclusion are cited as an exception to the lack of a general source of obligations based on the creation of legitimate expectations.[14]

(ii) Dutch *Plas/Valburg* and *CBB/JPO* decisions (*supra* Chap 2, nr. 34): Founded on the *Plas/Valburg* decision and, in the meantime, replaced by the *CBB/JPO* decision, it is a constant case law of the *Hoge Raad* that "the standard for assessing the obligation to pay damages in the event of broken-off negotiations is that each of the negotiating parties – who are obliged to have their conduct determined in part by each other's legitimate interests – is free to break-off negotiations, unless this would be unacceptable on the basis of the other party's legitimate expectation in the conclusion of the agreement or in connection with the other circumstances of the case."[15] Here, the legitimate expectations of the conclusion of some contract ("einigerlei contract") is the central criterion to establish an obligation to contract. The formulation, however, is open and also allows for "other circumstances of the case."

10 Staudinger/Feldmann (2018) BGB § 311 nr. 143.

11 Original text: "*Lorsque la confiance légitime que le contrat serait sans aucun doute conclu a été suscitée, elle peut impliquer la réparation de la perte des avantages nets attendus du contrat non conclu.*"/"*Wanneer het rechtmatig vertrouwen is gewekt dat het contract zonder enige twijfel gesloten zal worden, kan deze het herstel van het verlies van de verwachte netto-voordelen uit het niet gesloten contract inhouden.*"

12 See Maarten Herbosch, "Contractdwang bij onrechtmatig afgebroken onderhandelingen over de koop van onroerend goed? Het schijn geen brug te ver," *T.Not.* (2021). p. 314, nr. 4. for a different explanation.

13 Critical about the new provision Thomas Derval and Charles-Edouard Lambert, "La conclusion dynamique du contrat," in *Le Livre 5 du Code civil et le nouveau droit des contrats*, ed. Rafaël Jafferali (Bruxelles: Larcier, 2022). pp. 83–97, nrs. 24–29. In favour: Jafferali, "La formation dynamique du contrat." pp. 175–176, nr. 4.

14 Explanation to the law of 24 February 2021 containing Book 5 "Obligations" of the Civil Code, DOC 55 1806/001, p. 18. Confirming by one of the drafters of the new law of obligations Jafferali, "La formation dynamique du contrat." p. 176, nr. 4 and Stijns, *Verbintenissenrecht Boek 1*. nr. 102.

15 HR 12 August 2005, ECLI:NL:HR:2005:AT7337 (CBB/JPO), nr. 3.6. Free translation. Original text: "*als maatstaf voor de beoordeling van de schadevergoedingsplicht bij afgebroken onderhandelingen heeft te gelden dat ieder van de onderhandelende partijen – die verplicht zijn hun gedrag mede door elkaars gerechtvaardigde belangen te laten bepalen – vrij is de onderhandelingen af te breken, tenzij dit op grond van het gerechtvaardigd vertrouwen van de wederpartij in het totstandkomen van de overeenkomst of in verband met de andere omstandigheden van het geval onaanvaardbaar zou zijn.*"

What kind of circumstances can amount to relevant "other circumstances" remains rather unclear.[16]

(iii) German law and the deception of legitimate expectations: Under German law, the central criterion for declaring the breaking-off of contract negotiations wrongful may be the deception of a created legitimate expectation of contract conclusion by breaking-off those negotiations without sufficient reason (*supra* Chap. 3, nrs. 23–24). Relying on this reasoning pre-supposes an obligation to contract or at least to continue negotiations. Yet this obligation to contract is "only" relied on in order to establish liability and overcome the issue of causal uncertainty. Indeed, contrary to the Dutch and Belgian solution, the obligation to contract is not enforced. This is somewhat contradicting and generally explained by the fact that it would otherwise amount to an indirect obligation to contract ("*indirekter Kontrahierungszwang*"), though the finding of liability is based precisely on a pre-supposed obligation to contract.[17]

(iv) Italian law and the deception of legitimate expectations: Though Faggella, when first dealing with the question, had relied on some sort of implicit agreement to elaborate a contract in order to explain that the breaking-off of negotiations had become wrongful (*supra* Chap. 1, nr. 15), Italian courts now seem to rely on the same argument as German courts: the deception of legitimate expectations without sufficient justification.[18] Under Italian law, as much as under German law, the contract cannot be enforced (in nature or damages):

> "the traditional teaching of this Supreme Court, according to which the prejudice that can be compensated in the event of ascertained pre-contractual liability must be limited within the limits of the strict negative interest ("*id quod interest contractum non fuisse*"), represented both by the expenses unnecessarily borne in the course of

16 See for an overview Asser/Sieburgh 6-III 2022/196; Ruygvoorn, *Afgebroken onderhandelingen en het gebruik van voorbehouden*. p. 48: "Apparently, there are thus two bases that make it impossible to break-off negotiations unilaterally: legally justified establishment trust in the success of negotiations and 'other circumstances' that make breaking off negotiations unacceptable by the standards of reasonableness and fairness." Free translation. Original text: "*Kennelijk zijn er dus twee grondslagen die maken dat onderhandelingen niet meer eenzijdig kunnen worden afgebroken: rechtens gerechtvaardigd totstandkomingsvertrouwen in het welslagen van de onderhandelingen en 'andere omstandigheden' die maken dat het afbreken van de onderhandelingen naar maatstaven van redelijkheid en billijkheid onaanvaardbaar is*."

17 "In contrast, it is often argued in the literature that this practice clearly creates the risk of an indirect obligation to contract." MüKoBGB/Emmerich, 9. Aufl. 2022, BGB § 311 nr. 220. Free translation. Original text: "*Dagegen wird im Schrifttum vielfach eingewandt, dass diese Praxis unverkennbar die Gefahr eines mittelbaren Kontrahierungszwanges begründe*." Reference is made to Staudinger/Feldmann (2018) BGB § 311 nr. 175, which in turn refers to Stoll, "Tatbestände und Funktionen der Haftung für culpa in contrahendo." p. 445. The same argument under Dutch law reported and subscribed by Ruygvoorn, *Afgebroken onderhandelingen en het gebruik van voorbehouden*. p. 254.

18 As is reported by Cian, *Commentario breve al Codice Civile*. p. 1426, nr. V or *Febbrajo, Good Faith and Pre-Contractual Liability in Italy*. p. 292. I did, however, not find the exact wording in the case law I looked at.

negotiations with a view to the conclusion of the transaction, and by the loss of further opportunities to enter into an equally or more advantageous contract with others, without extending to the positive interest ("*quantum lucrari potuit*"), and in particular to the indemnifiable loss of profit (pursuant to arts. 1218, 1223 Civil Code and Art. 1453 Civil Code, para. 1) if the contract (if hypothetically concluded) had not been performed or had been terminated due to the other party's fault (see Court of Cassation no. 19883/2005, Court of Cassation no. 2525/2006, Court of Cassation no. 24625/2015, Court of Cassation no. 4718/2016, Court of Cassation no. 30186/2021, Court of Cassation no. 19202/2023)."[19]

6. POINT OF NO-RETURN – Essentially the same reasoning as that applied in the case of deceiving a legitimate expectation – deducting an obligation from a party's conduct – can be observed in the case of reaching a point of no-return. Indeed, a party is held to a prior appearance it had created, namely, that the contract would be concluded. This idea also lies at the root of the doctrine of *venire contra factum proprium* or forfeiture of rights, which provide that if a party acted contrary to what it had previously made think, it is held to this appearance, even though the party could *a priori* rightfully act the way it did (*supra* Chap. 6, nr. 31). In all these cases, the issue is identical: rights of parties are impaired absent a sufficient legal ground.

7. COMPARATIVE CONSIDERATIONS – From a comparative perspective, it is striking that, except for French law, all analysed legal systems rely on some form of obligation to contract. Though relatively isolated, the French law approach is structurally speaking coherent: it sticks to a monolithic structure and does not provide for a liability for the breaking-off of negotiations or the refusal to contract. The other – two-pronged – approach is that chosen by the Dutch and somewhat half-heartedly by the Belgian systems: here, it is recognized that at some point in the negotiation process, parties no longer are free to break-off negotiations, and by consequence, the sanction consists in enforcing the contract under negotiations, be it that the Belgian approach does not seem to want to go all the way down that road. Seemingly, the Belgian legislator could not decide

19 Cass.civ.it. 15 december 2023 nr. 35170. Free translation. Original text: "*L'operato inquadramento dell'istituto nell'ambito della responsabilità di tipo contrattualenon può, tuttavia, condurre alle conseguenze prospettate dalla ricorrente, rimanendotuttora fermo il tradizionale insegnamento di questa Corte Suprema secondo cui il pregiudizio risarcibile in caso di accertata responsabilità precontrattuale deve ritenersi circoscritto nei limiti dello stretto interesse negativo ('id quod interest contractum non fuisse'), rappresentato sia dalle spese inutilmente sopportate nel corso delle trattative in vista della conclusione del negozio, sia dalla perdita di ulteriori occasioni per la stipulazione con altri di un contratto altrettanto o maggiormente vantaggioso, senza estendersi all' interesse positivo ('quantum lucrari potuit'), e in particolare al lucro cessante risarcibile (ex artt. 1218, 1223 c.c. e art. 1453 c.c., comma 1) se il contratto (ove ipoteticamente concluso) non fosse stato poi adempiuto o fosse stato risolto per colpa della controparte (cfr. Cass. n. 19883/2005, Cass. n. 2525/2006, Cass. n. 24625/2015, Cass. n. 4718/2016, Cass. n. 30186/2021, Cass. n. 19202/2023).*"

to implement an obligation to contract. Difficulties in fully embracing a monolithic or two-pronged structure can also be observed under German and Italian law, where an obligation to contract is pre-supposed in the reasoning leading to liability but is then not enforced when it comes to the sanction. The unease of dealing with wrongful breaking-off of negotiations is palpable.

8. Choice of criterion – The widespread reliance on some form of an obligation to contract suggests that in most legal systems, scholars, judges, and occasionally, legislators perceive a need for such an obligation to contract. Generally speaking, I agree with this necessity. Yet the *way in which* this result is aimed for is flawed. Not only do scholars, courts, and legislators generally not recognize that they try to create obligations to contract or negotiate but they do so generally based on a not quite thoughtful criterion. Indeed, the choice for the criterion of deceived legitimate expectations is strange upon closer reflection. Sure, given the semantic trick it allows (pre-supposing an obligation, as explained *supra* Chap. 3, nr. 23), it is sensible. Yet the decision, based on which an obligation to contract can be granted, is a fundamental and political one (*supra* Chap. 1, nrs. 30–31). That some vague and, frankly, quite random criterion of deceived legitimate expectations is relied on for that purpose cannot convince. Socio-economically, no better reason for relying on this criterion comes to mind than some vague intuition that it is not quite upright to deceive legitimate expectations.

1.2. Content

9. Obligation to negotiate or to contract – So far, I have always referred to an obligation to contract or to negotiate as an aggregate. Yet "a claim to renegotiate does not result in contract enforcement."[20] Hence, both are distinct, and it matters which one is at stake, an obligation to contract or to negotiate. There is no absolute answer to this question; depending on the context, either an obligation to contract or to negotiate has been relied upon. Given that the obligation to negotiate or to contract, more often than not, is implied in the reasoning instead of being explicitly recognized, the clearest manifestation of the content of the obligation will be the granted remedy. If the remedy is one of forcing the continuation to negotiate, the underlying obligation is one to continue negotiations; if the remedy is on of forcing the conclusion of a contract, the underlying obligation is one to conclude a contract.

10. Obligation to negotiate – As negotiations are not an end in themselves but merely a means to reach a contract conclusion, an obligation to negotiate cannot be an obligation to reach a certain result. Instead, it is an obligation to provide all reasonable means to reach an agreement and act, if not cooperatively, at least constructively. That is what Annick De Boeck describes under Belgian

20 Ruygvoorn, *Afgebroken onderhandelingen en het gebruik van voorbehouden*. p. 255. Free translation. Original text: "*Een vordering tot dooronderhandelen levert dus geen contractsdwang op.*"

law.[21] She deducts therefrom that forced negotiations only make sense if it still is possible that a contract could be concluded.[22] Under Dutch law, Marcel Ruygvoorn interprets the case law of the *Hoge Raad* in the same sense:

> "Therefore, the possibility, accepted by the *Hoge Raad*, that a party who breaks off negotiations at a stage when it is no longer free to do so may be ordered to continue negotiating, does not imply any contractual compulsion on that party, but merely an obligation to try to agree with the other party, in accordance with the standards of reasonableness and fairness, on the outstanding issues."[23]

This corresponds to the French understanding of an agreement on the principle (of contracting) ("*accord de principe*"). As Gaël Chantepie and Mathias Latina explain, such an agreement on the principle obliges parties contribute in good faith to concluding a contract.[24] The Catala reform project for the French Civil Code even devoted an article to it:

> "Article 1104–1 The parties may, by an agreement in principle, undertake to negotiate the elements of which are to be determined, and to work together in good faith to determine them."[25]

21 De Boeck, "De tussenkomst van de rechter in de precontractuele fase: mogelijkheden en grenzen." pp. 233–245, nr. 29–63. Under German law: Robert Freitag, "'Specific performance' and 'causa-Lehre' über alles im Recht des Vorvertrags?" *AcP* 207 (2007). p. 306.

22 Many reasons can be thought of that would make such a future contract conclusion unthinkable. Either one of the parties has already contracted with a third party, the relations between parties have become too heated up, the position of one of the parties on the market has changed drastically, . . . De Boeck, "De tussenkomst van de rechter in de precontractuele fase: mogelijkheden en grenzen." 236, nr. 41. See also in the Netherlands Tjittes, *Commercieel Contractenrecht*. p. 82; Ruygvoorn, *Afgebroken onderhandelingen en het gebruik van voorbehouden*. p. 256 (see also examples there). For a comparative analysis Carlos Bollen, "Enforcement of the Duty to Carry on Neogtiations: (Schould It Be) a Possibility in Europe or Not?" in *Specific Performance in Contract Law: National and Other Perspectives*, ed. Jan Smits, Daniel Haas and Geert Hesen (Antwerp: Intersentia, 2008). pp. 231–248.

23 Ruygvoorn, *Afgebroken onderhandelingen en het gebruik van voorbehouden*. p. 254. Free translation. Original text: "*De door de Hoge Raad aanvaarde mogelijkheid dat een partij die in een stadium waarin dit hem niet meer vrij staat de onderhandelingen afbreekt, veroordeeld kan worden om door te onderhandelen, betekent dan ook geen contractdwang voor die partij, maar louter de verplichting om, naar maatstaven van redelijkheid en billijkheid, met de ander te trachten het eens te worden over de nog openstaande punten*."

24 Gaël Chantepie and Mathias Latina, *Le nouveau droit des obligations Commentaire théorique et pratique dans l'ordre du Code Civil* (Paris: Dalloz, 2018). p. 155, nr. 171. Also understood in this way by the Belgian author Bertrand De Coninck in his comparative analysis: "The agreement in principle does not oblige the parties to conclude the final contract, and either party may break-off negotiations provided it has complied with the obligation to negotiate in good faith." De Coninck, "Le droit commun de la rupture des négotiations précontractuelles." p. 44, nr. 37. Free translation. Original text: "*L'accord de principe n'oblige pas à conclure le contrat définitif, chacune des parties pouvant rompre les négociations pour autant qu'elle ait respecté l'obligation de négocier de bonne foi*."

25 Free translation. Original text: "*Les parties peuvent, par un accord de principe, s'engager à négocier ultérieurement un contrat dont les éléments sont à déterminer, et à concourir de bonne foi à leur détermination*."

Though having "to work together in good faith to determine" the remaining unsettled points may seem self-evident even absent an obligation to negotiate, it, in fact, is not, as negotiations, and so are parties, are free to enter negotiations merely to assess the opportunity of contracting. As a default situation, it appears contrary to the freedom from contract to require that parties constructively contribute to finding an agreement. Hence, an obligation to negotiate has an added value, at least theoretically speaking. Marcel Ruygvoorn illustrates what an obligation to negotiate may designate:

> "In any case, a party who has been ordered to continue negotiations should be expected to adopt a real, open and reasonable attitude to the remaining issues. Proposals made to overcome differences should be real and reasonable. There should be no sham offers and the proposals should not be rejected on unreasonable grounds. If the party ordered to continue negotiating frustrates the negotiations by adopting a very inflexible attitude, the court of fact will have to examine the extent to which the positions taken by that party in the negotiations are reasonable."[26]

Admittedly, the line between an obligation to negotiate and general duties of care may, at times, be particularly difficult to trace.

11. Obligation to contract – The traditional definition of an obligation to contract is provided by Hans Karl Nipperdey in *Kontrahierungszwang und diktierter Vertrag* from 1920:

> "The forced contract is the obligation imposed by a rule of law on a legal entity in the interest of a beneficiary, without the agreement of the obligated, to conclude a contract with the beneficiary with a specific content or a content to be determined by an impartial party"[27]

To Iris Houben, as she explains in her dissertation *Contractdwang*, this definition has been interpreted to designate an obligation to accept an offer (*infra* Chap. 7, nr. 12) instead of an obligation to contract. Rather than suggesting an alternative

26 Ruygvoorn, *Afgebroken onderhandelingen en het gebruik van voorbehouden*. p. 258. Free translation. Original text: "*In elk geval geldt dat van een partij die is veroordeeld om de onderhandelingen voort te zetten, een reële, open en redelijke opstelling mag worden verwacht ten aanzien van de nog overgebleven punten. Voorstellen die gedaan worden om meningsverschillen te overbruggen, dienen reëel en redelijk te zijn. Er mag geen sprake zijn van schijnaanbiedingen en de voorstellen mogen niet op onredelijke gronden worden afgewezen. Frustreert de partij die bevolen is om door te onderhandelen de onderhandelingen door een hele starre houding aan te nemen, dan zal de feitenrechter moeten onderzoeken in hoeverre de door die partij ingenomen standpunten in de onderhandelingen redelijk zijn.*"

27 Hans Carl Nipperdey, *Kontrahierungszwang und diktierter Vertrag* (Jena: Verlag von Gustav Fischer, 1920). p. 7. Free translation. Original text: "*Der Kontrahierungszwang ist die auf Grund einer Norm der Rechtsordnung einem Rechtssubjekt ohne seine Willensbindung im Interesse eines Begünstigten auferlegte Verpflichtung, mit diesem einen Vertrag bestimmten oder von unparteiischer Seite zu bestimmenden Inhalts abzuschließen.*"

interpretation, she gives an alternative *definition* which, particularly in the English translation, appears somewhat rudimentary:

> "I describe forced contracting simply as an obligation to contract."[28]

Jan Busche's definition appears more useful, as provided in in his habilitation, *Privatautonomie und Kontrahierungszwang*.[29] For him, an obligation to contract ("*Kontrahierungszwang*") means that "the provider who refuses to enter into a contract is obliged by law to conclude a private-law contract with the rejected prospective customer (obligatio ex lege)."[30] To this, he then adds the implications of an obligation to contract, namely:

> "In the case of a general obligation to enter into a contract, a legal obligation only exists for the party refusing to enter into the contract, as the party that wants to contract, even if it is the only supplier. In contrast to the party refusing the contract, the party interested in the contract is also free to refrain completely from concluding the contract. For the party refusing to enter into a contract, the legal obligation to enter into a contract means not only a restriction of his freedom to enter into a contract, but also a restriction of his freedom to amend and terminate the contract. Anyone who is obliged to conclude a contract must, for the same reasons, allow himself to be bound by the target contract to be concluded, as otherwise the effect of the obligation to contract could be undermined."[31]

Though this certainly helps to understand better what is at stake when an obligation to contract is enforced, it does not allow to understand what exactly the content of an obligation to contract is. Busche understands the obligation to contract as an obligation to be obliged ("*Verpflichtung zur Verpflichtung*").[32] That is to say

28 Houben, *Contractdwang*. p. 4. Free translation. Original text: "*Ik omschrijf contractdwang simpelweg als een contracteerplicht.*"

29 Busche, *Privatautonomie und Kontrahierungszwang*. XXIV+722 p.

30 Busche, *Privatautonomie und Kontrahierungszwang*. p. 240. Free translation. Original text: "*Aus dem Rechtsinstitut des allgemeinen Kontrahierungszwangs folgt für den vertragsverweigernden Anbieter die auf Gesetz beruhende Verpflichtung zum Abschluß eines privatrechtlichen Vertrages mit dem abgewiesenen Vertragsinteressenten (obligatio ex lege).*"

31 Busche, *Privatautonomie und Kontrahierungszwang*. p. 240. Citations omitted. Free translation. Orginal text: "*Ein Rechtszwang besteht beim allgemeinen Kontrahierungszwang immer nur für den vertragsverweigernden Teil, da der Vertragsinteressent gerade freiwillig mit dem Vertragsverweigerer abschließen will, auch wenn es sich um den einzigen Anbieter handeln sollte. Im Gegensatz zum Vertragsverweigerer ist der Vertragsinteressent auch frei, von dem Vertragsschluß vollständig Abstand zu nehmen. Für den Vertragsverweigerer bedeutet der Rechtszwang zum Kontrahieren nicht nur eine Beschränkung seiner Vertragsbegründungsfreiheit, sondern zugleich auch eine Einschränkung seiner Vertragsabänderungs- und -beendigungsfreiheit. Wer zum Vertragsschluß verpflichtet ist, muß sich aus den gleichen Gründen an dem abzuschließenden Zielvertrag festhalten lassen, da ansonsten die Wirkung des Kontrahierungszwangs unterlaufen werden könnte.*"

32 Busche, *Privatautonomie und Kontrahierungszwang*. p. 247.

that one has to conclude a contract; the content of that contract, however, is not fixed by virtue of the obligation to contract and, hence, must be established by the parties jointly.

Relying on such an obligation may be perceived as naive. If parties failed to come to an agreement in the first place, why should they mordaciously find an agreement after one of the parties has manifested its unwillingness to contract?

> "An obligation to conclude a contract as well as a judgement of the party refusing the contract to conclude a contract with the party interested in the contract without a more detailed determination of the consideration to be provided by the party interested in the contract or the procedure for its determination also appears, apart from the procedural problems raised by this, to be somewhat pointless in terms of substantive law, as it can hardly be expected that the contract will be concluded quickly due to the prior behaviour of the party refusing the contract. Finally, the fear that the party refusing the contract, as the economically stronger party, will evade the obligation to contract by demanding contractual terms that are unacceptable to the other party cannot be dismissed out of hand."[33]

This is not so much a question of the content of its obligation but of its enforcement.[34] Such enforcement mechanisms should be strong enough to convince parties to find an agreement that both can live with. A judge-imposed contract, as enforcement of an obligation to contract, hence, seems both coherent and useful. To the extent that the party who claims the contract conclusion will generally be clear about what it claims, it will mainly be the counter-performance of the refusing party that will have to be fixed by the judge.[35] This should put a credible incentive on the refusing party to find an agreement, where it maintains greater influence over its own rights.

12. Obligation to accept or to offer – Alternatively, an obligation to contract could be conceived as an obligation to accept or to emit an offer. The former, an

33 Busche, *Privatautonomie und Kontrahierungszwang*. p. 252. Free translation. Original text: "*Eine Verpflichtung zum Vertragsschluß wie auch eine Verurteilung des Vertragsverweigerers zum Vertragsschluß mit dem Vertragsinteressenten ohne nähere Bestimmung der von dem Vertragsinteressenten zu erbringenden Gegenleistung bzw. des Verfahrens zu ihrer Bestimmung erscheint, abgesehen von den damit aufgeworfenen prozessualen Problemen, auch materiell-rechtlich einigermaßen sinnlos, da aufgrund des Vorverhaltens des Vertragsverweigerers kaum zu erwarten ist, daß es zu einem zügigen Vertragsabschluß kommt. Schließlich ist auch die Befürchtung nicht von der Hand zu weisen, der Vertragsverweigerer als wirtschaftlich stärkerer Teil werde sich durch Fordern für die Gegenseite nicht akzeptabler Vertragsbedingungen dem Kontrahierungszwang entziehen.*" See also the references there.

34 This point seems to be missed by Busche and the authors he relies on in Busche, *Privatautonomie und Kontrahierungszwang*. pp. 251–251.

35 Busche, *Privatautonomie und Kontrahierungszwang*. p. 252.

obligation to accept an offer,[36] seems more advantageous to the party suffering the refusal to contract, as it will, logically, be the party emitting the offer. This right to have its offer accepted, however, should be paired with some competence of judges to control the reasonability of that offer. Otherwise, abuses of the parties entitled to have their offer accepted must be feared. Franz Bydlinski, in *Zu den dogmatischen Grundfragen des Kontrahierungszwanges*,[37] argues that by requiring reasonable offers, the freedom to decide the content of the contract is also being curtailed, as parties are no longer entirely free to decide the content of the contract.[38] Though that is true, it does not appear quite problematic today since correcting contracts with grossly imbalanced content is increasingly accepted under national legal systems.

If one prefers a system which is more favourable to the party who refused to contract, an obligation to emit an offer can be considered preferable. Such a way of proceeding leaves more control in the hands of the party that originally refused to contract and be more protective of its freedom from contract. Here, again, an *a posteriori* control by a judge should be possible in order to prevent abuses.

13. Obligation to perform – As an alternative to an obligation to contract, offer, or accept, a mere obligation to perform the obligations under the contract to be concluded may appear as a more pragmatic solution, as arguably, the purpose of a forced contract is the performance of the obligations within it. This indeed may occasionally be a pragmatic solution but only makes sense where the obligations under the contract to be concluded are already clear.[39] In fact, with Busche, it must be clarified that such an obligation to perform can occasionally satisfy the needs of the party suffering the refusal to contract but, in fact, fulfils another *function* than an obligation to contract. The latter serves to establish what the parties will owe each other in the future:

> "In the context of the general obligation to contract, the contract therefore has no other function than in general in contract law: it serves to implement the exchange of services. Only the conclusion of the contract creates clarity for the parties about all the conditions of the exchange transaction, in particular about the type and amount of the consideration."[40]

36 Staudinger/Bork (2020) Vorbemerkung zu §§ 145 ff. nrs. 29 and 33.

37 Bydlinski, "Zu den dogmatischen Grundfragen des Kontrahierungszwanges." pp. 1–46.

38 Bydlinski, "Zu den dogmatischen Grundfragen des Kontrahierungszwanges." p. 5. In the same sense Nipperdey, *Kontrahierungszwang und diktierter Vertrag*. p. 31.

39 Busche, *Privatautonomie und Kontrahierungszwang*. p. 248; Bydlinski, "Zu den dogmatischen Grundfragen des Kontrahierungszwanges." p. 24.

40 Busche, *Privatautonomie und Kontrahierungszwang*. p. 249. Free translation. Original text: "*Der Vertrag hat also im Kontext mit dem allgemeinen Kontrahierungszwang keine andere Funktion als im übrigen Vertragsrecht: Er dient der Durchführung des Leistungs- austausches. Erst der Vertragsschluß schafft für die Parteien Klarheit über alle Bedingungen des Austauschgeschäfts,*

14. JUDGE-MADE CONTRACT – The function of fixing the obligations of parties for the future may be put upon a judge who imposes what parties were to agree to. Subsequentially, the judges can enforce the obligation to perform. This begs obvious questions in terms of how the judge is to determine the content of the contract and inherently entails the freedom to decide the content of a contract. From this regard, such an approach appears more intrusive and less sustainable, hence, less desirable. In order to remain as faithful as possible to party autonomy, the judge must not decide the content of the contract based on what is normal in the market but based on what parties would have agreed to.[41] Though both criteria can lead to the same result, the distinction matters to the extent that it allows the judge to take into account specific circumstances of the concrete case.

Nevertheless, it remains quite intrusive for a judge to both decide upon the content of the contract to be concluded between parties and to declare them bound to it. Doing so only seems plausible if a prior obligation to contract has been infringed (*supra* Chap. 7, nr. 11), thus limiting the instances in which a judge would have to proceed to such an intrusive act. Granting this power to a judge subsequently to the non-performance of an obligation to contract seems confirmed in the phrasing of article 2932 *Codice civile*,[42] which interestingly provides specifically the judge's power to declare parties bound to a contract:

> "If the party who is obliged to conclude a contract fails to perform the obligation, the other party, if it is possible and not precluded by the title, may obtain a judgment producing the effects of the unfinished contract.
>
> In the case of contracts having as their object the transfer of ownership of a specific thing or the creation or transfer of another right, the application may not be granted if the party making the application fails to

---

insbesondere über Art und Höhe der Gegenleistung." See also Bydlinski, "Zu den dogmatischen Grundfragen des Kontrahierungszwanges." p. 18.

41 For a more detailed discussion, particularly to fix prices, see Busche, *Privatautonomie und Kontrahierungszwang*. pp. 257–262. Contra: Bydlinski, "Zu den dogmatischen Grundfragen des Kontrahierungszwanges." p. 27. His argument is based on equal treatment considerations.

42 See also § 894 ZPO in German law: "Where the debtor has been sentenced to make a declaration of intent, such declaration shall be deemed to have been made as soon as the judgment has attained legal force. Where the declaration of intent depends on counter-performance being made, this effect shall occur as soon as an enforceable execution copy of the final and binding judgment has been issued in accordance with the stipulations of sections 726 and 730." Original text: "*Ist der Schuldner zur Abgabe einer Willenserklärung verurteilt, so gilt die Erklärung als abgegeben, sobald das Urteil die Rechtskraft erlangt hat. Ist die Willenserklärung von einer Gegenleistung abhängig gemacht, so tritt diese Wirkung ein, sobald nach den Vorschriften der §§ 726, 730 eine vollstreckbare Ausfertigung des rechtskräftigen Urteils erteilt ist.*" In the context of forced contracting: Freitag, "'Specific Performance' and 'causa-Lehre' über alles im Recht des Vorvertrags?" p. 293. Under Dutch law, this also appears to be possible under article 3:300 NBW (Asser/Sieburgh 6-II 2021/352.). Under Belgian law defended in De Rey, *Herstel in Natura. Rechtsvergelijkende studie in het contractenrecht met buitencontractuele invalshoek*. p. 786, nr. 922. See also references for French law in footnote 4739. In the meantime, this could occur based on article 5.236 Be. Civ. C.

> perform or make an offer of performance in accordance with the law, unless performance is still due."[43]

Here, it is clear that the judge only proceeds to declaring parties bound to a contract by way of forced performance of an obligation to contract. Indeed, as Giorgio Cian explains:

> "Art. 2932 protects the holder of the ineffective performance of the consent to the conclusion of the final contract by giving it the power to obtain a constitutive judgment that produces the same effects as the final contract. The rule governs cases of breach of obligations to contract, whether of legal source . . . or negotiated (e.g., a settlement agreement between co-heirs for the division of a hereditary asset). The provision in question does not only concern the hypothesis of non-performance of a preliminary contract, but also any other case from which the obligation to give consent derives."[44]

15. Various approaches – It appears that the obligation to contract, the obligation to accept, or the obligation to emit an offer fulfils the function of fixing rights and obligations of parties for the future and thus fulfil the actual function of concluding a contract. The obligation to perform, however, only occasionally may serve the ends of the harmed party but do not fulfil the function of fixing rights and obligations. The line of distinction between both functions is not as rigid as it may seem. A Belgian case of the Court of Appeal of Antwerp illustrates this aptly.[45] An elderly couple bought an apartment in a residence for assisted living yet refused to conclude a contract with the provider of some of the services coming with the apartment. They had, however, agreed to an obligation to conclude that latter contract by means of their sales agreement. As they refused to conclude the contract, they also refused any payments

43 Free translation. Original text: "*Se colui che è obbligato a concludere un contratto non adempie l'obbligazione, l'altra parte, qualora sia possibile e non sia escluso dal titolo, può ottenere una sentenza che produca gli effetti del contratto non concluso.*

Se si tratta di contratti che hanno per oggetto il trasferimento della proprietà di una cosa determinata o la costituzione o il trasferimento di un altro diritto, la domanda non può essere accolta, se la parte che l'ha proposta non esegue la sua prestazione o non ne fa offerta nei modi di legge, a meno che la prestazione non sia ancora esigibile."

44 Cian, *Commentario breve al Codice Civile*. p. 3898. Free translation. Official text: "*L'art. 2932 tutela il soggetto titolare della prestazione infungibile del consenso alla conclusione del contratto definitivo, conferendogli il potere di ottenere una sentenza costitutiva che produce gli stessi effetti del contratto defi-nitivo. La norma regola le fattispecie di violazione degli obblighi a contrarre, siano essi di fonte legale . . . ovvero negoziale (es. accordo transattivo tra coeredi per la divisione di un bene ereditario). La disposizione de qua non riguarda le sole ipotesi di inadempimento di un contratto preliminare, bensì anche ogni altra fattispecie dalla quale derivi l'obbligazione di prestare il consenso.*"

45 Antwerp 8 November 2021, 2020/AR/836, unpublished.

under that contract. In the case at hand, the service provider merely claimed for the payment and not for contract conclusion in general. The court granted the claim but lowered the amount according to what is common on the relevant market (on which *supra* Chap. 7, nr. 14). Here, the claimant did not bother to obtain the contract conclusion but merely the performance of the contract. Yet the extent of that performance was fixed by the judge.

1.3. Validity

16. Determinability – The question of validity of the obligation to contract or negotiate will mainly focus on the question of whether the respective obligation is sufficiently determinable, as this may prove questionable. It should be said that this question of validity mainly rises in relation with obligations stemming from negotiation agreements (*supra* Chap. 7, nr. 1), as the validity of statutory obligations is generally not assessed. Yet the reflections made on such contractual obligations to contract may also prove relevant for the general design of statutory obligations to contract, as they concern the generally relevant question of their determinability.

17. Obligation to contract – As far as its validity is concerned, a possible issue with an obligation to contract could be its indeterminacy.[46] Indeed, if parties are merely obliged to contract, the content of that contract at this point is undetermined.[47] To be valid, the object of an obligation generally has to be determinate or at least determinable according to some more or less objective criteria. In the case of an obligation to contract, it is potentially very difficult to establish what such an obligation to contract actually is, given that the object of the contract may be unknown. To this, two possible answers exist: either the contract parties agree to conclude must already be determined or at least determinable or the fact of concluding the contract itself is considered as a determined object of the negotiation agreement. If neither of those two is retained, then the object of such an obligation to contract is not sufficiently determined or determinable, hence, the obligation to contract is not valid.[48] In that case, it could still possibly inform a liability claim[49] but not fulfil its intended function.

18. Contracting itself as object of the negotiation agreement – Busche overcomes this issue by opting for the second solution. He distinguishes between, on the one hand, the obligation to contract and, on the other hand, the content of that contract.[50] While it is clear *that* parties have to agree, it remains

46 Medicus and Lorenz, *Schuldrecht I Allgemeiner Teil*. p. 31, nr. 13; Staudinger/Bork (2020) Vorbemerkung zu §§ 145 ff. nrs. 57–58.

47 Fikentscher and Heinemann, *Schuldrecht Allgemeiner und Besonderer Teil*. p. 85, nr. 113; Staudinger/Bork (2020) Vorbemerkung zu §§ 145 idem nr. 15.

48 As is clearly explained in Fikentscher and Heinemann, *Schuldrecht Allgemeiner und Besonderer Teil*. p. 97, nr. 132; Staudinger/Bork (2020) Vorbemerkung zu §§ 145 idem nr. 59.

49 Fikentscher and Heinemann, *Schuldrecht Allgemeiner und Besonderer Teil*. p. 97, nr. 132; Staudinger/Bork (2020) Vorbemerkung zu §§ 145 idem nr. 83.

50 Busche, *Privatautonomie und Kontrahierungszwang*. pp. 247–248.

unclear *what* they have to agree to. Yet the fact that the *content of the contract* to be concluded is uncertain is distinct from the *obligation to contract* itself and, hence, not an issue in terms of validity. If, in a second phase and, subsequently, to a non-performance of the obligation to contract, a judge must impose a contract on parties, the claim as such, again, is sufficiently precise: it is a claim for fixing the contractual obligation.[51]

19. DETERMINED OR DETERMINABLE CONTRACT – Robert Freitag argues (in the context of negotiation agreements but his reasoning is extendable to all obligations to contract independent of their source) that a negotiation agreement, which already contains a determined or at least a determinable object, *is* actually the contract that supposedly remains to be concluded:

> "an agreement that merely obliges the parties to conclude a further contract cannot be conceived if the parties have already agreed on their mutual rights and obligations – the 'preliminary contract' to a consensual contract therefore in reality already constitutes the main contract itself."[52]

This only is convincing to the extent that parties already 'agreed on their mutual rights and obligations.' Then we are, indeed, not faced with an obligation to contract[53] but with a contract. In that case, the remedy would be an obligation to perform the contract in question (*supra* Chap. 7, nr. 13).

20. OBLIGATION TO NEGOTIATE – In the case of an obligation to negotiate, parties agree that they must provide their best efforts to reach an agreement.[54] Though such an obligation, in fact, remains quite abstract and vague, it is, generally speaking, not considered problematic in terms of determinability.[55] Of course, parties may also specify more clearly what conduct can, or cannot, give rise to liability in order to extend or limit their chances of holding or being held liable (*supra* Chap. 7, nr. 3).

51 Busche, *Privatautonomie und Kontrahierungszwang*. p. 269.

52 Freitag, "'Specific performance' and 'causa-Lehre' über alles im Recht des Vorvertrags?" p. 302. Free translation. Original text: "*eine Vereinbarung, die die Parteien lediglich dazu obligiert, einen weiteren Vertrag zu schließen, jedenfalls dann nicht gedacht werden könne, wenn die Parteien sich bereits endgültig über ihre wechselseitigen Rechte und Pflichten geeinigt haben – der 'Vorvertrag' zu einem Konsensualvertrag stelle daher in Wirklichkeit bereits den Hauptvertrag selbst dar.*"

53 Recognized by Robert Freitag: Freitag, "'Specific performance' and 'causa-Lehre' über alles im Recht des Vorvertrags?" p. 303. See the references there.

54 Fikentscher and Heinemann, *Schuldrecht Allgemeiner und Besonderer Teil*. p. 99, nr. 134; Freitag, "'Specific performance' and 'causa-Lehre' über alles im Recht des Vorvertrags?" p. 305. It must be noted that his reasoning falls short regarding his own criticism: he argues that scholarship generally has a too narrow perspective on what parties intended with their negotiation agreement to then posit an alternative but equally narrow vision of what parties intended. Instead, I here offer a perspective which leaves room for the actual intention of parties in their concrete circumstances.

55 Freitag, "'Specific performance' and 'causa-Lehre' über alles im Recht des Vorvertrags?" p. 306.

1.4. Strict liability

21. Obligation to contract – To the extent that an obligation to contract binds the party under that obligation to reach a relatively determined outcome, the question rises whether such an obligation formulates a strict liability, i.e. a liability which, independent of whether the conduct adopted in not reaching this result was a fault, holds the party failing to reach that result liable. As mentioned *supra* (Chap. 2, nr. 32), Thomas Krawitz argues in this sense in his dissertation, *Schutz vorvertraglicher Investitionen*:[56]

> "However, in addition to fault-based liability, strict liability should also be recognised."[57]

22. *MBO/De Ruiterlij* – Yet it seems to me[58] that such an approach is not common practice at this point. Rather, the opposite, and quite sensibly so, appears to be the case. The Dutch *MBO/De Ruiterij*[59] case decided by the *Hoge Raad* offers an insightful illustration of this point. In that case, parties negotiate about the extension of a hotel complex in Maastricht. Negotiations for the realization of these works appear to be particularly difficult and are ultimately broken-off because the mother company of the hotel complex is no longer willing to invest in the extension, as the economic prospects for the hotel market in Maastricht have changed.[60] In that case, the *Hoge Raad* accepted that even where a party was under an obligation to contract, it could – in the case of supervening unpredictable events – be justified to break-off negotiations in violation of its obligation:

> "The complaint correctly assumes that, if the other party to the party which breaks off negotiations on a contract to be concluded had a legitimate expectation that the contract would be concluded, that does not have to lead, in all circumstances, to the conclusion that the breaking off is unacceptable. Consideration should also be given to the extent to which and the manner in which the party terminating the negotiations contributed to the creation of that confidence and to the legitimate interests of that party; in this regard, it may also be relevant whether unforeseen circumstances occurred in the course of the negotiations."[61]

56 Krawitz, *Schutz vorvertraglicher Investitionen – Zur Haftung beim Scheitern von Vertragsverhandlungen*. 233 p.

57 Krawitz, *Schutz vorvertraglicher Investitionen – Zur Haftung beim Scheitern von Vertragsverhandlungen*. p. 97. Free translation. Original text: "*Neben einer verschuldensabhängigien Haftung sollte aber auch eine verschuldensunabhängige Haftung anerkannt werden.*"

58 In the same sense Ruygvoorn, *Afgebroken onderhandelingen en het gebruik van voorbehouden*. p. 254.

59 HR 14 juni 1996, *NJ* 1997/481 (*MBO/De Ruiterij*). In the same sense, the anlysis made in Ruygvoorn, *Afgebroken onderhandelingen en het gebruik van voorbehouden*. p. 58.

60 For a more detailed discussion of the facts, see Ruygvoorn, *Afgebroken onderhandelingen en het gebruik van voorbehouden*. pp. 123–126.

61 HR 14 juni 1996, *NJ* 1997/481 (*MBO/De Ruiterij*), nr. 3.6. Free translation. Original text: "*De klacht gaat terecht ervan uit dat, ingeval bij de wederpartij van degene die de onderhandelingen*

It seems that in relation to such an obligation to contract, no strict liability exists. This is often expressed by adding the requirement that no sufficient reason for the breaking-off must exist. Other than in this function and context, the frequent addition of "without sufficient reason" would make no sense, as Olivier Deshaye strongly formulates:

> "Does this mean that case law is schizophrenic? On the one hand, it affirms the freedom to terminate by deciding that only the circumstances surrounding the termination constitute fault. But on the other hand, it ensures that the person who terminated the contract had legitimate reasons for ceasing negotiations?"[62]

23. Breaking-off without sufficient reason – It indeed seems that by adding the requirement that there must be no sufficient reason for breaking-off negotiations, an assessment of the conduct in the given circumstances is included in the framing of the unlawfulness.[63] Such a reasoning can be commonly observed[64] but is particularly clear and thematized under German law:

> "Liability for culpa in contrahendo is ruled out if the party who induced the other party to trust in the conclusion of the contract has a valid reason to break off the contract negotiations."[65]

---

over een te sluiten overeenkomst afbreekt, het gerechtvaardigde vertrouwen bestond dat die overeenkomst tot stand zou komen, dit niet onder alle omstandigheden behoeft te leiden tot de slotsom dat het afbreken onaanvaardbaar is. Rekening dient ook te worden gehouden met de mate waarin en de wijze waarop de partij die de onderhandelingen afbreekt, tot het ontstaan van dat vertrouwen heeft bijgedragen, en met de gerechtvaardigde belangen van deze partij; hierbij kan ook van belang zijn of zich in de loop van de onderhandelingen onvoorziene omstandigheden hebben voorgedaan."

62 Deshayes, "La rupture des pourparlers." p. 8. Free translation. Original text: "*Faudrait-il alors que la jurisprudence soit schizophrène? D'un côté, elle affirme la liberté de rompre en décidant que seules les circonstances entourant la rupture constituent une faute. Mais d'un autre côté, elle s'assure que l'auteur de la rupture avait de légitimes motifs de cesser les négociations?*"

63 Olivier Deshayes explicitly argues in this sense: "It may be considered that in certain cases it is no longer possible to break-off talks. More precisely, it is only possible if there are grounds that the judge considers legitimate. In this case, the review of grounds would come into full play: it would make it possible to distinguish between legitimate and illegitimate, i.e. unlawful, terminations. The fault would no longer lie in the circumstances surrounding the termination but in the termination itself." Deshayes, "La rupture des pourparlers." p. 9. Free translation. Original text: "*On peut estimer que dans certains cas la rupture des pourparlers n'est plus possible. Plus exactement, qu'elle n'est possible que s'il existe des motifs qualifiés de légitimes par le juge. Le contrôle des motifs jouerait alors à plein: il permettrait de faire le départ entre les ruptures légitimes et les ruptures illégitimes, c'est-à-dire illicites. La faute ne résiderait plus dans les circonstances entourant la rupture mais bien dans la rupture elle-même.*"

64 For instance, under French law (Deshayes, "Le dommage précontractuel." p. 201, nr. 31.) but also more generally from a comparative perspective (Babusiaux, "Liability for Negotiations." p. 369, nr. 20.).

65 Staudinger/Feldmann (2018) BGB § 311 nr. 147. Free translation. Original text: "*Eine Haftung aus Verschulden bei Vertragsschluss scheidet aus, wenn derjenige, der beim anderen Teil das Vertrauen auf den Vertragsabschluss geweckt hat, einen triftigen Grund zum Abbruch der*

Adding this requirement, in fact, consists in adding a conduct criterion to the outcome-oriented unlawfulness (breaking-off of negotiations). Though the function of this added criterion might thereby be clarified, Thomas Krawitz's critique – that no reliable definition of such a sufficient reason can be provided[66] – persists. Indeed, the exact threshold that the necessity of an absence of good or sufficient reason installs is unclear.[67] In the *MBO/De Ruiterij* decision, this seemed to be a force majeure standard, as Tjittes argues.[68] The same seems to be applicable under German law, where it is argued that the standard should be the same as in the case of attributability of non-performance of a contractual obligation.[69] This makes sense that given that it is an obligation to reach a certain result, the general standard for lack of attributability is applied. The OLG Brandenburg, however, found that the fact that the party did not react rapidly to its counterparty justified that the latter broke-off negotiations in the case of legitimate expectations of future contract conclusion.[70] This appears as a rather lenient threshold and casts doubt on how strict the assessment of such "legitimate reasons" is, which is also defended in scholarship.[71]

The question, at this stage, seems to be open for discussion. Structurally speaking, both answers appear plausible depending on how such an obligation to contract is intended.

2. Enforcement

24. Enforcement of voluntary acts – The enforcement of an obligation to negotiate or to contract, predictably, can lead to issues, for there is an inherent contradiction in forcing what is conceived as a voluntary act. A recent example of this is a Curaçoan saga on forced contracting.[72] In essence, the operator of a beach, Papagayo, had agreed in a letter of intent to give to a company a lease right for a building on that beach to have a diving school installed there.

Vertragsverhandlungen hat." See also Stoll, "Tatbestände und Funktionen der Haftung für culpa in contrahendo." p. 446.

66 Krawitz, *Schutz vorvertraglicher Investitionen – Zur Haftung beim Scheitern von Vertragsverhandlungen*. pp. 78–81.

67 Staudinger/Feldmann (2018) BGB § 311 nr. 147 and Stoll, "Tatbestände und Funktionen der Haftung für culpa in contrahendo." p. 450.

68 Tjittes, *Commercieel Contractenrecht*. p. 92.

69 Staudinger/Feldmann (2018) BGB § 311 nr. 147; Stoll, "Tatbestände und Funktionen der Haftung für culpa in contrahendo." p. 450.

70 "Through its hesitant behaviour after receiving the draft contract of 11 December 2006, the plaintiff itself contributed to the fact that the defendant refrained from placing the order." OLG Brandenburg 27 November 2008–12 U 228/07, *BeckRS* 2009, 1224, nr. 2. Free translation. Original text: "*Die Klägerin hat durch ihr zögerliches Verhalten nach Erhalt des Vertragsentwurfs vom 11.12.2006 selbst dazu beigetragen, dass die Beklagte von der Erteilung des Auftrages Abstand genommen hat.*"

71 Fikentscher and Heinemann, *Schuldrecht Allgemeiner und Besonderer Teil*. p. 71, nr. 93; MüKoBGB/Emmerich, 9. Aufl. 2022, BGB § 311 nr. 195.

72 This development is based on what I have written in Hick, "Aansprakelijkheid voor afgebroken onderhandelingen in België en Nederland: Op koers voor toenadering." p. 254, nr. 27.

In this company, Watersports, there were (simplified) two parties. Ultimately, Papagayo signed the lease agreement not with Watersports but with one of the two parties privately. The other party demands compliance with the letter of intent. In 2017, the Court of First Instance in Curaçao ruled as follows:

> "5.1. declares that Papagayo acted unlawfully vis-à-vis Watersports by entering into the rental agreement not in the name of Watersports but in the name of [defendant in the action under subsection 1] privately;
>
> 5.2. orders Papagayo to enter into a rental agreement with Watersports concerning the diving school within two months of service of this judgment, in accordance with the provisions as included in the agreement submitted as exhibit 8 to the statement of reply[], under thread of a penalty payment of NAf 1,500 for each day or part of a day that Papagayo remains in default, with a maximum of NAf 150,000;"[73]

On appeal, Papagayo disputes having acted unlawfully, but the court does not follow. On the contrary, the court finds that Papagayo failed to take Watersports' interests into account sufficiently and by "deviating at the last minute from the line always followed – 'breaking-off negotiations' – acted unlawful."[74] However, the court is of the opinion that forcing parties to contract is not the appropriate sanction, as the relationship between the parties has been largely disrupted and, therefore, "will create more problems than solve them."[75] Instead, the performance interest will have to be compensated. Compensation of the performance interest involves "to determine the difference between the hypothetical situation that Watersports would have been in if the written lease had been put in its name and the actual situation as it existed when it was not."[76] To budget for this difference, a multitude of circumstances, such as the "difficult relationship between the

73 GiEA Curaçao 11 December 2017, ECLI:NL:OGEAC:2017:186, nr. 5.1. Free translation. Original text: "*5.1. verklaart voor recht dat Papagayo onrechtmatig heeft gehandeld jegens Waterports door de huurovereenkomst niet op naam van Watersports af te sluiten maar op naam van [verweerder in conventie sub 1] privé; 5.2. veroordeelt Papagayo om binnen twee maanden na betekening van dit vonnis een huurovereenkomst ter zake de duikschool met Watersports aan te gaan, conform de bepalingen zoals opgenomen in de overeenkomst overgelegd als productie 8 bij conclusie van antwoord[], een en ander op straffe van een dwangsom van NAf 1.500 voor iedere dag of gedeelte van een dag dat Papagayo hiermee in gebreke blijft, met een maximum van NAf 150.000.*"

74 GHACMB, 15 November 2019, ECLI:NL:OGHACMB:2019:257, nr. 2.4.4. Free translation. Original text: "*op het laatste moment afwijken van de steeds gevolgde lijn – het 'afbreken van de onderhandelingen' – onrechtmatig" was.*

75 GHACMB, 15 November 2019, ECLI:NL:OGHACMB:2019:257, nr. 2.6. Free translation. Original text: "*meer problemen zal creëren dan oplossen.*"

76 GHACMB, 15 November 2019, ECLI:NL:OGHACMB:2019:257, nr. 2.7. Free translation. Original text: "*dan om het vaststellen van het verschil tussen de hypothetische situatie waarin Watersports zou hebben verkeerd wanneer de schriftelijke huurovereenkomst wel op haar naam zou zijn gesteld en de werkelijke toestand zoals die bestond toen dat niet was gebeurd.*"

persons involved at Watersports and the likelihood that (further) conflicts would have arisen within Watersports, as well as whether Watersports, as Papagayo argues, can be blamed for its own fault,"[77] must be taken into account.

The case was referred to the *Hoge Raad*, particularly on the grounds that the Common Court of Justice of Aruba, Curaçao, Sint Maarten, and of Bonaire, Sint Eustatius, and Saba had allegedly gone beyond the bounds of the law on appeal. Indeed, Papagayo had not asked the court to reform the contracting order but to decide that it had not wrongfully broken-off negotiations. In this sense, the *Hoge Raad* decides that "the court therefore [was] not free to substitute another form of compensation for the court's order that [Papagayo] enter into a rental agreement with Watersports."[78] Be that as it may, this saga clearly shows how practically difficult the enforcement of an obligation to contract appears to be.

25. Practicability – Such practical difficulties do not come as a surprise. Nipperdey, in his *Kontrahierungszwang und diktierter Vertrag* in 1920, already stated that the enforcement of such voluntaristic acts is inherently problematic or vain:

> "an obligation to contract that would only require a legal entity to enter into a contract of a certain type with someone, e.g. a contract of employment, without either specifying performance and counter-performance or specifying how the terms of the contract are to be determined in the absence of an agreement, would be a legal anomaly. This is because the obliged party could then easily evade his obligation by imposing abnormal conditions while declaring his fundamental willingness to conclude the contract."[79]

Such a risk could be mediated by having the conditions to which parties must agree fixed by a third party (as, for instance, by a judge). This is the solution suggested by Nipperdey,[80] but I have earlier stated that this is more detrimental to the party's freedom of contract and should, therefore, not too hastily be relied upon. Instead, and as explained *supra* (Chap. 7, nr. 11), it is important to be mindful of how the enforcement of such an obligation to contract or to negotiate is constructed. This is, in my opinion, a matter of settings incentives in such a manner that the obliged party, a party which thus *a priori* no longer wants to

77 GHACMB, 15 November 2019, ECLI:NL:OGHACMB:2019:257, nr. 2.7. Free translation. Original text: "*moeizame verstandhouding tussen de bij Watersports betrokken personen en de kans dat het binnen Watersports tot (nadere) conflicten was gekomen, alsmede de vraag of Watersports, zoals Papagayo betoogt, eigen schuld kan worden verweten.*"

78 HR 11 juni 2021, ECLI:NL:HR:2021:860, nr. 3.2.3. Free translation. Original text: "*het hof daarom niet vrij [was] om een andere vorm van schadevergoeding in de plaats te stellen voor de door het gerecht uitgesproken veroordeling van [Papagayo] om een huurovereenkomst met Watersports aan te gaan.*"

79 Nipperdey, *Kontrahierungszwang und diktierter Vertrag*. p. 31. Free translation. Original text: "*ein Kontrahierungszwang der nur anordnen würde, dass ein Rechtssubjekt mit jemandem einen Vertrag bestimmter Art, z.B. einen Arbeitsvertrag abschliessen muss, ohne entweder Leistung und Gegenleistung zu bestimmen oder anzugeben, in welcher Weise die Vertragsbedingungen ohne Vereinbarung festzusetzen sind, wäre eine juristische Anomalie. Denn dann könnte der Verpflichtete, unter Erklärung seinder grundsätzlichen Abschlussbereitschaft sich ohne weiteres durch Stellung abnormer Bedingungen seiner Verpflichtung entziehen.*"

80 Nipperdey, *Kontrahierungszwang und diktierter Vertrag*. p. 31.

contract or to negotiate, has an interest in contracting or constructively taking part in the negotiations to prevent the conduct described by Nipperdey. This requires that the offers made must be reasonable, hence requiring a possible *a posteriori* control of the judge, and that in case one party does not act constructively to reach an agreement, the alternative is a judge-made contract – an outcome which is likely less advantageous to the obliged party.

Nevertheless, it may not seldom be the case that enforcing an obligation to negotiate or to contract indeed 'creates more problems than it solves' (*supra* Chap. 7, nr. 24). In those cases, compensation in damages may appear more suitable.

26. Compensation of performance interest – In the context of the compensation, it is useful to speak in terms of the performance interest (as opposed to cases of mere conduct-based liability *supra* Chap. 4, nr. 2–6). That interest describes the position a party would have been in had the obliged party performed duly. In the case of an obligation to negotiate, this is the position of the constructive continuation of negotiations. This should, then, be the compensation of the loss of a chance of concluding the contract under negotiations, where the loss of a chance doctrine is accepted (*supra* Chap. 6, nr. 12). Other than that, there does not really seem to be much to be compensated. That is different in the case of an obligation to contract. There, a party should be reinstated as good as possible in the position it would have been in had the contract under negotiations been concluded. This means that the equivalent of the net benefit, i.e. the benefit minus the costs that would have been made to perform one's own obligations, should be granted. Calculating this net benefit may, at times, be very difficult, as the content of the contract will not necessarily be known. It could be that these practical difficulties account for the very low number of Dutch courts granting the performance interest when parties were under an obligation to contract, as reported by Marcel Ruygvoorn.[81] These practical difficulties, however, are not a legally relevant argument against granting such compensation.

27. Performance of compensation? – Worth mentioning in this context is the quite peculiar approach the Belgian legislator has opted for in the second sentence of the second alinea of article 5.17 Be. Civ. C.:

> "If a legitimate expectation has been created that without any doubt the contract would have been concluded, this liability may include compensation for the loss of the expected net benefits from the contract not concluded."[82]

This liability relies on an implicit obligation to contract based on legitimate expectations (*supra* Chap. 7, nr. 5). Yet it does not seem *necessary* to grant the net benefits under the negotiated contract, as the compensation "*may*" cover this amount but

81 Ruygvoorn, *Afgebroken onderhandelingen en het gebruik van voorbehouden*. pp. 266–269.

82 Original text: "*Lorsque la confiance légitime que le contrat serait sans aucun doute conclu a été suscitée, elle peut impliquer la réparation de la perte des avantages nets attendus du contrat non conclu.*"/"*Wanneer het rechtmatig vertrouwen is gewekt dat het contract zonder enige twijfel gesloten zal worden, kan deze het herstel van het verlies van de verwachte netto-voordelen uit het niet gesloten contract inhouden.*"

does not necessarily do so. Quite frankly, this "may" is puzzling, as it is not obvious what the "may or may not" depends on. Furthermore, the article does not seem to grant a right to performance but instead a right to compensation only. Hence, the extent of the obligation is not one of granting performance but merely of granting compensation. A right to performance of compensation, thus. Admittedly, this peculiar obligation may be related to the fact that, practically speaking, it can be difficult to implement a forced contract conclusion, as has just been explained. Whether this justifies an *a priori* exclusion of the right to actual performance may be doubted. A classic case-by-case analysis appears more sensible.

Maarten Herbosch also tried to explain this second sentence, be it in a previous version of the sentence, which set accents slightly differently.[83] To him, it is an application of the doctrine of a loss of a chance.[84] This explanation, in turn, does also not allow to explain this provision consistently. Granted, in as far as the obligation created by the legitimate expectations could be one to negotiate, applying the loss of a chance doctrine to conclude the contract under negotiations is coherent and plausible (*supra* Chap. 7, nr. 26). Yet the loss of a chance doctrine does not rhyme with the possibility of being granted the full net benefits, which this provision "may"[85] give rise to, as this would pre-suppose a 100% chance, which then is a certitude and not a chance:

> "in the context of loss of a chance, there is no certainty. Indeed, the chance is the real possibility – not certainty – of gaining a benefit or avoiding a disadvantage. Whereas IPH and Neofibra assume that it is certain that the contract would have been concluded if the negotiations had not been erroneously stopped, on this basis they cannot claim compensation in the context of loss of a chance."[86]

Yet an obligation to negotiate does not give right to a conclusion of the contract and thus not to this certitude. No matter how one tries to explain it, this second sentence remains somewhat of a unicum.

83 Back then, the proposed provision read as follows: "Where a legitimate expectation has been created that the contract will be concluded without any doubt, it involves at most the recovery of the loss of expected net benefits from the contract not concluded." Free translation. Original version: "*Wanneer het rechtmatig vertrouwen is gewekt dat het contract zonder enige twijfel gesloten zal worden, houdt deze maximaal het herstel van het verlies van de verwacht nettovoordelen uit het niet gesloten contract in.*"

84 Herbosch, "Contractdwang bij onrechtmatig afgebroken onderhandelingen over de koop van onroerend goed? Het schijn geen brug te ver." p. 314, nr. 4.

85 Or in the previous version "at most."

86 Gent, 3 December 2014, *TBBR* 2018/1 (47) p. 51. Free translation. Original text: "*in het kader van het verlies van een kans, is er geen zekerheid. De kans is immers de reële mogelijkheid – en niet de zekerheid – van het verwerven van een voordeel of het vermijden van een nadeel. Waar IPH en Neofibra ervan uitgaan dat het zeker is dat het contract zou zijn gesloten geweest indien de onderhandelingen niet foutief waren stopgezet, kunnen zij op grond hiervan geen vergoeding vorde- ren in het kader van het verlies van een kans.*"

8 Alternative

Obliegenheit to contract

1. Forced will

1. Conceptually and practically problematic – As just explained, in a liberal legal system based on self-determination and free will of its subjects, enforcing a decision of free will turned out to beg some resolvable conceptual questions (validity *supra* nrs. Chap. 7, nrs. 16–20) but, more importantly, is practically problematic, as has already been illustrated (*supra* Chap. 7, nr. 24–25). Given that forcing parties to continue negotiations or to contract often appears to be unpractical, at least within the existing legal framework, the possibility of an alternative approach appears worthwhile exploring.
2. Incentivizing debtor of obligation to comply – Our contemporary legal systems are normatively based on the free will of parties. It has already appeared (*supra* Chap. 7, nr. 11–12) that in conceiving such obligations to negotiate or to contract, it matters particularly to conceive them in such a way that the debtor of this obligation (the party forced to negotiate or to contract which refused to do so) is incentivized to contribute constructively to the negotiations and/or contract conclusion. Only in that case could his own will be directed in the sense of continuing negotiating or contracting. In order to achieve this, the debtor must either be worse off if he refuses to negotiate/contract or better off if he continues to negotiate/contract, both relative to his *status quo* situation of breaking-off negotiations/refusing to contract.
3. Accept or negotiate – To achieve such a constellation of interests, I suggest the following: if a party unlawfully breaks-off negotiations or refuses to contract, it has to continue negotiations. If the party fails to act sufficiently constructive, it loses its right to refuse to contract, and hence, it has to accept the contract offered by its counterparty, provided it is a reasonable offer.

   Let me illustrate the case. Party A sells a house; Party B is interested in buying it. For whatever reason, Party A unlawfully breaks-off negotiations. Then Party A has to renegotiate the sales contract that it refused unlawfully to conclude. If these negotiations fail due to Party A acting in a non-cooperative way, Party A loses its right to refuse Party B's offer and has to conclude the sales contract, provided the offer made by B was reasonable. In this constellation of

DOI: 10.4324/9781003599166-12

interests, it is in the best interest of A to negotiate constructively with B, as otherwise, it will have to accept B's offer, again, provided that offer is reasonable.

4. Remaining questions – There are some remaining questions, notably with reference to the burden of proof. Does B have to prove that A did not negotiate constructively, or does A have to prove that, in fact, it did negotiate constructively and that the failure of the negotiation is not reproachable to Party A? In other terms, the question rises whether there is a presumption of lack of cooperation by A if negotiations fail. As such, this question needs no definitive answer in the present context; it merely matters that such a presumption *can* be used by a legislator were he to implement such an approach. The same – relying on a presumption or not – goes for the question of who has to prove that the offer made by B was reasonable and that, hence, A had to accept it. Is it upon A to prove that it was not if he intends to escape the contract, or does A have to prove that it was if it wants to see the contract enforced? Opting for one or the other will, of course, impact the ease with which this mechanism can be relied on by the party suffering the failed negotiations or contract conclusion.

5. Advantages – Though I cannot exclude that this approach would rule out all problems that may arise in enforcing a contract conclusion, the approach I here suggest has some undeniable advantages. The first and foremost is that it distributes interests in such a manner that parties themselves have a strong incentive to reach an agreement through renegotiations. Instead of plumply forcing parties to negotiate, fixing the alternative outcome of the negotiations will incentivize the party that is at the origin of the failure of the negotiations to provide best efforts to reach an agreement. In that sense, it leaves more room to party autonomy, as it relies on a negotiated contract – be it that those negotiations are led with a sword of Damocles over the head of the party that acted unlawfully in the first place.

   A second advantage, which is a consequence of the first, is that in this way, the imbalance of power between negotiating parties is – at least to some extent – re-balanced. Indeed, generally, the party that has to ask for the renegotiation is in a weaker negotiation position because it will, to some extent, depend on the conclusion or adaptation of a contract; otherwise, it would likely not have asked for it. This party in a weaker position then finds itself at the mercy of its counterparty. Quite obviously, this creates a very unbalanced starting position for the party in the weaker position. By providing that the party in the stronger position would have no choice but to accept the offer of the party in the weaker position, the power imbalanced is reversed, hence creating a more balanced starting position for the negotiations.

6. Legal implementation – This may all sound very good and well, or at least it does to me, but the question arises of how such a constellation of interests can be legally speaking implemented. Luckily, a doctrine exists in many legal system – be it that it remains somewhat under the radar – that allows specifically to reach this constellation of interests, namely, the so-called *Obliegenheit*. I suggest that instead of relying on an obligation to contract or to negotiate, it would be much more sensible to rely on an *Obliegenheit* to contract.

2. Obliegenheit to contract

2.1. Obliegenheit[1]

7. The notion – The ill-translatable notion of an *Obligenheit* – in French *incombance* or occasionally translated into English as "charge" – is subject of ongoing discussions. I, therefore, feel the urge to alert the reader that he may find variations of the here presented understanding of the *Obliegenheit.* These variations are mainly the result of many scholars or courts invoking the notion when it suits their purpose with relatively little to no further study of the notion, its relevance, and implications.[2] This leads to a particularly scattered and often almost mystified understanding of the *Obliegenheit.* If, in order to understand what an *Obliegenheit* is, a more in-depth study is required in the first place, that is because its technical meaning remains unclear; the notion is used "inflationary"[3] and is subject to relatively fundamental scholarly debate. As Susanne Hähnchen indicates in her habilitation, *Obliegenheiten und Nebenpflichten*:

> "Today's fundamental views on the *Obliegenheit* are diverse and not always free of contradictions."[4]

By consequence, I first need to clarify, to the extent necessary for the present purpose, how an *Obliegenheit* ought to be understood. Two approaches are possible for this endeavour: either historically rolling up the evolution of how *Obliegenheiten* have been understood throughout the time up until today, on the one hand,[5] or, on the other hand, providing the reader with a targeted and brief overview of the current state of affairs as can be found in contemporary literature. I opt for the second approach, which is more in line with my present purpose but not without a brief contextualization on the origin of the notion of *Obliegenheit.*

1 I hope to be able to dedicate a separate publication to the topic, which will go into more detail concerning some of the topics here merely mentioned. Going into too much detail at this point would lead astray from the actual purpose here pursued. Also, I would like to thank Violeta Kuzmanovic for the constructive and helpful discussions on this chapter.

2 Hähnchen, *Obliegenheiten und Nebenpflichten. eine Untersuchung dieser besonderen Verhaltensanforderungen im Privatversciherungsrecht und im allgemeinen Zivilrecht unter besonderer Berücksichtigung der Dogmengeschichte.* p. 35.

3 As argued by Hähnchen, *Obliegenheiten und Nebenpflichten. eine Untersuchung dieser besonderen Verhaltensanforderungen im Privatversciherungsrecht und im allgemeinen Zivilrecht unter besonderer Berücksichtigung der Dogmengeschichte.* p. 129.

4 Hähnchen, *Obliegenheiten und Nebenpflichten. eine Untersuchung dieser besonderen Verhaltensanforderungen im Privatversciherungsrecht und im allgemeinen Zivilrecht unter besonderer Berücksichtigung der Dogmengeschichte.* p. 35. Free translation. Original text: "*Die heutigen, grundsätzlichen Auffassungen zu den Obliegenheiten sind viel- fältig und nicht immer widerspruchsfrei.*"

5 Such as done in Thomas Ehrensperger, *Strukturen und Verletzungen von Obliegenheiten im Schweizerischen Privatrecht (unter Ausschluss des Versicherungsrechts)* (Zürich: University of Zurich, 2004). pp. 19–40.

8. Origin – The origin of the *Obliegenheit* is generally located under German insurance law. Yet Phillip Hellwege has argued that their origin reaches even further back into English naval insurance law.[6] More specifically, it was meant to protect the insurers – back then considered as in a weak position – from insurance fraud. From there, it found its way into German insurance law, was received under Swiss law, where it got its French translation – "*incombance*" – and finally was popularized for the general law of obligations by Reimer Schmidt in Germany with his habilitation, *Die Obliegenheiten: Studien auf dem Gebiet des Rechtszwanges im Zivilrecht unter besonderer Berücksichtigung des Privatversicherungsrechts*.[7] Relatively recently,[8] a few fundamental studies have appeared on the notion, chronologically: Thomas Ehrenspergher's *Strukturen und Verletzungen von Obliegenheiten im Schweizerischen Privatrecht (unter Ausschluss des Versicherungsrechts)*[9] in 2004 under Swiss law, Susanne Hähnchen's *Obliegenheiten und Nebenpflichten. eine Untersuchung dieser besonderen Verhaltensanforderungen im Privatversciherungsrecht und im allgemeinen Zivilrecht unter besonderer Berücksichtigung der Dogmengeschichte*[10] in 2010 under German law, and Barbara Freleteau's *Devoir et incombance en matière contractuelle*[11] in 2017 under French law. To me, Susanne Hähnchen's habilitation has been the most insightful and influential material on the subject matter.[12]

6 Phillip Hellwege, "Obliegenheiten im Versicherungsvertragsrecht aus historisch-vergleichender Perspektive," *RabelsZ* (2012). pp. 864–892.

7 Reimer Schmidt, *Die Obliegenheiten: Studien auf dem Gebiet des Rechtszwanges im Zivilrecht unter besonderer Berücksichtigung des Privatversicherungsrechts* (Karlsruhe: Versicherungswirtschaft, 1953). xxii+388 p.; Hähnchen, *Obliegenheiten und Nebenpflichten. eine Untersuchung dieser besonderen Verhaltensanforderungen im Privatversciherungsrecht und im allgemeinen Zivilrecht unter besonderer Berücksichtigung der Dogmengeschichte*. p. 4. In this context also relevant: Josef Esser, "R. Schmidt Die Obliegenheiten. Studien auf dem Gebiet des Rechtszwangs im Zivilrecht unter Berücksichtigung des Privatversicherungsrechts," *AcP* 154 (1955). pp. 49–52.

See on the evolution of the notion "*Obliegenheit*" Hähnchen, *Obliegenheiten und Nebenpflichten. eine Untersuchung dieser besonderen Verhaltensanforderungen im Privatversciherungsrecht und im allgemeinen Zivilrecht unter besonderer Berücksichtigung der Dogmengeschichte*. p. 113 *et seq*. and Ehrensperger, *Strukturen und Verletzungen von Obliegenheiten im Schweizerischen Privatrecht (unter Ausschluss des Versicherungsrechts)*. p. 9 *et seq*.

8 Slightly older is Mathias Edward Storme's dissertation, which also deals with the subject matter: Matthias Edward Storme, *De invloed van de goede trouw op de kontraktuele schuldvorderingen* (Brussel: E. Story-Scientia, 1990). XVI+544 p.

9 Ehrensperger, *Strukturen und Verletzungen von Obliegenheiten im Schweizerischen Privatrecht (unter Ausschluss des Versicherungsrechts)*. xxiv+145 p.

10 Hähnchen, *Obliegenheiten und Nebenpflichten. eine Untersuchung dieser besonderen Verhaltensanforderungen im Privatversciherungsrecht und im allgemeinen Zivilrecht unter besonderer Berücksichtigung der Dogmengeschichte*. XXI+351 p.

11 Barbara Freleteau, *Devoir et incombance en matière contractuelle*, ed. Yves Lequette, Bibliothèque de droit privé, (Paris: LGDJ, 2017). 633 p.

12 For a book review, see Herbert Roth, "Susanne Hähnchen: Obliegenheiten und Nebenpflichten. Eine Untersuchung dieser besonderen Verhaltensanforderungen im Privatversicherungsrecht und im allgemeinen Zivilrecht unter besonderer Berücksichtigung der Dogmengeschichte," *JZ* 18 (2010).

9. Behavioural requirement of lower intensity – Often, the *Obliegenheit* is presented as a 'behavioural requirement of lower intensity' ('*Verhaltensanforderung von geringerer Intensität*').[13] What is meant by "lower intensity" may seem rather vague. What is clear, however, is that an *Obliegenheit* is an incentive to act cooperatively or, perhaps broader, reasonably, in the exercise of one's right.

Indeed, two elements are distinctive: an *Obliegenheit* (i) is an incentive to act reasonably (ii) towards one's debtor in the exercise of one's right or some other prerogative. This (i) incentive to act reasonably is akin to duties of conduct, as Susanne Hähnchen clarified in her habilitation,[14] instead of an obligation.[15] The specificity of the *Obliegenheit* is (ii) that it is associated with the exercise of a right, or at least some prerogative, as Matthias Edward Storme specified in his dissertation, *De invloed van de goede trouw op de kontraktuele schuldvorderingen*, where he defines the *Obliegenheit* as "an duty to cooperate, usually on the part of a creditor, but more generally on the part of any person wishing to invoke a particular legal position."[16] Barbara Freleteau formulates this same idea succinctly as "the *Obliegenheit* is always on the holder of a right. It corresponds to the hypothesis that a specific behaviour will be required from the beneficiary of a legal advantage, if he wants to effectively benefit from it."[17] For the sake of convenience, I will refer to "rights" hereafter, but the notion must not be understood overly narrowly but to also comprise some legal prerogatives.

10. Relation to liability – Generally speaking, the infringement of duties of conduct give rise to liability to the extent that the remaining conditions of

13 Medicus and Lorenz, *Schuldrecht I Allgemeiner Teil*. p. 47, nr. 20. See for a more in-depth discussion Hähnchen, *Obliegenheiten und Nebenpflichten. eine Untersuchung dieser besonderen Verhaltensanforderungen im Privatversciherungsrecht und im allgemeinen Zivilrecht unter besonderer Berücksichtigung der Dogmengeschichte*. p. 2. See references there.

14 Hähnchen, *Obliegenheiten und Nebenpflichten. eine Untersuchung dieser besonderen Verhaltensanforderungen im Privatversciherungsrecht und im allgemeinen Zivilrecht unter besonderer Berücksichtigung der Dogmengeschichte*. pp. 233 and 247. See in the same sense Freleteau, *Devoir et incombance en matière contractuelle*. p. 28, nr. 25 and p. 48, nr. 53.

15 The distinction between obligations and duties of care is in and of itself rather unclear and by no means watertight.

16 Storme, *De invloed van de goede trouw op de kontraktuele schuldvorderingen*. p. 197, nr. 196. Free translation. Original text: "*een gehoudenheid tot medewerking, veelal van een schuldeiser, doch meer algemeen van elkeen die zich op een bepaalde rechtspositie wil beroepen*." See also in this sense Hähnchen, *Obliegenheiten und Nebenpflichten. eine Untersuchung dieser besonderen Verhaltensanforderungen im Privatversciherungsrecht und im allgemeinen Zivilrecht unter besonderer Berücksichtigung der Dogmengeschichte*. p. 258 and Freleteau, *Devoir et incombance en matière contractuelle*. p. 48, nr. 53.

17 Freleteau, *Devoir et incombance en matière contractuelle*. p. 48, nr. 53. Free translation. Original text: "*l'incombance pèse toujours sur le titulaire d'un droit. Elle correspond à l'hypothèse où un comportement spécifique va être exigé de la part du bénéficiaire d'un avantage juridique, s'il veut pouvoir effectivement en bénéficier*." Yet Freleteau does not seem to see that the holder of that right has to fulfil this act in the interest of its counterparty.

application for liability are fulfilled. Given that an *Obliegenheit* describes some form of conduct whose infringement is considered unreasonable or reprehensible, it would seem consistent that the infringement of an *Obliegenheit* would lead to liability, thus compensation of harm. However, that is not the sanction generally associated with an *Obliegenheit.*[18] Instead, the creditor loses his right or prerogative in the exercise of which he was under an *Obliegenheit.* In that sense, an *Obliegenheit* may appear as a pre-condition for the exercise of a right/prerogative, while at the same time formulating an imperative of conduct. This ambivalence translates into two opposing understandings of the *Obliegenheit* under German law. On the one side, the so-called pre-condition theory ("*Vorraussetzungstheorie*") – particularly relied upon within insurance law –understands an *Obliegenheit* as "the conditions to be fulfilled by the insured, in particular the policyholder, in order to receive his (insurance) claim."[19] To this theory is opposed the "obligational theory" ("*Verbindlichkeitstheorie*"), according to which an *Obliegenheit* is rather to be regarded as an obligation.[20] The relevance of choosing one or another theory has some implications under German law[21] but need not interest us here. For the time being, it suffices to understand that an *Obliegenheit* is an incentive to adopt a cooperative conduct which, when disregarded, leads to the loss of a right in relation to which it is imposed on the creditor.[22] Such a sanction is remarkable, as it goes beyond mere compensation of harm.

11. SANCTION – It is the peculiarity of the sanction of the *Obliegenheit*, which triggers its interest. Generally, this sanction is considered to be the loss of a right. In other words, if one does not comply with an *Obliegenheit*, one loses a right or does not get access to it; both describe the same reality but with a different focus. Such a sanction is quite radical and often described as an "all-or-nothing" approach.[23] Though it can sometimes be read that, as Reimer

18 Which does not necessarily imply that the sanction associated with an *Obliegenheit*, therefore, excludes a right to compensation.

19 Hähnchen, *Obliegenheiten und Nebenpflichten. eine Untersuchung dieser besonderen Verhaltensanforderungen im Privatversciherungsrecht und im allgemeinen Zivilrecht unter besonderer Berücksichtigung der Dogmengeschichte.* p. 23. Free translation. Original text: "*Voraussetzungen, die der damit Belastete, insbesondere der Versicherungsnehmer erfüllen müsse, um seinen (Versicherungs-) Anspruch zu erhalten.*" Find references and more in-depth discussion there. See on this also Ehrensperger, *Strukturen und Verletzungen von Obliegenheiten im Schweizerischen Privatrecht (unter Ausschluss des Versicherungsrechts)*. p. 11.

20 Hähnchen, *Obliegenheiten und Nebenpflichten. eine Untersuchung dieser besonderen Verhaltensanforderungen im Privatversciherungsrecht und im allgemeinen Zivilrecht unter besonderer Berücksichtigung der Dogmengeschichte.* p. 24. For references and more elaborate discussions, see there. See also Ehrensperger, *Strukturen und Verletzungen von Obliegenheiten im Schweizerischen Privatrecht (unter Ausschluss des Versicherungsrechts)*. p. 11.

21 On which see Hähnchen, *Obliegenheiten und Nebenpflichten. eine Untersuchung dieser besonderen Verhaltensanforderungen im Privatversciherungsrecht und im allgemeinen Zivilrecht unter besonderer Berücksichtigung der Dogmengeschichte.* p. 103 *et seq.*

22 Hähnchen, *Obliegenheiten und Nebenpflichten. eine Untersuchung dieser besonderen Verhaltensanforderungen im Privatversciherungsrecht und im allgemeinen Zivilrecht unter besonderer Berücksichtigung der Dogmengeschichte.* p. 263.

23 See in Hähnchen, *Obliegenheiten und Nebenpflichten. eine Untersuchung dieser besonderen Verhaltensanforderungen im Privatversciherungsrecht und im allgemeinen Zivilrecht unter*

Schmidt put it, *Obliegenheiten* are 'obligations of lesser intensity' ('*Pflichten minderer Zwangswirkung*')[24] or otherwise that it has 'less grave consequences' ('*minderen Rechtsnachteilen*'),[25] the consequences are rather far-reaching. In that sense, this terminology is deceptive. Indeed, the sanction goes beyond the compensation of harm and, hence, cannot be justified on general liability law but requires a specific legal basis. The mere qualification of some duties of conduct as an *Obliegenheit* does not suffice for that purpose; after all, the classification as an *Obliegenheit* in and of itself does not have any incidence. Paul Alain Foriers has put this succinctly when he criticizes the advent of the *Obliegenheit* under Belgian law:

> "Let us be clear: my intention is not to reject the explanatory role which the concept of incombance can play in illuminating certain mechanisms of positive law. It is simply to warn against the tendency of its proponents to transform certain duties – which are, moreover, indisputable – into incumbencies sanctioned by forfeiture, and thus by a civil penalty which would replace the rules of civil liability.
>
> It is surprising in this respect that some authors see incombances as duties of lesser intensity because they do not give rise to any recourse against those who are bound by them.
>
> The mechanism of incombance is, in fact, much more formidable. It is the economy of the principle of civil liability. If it does not give rise to any recourse, it is because it removes all usefulness. Its 'creditor' cannot suffer from its inobservation because its 'debtor' forfeits his right.
>
> It is against this radical sanction that I object."[26]

---

besonderer Berücksichtigung der Dogmengeschichte. p. 56; Ehrensperger, *Strukturen und Verletzungen von Obliegenheiten im Schweizerischen Privatrecht (unter Ausschluss des Versicherungsrechts)*. p. 116.

24 Schmidt, *Die Obliegenheiten: Studien auf dem Gebiet des Rechtszwanges im Zivilrecht unter besonderer Berücksichtigung des Privatversicherungsrechts*. p. 315. See also Hähnchen, *Obliegenheiten und Nebenpflichten. eine Untersuchung dieser besonderen Verhaltensanforderungen im Privatversciherungsrecht und im allgemeinen Zivilrecht unter besonderer Berücksichtigung der Dogmengeschichte*. p. 11 and Ehrensperger, *Strukturen und Verletzungen von Obliegenheiten im Schweizerischen Privatrecht (unter Ausschluss des Versicherungsrechts)*. p. 27. See also Marcel Fontaine, "Obliegenheit, incombance?," in *Liber Amicorum Hubert Claessens. Verzekering: Theorie en praktijk/Assurance: théorie et pratique*, ed. Herman Cousy et al. (Antwerpen: Maklu, 1998). pp. 254–255.

25 Hähnchen, *Obliegenheiten und Nebenpflichten. eine Untersuchung dieser besonderen Verhaltensanforderungen im Privatversciherungsrecht und im allgemeinen Zivilrecht unter besonderer Berücksichtigung der Dogmengeschichte*. p. 13.

26 Paul Alain Foriers, "Les incombances en droit positif belge – L'exemple d'une notion à bannir," in *Le droit du travail au XXIe siècle: liber amicorum Claude Wantiez*, ed. Marc Morsa and Philippe Gosseries (Bruxelles: Editions Larcier, 2015). p. 573. Free translation. Original text: "*Entendons-nous bien, mon propos n'est pas de rejeter le rôle explicatif que peut jouer la notion d'incombance pour*

12. Difficulties – Foriers draws a distinction between an explanatory role of the *Obliegenheit* and a second role in which the use of the notion of *Obliegenheit* leads to circumvent principles of liability law. Herewith, Foriers goes to the heart of the difficulties surrounding the notion of *Obliegenheit*. The notion is so puzzling because it relies on a circular reasoning: if the infringement of a duty to act cooperatively gives rise to the loss of a right, it is an *Obliegenheit*. In that sense, the sanction justifies the qualification which, in a backward loop, justifies the sanction in the first place. As Hähnchen put it:

> "Circular reasoning of the prevailing opinion, . . . which on the one hand concludes from the legal consequences that there are *Obliegenheiten* and on the other hand considers other legal consequences to be excluded because of the qualification as an *Obliegenheit*."[27]

Such a reasoning is, of course, possible when it is used to describe (explanatory function) an existing legal rule. For example, Article 5.179, al. 2 of the Belgian Civil Code provides that for an assignment of claims to be enforceable against the debtor of the obligation, the latter must have been notified of the assignment. In this case, the standard is one of cooperation with the assigned debtor; it is reasonable to notify the debtor of the change of creditor. If the new creditor fails to do so, he cannot rely on his right to claim against the debtor in question. The new creditor, therefore, has a legal advantage which he expects but loses the exercise of it if he fails to act in a cooperative manner. Whether or not this standard of cooperation is qualified as *Obliegenheit* will ultimately have no impact on the required cooperation and its application but may help understanding the underlying mechanism. In such a case, the qualification serves a pedagogical or classification purpose; it is the explanatory function Foriers refers to. Ultimately, however, this function is, legally

---

éclairer certains mécanismes de droit positif. Il s'agit seulement de mettre en garde contre la tendance qu'auraient ses partisans à transformer certains devoirs – par ailleurs incontestables – en incombances sanctionnées de déchéance, donc d'une pénalité civile qui se substituerait aux règles de la responsabilité civile. On s'étonnera à cet égard que certains auteurs voient dans les incombances des devoirs de moindre intensité car n'ouvrant aucun recours contre ceux qui en sont tenus. Le mécanisme de l'incombance est, en effet, bien plus redoutable. Il fait l'économie du principe de la responsabilité civile. S'il n'ouvre aucun recours, c'est qu'il en supprime toute utilité. Son 'créancier' ne peut souffrir de son inobservation puisque son 'débiteur' est déchu de son droit. C'est contre cette sanction radicale que je m'élève." In Belgian scholarship, Houben has seemingly, in reaction to this Fontaine's article, argued in favour of the incorporation of the *Obliegenheit* in Belgian law (Michaël Houbben, "Quelques considérations en faveur de l'intégration de l'incombance en droit privé belge," *Annales de droit de Louvain* (2016). pp. 91–139).

27 Hähnchen, *Obliegenheiten und Nebenpflichten. eine Untersuchung dieser besonderen Verhaltensanforderungen im Privatversciherungsrecht und im allgemeinen Zivilrecht unter besonderer Berücksichtigung der Dogmengeschichte*. p. 26. Free translation. Original text: "*Zirkelschluss der herrschenden Meinung, . . . die einerseits aus den Rechtsfolgen auf Obliegenheiten schließt und wegen der Qualifizierung als Obliegenheit andere Rechtsfolgen für ausgeschlossen hält.*"

speaking, irrelevant; after all, the sanction in question is legally fixed. Whether one qualifies the doctrine in question as an *Obliegenheit* or not does not alter the sanction that can ensue from its violation – and rightly so. It only serves a pedagogical or convenience function to qualify it as an *Obliegenheit.*

However, this circular reasoning becomes problematic in instances where the loss of a right is justified *merely* based on the qualification as an *Obliegenheit.* A decision of the Court of Appeal of Antwerp[28] aptly illustrates this danger: after a divorce of a couple, the ex-wife was allowed to remain in the home of the family and had to pay a compensation for that to her ex-husband. At some point, she has to move out of the old family home and cease to pay the compensations to her ex-husband from the moment she leaves the house. Yet she does not notify her ex-husband that she left the house. The ex-husband claims payments for the time between her actually leaving the house and notifying the husband of her moving out. The Court of Appeal, by stating that the duty to notify in that case would be an *Obliegenheit*, declares that the ex-wife, for having omitted to notify her ex-husband of her moving-out, has to pay:

> "the duty to notify counts as an *Obliegenheit*, i.e. a burden which, in case of non-compliance, leads to a curtailment or processing of rights, which makes non-compliance with this obligation imply a loss of rights, translated for this purpose into the still owing of the housing allowance."[29]

The Court should only proceed to such a sanction to the extent that this sanction, the loss of a right, is legally recognized as the legal consequence of the lack of notification. The mere qualification as an *Obliegenheit*, in and of itself, cannot justify any legal consequences. That would be a form of jurisprudence of terms ("*Begriffsjurisprudenz*"): deducting legal consequences from terminology instead of deducting terminology from legal consequences. Such an approach is outdated.[30]

13. Mechanism – In the cited passage earlier (nr. 221), Paul Alain Foriers calls the *Obliegenheit* a "*mechanism*."[31] In my opinion, this is a very convenient and instructive way of presenting the matter. Indeed, an *Obliegenheit* is best understood as a mechanism which brings about a specific constellation of interests. This constellation of interests is the following one: the fulfilment of cooperative acts by a creditor towards his debtor is in his own interest because the

28 Antwerp 14 March 2018, *T.Not.* 2018 (535).

29 Antwerp 14 March 2018, *T.Not.* 2018 (535). p. 545. Free translation. Original text: "*kennisgevingsplicht geldt als een Obliegenheit, d.i. een last die bij niet-naleving leidt tot een inkrimping of verwerking van rechten, wat maakt dat verzuim aan deze plicht een verlies van rechten impliceert, ten deze vertaald in het langer verschuldigd zijn van de woonstvergoeding.*"

30 Hähnchen, *Obliegenheiten und Nebenpflichten. eine Untersuchung dieser besonderen Verhaltensanforderungen im Privatversciherungsrecht und im allgemeinen Zivilrecht unter besonderer Berücksichtigung der Dogmengeschichte*. p. 234 and p. 242 *et seq.*

31 Foriers, "Les incombances en droit positif belge L'exemple d'une notion à bannir." p. 573.

creditor otherwise loses his right. In this sense, the imposition of an *Obliegenheit* allows to align – at least legally speaking – the interests of debtor and creditor.[32]

This mechanism operates in two times: first, the imposition of the norm of conduct, the *Obliegenheit* as such, and in a second time, the sanction of the loss of the right. The imposition of the norm of conduct is not in the interest of the person on whom it rests; it is to the advantage of the counterparty. But the fulfilment of that norm becomes in the own interest of whom it rests on because, in the case of non-fulfilment, that party loses its own right/prerogative.

When approached from this perspective, it opens the possibility of understanding and defining the *Obliegenheit* based on the constellation of interests which appears as the crucial element of the *Obliegenheit*.[33] From this perspective, sanctions other than the entire loss of the right become plausible. Such could be the loss of the exercise of a right in the specific circumstances instead of losing the right altogether.[34] That is, for instance, the case of the prohibition of abuse or rights (as described *supra* Chap. 6, nrs. 30–31). Another sanction could be the reduction of the right, again, as can be observed in the context of the prohibition of abuse of rights. Within insurance law, traditionally the area of law where *Obliegenheiten* are most recurrent, there is a tendency to favour reduction of the right over the loss of a right. At least I have observed it in the context of Belgian[35] and German laws.[36]

Another consequence of understanding the *Obliegenheit* based on the constellation of interests it creates is that its description remains somewhat vague and fluctuating. Still, I believe it to be more helpful in understanding what an *Obliegenheit* is to understand it as a mechanism.

14. LEGAL BASIS – It follows that an *Obliegenheit* does not find its legal basis in general liability law and certainly not through the qualification as an *Obliegenheit*. Instead, the mechanism of the *Obliegenheit* requires a specific legal basis providing for the norm of conduct related to the exercise of a right/prerogative and that it specifies that, in case of its non-respect, the creditor will lose his right, part of it, its exercise, or part of its exercise.

32 Ehrensperger, *Strukturen und Verletzungen von Obliegenheiten im Schweizerischen Privatrecht (unter Ausschluss des Versicherungsrechts)*. p. 44.

33 Ehrensperger, *Strukturen und Verletzungen von Obliegenheiten im Schweizerischen Privatrecht (unter Ausschluss des Versicherungsrechts)*. p. 45.

34 Mentionned by Ehrensperger, *Strukturen und Verletzungen von Obliegenheiten im Schweizerischen Privatrecht (unter Ausschluss des Versicherungsrechts)*. pp. 116–117.

35 Articles 58–60 of the law on insurances (30 avril 2014 *M.B.*) provide that if the policyholder fails to inform the insurer adequately about the insured risk, the insurer may reduce its benefit by the amount it would have paid had the policyholder been adequately informed. This is no longer a forfeiture but a reduction in the debtor's performance as a result of the creditor's failure to live up to the *Obliegenheit*.

36 On this Hähnchen, *Obliegenheiten und Nebenpflichten. eine Untersuchung dieser besonderen Verhaltensanforderungen im Privatversciherungsrecht und im allgemeinen Zivilrecht unter besonderer Berücksichtigung der Dogmengeschichte*. p. 160.

2.2. To contract

15. *Obliegenheit* to contract – This brief description of what an *Obliegenheit* is has allowed me to show that, and how, the interests of a right holder can be aligned with those of the party that has to undergo the exercise of that right, namely, by making the existence (or its exercise) of the right conditional upon the adoption of cooperative, or at least reasonable, conduct. Thereby, the interposition of an *Obliegenheit* incentivizes the right holder to act according to the interests of the party undergoing the exercise of the right. In the context of forced contract negotiations, that right, or more broadly, prerogative, is the freedom from contract. Hence, an *Obliegenheit* to contract would render the existence or exercise of the freedom from contract conditional upon the cooperative or constructive conduct in the negotiation process of the party whose freedom from contract is used unlawfully: Party A can only break-off negotiations/refuse to contract (freedom from contract) if it has acted cooperatively/reasonably in the negotiation process.

Such an *Obliegenheit* to contract can be conceived either as pre-existing any unlawfulness (I'll call it anticipatory *Obliegenheit*) or as a reaction to an unlawfulness (I'll call it remedial *Obliegenheit*).

16. Anticipatory *Obliegenheit* – It is conceivable that an *Obliegenheit* to contract exists prior to any unlawful breaking-off of negotiations. A generalized *Obliegenheit* to contract could apply in all cases of contract negotiations, or it could be restricted to some specific kinds of contract negotiations, as, for instance, in the context of economic dependence on contract conclusion. One could also think that the field of application could be delineated *rationae personae* by creating an *Obliegenheit* to contract in the context of a business contracting with a platform (B2P), a consumer with a bank, *et cetera.*

An *Obliegenheit*, by aligning the interests of a right holder and its counterparty, allows to re-balance a situation which, absent the *Obliegenheit*, would put one party more or less at the mercy of the other. By consequence, imposing an *Obliegenheit* mostly makes sense in contexts where one party, absent the existence of the *Obliegenheit*, would be particularly vulnerable or dependent on the contract conclusion.

17. Remedial *Obliegenheit* – It is also conceivable to approach an *Obliegenheit* to contract as a remedy: if a party has unlawfully broken-off negotiations or refused to contract, then the remedy is an *Obliegenheit* to contract. In that case, the field of application will be defined by the committing of the unlawfulness. Essentially, it will be an incentive to renegotiate the contract where negotiations failed but with a specific constellation of interests.

18. Non-respect of *Obliegenheit* – No matter whether the *Obliegenheit* is an anticipatory or a remedial one, the consequence of its non-respect (negotiation non-cooperatively) is the loss of the freedom from contract of the party on which the *Obliegenheit* rests (the *Obliegenheit*-debtor). Hence, the *Obliegenheit*-debtor can no longer refuse to contract. However, such a remedy can only be sensible where the offered contract by the *Obliegenheit*-creditor is reasonable, i.e. not (excessively) detrimental to the interests of the *Obliegenheit*-debtor. The aim of imposing such an *Obliegenheit* cannot be to overly disadvantage the *Obliegenheit*-debtor.

Such an approach has also been defended under Dutch law – be it not as an *Obliegenheit*:

> "On this basis, it is considered possible in the literature, in my view rightly, to order a party who rejects a reasonable proposal from the other party in the phase of compulsory renegotiation to conclude the contract on the basis of the rejected proposal. That obligation can then be enforced by real execution under Art. 3:300 of the Civil Code."[37]

19. LEGAL BASIS – To the extent that the typical sanction associated to an *Obliegenheit* is more far-reaching than the mere compensation of harm, it cannot be based on liability law and requires a specific legal basis. The proposal for an *Obliegenheit* to contract is *de lege feranda*, with the nuance that the constellation of interests typical for the *Obliegenheit* can also be achieved relying on the abuse of rights doctrine. Indeed, an *Obliegenheit* to contract could be seen as an abuse of the right to break-off negotiations in imposed renegotiations. Given the increased threshold of qualified fault in order to invoke an abuse of rights, such an alternative only appears as a second-best option. Instead, a specific *Obliegenheit* to contract appears preferable.

20. SCOPE OF APPLICATION – To the extent that such a specific legal basis is preferable, the question of the field of application becomes relevant. In that context, it should be borne in mind that an *Obliegenheit* is a means to grant more protection to a party in a position of weakness. By consequence, this consideration should dictate the delimitation of its field of application.

This means that for the anticipatory *Obliegenheit* to contract should be imposed in situations where a party is, as a baseline, in a position of weakness, such as a situation of dependence. This is but one suggestion to highlight the strength of the insight just presented: it opens the way to targeted means to combat unjust situations of power imbalance. Thomas Ehrenspergher speaks in this context of the steering effect ("*Lenkungswirkung*") that can be fulfilled with the imposition of an *Obliegenheit*.[38]

As far as a remedial *Obliegenheit* to contract is concerned, it appears that given the unlawfulness of the party breaking-off negotiations or refusing to

37 Asser/Sieburgh 6-II 2021/352. Free translation. Original text: "*Mijns inziens terecht, wordt in de literatuur op deze grondslag mogelijk geacht een partij die in de fase van verplicht dooronderhandelen een redelijk voorstel van de wederpartij afwijst, te veroordelen om op basis van het verworpen voorstel de overeenkomst te sluiten. Die verplichting kan dan door middel van reële executie op grond van art. 3:300 BW worden afgedwongen.*" See also comparably Ruygvoorn, *Afgebroken onderhandelingen en het gebruik van voorbehouden*. p. 258.

38 Ehrensperger, *Strukturen und Verletzungen von Obliegenheiten im Schweizerischen Privatrecht (unter Ausschluss des Versicherungsrechts)*. p. 122.

contract, the counterparty is already in a position of weakness following the unlawful exercise of the freedom from contract. Hence, it seems plausible to justify an *Obliegenheit* in that context.

I am aware that depending on ideological background and convictions, one may differ in opinion on the preceding points, i.e. the question of whether and where an *Obliegenheit* to contract would be justified. To the extent that the reader may perhaps not agree on the granting of an *Obliegenheit* in these contexts, I want to point out that the extent of an *Obliegenheit* can be modulated in such a way that it puts a greater or lesser "burden" on the party on which the *Obliegenheit* is imposed.

21. Extent of *Obliegenheit* – The extent of an *Obliegenheit* can be adapted along two variables: first, the standard of conduct that is expected; second, the standard against which the offer of the *Obliegenheit*-creditor is assessed. First, the requirement to act cooperatively can be set to a lower standard, such as acting reasonably in the context of negotiations. Admittedly, one may wonder whether this will really change much, as it remains an open norm for the interpretation of which a judge retains considerable leeway. Second, the threshold against which the offered contract is assessed can be modified. It could equally well be that the contract may not be detrimental, excessively detrimental, or manifestly detrimental to the *Obliegenheit*-debtor. Another alternative could be that the contract would be set by a judge or a designated third person.

These are examples, and one may find them more or less convincing. The main point I want to make is that there is leeway in how such an *Obliegenheit* can be designed. The limit which cannot be crossed in that design is that the *Obliegenheit* must still retain its function of aligning interests of parties.

22. Burden of proof – Another, and perhaps more practical, means of altering the strength of an *Obligenheit* is the allocation of the burden of proof (*supra* Chap. 8, nr. 4). The fact that an *Obliegenheit* to contract is applicable will always be for the party that wants to rely on it to prove it. Here, little variance can be expected. It is the question of who must prove that the party on whom the *Obliegenheit* rests has not lived up to it in case of failed contract conclusions. Theoretically speaking, it seems most straightforward that the counterparty has to prove the bad performance on the *Obliegenheit*-debtor, i.e. prove that negotiations failed because it did not act cooperatively. It is, however, also conceivable that from the result of failed contract negotiations, a presumption of lack of cooperation is drawn, putting the burden of proof on the *Obliegenheit*-debtor to prove that he, in fact, did act cooperatively.

Another question is who has to bear the burden of proving that the offer made by the *Obliegenheit*-creditor was reasonable. Here, it could be presumed that it is reasonable, hence charging the *Obliegenheit*-debtor with proving that the offer was unreasonable and that he, therefore, could still refuse it. Inversely, the burden could be put on the *Obliegenheit*-creditor to prove that his offer was reasonable.

9 Summary

1. The present part is based on the finding that much of the contemporary case law and scholarship pertaining to failed contract conclusion relies on a pre-supposed obligation to contract. This can mainly be (i) in the way the invoked fault is described or (ii) in the sanction that is applied. Concerning the (i) framing of the fault, the "deception of legitimate expectations of future contract conclusion" or the "having reached a point of no-return" are very common instances of such pre-supposed faults. As a matter of fact, it is quite understandable that scholars and case law alike rely on such a framing of the fault, as, absent a pre-supposed obligation to contract or to negotiate, the breaking-off of negotiations or the refusal to contract itself cannot give rise to liability due to the normative causal uncertainty following the freedom from contract. Yet the reasoning is technically flawed. In case of the (ii) enforcement of the obligation to contract, it is particularly the prohibition of the abuse of rights doctrine which, under the cover of the moderation of the abusive exercise of a right, allows to enforce an obligation to contract or to negotiate. It is precisely this possibility for the judge to moderate the abusive exercise of the right in question, which allows to side-line considerations of causality and, by consequence, be able to ignore these issues in cases of breaking-off or refusal to contract.

Circumventing the issue of normative causal uncertainty certainly is convenient but, once looked upon closely, cannot be reconciled with the structure of systems of the law of obligations. Obligations have to find their source in a recognized source for obligations and cannot be created *ex nihilo*.[1] This would give rise to very arbitrary decisions and, generally, a system of liability for contract negotiations which cannot be explained and delimited. That is, what can be observed too frequently in the analysed legal systems. Instead of trying to hide away these implied obligations to contract by relying on some semantic tricks

1 As Bydlinski puts it: "Surely one cannot award claims by judgement that have not yet arisen (and by no means have not yet become due)." Bydlinski, "Zu den dogmatischen Grundfragen des Kontrahierungszwanges." p. 17. Free translation. Original text: "*Man kann doch wohl Ansprüche nicht durch Urteil zusprechen, die noch gar nicht entstanden (keineswegs bloß noch nicht fällig geworden) sind.*"

DOI: 10.4324/9781003599166-13

in framing the fault or some compromise solution to enforce these obligations to contract, it appears preferable to me to overtly recognize the existence of such obligations to contract or to negotiate upfront. This bears a considerable advantage: it allows the topic to be addressed openly.[2]

This is of fundamental importance, as it allows for an open discussion of the extent of such obligations to contract or negotiate and, in my eyes, even more importantly, the considerations on which such an obligation can or should be based. This gives access to a fundamentally political discussion which is presently hidden under some quite random and purely legal technical discussions, leaving a discussion as fundamental as that of protecting parties' freedom to contract to the whims of discussions which often fail to see what actually is at stake: the freedom of contract of the parties facing the refusal to contract or breaking-off of negotiations.

2. In the present part, I have tried to build a basic structure of such obligations to contract or to negotiate and to highlight the relevant structural questions. To the extent available, I have also fleshed out this structure with the existing literature and case law. This exercise of fleshing out, however, is rather tentative and meant to open a discussion which, in my eyes, needs to be had. To overcome some inherent issues with enforcing a supposedly free will, I have suggested to rely on an *Obliegenheit* to contract or to negotiate instead of an obligation to contract or to negotiate. By setting incentives in such a way that the party which, by breaking-off negotiations or refusing to contract, has testified its disinterest in concluding the contract in question, actually gets an own interest in constructively taking part in its negotiations, the *Obliegenheit* allows to overcome this inherent issue of forcing a free will. In this context, it is important to see such an *Obliegenheit* more as a blueprint for a way to incentivize parties, which can be adapted to the convictions of lawmakers. This should allow for it to be adaptable to the corresponding political intentions.
3. In its essence, Jan Busche has already defended the same approach, only the technical structuring he relied on was different:

> "It is not a matter of steering the parties towards a heteronomously formulated contractual goal that is founded in the social network of the partnership, but of balancing individually formulated interests. The task of the general obligation to contract is not the redistribution of spheres of freedom, but the preservation of individual freedom according to the design plan of general contract law. The specification of concrete contractual conditions is not compatible with this. The purpose of the general

2 Or as Busche puts it in *Privatautonomie und Kontrahierungszwang*: "The derivation of the general obligation to contract from the functional conditions of contract law makes it advisable to reflect again on its normative foundation." Busche, *Privatautonomie und Kontrahierungszwang*. p. 651. Free translation. Original text: "*Die Ableitung des allgemeinen Kontrahierungszwangs aus den Funktionsbedingungen des Vertragsrechts läßt es angeraten erscheinen, abschließend erneut über sein normatives Fundament nachzudenken.*"

> obligation to contract is to overcome an impediment to the conclusion of a contract caused by a refusal to contract in the confidence that the parties, aware of the obligation to contract, will decide privately and autonomously on a balance of interests that is appropriate for them. Only if the parties fail to reach agreement does the right to unilateral determination of the content of the contract by the obligated party or, alternatively, judicial determination take the place of private autonomous negotiation."[3]

That such an *Obliegenheit*, and actually an obligation as well (though it, in fact, is already commonly relied upon), may still appear as a far-reaching encroachment upon the freedom from contract may not dissuade scholars, judges, or legislators from engaging in this discussion. Admittedly, the discussion may seem thin-iced, as it is always presented as yet another limitation of freedom from contract. This is, however, a very one-sided presentation, as Jan Busche explains. What is left out in this discussion is that the exercise of one's freedom *from* contract always implies the negation of someone else's freedom *to* contract in that very instance. Leaving this perspective out creates a biased description of the state of the law. In this biased description, the failure to conclude a contract is ascribed to the laws of offer and demand, bad fortune, or bad negotiating skills. This is too simplistic a perspective, leaving out the very considerable issue of power relations within no-contract law. Striking the balance in the way it is currently done, however, is not an immutable truth but a political choice. Hence, the decision of providing for an obligation to contract or to negotiate is a fundamental and important political choice. Understanding that, presently, this decision is only half-heartedly made and based on a criterion which, socio-economically speaking, is as random as that of the deception of legitimate expectations, should cast doubt on the current approach. But that is a question for another book.

3 Busche, *Privatautonomie und Kontrahierungszwang*. p. 648. Free translation. Original text: "*Es geht nicht um die Lenkung der Parteien zu einem heteronom formulierten und im Sozialverbund der Sozietät fundierten Vertragsziel, sondern um den Ausgleich individuell formulierter Interessen. Nicht die Umverteilung von Freiheitssphären, sondern die Bewahrung individueller Freiheit nach dem Gestaltungsplan des allgemeinen Vertragsrechts ist die Aufgabe des allgemeinen Kontrahierungszwangs. Damit verträgt sich die Vorgabe konkreter Vertragsbedingungen nicht. Der allgemeine Kontrahierungszwang bezweckt die Überwindung einer durch Vertragsverweigerung eingetretenen Vertragsabschlußsperre im Vertrauen darauf, daß sich die Parteien im Bewußtsein der Abschlußverpflichtung privatautonom zu einem für sie angemessenen Interessenausgleich entschließen. Lediglich für den Fall des Versagens der Privatautonomie bei Nichteinigung der Parteien tritt an die Stelle der privatautonomen Aushandlung das Recht zu einseitiger Bestimmung des Vertragsinhalts durch den Verpflichteten bzw. ersatzweise die gerichtliche Festsetzung.*"

Conclusion

Summarizing

1. At the outset of this book, I have not promised answers but questions, namely, what relevant questions to ask regarding liability for failed contract negotiations. It is now time to review how I have found the questions to your answers or at least the questions which should allow to reach right answers.
2. First, the *function* of liability for contract negotiations. Based on a historical-comparative approach, I have singled out two distinct interests that are considered worthwhile of protection: either the patrimonial damage suffered or the freedom to contract that has been annihilated by the decision to break-off negotiations or to refuse to contract (*supra* Chapter 1, nrs. 27–35). Those two interests are looked at in conjunction and so are the means to protect them. That is generally done by relying on what is commonly called *culpa in contrahendo* or pre-contractual liability, a conduct-based liability law system (*supra* Chap. 2, nrs. 1–11). Yet dealing with both questions interchangeably does not help a better understanding, and I have thus decided to deal with both separately, asking the question what legal framework is necessary to accommodate their protection in the context of failed contract conclusion in the different analysed legal systems (Belgium, France, the Netherlands, Germany, and Italy).
3. I have found that to *protect the patrimonial integrity*, all legal systems I have dealt with rely on a conduct-based liability law system (*supra* Chap. 2, nr. 12–24). Where the extra-contractual liability law system provides for a conduct-based system, extra-contractual liability is mainly referred to as relevant liability law system; where that is not the case, another system must be relied upon ("relativity of liability for contract negotiations"). Hence, under Belgian and French law, the legal basis clearly is extra-contractual liability, as their extra-contractual liability law is conduct based. Yet superfluously, they know a specific duty of care of acting in good faith during contract negotiations. Dutch law historically, but superfluously, too, bases its liability for contract negotiations on good faith instead of their extra-contractual liability law, which could accommodate liability for contract negotiations (as it is conduct-based in the relevant parts). Dutch scholars increasingly seem to agree that liability for contract negotiations could

DOI: 10.4324/9781003599166-14

be based on extra-contractual liability. As Italian extra-contractual liability law is seen by some as conduct-based and by others as not, the legal framework for their liability for contract negotiations varies depending on the scholar or composition of the *Corte di Cassazione*. German extra-contractual liability law, at last, clearly is not conduct-based, and hence, their liability for contract negotiations must be accommodated elsewhere, namely, in the contractual context.

4. To *protect the freedom to contract* of the disappointed negotiator, the breaking-off of negotiations or the refusal to contract itself must become unlawful (*supra* Chap. 2, nr. 25). Yet a conduct-based liability cannot do so: due to freedom from contract, no causal link can be established between the breaking-off/refusal itself and any potential harm, as in the hypothetical alternative scenario relied upon to establish a causal link in conduct-based liability law systems, the party could still have broken-off negotiations. In that case, the same or greater harm would have risen. Hence, in the scenario without the breaking-off/refusal, the same or greater harm could also have occurred (*supra* Chap. 2, nr. 26–32). This hypothesis cannot be excluded unless one pre-supposes an obligation to contract or to negotiate, in which case, the hypothetical alternative scenario would be normatively determinate: contracting/continuing negotiations. In that case, liability can be established, and its consequence should be the conclusion of the contract in question or the continuation of negotiations, depending on what has been pre-supposed (*supra* Chap. 2, nrs. 33–34).

Such an obligation to contract quite clearly exists under Dutch law and the new Belgian code, be it with some reserves on the enforcement in kind of that obligation. In German and Italian law, such an obligation to contract is often indirectly relied upon to explain that the breaking-off of negotiations was unlawful, without extending this reasoning into the granted remedies. French law, at last, does not know such an obligation to contract or negotiate in any form whatsoever (see nuance *infra* Conc. nr. 7).

5. Hence, to protect the two interests considered worthwhile of protection in case of failed negotiations, a general fault-based liability and an obligation to contract/to negotiate are required. Therefore, the structure of liability for contract negotiations in Belgium, France, Germany, Italy, and the Netherlands is and ought to be two-pronged (*supra* Chap. 2, nrs. 33–34). First, a general conduct- or fault-based liability that can compensate pure economic loss suffered in the context of contract negotiations and often due to the failure of contract negotiations. Second, an obligation to contract or to negotiate, being understood that both are distinct obligations but that it is not always very clear which one of the two is relied upon (*supra* Chap. 2, nrs. 35–37).

These two parts of liability for contract negotiations are necessary because a conduct-based liability alone cannot justify that the breaking-off of negotiations or the refusal to contract itself gives rise to liability. Hence, if, and to the extent that, the breaking-off of negotiations or the refusal to contract itself should give rise to liability, an obligation to contract or to negotiate is necessary.

6. A conduct-based liability law system is needed to accommodate for the compensation of pure economic loss in the context of contract negotiations. In looking at how the different national legal systems go about explaining and structuring this conduct-based liability, it has been shown that the clearest and most coherent structure results of a mere application of very basic principles of the law of obligations (*supra* Chap. 3, nrs. 1–2). As Carsten Nickel wrote programmatically in the introduction to his dissertation, *Die Rechtsfolgen der culpa in contrahendo*:

> "By going into the case groups of c.i.c. in more detail, it is to be shown that their legal consequences deviate, if at all, only to a marginal extent from the initial situation resulting from §§ 249–252 BGB."[1]

What he set out to show under German law can be confirmed under all analysed national systems (*supra* Chap. 3, nrs. 3– Chap. 4, nr. 7). Deviations do exist but generally sit oddly in the broader structure of the law of obligation systems and seem to be the result of the misunderstanding *that* and *how* liability for contract negotiations conclusion is essentially a mere application of the two respective liability law systems. This tendency to autonomize liability for contract negotiations has, from this perspective, rather contributed to complicating matters, instead of making the structure of this liability clearer and more comprehensible.

7. It is via the imposition or recognition of the existence of an obligation to contract/negotiate that the freedom of contract of parties to the negotiations can be protected but not merely based on a conduct-based liability. Though such an obligation to contract/negotiate often is perceived as a particularly far-reaching limitation of freedom from contract of some parties, this limitation is, in fact, already present in all legal systems. Either it is pre-supposed in the way the fault is conceived or it is indirectly enforced via the remedy in question, typically an abuse of rights (*supra* Chap. 5, nrs. 1– Chap. 6, nr. 35). Instead of hiding away these obligations to contract or negotiate, I suggested to address them directly so as to be able to clarify what is actually done in the different legal systems while also allowing to discuss more sensibly the legal basis and extent of such obligations to contract or negotiate (*supra* Chap. 6, nrs. 36–38). In light of the preceding, I then drew a blueprint for an obligation to contract and for an obligation to negotiate based on what I could observe in the different analysed legal systems (*supra* Chap. 7, nrs. 1–27).

8. As the enforcement of an obligation to contract or to negotiate often is perceived as not only ideologically difficult but also practically unworkable (*supra* Chap. 8, nrs. 1–6), I have suggested an alternative approach by relying on an *Obliegenheit* to contract. Essentially, such an *Obliegenheit* to contract works in three steps: first, parties have to renegotiate once negotiations have failed. If the party

1 Nickel, *Die Rechtsfolgen der culpa in contrahendo*. p. 22. Free translation. Original text: "*Durch näheres Eingehen auf die Fallgruppen der c.i.c. soll gezeigt werden, dass ihre Rechtsfolgen, wenn überhaupt nur in marginalem Ausmaß von der aus den §§ 249–252 BGB ergebenden Ausgangslage abweichen.*"

under the *Obliegenheit* to contract fails to live up to the required care/constructive participation in the negotiation process, it loses its freedom to refuse the offer made by the party benefiting from the *Obliegenheit*. So doing, the party under the *Obliegenheit* to negotiate is incentivized constructively to take part in the negotiation process and protect party autonomy as much as possible.

9. An insight which was striking in the course of the present book project was to find how much focus is laid on protecting parties to failed negotiations from pure economic loss by distributing the losses via liability law and how, within national systems of the law of obligations, little focus lies on the protection of parties' freedom to contract. This may be due to the general perception that protecting the freedom of contract of individuals, which requires an obligation to contract, would be alien to the system of private law and an excessive encroachment upon freedom from contract. Yet the limitation of one's freedom from contract always occurs in the interest of protecting someone else's freedom of contract. In that way, it is necessary to maintain a legal framework within which parties enjoy a material freedom of contract instead of one within which strong economic actors structurally come to stand in a position in which they can abuse their freedom from contract at the expense of relatively weaker parties. Structurally preferring the freedom *from* contract of one over the freedom *to* contract of the other is not a neutral or self-evident position but one which can and should be part of the discussion.

Formulating questions

10. Questions are asked by an individual with a specific interest in mind. Depending on who that individual is and with what interest in mind, questions will vary. To account for this variance, I will first deal with questions a legislature may ask (*infra* Conc. nr. 11) to then deal with those of an individual who had to undergo the failure of negotiations or a refusal to contract (or her or his lawyer) (*infra* Conc. nr. 12) and, lastly, a judge confronted with deciding such a case (*infra* Conc. nr. 13).

11. A *legislature* should first ask itself whether its extra-contractual liability law can lead to the compensation of pure economic loss based on negligent conduct for the protection of the patrimonial integrity of negotiators.

If that is the case, and this should, in principle, be a rather straightforward answer, no further steps must be taken to protect the patrimonial integrity of negotiators. What is more, it will be preferrable to not regulate anything specific for failed contract negotiations to prevent the risk of inadvertently compromising the flexibility and nuance of conduct-based liability law systems.

If that is not the case, then two options exist. Either the legislature links the liability for failed contract negotiations to an existing system of conduct-based liability, as did the German legislature in the *Schuldrechtsreform*, or a system of conduct-based liability is created (expectation-based liability for instance) to accommodate liability for a failed contract conclusion. To the extent possible, the former approach should be preferred, as it will allow to build on a pre-existing and well-established body of liability law instead of having to create a new one.

As all analysed legal systems have such a conduct-based liability applicable to contract negotiations, the preliminary question of whether the protection of the patrimonial integrity of negotiators is considered worthwhile seems rather theoretical. This is not the case for the protection for the freedom of contract of negotiators. Only Dutch and Belgian laws appear to consider it meriting protection under certain circumstances. French law, most clearly, does refuse such protection. From a legal-technical perspective, both approaches can be defended.

If a legislature wants to protect freedom of contract, it needs to reflect primarily on (i) the considerations such protection should be based and on (ii) the extent of the granted claim to protect this interest. (i) Considering the instances of affording protection, legitimate expectations of the future conclusion of a contract appear as widely accepted. I have doubts about the clarity of this criterion and, more importantly, about its soundness (though it has an intuitive appeal). Instead, it seems much more plausible to take socio-economic considerations, such as dependence or unequal bargaining power, into account when deciding whether protection should be granted. This requires further study, which shall be published elsewhere. (ii) As far as the extent of the protection goes, different degrees are imaginable. First, a choice can be made between an obligation to contract or to negotiate, which imply different degrees of constraint. Second, the chosen obligation can be limited to mere compensation of damages or a performance in kind. As the latter appears difficult to apply in practice and is generally met with scepticism, I have suggested working with an *Obliegenheit* instead.

If a legislature does not want to protect freedom of contract, it quite simply does not need to take any steps, as by default, no such protection can be afforded on a conduct-based liability law system. Where applicable, it is important to mention that the prohibition of abuse of rights and the loss of chance doctrine can allow to reach functionally similar results by relying on a different reasoning – beating around the bush of causal uncertainty.

12. A *party* seeking compensation should first consider the order of its claims. (i) First, performance of the contract, which must be tried to be proven concluded. If that is not successful, the present book becomes relevant. (ii) Second, one should then claim a right to the conclusion of the contract either based on a negotiation agreement or a general obligation to contract if applicable. Performance of this right can then be granted in kind or by way of compensation (in kind or damages). (iii) Should this fail or be unavailable, the doctrine of loss of a chance and the prohibition of abuse of rights can provide a functionally similar alternative. (iv) Fourth, compensation for the suffered pure economic loss should be claimed. Here, it is crucial to pay close attention to the invoked fault, as it should, in theory, be the fault, which determines which harm is causally linked to it and thus compensable. (v) A fifth avenue, which I could not comprise in the restricted space of this book but will deal with elsewhere, are claims based on enrichment law. They may prove to be a valuable alternative, though being currently underexplored.

13. A *judge* confronted with deciding a case of failed contract conclusion should first ask the question whether there exists, or not, an obligation to contract or to negotiate, stemming from whatever accepted source for such an obligation. If that is the case, he should establish the extent of this obligation and the most appropriate way of enforcing it, in function of the national rules on the enforcement of obligations. If no such obligation to contract or negotiate can be found to exist in the individual case, he will, alternatively, have to assess what damage can causally be linked to the invoked fault. Here, crucially, no harm can be causally linked to the breaking-off of negotiations or the refusal to contract. Coherence requires that this be applied rigorously and not be overcome by pre-supposing an obligation to contract or to negotiate (deception of legitimate expectations). Hence, only acts or omissions *related to* the breaking-off or refusal can be causally linked to any kind of harm, and it is crucial to establish *which* invoked harm can be.

14. I have now focused on the, as a result of the preceding, right questions to ask, not on the wrong questions. There are too many wrong questions to potentially be asked, and it thus wouldn't be sensible to take such an approach. Two recurrent ones should nevertheless be briefly addressed.

First, the positive and negative interest. It has repeatedly been stated: distinguishing between the positive and negative interest has, at most, some approximate descriptive value but not a normative one. As this value is rather limited and the risk of being misled by those notions is far greater, I strongly advocate for leaving them aside in the context of failed contract negotiations.

Second, the legal basis of liability for failed contract negotiations. This has been the predominant discussion overshadowing the whole domain, regardless of its quite limited relevance. The main debate should be had on the way this liability, which must be a conduct-based one, is applied. The legal basis of a conduct-based liability law system is a fairly easy and quickly answered one. It is answered relatively to the existing framework of extra-contractual and contractual liability. Whether it is of contractual or extra-contractual nature will then only have incidental influence on prescription periods or similar technicalities.

15. With all of the preceding being written out, I hope that this book has contributed to getting the questions right in relation to failed contract negotiations.

Alphabetical bibliography

Ahrens, Hans-Jürgen and Andreas Spickhoff. *Deliktsrecht*. Vols. XLVIII+723. München: C.H. Beck, 2022.

Alpa, Guido. "Unjust Damage and the Role of Negligence: Historical Profile." *Tulane European and Civil Law Forum* 9 (1994): 147–177.

Babusiaux, Ulrike. "Liability for Negotiation." In *Commentaries on European Contract Laws*, edited by Nils Jansen and Reinhard Zimmermann, 348–373. Oxford: Oxford University Press, 2018.

Baeyens, Sander. "De Theorie Van Het Verlies Van Een Kans: Een Rechtsvergelijkende Analyse Toegepast Op De Zuivere Vermogensschade." *RW* (2016): 363–378.

Ballerstadt, Kurt. "Zur Haftung Für Culpa in Contrahendo Bei Geschäftsabschluss Durch Stellvertreter." *ACP* (1950/1951): 501–531.

Baudenbacher, Laura Melusine. *Vom Gemeineuropäischen Zum Europäischen Rechtsmissbrauchsverbot*. Baden-Baden: Nomos, 2016.

Benatti, Francesco. *La Responsabilità Precontrattuale*. Milano: Giuffrè, 1963.

Benedict, Jörg. *Culpa in Contrahendo*. Vol. I. Tübingen: Mohr Siebeck, 2018.

Berg, Olivier. "Le Dommage Dans Les Projets De Réforme Français Et Belge. Perspectives D'outre-Rhin." In *La Réforme Du Droit De La Responsabilité En France Et En Belgique*, edited by Bernard Dubuisson, 445–452. Bruxelles: Bruylant, 2020.

Bieri, Laurent. "Perte D'une Chance Vs Responsabilité Précontractuelle À La Probabilité De La Causalité." *Jusletter*, 27 August 2007 (2007). https://jusletter.weblaw.ch/juslissues/2007/436/_5888.html__ONCE&login=false

Bocken, Hubert, Ingrid Boone, and Marc Kruithof. *Inleiding Tot Het Schadevergoedingsrecht*. Brugge: Die Keure, 2014.

Bollen, Carlos. "Enforcement of the Duty to Carry on Neogtiations: (Schould It Be) a Possibility in Europe or Not?" In *Specific Performance in Contract Law: National and Other Perspectives*, edited by Jan Smits, Daniel Haas and Geert Hesen, 231. Antwerp: Intersentia, 2008.

Bollen, Carlos. "Precontractuele Aansprakelijkheid Voor Het Afspringen Van Onderhandelingen, in Het Bijzondere M.B.T. Een Acquisiteovereenkomst." *TBBR* (2003): 136–160.

Brun, Philippe. *Responsabilité Civile Extracontractuelle*. Paris: LexisNexis, 2023.

Busche, Jan. *Privatautonomie Und Kontrahierungszwang*. Jus Privatium. Tübingen: Mohr Siebeck, 1999.

Busnelli, Francesco D. and Giovanni Comandé. "Causation under Italian Law." In *Unification of Tort Law: Causation*, edited by J. Spier, 79–92. The Hague: Kluwer, 2000.

Busnelli, Francesco D. and Giovanni Comandé. "'Wrongfulness' in the Italian Legal System." In *Unification of Tort Law: Wrongfulness*, edited by Helmut Koziol, 69–82. The Hague: Kluwer International, 1998.

Bussani, Mauro and Vernon Valentine Palmer. "The Liability Regimes of Europe – Their Façades and Interiors." In *Pure Economic Loss in Europe*, edited by Mauro Bussani and Vernon Valentine Palmer, 120–159. Cambridge: Cambridge University Press, 2003.

Bussani, Mauro and Vernon Valentine Palmer. "The Notion of Pure Economic Loss and Its Setting." In *Pure Economic Loss in Europe*, edited by Mauro Bussani and Vernon Valentine Palmer, 3–24. Cambridge: Cambridge University Press, 2003.

Bussani, Mauro, Anthony J. Sebok, and Marta Infantino. "Compensation for Pure Economic Loss." In *Common Law and Civil Law Perspectives on Tort Law*, edited by Mauro Bussani, Anthony J. Sebok and Marta Infantino, 143–176. Oxford: Oxford University Press, 2022.

Bydlinski, Franz. "Zu Den Dogmatischen Grundfragen Des Kontrahierungszwanges." *ACP* (1980): 1–46.

Canaris, Claus-Wilhelm. "Ansprüche Wegen 'Positiver Vertragsverletzung' Und 'Schutzwirkung Für Dritte' Bei Nichtigen Verträgen. Zugleich Ein Beitrag Zur Vereinheitlichung Der Regeln Über Die Schutzpflichtverletzungen." *JZ* 15/16 (1965): 475–482.

Canaris, Claus-Wilhelm. *Die Vertrauenshaftung Im Deutschen Privatrecht (Unveränderter Nachdruck 1981). Claus-Wilhelm Canaris, Gesammelte Schriften*, edited by Grigoleit Hans Christoph and Neuner Jörg. De Gruyter, 1981. https://doi.org/10.1515/9783110274035.1005.

Cane, Peter. *The Anatomy of Tort Law*. London: Hart Publishing, 1997.

Cartwright, John and Martijn Hesselink. *Precontractual Liability in European Private Law*. Cambridge: Cambridge University Press, 2008.

Cassan, Hervé and Marie-Pierre de Bailliencourt. *Traité Pratique De Négociation*. Bruxelles: Larcier, 2019.

Castronovo, Carlo. "The Italian Law of Obligations from the Civil Code of 1942 to Today Profiles of an Evolution." *RFJ* 9 (2021): 79–104.

Castronovo, Carlo. *Responsabilità Civile*. Milano: Giuffrè, 2018.

Chantepie, Gaël and Mathias Latina. *Le Nouveau Droit Des Obligations Commentaire Théorique Et Pratique Dans L'ordre Du Code Civil*. Paris: Dalloz, 2018.

Cian, Giorgio. *Commentario Breve Al Codice Civile*. Padova: Cedam, 2022.

Coggiola, Nadia. "The Influence of Foreign Legal Models on the Development of Italian Civil Liability Rules from the 1865 Civil Code to the Present Day." *Italian Law Journal* 2 (2019): 441–470.

Cornelis, Ludo. "La Responsabilité Précontractuelle, Conséquence Éventuelle Du Processus Précontractuel." *TBBR* 6 (1990): 36.

De Boeck, Annick. "De Precontractuele Fase Als Ontmoetingsplaats Voor Buitencontractuele En Contractuele Aansprakelijkheid: De Schade Ten Gevolge Van Tekortkomingen Tijdens De Precontractuele Fase Nader Geanalyseerd." In *Raakvlakken Tussen De Contractuele En Buitencontractuele Aansprakelijkheid*, edited by Sophie Stijns and Patrick Wéry, 30. Brugge: Die Keure, 2008.

De Boeck, Annick. "De Tussenkomst Van De Rechter in De Precontractuele Fase: Mogelijkheden En Grenzen." In *Le Juge Et Le Contrat – De Rol Van De Rechter in Het Contract*, edited by Sophie Stijns and Patrick Wéry, 221. Brugge: die Keure, 2014.

De Boeck, Annick. "Onderhandelen Met De Rem Op: Het Gebruik Van Voorbehoudmechanismen in De Precontractuele Fase." *TBBR* 1 (2018): 11.

De Boeck, Annick. "Precontractuele Aansprakelijkheid Anno 2010." *Themis* (2010): 24.

De Boeck, Annick and Tom Hick. "Totstandkoming Van Contracten: Het Komend Recht in De Rechtspraak." In *Verbintenissenrecht Themis 2021–2022 Nr. 120*, edited by Annick De Boeck and Sophie Stijns, 1–42. Antwerpen: Intersentia, 2022.

De Coninck, Bertrand. "Le Droit Commun De La Rupture Des Négotiations Précontractuelles." In *Le Processus De Formation Du Contrat – Contributions Comparatives Et Interdisciplinaires À L'harmonisation Du Droit Européen*, edited by Marcel Fontaine, 17. Bruxelles: Bruylant, 2002.

De Rey, Sébastien. *Herstel in Natura. Rechtsvergelijkende Studie in Het Contractenrecht Met Buitencontractuele Invalshoek*. Brugge: die Keure, 2019.

Derval, Thomas, and Charles-Edouard Lambert. "La Conclusion Dynamique Du Contrat." In *Le Livre 5 Du Code Civil Et Le Nouveau Droit Des Contrats*, edited by Rafaël Jafferali, 73–102. Bruxelles: Larcier, 2022.

Descamps, Olivier. "La Responsabilité Dans Le Code Civil." *Histoire de la Justice* 19 (2009): 291–310.

Deshayes, Olivier. "La Rupture Des Pourparlers." *Petites Affiches* 203 (2008).

Deshayes, Olivier. "Le Dommage Précontractuel." *RTD Com* Avr./Juin (2004): 187–204.

Dirix, Eric. "Gentlemen's Agreements En Adnere Afspraken Met Onzekere Rechtsgevolgen." *RW* (1985–1986): 27.

Drion, C.E. "Ons Onderhandelingsrecht Onder Handen." *NJB* 34 (2005).

Dubuisson, Bernard. "Les Mystères De L'alternative Légitime." *RGAR* 9 (2021): 15819–15833.

Dubuisson, Bernard. "The Projet De Réforme Du Code Civil Belge and the Reform of the French Civil Code – a Comparison of Selected Topics." In *French Civil Liability in Comparative Perspective*, edited by Jean-Sébastien Borghetti and Simon Whittaker, 397–424. Oxford: Hart Publishing, 2019.

Durant, Isabelle. "La Rupture Unilatérale Des Pourparlers Ou L'exercice D'une Liberté Surveillée." In *La Volonté Unilatérale Dans Le Contrat*, 39. Bruxelles: Editions du jeune barreau de Bruxelles, 2008.

Ehrensperger, Thomas. *Strukturen Und Verletzungen Von Obliegenheiten Im Schweizerischen Privatrecht (Unter Ausschluss Des Versicherungsrechts)*. Zürich: University of Zurich, 2004.

Eichenhofer, Philipp. *Rechtsmissbrauch Zu Geschichte Und Theorie Einer Figur Des Europäischen Privatrechts*. Tübingen: Mohr Siebeck, 2019.

Esmein, Paul. *Droit Civil Français*. Aubry & Rau. Vol. 6, Paris: Juris-classeurs, 1951.

Esser, Josef. "R. Schmidt Die Obliegenheiten. Studien Auf Dem Gebiet Des Rechtszwangs Im Zivilrecht Unter Berücksichtigung Des Privatversicherungsrechts." *ACP* 154 (1955): 49–52.

Esser, Josef. "Wandlung Von Billigkeit Und Billigkeitsrechtsprechung Im Modernen Privatrecht." In *Summum Ius Summa Iniuria; Individualgerechtigkeit Und Schutz Allgemeiner Werte Im Rechtsleben*, 22. Tübingen: Mohr Siebeck, 1963.

Faggella, Gabriele. "Dei Periodi Precontrattuali." In *Studi Giuridici in Onore Di C. Fadda, Iii*, 269–342. Napoli, 1906.

Faggella, Gabriele. *I Periodi Precontrattuali E La Responsabilità Precontrattuale*. Roma: Società Cartiere Centrali, 1918.

Fagnart, Jean-Luc. *La Causalité*. Waterloo: Kluwer, 2009.

Febbrajo, Tommaso. "Good Faith and Pre-Contractual Liability in Italy: Recent Developments in the Interpretation of Article 1337 of the Italian Civil Code." *Italian Law Journal* 2 (2016): 291–312.

Feenstra, Robert. "Grotius' Doctrine of Liability for Negligence: Its Origin and Its Influence in Civil Law Countries until Modern Codifications." In *Histoire Du Droit Savant (13e–18e Siecle) Doctrines Et Vulgarisation Par Incunables*, edited by Robert Feenstra, 129–171. Aldershot: Variorum, 2005.

Fikentscher, Wolfgang and Andreas Heinemann. *Schuldrecht Allgemeiner Und Besonderer Teil*. Leck: De Gruyter, 2022.

Fleischer, Holger. "Der Rechtsmissbrauch Zwischen Gemeineuropäischem Privatrecht Und Gemeinschaftsprivatrecht." *JZ* 18 (2003): 865–874.

Fleischer, Holger. "Schadensersatz Für Verlorene Chancen Im Vertrags- Und Deliktsrecht." *JZ* 54, no. 15/16 (1999): 766–775.

Fontaine, Marcel. "Obliegenheit, Incombance?" In *Liber Amicorum Hubert Claessens. Verzekering: Theorie En Praktijk/Assurance: Théorie Et Pratique*, edited by Herman Cousy, Caroline Van Schoubroeck, Colette Uytterhoeven and Annie Robijns, 151–163. Antwerpen: Maklu, 1998.

Foriers, Paul Alain. "Les Incombances En Droit Positif Belge – L'exemple D'une Notion À Bannir." In *Le Droit Du Travail Au Xxie Siècle: Liber Amicorum Claude Wantiez*, edited by Marc Morsa and Philippe Gosseries, 565–573. Bruxelles: Editions Larcier, 2015.

Freitag, Robert. "'Specific Performance' and 'Causa-Lehre' Über Alles Im Recht Des Vorvertrags?" *ACP* 207 (2007): 287–313.

Freleteau, Barbara. *Devoir Et Incombance En Matière Contractuelle*. Bibliothèque De Droit Privé. Edited by Yves Lequette. Paris: LGDJ, 2017.

Frenda, Daniela M. "Il Danno Da Mancata Realizzazione Di Un Risultato Atteso: Ai Confini Tra La Perdita Di Chances E Il Lucro Cessante?." *Danno e responsabilità* 1 (2024): 15–23.

Fuller, L.L. and W.R. Perdue. "The Reliance Interest in Contract Damages: 1." *Yale LJ* 46 (1936): 52–96.

Gazzoni, Francesco. *Manuale Di Diritto Privao*. Napoli: Edizioni Scientifiche Italiane, 2015.

Ghestin, Jacques. "L'abus Dans Les Contrats." *Gazette du Palais* 2 (1981): 379–384.

Ghestin, Jacques. "La Responsabilité Délictuelle Pour Rupture Abusive Des Pourparlers." *JCP. (éd Gen.)* 20–21 (2007).

Ghestin, Jacques, and Hugo Barbier. *Introduction Générale Tome Ii – Droit De La Preuve, Abus De Droit, Fraude Et Apparence*. Paris: LGDJ, 2020.

Giaro, Tomasz. "Culpa in Contrahendo: Eine Geschichte Der Wiederentdeckung." In *Das Bürgerliche Gesetzbuch Und Seine Richter*, edited by Ulrich Falk and Heinz Mohnhaupt, 113–154. Frankfurt am Main: Vittorio Klostermann, 2000.

Gordley, James. "The Rule Against Recovery in Negligence for Pure Economic Loss: An Historical Accident?" In *Pure Economic Loss in Europe*, edited by Mauro Bussani and Vernon Valentine Palmer, 25–56. Cambridge: Cambridge University Press, 2003.

Graziadei, Michele. "Liability for Fault in Italian Law: The Development of Legal Doctrine from 1865 to the End of the Twentieth Century." In *The Development and Making of Legal Doctrine*, edited by Nils Jansen, 126–163. Cambridge: Cambridge University Press, 2010.

Großerichter, Helge. *Hypothetischer Geschehensverlauf Und Schadensfeststellung – Eine Rechtsvergleichende Untersuchung Vor Dem Hintergrund Der Perte D'une Chance*. Münchener Universitätsschriften. Edited by Claus-Wilhelm Canaris. München: C.H. Beck, 2001.

Guski, Roman. *Rechtsmissbrauch Als Paradoxie – Negative Selbstreferenz Und Widersprüchliches Handeln Im Recht*. Tübigen: Mohr Siebeck, 2019.

Hähnchen, Susanne. *Obliegenheiten Und Nebenpflichten. Eine Untersuchung Dieser Besonderen Verhaltensanforderungen Im Privatversciherungsrecht Und Im Allgemeinen Zivilrecht Unter Besonderer Berücksichtigung Der Dogmengeschichte*. Jus Privatum. Tübingen: Mohr Siebeck, 2010.

Halpérin, Jean-Louis. "French Doctrinal Writing." In *The Development and Making of Legal Doctrine*, edited by Nils Jansen, 73–95. Cambridge: Cambridge University Press, 2010.

Hausmaninger, Herbert and Walter Selb. *Römisches Privatrecht*. Wien: Böhlau Verlag, 2001.

Hellwege, Phillip. "Obliegenheiten Im Versicherungsvertragsrecht Aus Historisch-Vergleichender Perspektive." *RabelsZ* (2012): 864–892.

Herbosch, Maarten. "Contractdwang Bij Onrechtmatig Afgebroken Onderhandelingen Over De Koop Van Onroerend Goed? Het Schijn Geen Brug Te Ver." *T.Not.* 4 (2021): 308–325.

Hesselink, Martijn W. *De Redelijkheid En Billijkheid in Het Europese Privaatrecht*. Den Haag: Kluwer, 1999.

Hick, Tom. "Aansprakelijkheid Voor Afgebroken Onderhandelingen in België En Nederland: Op Koers Voor Toenadering." *NTBR* 29 (2022): 243–255.

Hol, Antoine. "Fault in Legal Doctrine in the Netherlands." In *The Development and Making of Legal Doctrine*, edited by Nils Jansen, 164–182. Cambridge: Cambridge University Press, 2010.

Hosemann, Eike. "Article 1:102: Freedom of Contract." In *Commentaries of European Contract Laws*, edited by Nils Jansen and Reinhard Zimmermann, 30–51. Oxford: Oxford University Press, 2018.

Houbben, Michaël. "Quelques Considérations En Faveur De L'intégration De L'incombance En Droit Privé Belge." *Annales de droit de Louvain* (2016): 91–139.

Houben, Iris S.J. *Contractdwang*. Deventer: Kluwer, 2005.

Jafferali, Rafaël. "La Formation Dynamique Du Contrat." In *La Réforme Du Droit Des Obligations*, edited by T. Derval, Rafaël Jafferali and Benoit Kohl, 169–194. Bruxelles: Larcier, 2023.

Jafferali, Rafaël. "La Réforme Du Droit Des Contrats – Les Principales Nouveautés." *JT* (2023): 22–56.

Jansen, Nils. "Developing Legal Doctrine: Fault in the German Law of Delict." In *The Development and Making of Legal Doctrine*, edited by Nils Jansen, 96–125. Cambridge: Cambridge University Press, 2010.

Jansen, Nils. *Die Struktur Des Haftungsrechts*. Tübingen: Mohr Siebeck, 2003.

Jansen, Nils."Dogmatik, Erkenntnis Und Theorie Im Europäischen Privatrecht." *ZEUP* (2005): 750–783.

Jansen, Nils. "Gesetzliche Schuldverhältnisse Eine Historische Strukturanalyse." *ACP* 216 (2016): 112–223.

Jansen, Nils. "The Idea of a Lost Chance." *Oxford Journal of Legal Studies* 1, no. 2 (1999): 271–296.

Jansen, Nils. "Konturen Eines Europäischen Schadensrechts." *JZ* 4 (2005).

Jansen, Nils. *The Structure of Tort Law*. Oxford: Oxford University Press, 2021.

Jansen, Sanne and S. Stijns. "Contractweigering Kan Rechtsmisbruik Uitmaken (Noot Onder Cass. 7 Oktober 2011)." *RW* (2012–2013): 1182–1186.

Jhering, Rudolf. "Culpa in Contrahendo Oder Schadensersatz Bei Nichtigen Oder Nicht Zur Perfection Gelangten Verträgen." *Jahrbücher für die Dogmatik des heutigen römischen und deutschen Privatrechts* 4 (1861): 112.

Joisten, Céline. *L'incertitude Causale En Droit De La Responsabilité Civile*. Bruxelles: Larcier-Intersentia, 2024.

Jourdain, Patrice. *Les Principes De La Responsabilité Civile*. Paris: Dalloz, 2021.

Jourdain, Patrice. "Préjudice Consécutif À La Rupture Fautive Des Pourparlers." *RTD Civ.* (2006): 770–773.

Knetsch, Jonas. "Les Effets De La Responsabilité Et La Réparation Des Dommages. Unité Ou Diversité Des Formes De Réparation Dans Les Projets Français Et Belge. Point De Vue Du Droit Allemand." In *La Réforme Du Droit De La Responsabilité En France Et En Belgique*, edited by Bernard Dubuisson, 535–541. Bruxelles: Bruylant, 2020.

Koziol, Helmut. "Compensation for Pure Economic Loss from a Continental Lawyer's Perspective." In *Pure Economic Loss*, edited by W.H. van Boom, Helmut Koziol and Christian A. Witting, 141–161. Wien: Springer, 2004.

Koziol, Helmut. "Conclusions." In *Unificatio of Tort Law: Wrongfulness*, edited by Helmut Koziol, 129–135. The Hague: Kluwer International, 1998.

Kraakman, Reinier, John Armour, Paul Davies, Luca Enriques, Henry Hansmann, Gerard Hertig, Klaus Hopt, et al. *The Anatomy of Corporate Law a Comparative and Functional Approach*. 3rd ed. Oxford: Oxford University Press, 2017.

Krawitz, Thomas. *Schutz Vorvertraglicher Investitionen – Zur Haftung Beim Scheitern Von Vertragsverhandlungen*. Berlin: Duncker & Humblot, 2015.

Kreutz, Giannina. *Hypothetische Verträge Im Rahmen Des Schadensausgleichs*. Baden-Baden: Nomos, 2016.

Küpper, Wolfgang. *Das Scheitern Von Vertragshandlugen Als Fallgruppe Der Culpa in Conrahendo*. Berlin: Duncker & Humblot, 1988.

Lange, Hermann and Gottfried Schiemann. *Schadensersatz*. Tübingen: Mohr Siebeck, 2003.

Léonard, Thierry. *Conflits Entre Droits Subjectifs, Libertés Civiles Et Intérêts Légitimes. Un Modèle De Résolution Basé Sur L'opposabilité Et La Responsabilité Civile*. Bruxelles: Larcier, 2005.

Léonard, Thierry."L'abus De La Liberté De Ne Pas Contracter: Une Application Excessive De La Théorie De L'abus De Droit (Note Sous Cass. 11 October 2011)." *RCJB* (2013): 542–593.

Léonard, Thierry. "L'interdiction De L'abus De Droit Dans Le Nouveau Code Civil: Requiem Pour Un Principe Général De Droit?" In *Les Principes Généraux Du Droit Privé*, edited by J. Van Meerbeeck and Y. Ninane, 67–113. Limal: Anthemis, 2023.

Lequette, Yves, François Terré, Philippe Simler and François Chénedé. *Droit Civil Les Obligations*. Paris: Dalloz, 2022.

le Tourneau, Philippe, Cyril Bloch, André Giudicelli, Guettier, Christophe, Jérôme Julien, Didier Krajeski and Matthie Poumarède. *Droit De La Responsabilité Et Des Contrats*. Paris: Dalloz, 2023.

Lorenz, Stephan. "Grundwissen – Zivilrecht: Culpa in Contrahendo (§311 Ii, Iii Bgb)." *JUS* (2015): 398–401.

Magnus, Ulrich. "Comparative Report on the Law of Damages." In *Unification of Tort Law: Damages*, edited by Ulrich Magnus, 181–217. The Hague: Kluwer Law, 2001.

Mäsch, Gerald. *Chance Und Schaden*. Tübingen: Mohr Siebeck, 2004.

Mazeaud, Denis. "Rupture Fautive Des Pourparlers." *Revue des contrats* 2 (2004).

Mazzamuto, Salvatore. "Spunti in Tema Di Danno Ingiusto E Di Danno Meramente Patrimoniale." *Europea e diritto privato* 2 (2008): 349–400.

Medicus, Dieter. "Zur Entdeckungsgeschichte Der Culpa in Contrahendo." In *Iuris Professio Festgabe Für Max Kaser Zum 80. Geburtstag*, edited by Hans-Peter Benöhr, Karl Hackl, Rolf Knütel and Andreas Wacke, 169–181. Wien: Hermann Böhlaus, 1986.

Medicus, Dieter and Stephan Lorenz. *Schuldrecht I Allgemeiner Teil*. München: C.H. Beck, 2021.

Medicus, Dieter, and Jens Petersen. *Grundwissen Zum Bürgerlichen Recht*. München: Vahlen, 2019.

Menke, Christoph. *Kritk Der Rechte*. Suhrkamp Taschenbuch Wissenschaft. Berlin: Suhrkamp, 2018.

Mommsen, Friedrich. *Beiträge Zum Obligationenrecht Ii: Zur Lehre Von Dem Interesse*. Braunschweig: Schwetschke, 1855.

Müller, Christoph. *La Perte D'une Chance*. Bern: Staempfli editions, 2002.

Müller, Christoph. "La Perte D'une Chance N'a Pas Perdu Sa Chance En Droit Suisse (Commentaire De L'atf 133 Iii 462)." *Responsabilité et Assurances* (2008): 55–60.

Neumann, Franz L. "Der Funktionswandel Des Gesetzes Im Recht Der Bürgerlichen Gesellschaft." *Zeitschrift für Sozialforschung* 6 (1937): 542–596.

Nickel, Carsten. *Die Rechtsfolgen Der Culpa in Contrahendo*. Berlin: Buncker & Humblot, 2004.

Nipperdey, Hans Carl. *Kontrahierungszwang Und Diktierter Vertrag*. Jena: Verlag von Gustav Fischer, 1920.

Nuninga, W. Thijmen. "Het Recht Op Een Kans." *NTBR* 8 (2019): 41–52.

Nuninga, W. Thijmen, D. Verheij, Caroline Kahn, F. Auvray, and Christopher Borucki. "Chances as Legally Protected Assets." *ERPL* 2 (2020): 375–406.

Nüsslein, Elke. *Die Integration Der Culpa in Contrahendo in Das Bgb Nach Der Schuldrechtsrefomr*. Berlin: Peter Lang, 2018.

Orlandi, Mauro. "Responsabilità Precontrattuale." *Enciclopedia del diritto* (2021): 996–1031.

Pannebakker, Ekaterina. *Letter of Intent in International Contracting*. Ius Commune Europaeum Rotterdam: Erasmus University Rotterdam, 2016.

Pannebakker, Ekaterina. "Offer and Acceptance and the Dynamics of Negotiations: Arguments for Contract Theory from Negotiation Studies." *Erasmus Law Review* 6, no. 2 (2013): 131–141.

Pitotet, Paul. *Culpa in Contrahendo Et Responsabilité Précontractuelle En Droit Privé Suisse*. Bern: Staempfli, 1963.

Planiol, Marcel. *Traité Élémentaire De Droit Civil*. Vol. 2, Paris: LGDJ, 1949.

Radermacher, Lukas. "Authority of Agents." In *Commentaries on European Contract Laws*, edited by Nils Jansen and Reinhard Zimmermann, 587–648. Oxford: Oxford University Press, 2018.

Röckrath, Luidiger. *Kausalität, Wahrscheinlichkeit Und Haftung – Rechtliche Und Ökonomische Analyse*. München: C.H. Beck, 2004.

Roth, Herbert. "Susanne Hähnchen: Obliegenheiten Und Nebenpflichten. Eine Untersuchung Dieser Besonderen Verhaltensanforderungen Im Privatversicherungsrecht Und Im Allgemeinen Zivilrecht Unter Besonderer Berücksichtigung Der Dogmengeschichte." *JZ* 18 (2010): 893.
Ruygvoorn, Marcel R. *Afgebroken Onderhandelingen En Het Gebruik Van Voorbehouden*. Recht En Praktijk. Deventer: Kluwer, 2009.
Saleilles, Raymond. "De La Responsabilité Précontractuelle – a Propos D'une Étude Nouvelle Sur La Matière." *RTD Civ*. VI (1907): 697–751.
Salvi, Cesare. *La Responsabilità Civile*. Milano: Giuffrè Francis Lefebvre, 2019.
Schlinker, Steffen, Hannes Ludyga and Andreas Bergmann. *Privatrechtsgeschichte*. München: C.H. Beck, 2019.
Schmidt, Reimer. *Die Obliegenheiten: Studien Auf Dem Gebiet Des Rechtszwanges Im Zivilrecht Unter Besonderer Berücksichtigung Des Privatversicherungsrechts*. Karlsruhe: Versicherungswirtschaft, 1953.
Scholz, Philipp. "Haftungsbegründende Und Haftungsausfüllende Kausalität Im Zivil- Und Zivilprozessrecht." *JUS* (2021): 914–917.
Schrans, Guy. "Praecontractuele Verhouding Naar Belgisch Recht." *Vereniging voor de vergelijkende studie van het recht van België en Nederland* (1968): 39.
Schwarze, Roland. *Das Recht Der Leistungsstörung*. Berlin: De Gruyter, 2022.
Siebert, Wolfgang. *Verwirkung Und Unzulässigkeit Der Rechtsausübung*. Marburg in Hessen: Elwert'sche Verlagsbuchhandlung, 1934.
Simoens, Dries. *Schade En Schadeloosstelling*. Beginselen Van Belgisch Privaatrecht. Antwerpen: E. Story-Scientia, 1999.
Sirena, Pietro. "The Concepts of 'Harm' in the French and Italian Laws of Civil Liability." In *French Civil Liability in Comparative Perspective*, edited by Jean-Sébastien Borghetti and Simon Whittaker, 205–221. Oxford: Hart Publishing, 2019.
Spier, Jaap and Olav A. Haazen. "Comparative Conclusions on Causation." In *Unification of Tort Law: Causation*, edited by J. Spier, 127–154. The Hague: Kluwer International, 2000.
Stijns, Sophie. "Abus, Mais De Quel(S) Droit(S)?." *JT* (1990): 33–44.
Stijns, Sophie. *Verbintenissenrecht Boek 1*. Brugge: die Keure, 2024.
Stijns, Sophie and Françoise Auvray. "L'abus De Droit Dans Le Livre 1er Du Code Civil." In *Le Livre 1er Du Code Civil: Dispositions Générales*, edited by Patrick Wéry and Eric Dirix. Bruxelles: Larcier, 2024.
Stijns, Sophie and S. De Rey. "Het Nieuwe Verbintenissenrecht in Boek 5 Bw – Deel I." *RW* 24 (2023): 923–946.
Stoffel-Munck, Philippe. *L'abus Dans Le Contrat – Essai D'une Théorie*. Bibliothèque De Droit Privé. Edited by Jacques Ghestin. Paris: L.D.D.J., 2000.
Stoll, Hans. "Tatbestände Und Funktionen Der Haftung Für Culpa in Contrahendo." In *Festschrift Für Ernst Von Caemmerer Zum 70. Geburtstag*, edited by Hans Claudius Ficker and Detlev König, 435–474. Tübingen: Mohr Siebeck, 1978.
Storme, Matthias Edward. *De Invloed Van De Goede Trouw Op De Kontraktuele Schuldvorderingen*. Brussel: E. Story-Scientia, 1990.
Swaenepoel, Elke. *Toetsing Van Het Contractuele Evenwicht*. Antwerpen: Intersentia, 2011.
Tjittes, Rieme-Jan L. *Commercieel Contractenrecht*. Den Haag: Boom Juridisch, 2018.
Tjong Tjin Tai, Eric. "Schadebegroting, Verlies Van Een Kans En Proportionele Aansprakelijkheid." *NJB* 31 (2016): 2239–2244.
Tjong Tjin Tai, Eric. *Tort Law a Comparative Introduction*. Celtenham: Edward Elgar, 2022.
Trabucchi, Alberto. *Instituzioni Di Diritto Civile*. Milano: Wolters Kluwer, 2022.
Troiano, Paolo. "Art. 1337 C.C. Trattative E Responsabilità Precontrattuale." In *Codici Civile Commentato Online*, edited by Carlo Cicala. Kluwer, 2023.
van Dam, Cees. *Aansprakelijkheidsrecht*. Den Haag: Boom Juridisch, 2023.
Van Oevelen, Aloïs. "Juridische Verhouding En Aansprakelijkheid Bij Onderhandelingen Over (Commerciële) Contracten." *DAOR* (1990): 43–63.

Verkempinck, Brecht. *Schadevergoeding Wegens Wanprestatie in Europese Perspectief.* Brugge: die Keure, 2017.

Viney, Geneviève. *Introduction À La Responsabilité.* Traité De Droit Civil. Edited by Jacques Ghestin. Paris: LGDJ, 2019.

Viney, Geneviève. "L'appréciation Du Préjudice." *Petites Affiches* 99 (2005).

Vitale, Laura. *La Perte De Chances En Droit Privé.* Paris: LGDJ, 2020.

von Bar, Christian. *The Common European Law of Torts.* Vol. I. Oxford: Clarendon Press, 1998.

von Bar, Christian. *The Common European Law of Torts.* Vol. II. Oxford: Clarendon Press, 2000.

Wagner, Gerhard. "Comparative Tort Law." In *The Oxford Handbook of Comparative Law*, edited by Mathias Reimann and Reinhard Zimmermann, 996–1030. Oxford: Oxford University Press, 2019.

Widmer, Pierre. "Comparative Report on Fault as a Basis of Liability and Criterion of Imputation (Attribution)." In *Unification of Tort Law: Fault*, edited by Pierre Widmer, 331–367. The Hague: Kluwer, 2005.

Willems, Kurt. "Gentlemen's Agreements." In *Gemeenrechtelijke Clausules, Vol. I En Ii.* Contractuele Clausules, 43. Mortsel: Intersentia, 2013.

Zimmermann, Reinhard. *The Law of Obligations. Roman Foundations of the Civilian Tradition.* Cape Town: Juta & Co, 1990.

Zimmermann, Reinhard. *Roman Law, Contemporary Law, European Law: The Civilian Tradition Today.* Oxford: Oxford University Press, 2001.

Zuloaga, Isabel. *Reliance in the Breaking Off of Contractual Negotiations.* Intersentia, 2019.

Index

FSC
www.fsc.org
MIX
Papier | Fördert
gute Waldnutzung
FSC® C083411

Kolibri 360 GmbH
Ferdinand-Jühlke-Straße 7
99095 Erfurt, Deutschland
produktsicherheit@kolibri360.de